331.4816584
H21s

142192

SUCCESS
AND
BETRAYAL

SUCCESS
AND
BETRAYAL

*The Crisis of
Women in
Corporate America*

**Sarah Hardesty
Nehama Jacobs**

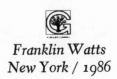

*Franklin Watts
New York / 1986*

Excerpts from "I'm the Breadwinner, My Husband Stays at Home"
by Luci Koizumi in *Glamour*, December 1985
Copyright © by the Condé Nast Publications, Inc.
Reprinted with permission of the author and Condé Nast.

Excerpts from *I've Done So Well—Why Do I Feel So Bad?*
by Celia Halas and Roberta Matteson
© 1978 Celia Halas and Roberta Matteson reprinted with
permission of MacMillan Publishing.

Library of Congress Cataloging in Publication Data

Hardesty, Sarah.
Success and betrayal.

Bibliography: p.
Includes index.
1. Women executives—United States.   2. Women in
the professions—United States.   I. Jacobs, Nehama.
II. Title.
HD6054.4.U6H37   1986   331.4'816584'00973   86-13243
ISBN 0-531-15027-5

*To my mother and father,
and to Elizabeth*
S.H.

To Mother, and to Peter
N.J.

ACKNOWLEDGEMENTS

The authors gratefully acknowledge the help and support of the following people:

First and foremost, the many quietly outstanding women whose openness and honesty in discussing their career ambivilence with two strangers is immeasurably appreciated. We respect their privacy in not printing their names and affiliations. We gratefully, and collectively, thank each one from whom we learned.

Secondly, the many successful men and women who shared insights for the record and dedicated time from their busy schedules to discuss a controversial subject: Lois Appleby, Joanne Black, Broward Craig, Coy Eklund, Malcolm Forbes, Jr., William Greenough, Alice Hennessey, Juanita Kreps, Russell Marks, Jr., Nancy Reynolds, Roy Rowan, Herbert S. Schlosser, Anne Wexler, Rosalie Wolf and Lois Wyse.

Several psychiatrists and psychologists gave willingly of their time and ideas where little previous research existed: Dr. Carol Galligan, Dr. Willard Gaylin, Dr. Frederick Hauser, Dr. Ethel Spector Person, and Dr. Ann Belford Ulanov. In addition, we are indebted to Dr. Milton Malev for first pointing out the concept of career landings from which women reassess, as well as calling to our attention the "living on the edge" syndrome. Among the many psychologists whose secondary work proved invaluable are Dr. Srully Blotnick, Dr. Carol Gilligan, Dr. Roger L. Gould, Drs. Celia Halas and Roberta Matteson, and Dr. Jean Baker Miller, all acknowledged at greater length elsewhere.

Of the many books on women in management, perhaps none has influenced us as much as Margaret Hennig and Anne Jardim's *The Managerial Women*. In attempting to update their theories and break fresh ground, we built on the solid foundation of their first inquiries into the subject. We also built on comprehensive research by Barbara Ehrenreich, Marilyn French, and Carolyn Heilbrun. Executive recruiters Ann Barry, Pendelton James, Gary Knisely, Judy Mapes and Leonard Pfeiffer all shared candidly their professional assessments, as did career counselor Nella Barkley. Radcliffe College's Margaret Touborg and Duke University's Jean O'Barr generously contributed a wealth of information on the attitudes of recent graduates and the next generation of management women.

Richard Cheney, Robert Dilenschneider, Robert Taft, and Jan Van Meter, all of Hill and Knowlton, Inc., were especially supportive. Anne Owen deserves special praise for her tireless work in typing the manuscript, as well as for handling, along with Laura Mulcahy, a number of tedious yet crucial editorial details with humor, grace and exceptional efficiency.

We're also grateful to the other friends and family who gave advice, patient understanding and, often, much appreciated hospitality throughout the many months of the book's development. In particular, we'd like to cite Alison Gardner, as well as Laura Meyer Wellman and Nancy Conroy.

Finally, Peter Binney patiently waded through several drafts with a fresh and telling eye, and contributed a balancing male perspective. Charlotte Sheedy, our agent, added her experience and expertise. Ellen Joseph, our editor, believed in this project from the very first, and provided judicious editing and unflagging moral support.

To all, our deepest gratitude.

CONTENTS

SUCCESS
AND
BETRAYAL

INTRODUCTION

A couple of years ago, two female executives in their early thirties, both vice presidents of their respective companies, got together to compare notes over drinks in the august, wood-paneled, predominantly male domain of a distinguished Ivy League club in New York City. The appointment to exchange insights about what was happening to them in this, their ascent into successful business careers, had been several times penciled in, postponed, erased, rescheduled. Finally, the long-delayed meeting between good friends had occurred. As always, they rejoiced with each other in the daily victories of their careers, the challenges confronted and surmounted, the professional relationships formed and sealed.

But for the first time, they shared with each other—at first haltingly and then with surprising intensity—what each had sensed separately but had not truly acknowledged even to herself: the vague, insistent questions, doubts, and dissatisfactions about the nature of the "success" that each had achieved in her career as well as the success of female peers. Why, they asked each other, did they feel this odd ennui, this disconcerting disappointment, this clichéd sense of "Is this all there is?" What was their problem? It was too early and they were too successful to be confronting the midlife crisis men have so long experienced. They both had good jobs at fine companies that had treated them well. So why did they feel that success should be something more, or at least, something *else?*

We, these two women managers, did not set out that night to write a book. But in our jobs as advisers to many of the top corporations in America, we regularly came into contact with many other women executives. They also suggested, at first only through vague remarks and quick asides, then with increasing candor, that the glowing opportunity to enter top American corporations and compete side by side with men, made possible for the vast majority of women not much more than a decade or so earlier, had fallen far short of their expectations. We also started to hear similar comments from many female friends in management positions at leading corporations throughout the country.

We had all benefited from a decade of unprecedented opportunities for women, supported by almost weekly polls and articles in the press, in all aspects of the work force. We had all confronted virtually every day through the media, at the office, and all about us the image of the confident, successful, corporate Amazon who climbed company ladders and performed other feats, such as the balancing act of a family and a baby from that high wire, just as effortlessly. We heard everywhere that the women who had entered the brave new world of corporate life had never had it so good—and that it could only get better. We were assured that the corporation would proffer endless rewards and opportunities for personal fulfillment, if women only understood the rules and played the right games. Business articles were handbooks and offered tips on how to jockey for a raise like the best of the boys or play on the right executive team; they sought to provide women with maps to the offices of the corporate stars. And they promised that the most glittering prizes could be ours—if we just followed their simple advice. And we did.

In many cases, the advice worked. Women succeeded. So why did it increasingly appear that so many women harbored secret doubts about the nature and degree of their success, a private sense they were oddballs, exceptions to the rule of euphoric achievement and boundless fulfillment in the corporation? As the women we dealt with began to realize that other women shared their secret, they began to speak out to us with increasing candor. The most vocal were not those in consulting firms, law firms, and smaller businesses, but rather the apparently most successful women managers at the corporations in the *Forbes* or *Fortune* 500 or 1000. They spoke of frustration, of emptiness, of exhaustion, of a sense they had somehow failed. Or had the corporation failed them? What was indeed the problem—if there was a problem? And who, if anyone, was to blame?

As we heard countless, similar stories, we began to wonder whether what was wrong with this picture was the image that had so long been perpetuated, not the women themselves who felt so frustrated and dejected for failing to live up to it. Had the reality not lived up to the image? What actually *was* the reality?

Seeing this pattern gradually emerge, like a photograph in the developer's tray, we decided it merited more serious and formal investigation. And we began conducting in-depth interviews with men and women working in all parts of the country. We wondered whether this phenomenon was limited to New York, hardly a representative American city. But, as we traveled to places like San Diego, and San Francisco, Boston, Durham, Chicago, and St. Paul, we found that the success and betrayal syndrome was national, not local. Was this phenomenon limited to a particular generation? We interviewed women from age nineteen to sixty-five, ranging from college students to interns to board members of America's most prestigious companies and women grappling with aging and retirement. We talked to pioneers and neophytes, single and married mothers, managers and trainees to get a sense of the sweep and scope of changes and sentiments—and to put our nascent theories to the test. We interviewed more than one hundred women in staff jobs and line jobs, in advertising and aerospace, in banking and broadcasting, chemicals and construction. We spoke with a woman college student in Los Angeles who was struggling with self-doubt and indecision before entering the work world. We talked with a

New York bank vice president in her fifties who had returned to corporate life after raising two children. In Chicago, we visited a thirty-five-year-old forest products company executive who had dropped out of the corporation to stay home with her new baby. And we heard from a twenty-seven-year-old black woman who had started her career on the plant floor of a large midwestern corporation before shifting to a staff position at a conglomerate. Of all the people we interviewed, more than three quarters had worked at one or more *Forbes* or *Fortune* 500 corporations, although some had dropped out to pursue other options, such as smaller companies or consulting firms.

We tried to avoid talking just with the top-level "name" executives who are often mentioned in the media. We tried not to round up the usual suspects, that cadre of women who are endlessly interviewed. We wanted to obtain a wider perspective from the broad mass of women who have never had a voice. We wanted to hear from the rest of us. These are the women who are experiencing the nitty-gritty reality of corporate life daily and who could give us honest appraisals rather than stock company-approved responses. Many of our interviewees requested anonymity due to the obviously sensitive nature of their attitudes and opinions about their careers. In respecting their privacy, we have given them pseudonyms throughout the book. In return, we gained their most honest corporate experiences and entrée to a whole new side of their careers—the side not heard when they are quoted for the record.

They also gave us a few surprises. We were particularly struck by how pervasive the success and betrayal syndrome actually is. Certainly not every woman who works in a corporation experiences success and betrayal, and a few—particularly those who have broken through to the top—report only positive experiences and a strong sense of fulfillment. But whatever their age, however long they had been in the work force, wherever they live and work, whatever their titles or industries, the majority of women describe a similar pattern. As we continued our interviews, the media started getting the same message. More stories appeared on women burning out or dropping out of corporate life or questioning for the first time why women weren't getting to the top. But no one explored the dynamic of women's recent progress in the corporation in enough depth to provide many insights and answers.

Through interviewing such a broad range of women at length, however, we were able to see that the dynamic can be charted and that the pattern extends beyond the success and betrayal phenomenon itself. We discovered that there is a process, or life cycle, of integrating women managers into corporations, which no one has yet identified and which almost inevitably leads to success and betrayal. This life cycle is characterized by a series of "landings" or evaluative points specific to women's careers, which are widely shared by women managers—particularly those who began their careers in the late sixties to early seventies and those who have since followed them into business. Daniel Levinson has charted male passages, and Gail Sheehy and Srully Blotnick have identified certain inevitable stages we all pass through in our lives. But the specific landings we discovered are trackable reactions particular to the shared experiences of *women in corporations,* and are based on inherently female myths and misconceptions, and the inevitably overly optimistic expectations that women bring to the workplace.

The myths and expectations create a romanticized larger-than-life view of the corporation and the possibilities it offers for success. In turn this perception has led women toward the new dependency of a marriage to the right corporation, replacing the old dependency of a marriage to Mr. Right. The marriage is perceived as a liaison with unlimited potential, creating in the process a whole new set of emotional and economic dependencies and a concomitant pressure to perform, to make the commitment last. But as women from the pioneer to the post-feminist make their corporate climb, most of them hit a landing that combines both their own burn-out of enthusiasm with hard evidence of an actual middle management topping-out at the very time women should finally be reaping the bountiful rewards of success. When the corporate mystique fails to live up to its billing, there is a subsequent sense of loss, and betrayal; priorities are reconsidered, and the roller-coaster phenomenon of success and betrayal by the corporation and by women is set in motion.

The more we talked with women executives, the more we realized we had only half the story. So with some trepidation about being able to coax an honest dialogue out of them, we called forty men, "new men" and old, from trainees to CEOs, household names and some less renowned entries from our own Rolodexes, to get their candid appraisals of women's corporate careers. These interviews brought more surprises, the most important being that men still carry a lot of pent-up and admittedly conflicting emotional baggage about women in corporations. Virtually every man, for example, insisted at some point in the interview that he would be the "only man to tell you this." We discovered that few current CEOs or top male corporate executives were willing to go on the record. Instead, our greatest sources of insight were *former* chairmen, CEOs, and presidents of the nation's largest corporations who felt most free to talk candidly with us and were able to give us honest, unguarded appraisals. And we found that, while there are always exceptions, men and women generally do differ in their myths and expectations as well as their career life cycles —and that women are indeed on rather separate emotional and psychic pathways as well as on separate corporate tracks. The experiences are superficially similar, and men obviously hold their own myths and experience their own disenchant-ment. But male corporate career patterns identified by writers such as Daniel Levinson and Michael Maccoby do not neatly fit most women as well.

The specific landings we identified that constitute wo-men's corporate life cycle do not correlate with the age of women but rather with their length and depth of experience in the workplace. Briefly defined here, these landings are:

• **Wooed and Won.** *How do women choose corporate culture, and what do they find when they get there?*

- **Proving Up.** How do women's experiences in the early stages of their career influence the crisis to come?

- **The Seeds of Disenchantment.** When and why do women first doubt the value and substance of their corporate contributions and rewards?

- **Success and Corporate Betrayal.** Why are women not reaching the top in America's top corporations? What inherent barriers in corporate culture limit their ascent?

- **Success and Self-Betrayal.** How does women's reassessment of corporate power and reward influence their lessened expectations of success and desire to remain within the system?

- **The Pivot Point.** Where do women go after they leave corporate culture and what happens next? Is there life after the fast track?

- **Reconcilable Differences.** When women stay within the corporation after recognizing the limits of their success, how do they adjust emotionally and professionally?

Some positive, constructive lessons can be learned from the recurring landings at which women find themselves. The conclusions will no doubt be controversial in part because of the necessary defensiveness of women who have gained their status via the women's movement, and who fought so hard not to see themselves singled out of the work force for special evaluation. And in part because in this time of experiment and flux in their role in the corporate domain, many women can hold conflicting and contradictory attitudes toward the specific subjects and issues we raise.

But for women to advance and contribute in the male-dominated corporation, the lessons should be considered; discussion should at least begin. These lessons include a positive recognition that the corporation is not a stand-in for emotional needs, companionship, self-esteem, or personal rewards; that women must understand their conflicting expectations of work, the corporation, and success; that women must reassess their time lines for achievement and set more appropriate, realistic goals. There are equally significant issues for the corporation—signals that cannot be ignored if they are to attract the brightest and the best gender-blind talent in order to remain economically creative and competitive. These issues include the potential for growth for women in the executive ranks; rewarding women to attract and hold them for the long haul; corporate structural changes, including adopting flextime to retain talented women who plan to raise families.

A better understanding of the dynamic between women and men within the corporation can improve the workplace for all of us. Such an understanding begins with an awareness of the scope of the problem—and the forces that brought women to the current ambivalent threshold of success in America's top corporations.

CHAPTER 1

BENCHMARKS AND BROKEN HEARTS

*Lots of people think the goals have
been reached for women in business,
that complete equality exists.
But there's still a long way to go.
We men, who just happen to have
been there first, are so innocent,
so ignorant.*

Coy Eklund
Former Chairman, The Equitable
Life Assurance Society
of the United States

I was one of four women in a class of four hundred at Wharton in 1964," recalls one corporate strategic planner who is now in her forties, "and the men's perception was that we shouldn't be there—that we would be depriving them of jobs after graduation." In 1986, a twenty-four-year-old advertising executive vowed, "By the time I'm thirty, I won't be working for anyone else. I'll be independent. My mother tells me I'm entirely unrealistic about my ambitions, and I keep thinking she settled all the way around. I think I overwhelm her, and she just doesn't understand why I need to do so much." That same year, a San Franciscan writes, "So much has been written about pushing ourselves to success; very little about finding our way to peace and serenity. Power lunches, executive stress, aerobics, ambition, super-Momming, keeping up until the strain is bursting our temples."[1]

Between 1972 and 1983, the number of women managers doubled to 3.5 million[2] and the number of executive women rose 143 percent. *Time* trumpeted, "A new class of women executives are heading up U.S. companies. . . . Women are more likely to be judged solely on their performance." Rand Corporation economist James P. Smith announced, "They're in the pipeline in middle management now. It's inevitable that after twenty years of work experience, a good number of those women will be at the top."[3] As recently as 1984, one survey of executive women quoted 82 percent as saying they were "highly satisfied" with their careers. Women have discovered in corporate culture the new frontier. It appears to be a manifest destiny, embracing simultaneously the values of individuality, independence, and self-direction.

But there is trouble in paradise. In 1985, of 1,362 senior corporate executives surveyed by Korn/Ferry International, only 2 percent, or twenty-nine, were women.[4] "Although women now hold roughly 30 percent of executive, administrative and managerial jobs, they are largely in the entry and middle ranks," observes the *Los Angeles Times*.[5] Currently, women hold only 4 percent of the twelve thousand directorships in America's top companies, and of the sixty-five hundred public companies in the United States, only fifteen are headed by women, most of whom inherited the job from a family member.[6] "The key issue now is whether women will go to the top ranks or just infiltrate into the middle," states R. Gordon McGovern, president and CEO of Campbell's Soup Company.[7] Argues Joan Ganz Cooney, co-founder and president of Children's Television Workshop and board member of five major corporations, "We've come a long way *maybe*. . . . Lots of women are in midlevel management jobs but still are almost never found in top decision-making slots."[8] One recent self-help book for women darkly warns against "the myth that the apex of self-realization and achievement can only be found through autonomy, independence and career."[9] Clearly, women have hit a wall. Most have advanced almost as far as they are likely to go. Half the "pioneer" corporate women surveyed in a recent *Wall Street Journal* poll cited slow advancement, "anti-feminist executives," and not being part of a male club as obstacles to their further advancement. Only 27 percent of young executives, "despite high salaries and excellent prospects, claim to be wholly satisfied (within their corporations)." Summed up one forty-three-year-old top manager in communications, "The business world doesn't consider women seriously. We're a social issue, not a business issue."[10]

What's going on here? Most of America's successful corporate women are just beginning to recognize they've been sold a bill of goods; the success that has sustained men for years proves mysteriously unsustaining to women. Women have become increasingly sensitized to the gap between expectation and reality ironically at the precise moment when men redouble their efforts in pursuit of title, money, and glory. As their corporate experience diverges from that of men, each level for women becomes less and less a reinforcement of expectations and more and more a benchmark of disillusionment. Is it possible that these spontaneous reactions are not isolated episodes at all, but predictable universal reactions that most women experience at the very moment in their careers when they've finally made it? More and more corporate women are coming to the same conclusion. And coming to it earlier in their careers. "When I started out, whatever we did was going to be good—for a girl," observes one senior energy-industry manager who is in her late thirties. "You didn't have to be CEO to be successful as a woman. Whatever you did above the rank of secretary was successful. Now women have to take up the same CEO burden men have always had to measure themselves against. And that's a very high target." Twenty years ago women could blame society for the limitations and constraints on their chances to realize their potential. Now society offers a lot of apparent opportunity—and women are forced to conclude that the whole problem doesn't lie "out there" somewhere; part of it resides within themselves.

For most corporate women, success has been a curious paradox. In the course of realizing self-fulfillment within the corporation, women also confront the limits of that fulfillment, as well as real ceilings on their corporate ascent. Corporate life dazzles women far beyond their hopes of economic independence, but at heart it fails to measure up to their early expectations. Although corporate life has furnished the vehicle for upward mobility, it has withheld the controls by which to steer it. It provides the stage for dramatic successes; and as women wait in the wings for more, it writes the script of their discontent.

How are corporations failing women? And how are women failing themselves?

The answer lies in the complex nature of what women today perceive as corporate betrayal. Part of their frustration, as the record shows, lies in the actual topping-out experienced by almost all women from the middle-management level on up. Such limited potential, coming on the heels of years of advancement, is exacerbated by the internal ticking of women's own clock, as they look to a career in their thirties to provide overt reasons not to surrender to biology. Instead, women discover that the slowing promotion track appears to be a punishment for success, and that the long-anticipated rewards of title and money are insufficient compared to the desire to live a well-rounded life. They begin to lose interest in proving to the corporation and to themselves that workaholism and sacrifice will result in rewards. Work in any industry gradually becomes monotonous. Women take a cynical view of the political maneuvering that is necessary to break through to top management. The pipeline seems hopelessly bottled up; the competition among women for a token spot hardly seems worth the effort.

Real and perceived corporate betrayal provides the backdrop for women's own self-limiting behavior—the phenomenon we call self-betrayal. As their careers plateau in a velvet ghetto, women gradually recognize the limits of their own ambition, the extreme sacrifice the corporation exacts in return for promotion to the top spot. Recalculating, they take themselves out of the running just as seniority would seem to guarantee success. In essence, they self-select out of the power game.

Notes Joan Ganz Cooney, "Many women don't *want* to be in the fast track, working eighteen hours a day, seven days a week, as fiercely competitive as men." It appears increasingly obvious that women experience a different dynamic within the corporate culture—a series of unique landings that differ substantially from the male experience. In these separate realities lie the stages of a separate life cycle for women of the corporation, and their disenchantment with limited prospects for success. How did we come to this?

Today's corporate woman—torn between expectations of success and the reality of continued limitations—is the product of an independent combination of historical forces, media hype, and the myths and expectations with which they were raised. Each plays a role in setting the stage. While the story of women's entry into the corporate culture begins with a generations-old patriarchal economy, the benchmark of women's current corporate condition is a scant twenty years old. It was as recently as 1963 that Betty Friedan first pieced together the modern patchwork quilt of women's discontent— "the problem that has no name."[11] The problem, feminism would soon explain to women, was the missing opportunities for independence and self-esteem that men were ostensibly receiving from their careers. Why be tied to a dishwasher when you could be tied to a desk instead?

It was not long before the problem with no name had a solution—and its own literature. "It was Helen Gurley Brown, more than anyone else, who was responsible for that transformation of the 'spinster' [executive] of the forties and fifties into 'the newest glamour girl of our times.'. . . Brown, perhaps more than feminist Betty Friedan . . . sensed the profound misogyny which was spreading under the suburban 'dream houses' like seepage from a leaky septic tank," write Barbara Ehrenreich and Dierdre English.[12] Helen Gurley Brown's vision of the career "girl," as she happily called herself then, was "the old feminist ideal of the independent woman with a new twist—she was sexy." In Brown's own words, "She supports herself. . . . She is not a parasite, a dependent, a scrounger, a sponger or a bum. She is a giver, not a taker, a winner and not a loser."[13]

Suddenly the career woman was elevated from pitiable to enviable in one short decade. Who wouldn't want to be in her place? Smart women abandoned housewifery for the workplace, paying their dues as secretaries—the only entry-level jobs then available to them. One woman, who married "the first man who was interested in having for a wife a woman who had a career" recalls, "We went to a dinner party where all the other women had Ph.D.'s and I had a career, but we spent one hour discussing how the brand-new perma-press cycle on washing machines worked. The people who were doing the interesting vocational things were men. In fact, lots of those women now have interesting careers, too. But I concluded at the time—and I'm not too proud of it—that I was going to work because I wanted to be a part of the more interesting half of the population."

In Hollywood, where the career woman had gone out with the forties, career stereotypes were reinforced on television, where she was just coming in. The new culture had its own small-screen icon; her name was Mary Tyler Moore. Her character, Mary Richards, became a metaphor for all the rich experience women hoped a career would bring. In that simple time, there was no career problem that Rhoda Morgenstern and common sense couldn't cure.

Meanwhile, the quagmire that was Vietnam ironically served, as all wars have, to open wide the windows of business opportunity for women. Women who opposed the war on moral grounds found themselves almost immorally well positioned to profit by it. The selective service, with its loopholes and its capricious lottery system, forced younger men to defer their corporate dreams. "By the time I got out of the service I felt as if the world had passed me by," recalls one male manager of that era. Well-educated women rushed to fill the vacuum of entry-level corporate vacancies. *This* war would provide a very different, very permanent kind of opportunity for women. It was their big chance; they were not about to blow it.

The second awakening of the early seventies was the fruition of the civil rights movement of the sixties. As one male manager observes, "It helped women's causes, I think, because vicariously all the people in our generation had to rid ourselves of the prejudices our parents had held against blacks, chicanos, homosexuals, and so forth. And once you have conquered the racial barriers . . . once you have become open-minded enough to see the individual as an individual, you can apply the same standards to women."

The debut of *Ms.* magazine in 1972—a short decade after the Harvard Business School opened its doors to women for the first time—became the third great contributor to women's corporate awakening. *Ms.* overcame the isolation of solitary dreams and created a culture of women prepared to build something, to "go for it" together. While relatively few women consciously identified with "women libbers," unconsciously women all over America had internalized the message, preparing to live it every day in corporate America. "Everyone was single, everyone was talking about this new magazine called *Ms.* and about Gloria Steinem," reminisces one woman marketing executive. "I had an adoring crush on her. I realized I could aspire to be like that—she was ladylike, nonabrasive,

yet militant—without compromising what I'd grown up with."
Yet, looking back, many of the corporate managers we interviewed hold feminism responsible for raising women's expectations far beyond what was realistically possible to achieve on all fronts. "*Ms.* founded a 'cause' based on one part of being a woman," comments Ricki, a marketing vice president now in her early forties and mother of two. "Remember, Steinem is single—without children. Nobody said, 'Let's look at what being fulfilled as a woman is all about.' It was simply, 'Here's a role women are denied, and they shouldn't be. Let's open up that [career] role so they can *choose between* being homemakers and having careers.' *Choose* means giving up one of those alternatives. Nobody asked, 'Do women want to give up motherhood?' What's the role of motherhood in an emotional portfolio? Nobody bothered to do any strategic planning for the future. Nobody ever thought to ask, 'How do you do both?'"

With *Ms.*'s daughters, *Savvy* and *Working Woman,* came a new kind of women's literature—the literature of women in business. Since there were few role models for women to follow, the best-educated, most information-hungry generation of women in history was prepared to read its way to the top. What it got was a mish-mash of advice, information, and manifesto. The available literature perpetuated the good news —the upside potential of women's success. With no historical track record and little perspective, the literature ignored—or simply never perceived—the ambivalence and sacrifice associated with becoming a managerial woman. Books encouraged women to believe in the myth of meritocracy based on macho rules that, if followed, could propel women to the top by somehow coaxing men into forgetting their traditional biases and accepting women as team players. An entire generation of pioneer women was misled, however inadvertently, into believing there were no barriers women could not overcome through canny gamesmanship and a thorough initiation into the rules. The concentration on style to the exclusion of substance foreshadowed some of the problems to come—a fact of life not lost on sociologist Barbara Ehrenreich, who notes that the most striking aspect of contemporary literature "for and about the corporate woman is how little it has to say about the purposes, other than personal advancement, of the corporate 'game.' [No one] ever voices a transcendent commitment to, say, producing a better widget."[14]

At the same time, a new business ethic was being promoted in books that suggested women could become less "womanly" and that corporations might in turn become less male. While some books counseled women to change their inherent values and style, others held out hope that the environment might change, sparing women unnecessary psychic surgery on themselves. The male literature of business suggests few of the same problems. Instead, it reflects the fact that while men, too, experience self-doubt, disillusionment, and periods of reassessment, the causes, symptoms, timing, and expression of male disenchantment register differently.

The corporate disillusionment women are now experiencing is largely different from the doubts corporate men have traditionally confronted. Women bring a second, private agenda to their corporate experience—an agenda of which men are largely unaware. It combines the myths and expectations of a tumultuous two decades and the unprecedented promotional hype the media has accorded working women.

Under the media microscope, women are daily bombarded by images of blatant success and self-fulfillment, from cover story profiles to credit card commercials. As a result, there is a largely ignored dichotomy between women's career images as the media report them and the reality of women's day-to-day behind-the-scenes confrontations with the vastly more confusing paradoxes of success. Few women find much of their own experience reflected in the current business press. One business weekly interviews a handful of successful women in the financial community in its "Careers" column and closes by asking "What has been the cost of your success?" Replies one forty-six-year-old first vice president, "There has been no cost at all. It's a better and happier way of living all around." A thirty-three-year-old investment counsel adds, "I second that."[15] No wonder so many women feel guilty sharing the doubts and psychological costs of their own achievement. Any woman who claims to have solved the problem evokes snorts of derision. "I've seen those profiles," commented one vice president for human resources at a major New York City bank. "Usually they're the women with one foot out the door the week after the interview." Other women are equally vehement in their denouncement of such "positive" role models. "If I see one more of those profiles, I'll scream. They're the women you don't want to turn out to be," says another.

Women's perception of success has fallen victim to what columnist Michael Kinsley terms "executive porn"—magazine profiles of men that "regularly feed their readers' gray-flannel fantasies with salacious photos of high-powered executives posed with suggestive self-importance against a backdrop of corporate luxury."[16] When applied to the public fascination with women business celebrities who lend their blue-suited bodies to feed the private fantasies of the eighties, Kinsley's interpretation assumes even more suggestive implications: Superwoman as centerfold. "It's much more subtle and insidious than you think," reports one cable television executive. "I saw it all the time on my job. When I would meet these women before they went on the set, their lives were just as real as mine. But stick a camera in their face, and they come across on the screen like they don't ever have to do any laundry. The true reality of their lives never comes across." Considering the current limited opportunities for upward mobility, what woman can risk parading her own career ambivalence in the press, fulfilling the male stereotype that women aren't macho enough to take the heat? One commodities executive suggests the role model created by such media pressure takes its toll: "There's an intolerance among women who have done very well. They are paid very high salaries, and then they turn around and ask of the rest of us, 'Who is this woman with all these cracks in the facade, trying to relate to me?' They sense that their lives are a house of cards. As a result, they're following rigid rules like a Prussian general, and they fear any questions. They're operating so much on sheer will and rules and gamesmanship that anything that doesn't operate on the same set of rules is a threat to their fragile fingertip control. A lot of women have their lives down to a little box that consists of their wealth and their career plans—and that's it." The public sees only the mastery, never the misery—unless something goes spectacularly awry, as it did with Mary Cunningham. No wonder the sense of betrayal sneaks up on so many women. They are congratulated so publicly on every achievement as celebrated in the media, that the vast majority of women—who don't thrive on imbalance, who question daily their reasons for going to the office—are intimidated into silence. Like Betty Friedan's housewife of twenty years ago, they, too, suffer a "problem that has no name."

It is now abundantly clear to America's first-generation corporate pioneers that playing by the rules does not preordain success. Games are not enough. Nor does becoming the corporate equivalent of Marabel Morgan's Total Woman necessarily engender happy-ever-after corporate marriages. Increasingly disillusioned female "successes" are questioning their corporate history, their goals and values, and the trade-off needed just to survive, let alone to thrive. As women reach and surpass the point of professional maturity, experience is shaking their previously unchallengeable assumptions about how far they will rise and the value of the rewards they have received and will receive from America's biggest and best corporations.

If history suggests anything, it is that we are again at a turning point in understanding women's identity. Today's corporate woman is just confronting the costs of corporate affiliation. Like Nora in Ibsen's A *Doll's House*, women managers perceive themselves as trapped in a corporate home of glass walls (and ceilings) through which they can see but which they cannot penetrate. These are the seeds of a new and insistent crisis of success and betrayal. Its origins lie in the carefully nurtured myths and extravagant expectations that women bring to life today in corporate America.

CHAPTER 2
MYTHS AND EXPECTATIONS

I think my generation, those of us who work with young women to encourage their aspirations—in contrast to the silent treatment we got in our youth—probably haven't said enough about the constraints that nevertheless apply in the new era.

Juanita Kreps
Former United States
Secretary of Commerce

I think it's the Myth of the Great Potential, as Snoopy likes to call it," Rachel, thirty-four-year-old corporate counsel with a large midwestern manufacturer, comments. "If you are raised to be an achiever, you constantly feel bad because you haven't achieved all those expectations. You don't feel, 'Wow, I got this far,' but disappointed: 'Oh, I only got this far.'" Adds Sheila, a thirty-four-year-old corporate vice president, "The myths become a self-fulfilling prophecy. You don't want to think about the reality, and its implications, so you choose not to examine the myths too closely. I poured so much of my life into a career at the expense of other areas of my life that I need to hang on to the myths irrationally, to defend those choices. Even though I know rationally those myths are no longer true. The myths reinforce the direction you've gone in." Theirs is the dilemma of a generation groping with the myths of extravagant promise with which they were raised—myths that fell short of reality.

Myths determine the corporate experience of women in America's largest companies and the same myths predetermine their enormous sense of betrayal and estrangement often at the very moment of their greatest success. These myths represent an amalgam of mothers' expectations, the incredible economic revolution that has fueled society's willingness to accept working women, and a parallel social evolution that encouraged women to find "self-actualization" in the same domain from which men had derived their self-esteem for years.

Yet men seldom begin their corporate careers burdened with such baggage. Because they are less conditioned to dependency and offered many more role models, they are far less dependent on myth as a means of projecting reality. They are raised on myths grounded in mastery that seldom culminate in self-limiting behavior, as do women's myths. As a result, while women's goals within corporate culture sometimes overlap men's, there are key differences in attitude and expectation. The gap between the myths on which women were raised and reality eventually creates more and more distance between corporate men and women precisely because these myths are so proprietarily female.[1] The longer men and women work together in the corporation, the less similar are their experiences and, more important, their perception and interpretation of these experiences. As a result, the most androgynous experience men and women share is at both extremes of the hierarchy—at the entry level, where the expectation gap is lowest, and in the rarefied winner's circle of the corporate boardroom, where the natural selection process has eliminated any other kind of corporate behavior.

Understanding the uncertainty with which women confront the corporate dream makes it easier to appreciate the mythic safety and security with which they invest that dream. "The illusions of our twenties," writes Gail Sheehy in *Passages*, "may be essential to infuse our first commitments with excitement and intensity, and sustain us in those commitments long enough to gain us some experience in living."[2] Paradoxically, at the root of much discontent among today's corporate realists are the highly romanticized myths and expectations women thought they'd dispensed with years ago. An examination of these myths illuminates the complex reasons behind women's sense of corporate betrayal.

Like so much else, women's myths of success were shaped by a largely innocent but highly respected source: mothers. While a recent University of Texas survey of fifty women reports that "female leaders . . . saw their fathers as primary role models,"[3] our more extensive interviews found in almost all cases that women's concepts of their future success came from maternal influences—both positive and negative (hardly surprising, when fathers of the fifties and sixties were seldom at home). One communications executive says, "I've read a lot of studies saying that Daddy's girl is always the most successful. In my case, nothing could be further from the truth." Most women agree. The grandiose fantasies women wove for themselves—in all generations from pioneer through today's post-Yuppie—derive much more from mother's influence than from father's. "My mother's very smart; she has a degree from Wellesley, but she does a lot of things she doesn't get paid for. And she keeps reinforcing that work is the living end," says Marcie, a thirty-seven-year-old research director. Hers was not the only mother whose messages, tacit and overt, fueled the mythic conception of work: "My mother should have been running GM instead of running me," sighs Dana, a cosmetics industry veteran. "And she spent her entire life trying to make something out of her children's lives. In junior high when everyone else was baby-sitting for fifty cents an hour, my mother suggested I give piano lessons for ten dollars. And she kept her foot in my back."

For three generations of women in the work force—the pioneer careerists, the "accidental careerists" who fell into corporate opportunities, and the post-feminists—the perpetual allure of the corporate mystique corresponds with long-held fantasies of success and justifies the effort it took to get and stay there, whatever the eventual reality. The pioneers felt the pressure to trailblaze with myths that drove them to bold accomplishments in the corporate world. As MasterCard International senior vice president Joanne Black puts it, "For us, it was the brink of a new frontier, like being the first into space." For the Accidental Careerists, there was an added pressure. "I was just lucky that this job I fell into became a career," Marcie admits. "That recognition made me both need and resent the job more—sort of love/hate." For the post-feminist generation, the pressure is of a different and more intense nature: "I felt a lot of peer pressure at college. So many of my friends were business majors and interviewing like crazy," one young bank vice president admits. "My roommate was an electrical engineer and had more job offers than she knew what to do with. So I did feel pressure in terms of getting a job and the competition." Says Kyle, a young systems analyst. "If I were to stop working, because of the societal stigma attached, I'd be worried people would think there was something wrong with me. The pressure is on to maintain a business career."

Swept up in a tidal wave of unlimited potential, today's post-collegiate woman is carried along out of a need to "fit" some pattern, a need set up by those same myths and expectations on which she's been nurtured.

The Myths on the Way to Making It

Myth provides the drama, and history puts the show on the road," writes cultural historian Warren Susman.[4] Myths help set goals. They explain our choices. They thread through corporate careers, each a foundation of or a springboard to the next landing, where the myth receives yet more embroidery in woman's effort to direct reality to mesh with her expectation. But myths almost always overpromise and underdeliver. Their function is largely utopian. In the present predominantly male corporate culture, women's myths, far from enhancing fulfillment, almost preordain disenchantment. Myths also operate paradoxically. They can be both motivating and limiting, both productive and self-defeating, both "right" and "wrong." The same myths that earlier propel women upward later contribute directly to their disillusionment and deacceleration. Myths also exert tremendous influence as guarantors of society's esteem. As Amanda, a thirty-three-year-old textile executive puts it, "My career gives me a great sense of self-worth. I'd be single all my life if marriage meant I had to give up my career. I am very dependent on the feedback I get." Psychologist Maggie Scarf illuminates the connection between self-esteem and the extent to which a woman is loved and liked and valued by others: "Take away the gratifying input from the outside—from . . . co-workers—and she may collapse."[5] As we trace the course of women's career landings, it becomes obvious that women are conditioned from childhood to a series of expectations grounded in myth and misinformation. Twenty years later, women barely recall that they have struck a "unilateral bargain with the world" predicated on the complex myths that, one by one, come to govern their corporate lives.

The Myth of Unlimited Potential

My innate lack of confidence has been the bane of my existence," bemoans Megan, a thirty-four-year-old assistant vice president at a major midwestern bank. "To counteract it, my mother even painted a drawing of the Little Engine That Could on my nursery room wall." Twenty years later, an enchanting young girl dressed for success in bow tie and pearls, and carrying an attaché case poses for a full-page ad whose headline for today's Barbie Doll reads: "We girls can do anything, right, Barbie!" For years, women have bought a variation of that myth, the Myth of Unlimited Potential. In the wake of a glut of publicity announcing ever-widening horizons for women, parents and teachers eagerly exhort their charges to make up for lost time and the missed opportunities of prior generations. There are suddenly no barriers a strong will can't conquer. So ingrained is the classic overachiever pattern that women have for years accepted on faith, and despite all reality to the contrary, that theirs was the generation destined to take on the world—and win. The internalizing of responsibility for one's own destiny seemed the inevitable outcome of a me-generation mentality that favored individual accountability over collective complaining.

Ultimately, the Myth of Unlimited Potential is closely tethered to the myth that follows—the Myth of Individual Recognition. For the Myth of Unlimited Potential depends on women believing that the key to success lies primarily within themselves.

The tacit quid pro quo of the Myth of Unlimited Potential is the relatively new notion that if women actively assume responsibility for achieving their own success, the very act of assumption will itself be rewarded. As Margaret Touborg, executive assistant to the president of Radcliffe College comments, "High expectations for a career is a form of arrogance. All their lives, women have been told, 'You're the best, you're the brightest, much is expected of you.' Who can blame each generation for thinking that the future is just a little bit brighter for them than it was for those who went before?"

The Myth of Individual Recognition

"When I was first hired, I felt the company must have recognized some special quality in me—my good education, my communication skills," Tina, age twenty-two, begins hesitantly. "I thought they were recognizing me not for my ability to type a perfect page, but for my intellect—and that part of me would be very stimulated by my work." To no small extent, women have perenially excelled within the context of individual recognition, particularly in academic environments. Mastery experiences from an early age reinforce women's belief that individual talent and effort will be recognized and rewarded. And women continue to project onto the corporate experience this expectation, which has so richly rewarded them in the past. "That's the gender difference," asserts Dr. Carol Galligan, psychologist/psychoanalyst and director of the Women's Institute, a collective of women psychologists dedicated to redefining the psychology of women. "And I hear it over and over again from women patients: 'I worked all weekend and every night for five weeks, and no one appreciates it. No one says thanks. They just used me.' Women are surprised when I tell them that's what they pay you for."

It is not only entry-level women like Tina for whom the Myth of Individual Recognition lives. Ruth, at forty the manager of investment data services for a large commercial bank, says, "I felt the corporation recognized I was valuable. I've always worked for people who appreciated my efforts." This need for individual recognition and achievement —more than the cliché that women without a team sports background don't appreciate teamwork—goes a long way toward understanding why women measure success in *individual* terms.

Ownership of a task, project, title, or idea—critical to the life of this myth—comes to dictate women's sense of self-esteem inside the corporate environment. "People can't sell the product without you. And you get that recognition," explains Diana, a thirty-four-year-old bank vice president in international finance. With the Myth of Individual Recognition, women condition themselves to anticipate a standard of appreciation corporations are unprepared and unable to reward. To obtain individual recognition, women will often accept staff jobs or limited-duration "loans" to nonprofit organizations or task forces—so-called opportunities that men, unencumbered by the Myth of Individual Recognition, immediately perceive as the dead-ends they are. The Myth of Individual Recognition is hard to shake. Among successful corporate women, the wolf of ambition and recognition stalks hungrily for reward. Conditioned to look for that individual stroke, which becomes increasingly elusive the higher they climb, women end up betrayed by the very environment into which they have read many of their fantasies of individual fame and recognition. Comments Diana, "You start to develop something that isn't immediately associated with you. People don't say, 'Oh, that's Diana's idea,' and, 'Wow, that was terrific you did that.' I had to learn to be in the background and still be effective." Men see it differently. Offers Jason, a thirty-year-old male public relations executive: "Men don't take it so personally. It's more a sense of 'I'm going to win this game!' That's a different attitude than 'I want to be wonderful at what I do.' For women, the concentration is on me, not on the game." The sense of having been recognized, or "chosen" to trailblaze feeds women's need for individual recognition and reward.

The latest generation of corporate arrivals has been no more successful in dispelling the Myth of Individual Recognition, despite their apparent enhanced sense of mastery. "They have a confidence, a spirit of independence that women ten years ago didn't have," reports one vice president of her newer corporate arrivals. "They're *individually excellent* but often have no desire to be part of the team. So in a short period of time they either get religion, dig in and stay, or they'll say there isn't enough opportunity to move up, and they'll leave to go to smaller companies, or to do something entrepreneurial"— where there is perceived to be greater recognition. The Myth of Individual Recognition encourages women to believe they are leaving a uniquely personal stamp on a largely impersonal environment. Oblivious of the wave of anonymity that will ultimately wash over them, corporate women carry with them throughout their careers the illusion that they are leaving indelible footprints in the sand.

The Myth of Irreplaceability

The Myth of Irreplaceability is characterized by the urgent need to feel that one is materially contributing to the success and well-being of the organization. It is an illusion grounded in the uniquely egocentric experiences women have as a pampered child—often their mother's. And the myth is a prelude to women's truly irreplaceable role as birth-giver and nurturer, an experience men can never duplicate. Says one senior executive of her early ambition, "I thought I could make myself indispensable to some company as an analyst, not recognizing it was axiomatic, of course, that you couldn't put a woman in a position of managing men—there would be too much anxiety on the men's part." There is no role in the Myth of Irreplaceability for women on the corporate periphery— where they usually end up, despite their success.

"I was only twenty-six or twenty-seven, and I was on such a high," reports Denise, a former Washington aide now in a packaged goods conglomerate. "I loved it. I was really making a contribution to the national debate on key issues for this country. I look back and see I was highly inflating my importance, but then I really did feel like part of the action. And even today, it's still terribly important to me to be well used, in the good sense of the word. And my boss utilizes me well."

Comments Dr. Carol Galligan, "I think the irreplaceability syndrome is really an equivalent or carryover of the old womanly wish, 'I want him to be helplessly in love with me.' And when you ask women what they mean by 'helplessly,' they really mean, 'so he'll need me so much the bonds will never be broken; he can't leave because the thought of separating from *moi* is intolerable.' That's a good example of the conflict between women's fantasies and reality in the corporate culture."

Dr. Celia Halas and Dr. Roberta Matteson confirm that women invest emotionally in relationships, "hoping their unselfish commitments will pay generous dividends in the form of love and appreciation, which will in turn boost their sense of self-worth. All too often, their relationships go bankrupt. After a while a woman says to herself, 'I've done everything that was expected of me . . . and I haven't asked for much in return. How come I feel so bad?' "[6] In interview after interview, corporate women set up the same no-win relationship by projecting onto the corporation a need of their irreplaceable services that doesn't exist.

The Myth of the Meritocracy

The quest for the holy grail of individual recognition and irreplaceability leads naturally to the assumption that skilled performance will get you there. "I thought if I was good, everything would flow from that," recalls Trish, a publishing executive now in her late thirties. "I actually thought that if you were fair to other people in life, life would be fair to you. And although that's not the case, I am not quite willing to give that up." The myth that recognition rewards achievement is one of the most potent and pervasive among women at all levels within the corporate hierarchy. For many women, their belief in an operative meritocracy began in school, where talent and hard work were always rewarded, and that belief persists against all odds. Comments Dr. Frederick Hauser, clinical psychologist and chairman of the Department of Graduate Management at Pace University, "The Myth of the Meritocracy is a hangover from the old days of academic conditioning—an environment in which girls traditionally do better than boys, and which allows women to exercise their perfectionistic tendencies. In school, women learn they can compete very effectively with a *system* in which the goals and objectives are self-set. But that's significantly different from the corporate culture in which they must compete head on with others, a situation men are used to within an organization."

This sense of quid pro quo reward in exchange for hard work is further fueled by women's ordinal position—that is, where they stand in the birth order. An uncannily high number of corporate women interviewees are firstborns, and as Dr. Jerome Kagan, professor of Human Development in Harvard University's Department of Psychology, points out, "Studies show that first children tend to trust authority and believe in the legitimacy of authority more deeply because of their relation of privilege with the parents. For the firstborn, all seems orderly; it seems to be a just world. Therefore first children are unusually conscientious, because they've had parental guarantees—backed by early experience—that for them, all will turn out well."

"Almost all the women in my class at business school were firstborns," confirms Nina, illustrating Dr. Kagan's thesis with an ancedote out of her own experience as a management trainee at a major international bank: "At the time I started, I was relatively optimistic about women's opportunities at the bank, especially relative to other industries. I was very young and was still in the mode that life was a meritocracy. By the time I left the training program, my sense of meritocracy had already been violated. You realize that things no longer work the way they did in college."

It comes as no surprise that many men reject early on any belief in a corporate meritocracy; they then embrace and often thrive on gamesmanship. Is it any wonder in the face of a different male concept of rules and reward that women cling ever harder to the Myth of Meritocracy? Michael Maccoby celebrates at length man's subliminal fever for corporate gamesmanship: "He sees a developing project, human relations, and his own career in terms of options and possibilities, as if they were a game."[7] Men seldom fall prey to the Myth of Meritocracy— or, if they do, they outgrow the illusion sooner. "It's the flotsam theory of advancement," suggests former Phelps Dodge International president Russell E. Marks, Jr. "Someone simply floats to the top. And the way men work, it's not just innate ability, because people who have risen to a certain level have all demonstrated ability, so you have a pool of people all of whom have demonstrated they can run the company." After that, says Marks, now a senior vice president with executive search consultants Haley Associates, politics takes over.

"Because promotion is often pure chance—you happen to be in mind at a moment of pure need on the part of the company." In the mythic meritocracy that women carry about in their heads, women work hard to be chosen . . . and then they wait. And wait.

The Myth of Reward

You think, 'If they only know I'm trying hard and eating Rolaids over my anxiety, then I'll get fed,' " sighs Sheila, an account supervisor in her mid-thirties. For women who perceive corporate life as a pyramidal meritocracy, the corollary myth of reward inevitably follows. "I was looking forward to something that had a direct ladder up," corroborates Diana, a bank vice president. "Where I had clear opportunity ahead of me. Obviously, there are titles, but that's not as important as seeing that if you are good at what you do they will give you more responsibility. If you are good, you'll be rewarded for it." In this scenario, women managers, having endowed corporations with a humanistic perspective, believe that a tacit quid pro quo exists. "What keeps me at my company," admits Molly, a midwestern bank vice president, "is a tremendous amount of personal pride more than anything. It's fairly self-centered, but I get tremendous amounts of positive reinforcement from customers and the people I work with—the feeling that I'm doing a good job. It's not the salary or the feeling I'm doing something constructive. I have never been that motivated by salary."

The Myth of Reward reconfirms the observation that most women *are* working for different strokes than male peers. Although women, like men, are working for economic self-sufficiency, they are really in the game for more psychic rewards: "I love being in the situation I am in where I am being rewarded for performance," says Heidi, a young assistant product manager with a New Jersey packaged goods company. "It adds pressure because you realize you have to perform, but you feel that even here at my company—a corporation where you aren't going to get direct rewards for the efforts put in, because they can't really reward you in excess of how they are rewarding others—you do feel that your input really does to some extent determine what you receive." It is this blind optimism about the rewards of dedication that sets women up for disappointment. Heidi typifies the pattern: "Reward isn't in the salary. But the way the company handles it is that they give you a lot of intrinsic rewards. They create this real sort of team feeling and you can become a star on the team. People are really spoken of highly when they fit and are doing well, and there is a lot of verbal reinforcement."

Men, on the other hand, are far more realistic about how, and why, reward is doled out. Observes one oil company executive in his late thirties, "You all take the early train in together, and leave on the same train home to play golf. You have to be accepted by the group to do well." It is "fit," men recognize, not fastidiousness that brings the ultimate goodies.

For women, the Myth of Reward creates a cruel paradox: because the rewards for which they toil are so intangible, corporations have a difficult time identifying the source of women's frustration as they rise through the ranks. Women are equally mystified, as the fulfillment gap between expectation and reward widens the higher they climb. Few women consciously recognize that the traditional corporate rewards for which men work are not the psychic rewards for which they strive. The most ubiquitous answer to a corporate problem— throw more money or another title at it and hope the irritation will go away—is exactly the least satisfying reward to most of these women. Women are loaded for a different bear—largely unconscious that their expectation of recognition is another dead-end in the maze.

The Myth of Growth

Among the intangible rewards which women seek in a corporate career is an inherently female yearning for self-improvement. While entry-level men are negotiating starting salary, even the brightest women are often evaluating the job in terms of how much they will be challenged and how much they will grow: "I had always been a sucker for 'steep learning curves' and the opportunity to make a 'lasting contribution'—not to mention being 'mentored' by the chairman of the board of a Fortune 100 company," wrote Mary Cunningham recently.[8] Molly, a Chicago executive, thinks the Myth of Growth derived from years of lessons by anxious parents—lessons designed to make daughters more well rounded, "interesting" women. "Most of our parents had been raised during the Depression, and they wanted to expose us to as much as possible. I was sent to ceramics, ballet, this, that. . . . I was always bouncing around from subject to subject, no permanency. I was always trying things out. And I still go at things in that kind of experimental way." Amanda, a textile executive explains: "I never perceived my now-labeled 'ambition' as ambition per se. I always thought of it as the challenge of adversity. If you don't know anything about economics, why not get an M.B.A.? I have always respected things I don't know very much about."

Ultimately, the significance of a job and women's happiness in it is measured not just in titular and salary terms, if she is honest with herself, but at a deeper, more uniquely female level of satisfaction. She measures success in how much she grows from or is enriched by the experience. Molly continues to say of her job as a cash management advisor at a midwestern bank: "What has always been important to me is what I am learning. And as long as the learning process in one shape or form is continuing, I haven't felt a great motivation to seek out a new environment." The myth of growth still survives despite greater contemporary pressure for recognition and economic rewards. Regardless of the growing sophistication of women managers, the "learning curve mystique" is still a vibrant part of the mix.

Related to this is the avowed need for creative contribution. One corporate counsel told us, "What I like about my job is the creativity. You are solving problems all the time, anticipating problems. How to get from point A to point B." Ironically, as the literature from *The Organization Man* to *Something Happened* to *The Arrangement* vividly illustrates, women have inadvertently sought out a peculiar environment for the proving ground of their own creative impulse. If the target most women seek is creativity and challenge, repetition and tedium are the first disillusioning corporate enemies. Repetition aversion emerged as a strong motif in almost every interview. Janice, a human resource executive, describes an early assignment to redesign career paths within her firm: "I was so good at it that they asked me to do it over and over again in other departments. And my eyes glazed." A network television executive admits, "If I have done something a couple of times, I am ready to move on. Staying power is one of my weaknesses. I sort of like the new challenge—just to keep growing, I guess."

Women have a need not just to nurture but to *be* nurtured, to grow and flower within the corporation, that contributes to their eventual corporate disappointment and disillusionment. Few men suffer the same feelings. "Frankly, after business school, I wasn't interested in learning anymore," reminisces one airline executive in his mid-thirties. "I'd been doing that for years. I wanted to go out and *do* something." For men, success is measured not by learning something, but by controlling it.

The Myth of the
Corporation as Family

Searching for security, separating from one family, women inadvertently embrace another. They bond with the big strong corporate environment, which they imagine to be "safe," safer today than marriage, certainly. "Offices provide substitute families," observes publishing magnate Clay Felker, "a great attraction for a 'Peter Pan' generation of people who see divorce as inevitable and are reluctant to grow up and commit themselves to more traditional institutions."[9] Over and over again, we heard the "family" sentiment from women: "As a single person, I see my job as my point of continuity," says Elaine, a forty-three-year-old cosmetics marketing director. Paula Bernstein describes in *Family Ties, Corporate Bonds*, the androgynous desire to recreate the family environment in which most of one's early learning and achievement have taken place, to impose it on the workplace even though "the corporation cannot love us back. It makes no lifetime commitment to us, the way a family does—or should."[10] Women do even more. They develop a familial attachment to the *corporate entity as a whole*. The root of much of the eventual damage to corporate women's self-esteem comes from early, unconscious tendencies to anthropomorphize the company itself —the *inanimate* corporate entity—and to cast the corporation as either a proud father or a demanding lover, expecting the appropriate emotional feedback in return. Unlike family affiliations, the corporate family is presumed "safer" because one can theoretically close the door on responsibility at day's end.

Many women recognize themselves in this comment from Sheila, a ten-year veteran at her company: "I *have* to personify the corporation at this point to feel I'm getting something back even if I'm not. I truly believed that if I worked hard, I'd be rewarded with long-term employee security. This is like a family. And my love-hate relationship with it is really like a parental conflict. Part of me wants to break away from the family. And part can't."

While men describe themselves as "units" or "islands" within the corporation, women see themselves as tethered by a web of connections. These connections, as complexly woven as a Flemish tapestry, serve a variety of affiliative demands without which work within the corporation would become meaningless for most women.[11] "I guess I like the interaction with people," one television executive admits. Even the most independent woman is disappointed by the isolation: "I've only known two environments—the bank and the conglomerate," says Faye. "But at the latter, there wasn't a peer group like I was used to having. The first day on the job I assumed my boss would take me to lunch. Instead, I went across the street to Burger King and ate a hamburger alone."

What of women for whom the corporation *becomes* the father—an unfeeling, largely unresponsive patriarchal entity into which women invest their emotions, their need for approval and their dreams? Whatever the relationship or role model of their fathers, many women arrogate to the corporation paternal superiority as well as approval and validation as a good daughter. Contrary to studies suggesting that a healthy father-daughter relationship is the model that drives most women in corporate life, our interviews revealed a striking pattern of women who enter corporate life determined to prove something to a *weak* or *absent* father.[12] As detailed in the next chapter, a disproportionately high percentage of successful corporate women come from matriarchal households or divorced parents. Why was the myth of an infallible corporate daddy embraced unconsciously and universally? Was it to replace the all-too-fallible real-life role model who had failed to provide the necessary financial and emotional security such gifted women needed? Janice, a twelve-year veteran with one of the country's largest oil companies, recalls of her adolescence: "I felt sorry for and protective of my father, because my mother always yelled at him. He was always trying to please her." For such women, where a father was unreliable, the corporation is sure and secure. Here today, here tomorrow. So women continue to replay scenarios of failed father-daughter relationships hoping, this time, to make it come out right.

Ironically, as Paula Bernstein observes, "fathers" in corporations select "sons" to mentor to the top, but treat virtually all women as "daughters," consigning them to second-class status. Yet so powerful is the belief in infallible corporate fatherhood that when women "fail," they internalize the blame, having failed as dutiful daughters.

Realization of the failure of filial myths can lead to almost violent emotional reactions. Ann S. Barry, director of research at the executive recruiting firm of Handy Associates, characterizes the inadvertent self-sabotage this way: "I've seen women just self-destruct. They become too defensive. Criticism becomes a personal affront to women who like to be Daddy's good girl." As Sheila admits of her corporate relationship over time: "I've won every one of my promotions for being a good girl. I've only seriously complained twice in eight years, when they didn't promote me to account supervisor. I threatened to quit. And the second time, recently, I demanded a timetable for promotion to vice president. And you know what I found? Men give ultimatums years earlier than women."

The Myth of the
Corporation as Lover

Because corporations are still so overwhelmingly culturally male, it is not surprising that the role women unconsciously assign the corporation is not restricted to Daddy. There is the "corporate bride," the woman who has elevated corporate affiliation to the level of surrogate lover—a loyal, steady, reliable, and endlessly challenging companion in a fifty-fifty partnership. Small wonder, in a corporate society in which only 41 percent of the women executives are married (as against 90 percent of the men), 28 percent have never been married, and most women are married to their jobs an average of fifty-three hours each week.[13] Observes Sheila, "For a lot of us, the company's the only spouse. If you look at the women who've made it in our company, there isn't one with a happy normal marriage. And most are single." As in all modern relationships, the corporation is tacitly expected to contribute its fair share to the partnership. This unilateral prenuptial contract is another psychic bargain unconsciously struck between women and the corporation.

Why do young women find themselves attracted by this myth? And why, once women have been in the market longer, don't they wise up faster, instead of becoming so many corporate spinsters? The classic answer is fear of commitment. Caught in the rule change where neither marriage nor love was forever, the answer to this generation was never to trust its destiny to a man. An entire literature has risen to the challenge of exploding women's romantic notions about marriage. Next to nothing has been written to explore and explode women's romantic fantasies about work—and more specifically, fantasies that apply to the corporate world. The corporation has become the first husband, sometimes the sole contemporary focus of identity and gratification. Women become inadvertent victims of the "myth of independence," in which women assume that "the prioritizing of goals in a woman's life should be her search for self—and that that search must be done alone."[14]

"I never wanted to be economically dependent, and I still don't," proclaims Hillary, a thirty-seven-year-old energy executive. "Because, by God, at the office I can accept eight or even sixteen hours of someone telling me how high to jump. Fine. They're paying me for the privilege. And I can always vote with my feet and go elsewhere. But when you marry someone, it's a lot rougher emotionally because you live with it twenty-four hours a day. You don't just leave it. You carry great scars with you. So it's very important someone can't tell you how high to jump in your personal life." In transferring their expectations for happiness and fulfillment to a corporation, women create a new paradox: a job can't hurt you as a man can, women reason. But how could it be expected to respond compassionately?

Cashing in one dependent relationship for another, women are haunted by the same negative aspects of dependency from which they were running in their personal lives. Celia Halas and Roberta Matteson warn: "Women have confused the capacity for affiliation with the need for affiliation. . . . It is the connection with someone else's power that relieves our sense of disconnectedness."[15] Substitute the word *corporation* for the word *person*, and we have an accurate portrait of all too many of today's unhappy women managers. In setting out to avoid one dependency, women simply run into another. In establishing their identity as corporate brides, women too often lose their own. When the corporation becomes the lover, leaving is more than quitting; it represents a largely unexamined, heretofore inexplicable loss of self.

Myth of the Loyal Retainer

As with almost all of these myths, one paves the way for another. Why do so many women stay on in their corporate positions long after the bloom is off the rose? The Myth of the Corporate Family, fueled by the Myth of Irreplaceability spawns the Myth of the Loyal Retainer. Like the dutiful Mrs. Danvers in Alfred Hitchcock's *Rebecca*, corporate women, out of a misplaced sense of responsibility, hang around long after the body is cold. Kyle, a twenty-four-year-old systems engineer with a large computer manufacturer comments, "From the day you start here they impress on you your value as an individual and corporate asset—that we're one happy family—and the value they've invested in you. So I feel a responsibility to stay." This same investment/responsibility ratio also explains why so many women stay in companies with which they are only marginally satisfied. One commodities executive confessed, "I *do* owe the company a lot. I shouldn't rock the boat. My mother had told me not to push the company for any special treatment after my maternity leave—they'd given me enough already. If the recruiter calls? I'd tell them not now. Can you imagine starting fresh at this point and trying to set the same terms I have now?"

The "web" mentality encourages women to view the time and loyalty given to a corporation as an incremental process. "I really felt I was building something," said one marketing manager with a national packaged goods manufacturer, "and I hated to leave. To just walk away." Comments Dr. Carol Galligan, "Even women who work as secretaries to subsidize an acting career have said to me, 'I hate to go to a new job.' The single biggest cause of depression among women is un-familiarity. Their unwillingness to leave a job is a reluctance to break bonds and sever connections, an unwillingness to tolerate change and unfamiliarity." Whereas corporations see contributions in sequential terms—"You're only as good as your last marketing plan"—women's nurturance of the ideal of connection forces them to order their experience in con-tinuous terms—"I felt I was building something." The web of connectedness becomes a safety net, a personal insurance policy against failure on the corporate high wire.

The corporation, however, doesn't perceive it that way. Writer Carol Gilligan has established that when hierarchal relationships finally destroy the web of connectedness, "when nets are portrayed as dangerous entrapments, impeding flight rather than protecting against the fall" women find their long-term assumptions and experiences undermined.[16]

To put it another way, too many women imbue the corporation with the same mystique they would a long-term marriage. When the corporation signals it is ready to sever ties most women have long regarded as sacrosanct, they respond like any jilted wife, "After all we've meant to each other?"

The Myth of the Peaceable Kingdom

Unlike the pioneer careerists, today's new corporate women, products of egalitarian educational experience, expect to compete equally against men and to be equally rewarded for performance. Women of the eighties anticipate being treated as professionals, irrespective of gender. "It seems to me you read women's issues into situations that aren't really there like male-female boss problems," Kelly, a twenty-four-year-old junior manager comments. "I don't want to be treated like a woman. I expect to be treated like a manager." Sex is a largely irrelevant component of what they perceive as one big, happy corporate kingdom. "We're all in this together," they reason. Recalls Bonnie, a banking executive in her mid-twenties, "I remember having a conversation over drinks last year with a male friend, and a friend of his who was British. And this British friend said, 'There's no place for a woman in business. Because whenever I deal with a woman, I can't get past wanting to fuck her brains out.'" She continues, "We're not aware that we're being perceived as women first—as symbols—before we're being perceived as professionals. And I remember saying to this British fellow, 'Maybe women aren't making it in business because you don't want them to.'"

A truly egalitarian society is still only a wistful dream: "Studies show that while the vast majority of Americans want a balanced family (a child of each sex) most want a boy first. Ninety-four percent of men and 81 percent of women said they would choose a firstborn son, in one recent study by social psychologists Roberta Steinbacher, and Faith D. Gilroy."[17] Yet the Myth of the Peaceable Kingdom persists against all odds. Because this myth is vital to women's eventual disillusionment with corporate life, we will discuss it later in "The Uneasy Peace."

Myth of the Mentor

"It really comes down to the fact that you need a champion, a rabbi, a mentor," one male executive recruiter told us. "And it's a big problem because obviously the guy 'must' be sleeping with the lady if it is a male-female thing. Whereas no one ever accuses him of having a homosexual relationship with a guy if he is *his* mentor." Central to the success and betrayal cycle is the cliché of the *eminence grise*—the wise father figure ready and willing to launch a bright young woman into the intoxicating corporate stratosphere. Yet today, most women—even Mary Cunningham—put the word "mentor" in quotation marks. *Is* there the realistic possibility of a mentor for women? Or is what works for men just another myth for women? "Men feel they can develop bonds with other men—father-son relationships—that women can't because underlying sexual tension will eventually destroy the camaraderie that's necessary between two corporate individuals to play the game," one *Fortune* 500 executive in his late thirties admits candidly. When women look to the male promotion dynamic as a model against which to measure their own success, they set themselves up for betrayal. Wondering what has gone "wrong" because they've been unable to attract a mentor, women blame themselves. They fail to see that the system works differently for women, that mentoring in its purest sense is more myth than reality for most women. Recalls Becka, a senior banking executive, "You can only have a mentor if you earn a mentor. The only way to do that is by doing good work for someone in a position of responsibility. And if you're that visible, chances are you probably could have made it without a mentor."

Yet surrendering the Myth of the Mentor is a wrenching

concession, considering the alternative. Comments Marian, principal at a prestigious national consulting firm, "I think the most difficult thing is that I feel I'm always learning on my own. I don't know what a mentor situation is. You only develop that relationship over time—by playing golf together, drinking together, and I don't think many women have that. Added to which, a partner can only champion so many people." Yet the myth persists. A New York advertising agency vice president has written in her marketing career book that the mentor "will be obvious to the alert woman. The mentor is the one person in the firm who, for purely nonselfish reasons, will stand out for another as a supporter and champion. Often the role is sought out by the mentor as a means to surrogate for some void in his or her own life. The motivation, though, is almost always sincere."[18] Fortunately, women are becoming more sophisticated. One Harvard Business School class recently spent the entire session heatedly debating whether male mentors for women create more trouble than they're worth because of "real, potential, or perceived sexual pressures."[19]

Myth of the Androgynous Manager

Given the mythic conceptions of the Peaceable Kingdom and the platonic Mentor, it is not surprising that women have also brought into corporate culture the utopian belief in an androgynous management style in which gender is scarcely distinguishable if one carefully follows the rules. One woman executive recruiter interviewed advises women, "You can't put your heart on your sleeve. You must withhold your feelings. Let less be mirrored in your face. Women have a tendency to take things personally. That's a tip-off to whether you're emotionally mature or not." In a predominantly male culture, the premium is put on women's ability to set aside traditional biases toward caring, individual responsibility, and sensitivity in favor of more androgynous behavior. In reality, "androgyny" becomes a one-sided bargain—a code word to force women to conform to male views and expectations. When women fail to achieve that goal, they blame themselves.

Is that demand realistically either desirable or attainable? Increasingly, experience suggests it is not. Women grow up with an inherent ethic of caring that men do not have.[20] Such values do not automatically terminate when a woman is handed the keys to the corporate kingdom. Moreover, women who do deny this side of themselves in pursuit of competitive success are maligned by both sexes as unfeminine, hardhearted misfits within their gender. The choice leaves women in an untenable position. As Alice Sargeant notes, "As a result, [a woman] views the problem as hers, and her solution is to try to change herself. The system is not questioned."[21] Today, the notion of androgynous management has been perverted by corporations using androgyny as an excuse to force one-sided change in women's behavior without offering any concurrent hope for an evolution in corporate values. As a result, women become disillusioned, then angry. They perceive betrayal in being asked to adopt chameleon colors as the price of self-protection.

The Living-on-the-Edge Myth

I know it's stupid," says one woman in her late twenties, "but every time I open my paycheck, I wonder if it's the last one I'm going to get from the company. I guess it's just me," she concludes. But she's not alone. A remarkable number of successful women who have clearly made it in their companies still perceive themselves as precariously balanced at the edge of a psychological precipice that could give way any minute. "I want to be financially secure; I don't want to be a bag lady," says Catherine, a young banker. Her perception is echoed by her older counterparts who subconsciously believe they, too, are living right at the edge of potential career disaster. "It has always been a source of comfort for me to know that no matter what happens, I have my little co-op that I am subletting, and that I can still carry it no matter what, because I always want to have a place to live," says Hillary, one of the top oil multi-nationals most senior women executives. Like many, she worries that all her hard-won rewards can be swept away by a single slipup. Month after month, when the guillotine doesn't fall, she regards her continued presence as a reprieve for which she is duly grateful.

Why do women feel so precariously balanced? The answers start at home. "My father was a photographer," recalls Carla, a research director, "and we never knew from one month to the next if we'd have money to follow our dreams, or even have food on the table. I can even remember my mother begging him for grocery money." Recalls Cindy, "My father came over on the last boat from Germany in 1940, and no matter how successful the manufacturing business he started was, he always raised us to believe we could lose everything tomorrow." As a result of such conditioning, women take longer than men to feel they've "made it." They're more skeptical of their status and the security it can buy. And they're more vulnerable —to being fired, to topping out, to being excluded. They've absorbed a subliminal message: With few successful role models ahead, they, like Cindy's immigrant father, sense the danger of derailment and disaster implicit in the opportunity for success.

The ultimate irony of the Living-on-the-Edge Myth is that it forces women to live in one of two extremes—in an effort to escape the edge of disaster, they often cling to the security of the corporation. Eventually, they confront inevitable disappointment at never getting the degree of reassurance they need to feel "successful."

The Myth of Ideal Industries

For years, well-intentioned men have shuttled women toward certain "receptive" industries, mistakenly assuming the ubiquitous presence of women is a guarantee of their equality. Explains Pace University's Frederick Hauser, "Part of the problem is male managers in their late thirties to forties who view their own feminism positively, yet are perpetuating myths without even being aware they're part of the problem. They consciously mean their advice very sincerely—which is what makes the mythology so powerful and so much more destructive." Typical of this attitude is Ted, a financial services executive: "Banking is the perfect career for women, because it requires someone with strong interpersonal and marketing skills. Fifty percent of banking is personal selling skills. And women can bring those skills never matched by another boring guy in a gray suit." Yet a large percentage of the women interviewed started in banking, and their disillusionment seems no less than that of women who have careers in industries that are regarded as less receptive. The dropout rate remains constant across the board. Ditto for women in publishing, advertising, and other so-called women's fields. Retailing provides another object lesson. Says one former retailing executive who left the field for a job in financial services, "Women in retailing can be excellent, but they're simply overlooked even though they've excelled compared to their peers. And even though it's a quantifiable environment."

And, do women's own more perfectionistic expectations create a need to project perfection on the industries they join? One magazine yearly chooses an honor roll of the ten best companies for women. To prove a point, we interviewed several women from almost all the companies cited by the magazine. Is there such a thing as a "better" company for women? To judge from this list, the answer is no. Most of the women at the so-called best companies for women, as discussed later, are cynical. They conclude that too often the safety of a "good" reputation vis-à-vis women allows senior male management to knock off the few women who are threatening to really beat down the doors of the executive suite. As Dr. Frederick Hauser notes, "People responsible for a company's corporate communications feed this image of progressiveness toward women because it fits the current societal ethic of equity between men and women. The corporation is eager to spread the message, so women (and men) have been seduced into believing the message that things have changed more than they have."

Alongside myth in the psychic landscape lies expectation. Whereas myths are defined as ill-founded beliefs not grounded in fact, expectations are assumptions grounded in anticipation of a likely outcome, often with an attendant reward. Myth is grounded in fantasy. Expectation is grounded in experience. Together they form a game plan for a generation that was promised unlimited opportunity. Irrespective of generation, as women advance through corporate America, the impact of these expectations and assumptions on their eventual disillusionment becomes increasingly obvious.

The Moral Universe, the Moral Voice

Says Phil, in his thirties already treasurer of a large midwestern corporation, "I think a lot of people of my generation are frustrated because they brought to the workplace a sense of moral commitment, and they discover that there is no moral framework at all. Business is ultimately a transaction-type process. Very few people in business have a sense of ideological commitment." Except women. One of the key insights into women's disillusionment with corporate life is our discovery of a moral or judgmental voice that pervades women's analysis of their status within the company—and of the company itself. Over and over again, we heard women analyze their corporations in terms of approval and disapproval. Denise, director of issues management with a consumer products company, recalls: "It was the perfect fit. The job had a community and corporate orientation, it had political and writing aspects—all the stuff I loved. The company just fit like a glove."

Implicit in the different voice inherent in women is "an injunction to care, a responsibility to discern and alleviate the 'real and recognizable trouble' of this world."[22] We found women's judgmental voice to be a dominant and influential characteristic in their eventual response to success, setting up a self-defeating expectation spiral. Whereas for men, the judgmental voice is a passive disaster-check—a kind of corporate Jiminy Cricket preventing them from doing wrong in an extreme—for women the moral voice is an active injunction to do right. So important is that moral imperative for most women that they will invent, if necessary, a moral context for their work, a context that becomes a rationale for the clash between what must be done and what women feel *should* be done. One high-ranking woman manager in the defense industry whose daily responsibilities include refining a variety of complex weapons systems recalls: "I remember sometime early on in the job thinking to myself, 'Somewhere there's a woman in Moscow with the same name,' and thinking 'I'm protecting us against them because I'm a defense contractor.' At the time, I was engineering a B-52 target system, and they gave us the silhouette of a Russian fighter to work from. If you scored a hit on the fuselage, that was considered very good because the pilot would be in that part of the plane. And I was really very stunned. I dropped my pencil at that and thought, 'What am I doing?' And that was the first time I, as a woman, questioned what I was doing there."

The emergence of the moral voice changes forever one's pragmatic illusions of being willing to do whatever a male peer would do to succeed.[23] Many men will do whatever it takes, often consciously submerging ethical standards or insisting those standards are not compromised. Suggests Dr. Hauser, "Men consider compromises, the commission of small sins, to be a reasonable price for acceptance within the corporation. Whereas women's sense of morality is more monolithic, less group-oriented—and related to a more immediate context. They feel they're responsible for their behavior within the family rather than on the team." This moral voice within women is one the male corporate culture has long acknowledged, but seldom respected. To the extent that successful women participate in board directorships of corporate America, they usually serve as the "ethics experts." Often culled from nonthreatening backgrounds such as government or academia, these women are given the thankless job of serving as modern-day Cassandras prophesying the right moral road in the wilderness.

Yet when women desert their moral voice in favor of power in-fighting, they are punished, harassed, or simply viewed with suspicion. As a male oil company executive notes, "You've got to ask yourself which women have been successful in the corporate world. More than anything else, if a woman is willing to do all the things a man is willing to do, she has the added burden of having to answer the questions men have about why she's willing to." Women are placed in a no-win bind. Cast in the corporate equivalent of a madonna-whore image, they can't afford not to care, because men expect them to, then pass over them for promotion because women's values and goals for the corporation are different from men's. Or, put simply, she's too soft. Later in one's career when the Moral Voice fails to exercise its potential to "make things better," or the professional cost of doing so becomes unacceptably high, women are caught in an untenable dilemma between success and betrayal.

The Faster Clock

Like a mysterious circadian rhythm, a special clock ticks subliminally within women, impatiently hurrying them along to their career destinations. But only they can hear it ticking away. "The world of finance and business—so antithetical to what I'd been brought up with—was passing me by," says Amanda, a former textile conglomerate executive who switched to financial consulting. In interview after interview, the notions of time passing, the fear of being left behind once the circus had passed, alerted us to this subliminal pacemaker, operating separately and independently of the infamous biological clock. Where does such a demanding internal time-keeper come from? "Maybe it's because women have real beginnings and endings so much more than men: Women have to pay attention to monthly clocks, to the onset of menstruation, to the clock of menopause. I think all of that has made women more sensitive to the urgency of time," theorizes one executive. Offers another, "I always had too much of a work ethic to waste time."

Subliminal awareness of the time clock, the internal gate-keeper of women's satisfaction, dogs women throughout their career, fueling their discontent at every level as they confront the "waste" involved. "It's like the scene in *Our Town*, where the girl goes back and sees all that time passing," confesses one young executive. "Your priorities come into focus more. I really ask myself now, 'What do I want to get out of the corporation?'" Tick. Tick. Tick. Janice, a human resources manager, confesses, "I don't relax for even a second during the day. And my boss will ask me, 'Are you gonna calm down today? Ease up on everybody?' My boss gives me lectures about the hours I put in—I'm considered a workaholic." Because the meter is running, women bring to corporate life a furious intensity, a need to "get on with it." They have a hard time tolerating the perceived casualness with which corporations and male peers treat time: "Meetings were my first taste of corporate life, and I don't even know what they were exercises in. I suppose you could call them a number of things—like masturbation or jerking off—but they were not held to make decisions."

The sense of immediacy—the legacy of a preoccupation with time passing—foreshadows the corporate disillusionment to come. Demanding immediate gratification, the time clock ironically prohibits women from projecting ahead. Time and again, otherwise successful women would stumble over the question, "Have you ever done a five-year plan for yourself?" Says one executive in her early thirties, "I never think about what I'm going to do in the future. I hate those kinds of questions in job interviews. Because your options change. Maybe it's a fear that if I decide to be VP in charge of widgets, I'll miss other outside opportunities." Each woman believes herself to be unique in her inability to project the future. "I am just not a person who plans," says Marian, principal with a consulting firm whose specialty is strategic planning. Having abjured five- and ten-year plans for themselves, women have little conception of an appropriate timetable for success, so they end up living in extremes—either demanding approbation sooner than they should or lingering in dead-end jobs far too long. In both cases, the subliminal clock is dominating them, driving them inexorably forward. With few role models at the top, women have no realistic conception of how long "success" should take. And with the wind of the EEOC at their backs, they had an often unrealistic track record of advancement in the seventies that fueled an appetite for even faster advancement through the eighties. In the end, like the casing of an overwound watch, they can no longer contain the jumble of turning wheels. Something snaps.

Asks one twenty-four-year-old marketing executive rhetorically, "All I have in this life is my time. What am I doing with it?"

Style versus Substance

As comedian Lily Tomlin ruefully admits, "I always wanted to be somebody. I see now that I should have been more specific."[24] Among most women with whom we spoke, the spontaneous attraction to a corporate career was far more in the conception than in the execution. Comments Dr. Carol Galligan, "Even today, how many people ask a little girl what she's going to be when she grows up?" Small wonder that several women in high-tech industries agreed with this systems analyst's job assessment: "I really don't give a damn about microchips." Women are inadvertently encouraged to glamorize work, to invest in a career less for practical reasons, as men do, than as a vehicle to individual recognition and self-satisfaction. A certain vagueness pervades their goals. Says one senior woman banking executive, "I decided I wanted to be successful—to make money, sit on a board of directors, make decisions." Confesses Hillary, a senior-level oil company executive, "I had always wanted to be independent financially, and this was obviously a means to do it. I never thought of it as 'getting into business' . . . The subject matter didn't really matter that much."

The younger the woman, the greater the disparity between the auspicious vision she has of her eventual success and the reality of what it will take to get there. Says twenty-two-year-old Tina, "Somehow I would be a hero of my profession; somehow I'd be known for something in a work context. But I didn't really know what it was to work." Comments Dina, a twenty-six-year-old public relations manager, "My definition of success is achieving prominence within the company . . . becoming known as an expert in the public's eye." She considers that statement for a moment, then adds, "One big realization I've come to is that success takes a lot longer than I thought. I always thought I'd move quicker." One management consultant, on the verge of making partner at one of the country's most prestigious firms, says bluntly, "I'm certainly interested in the trappings of partnership. I'm not driven to it as a route to the presidency of the firm, but as a recognition of what I've done." The trappings are proof of mastery as the day-to-day substance of her achievements is not. Such trappings often become the end in and of themselves, a latter-day *Good Housekeeping* Seal of Approval to male peers. Molly expresses a typical drive for the instant mastery corporate affiliation can bestow: "I wanted to be a neurosurgeon originally, which is sort of a joke at this point. But all of a sudden I got concerned about how long it was going to take. It seemed like a lot of time invested, so I went into banking instead."

When women discover that the corporate road will take longer than expected, and that real success transcends imposing titles and important-looking business cards, they feel betrayed by their own unrealistic expectations. As one male executive recruiter comments, "I don't think women are raised to think they're going to have to pay their dues as men do." Which leads one fifty-six-year-old woman banker to this observation, not without some justification: "I think exceedingly ambitious young women are interested in the image, not in the company, because they are so interested in competing professionally." As futures forecaster Steven Custer puts it, "We're a generation that's more interested in what's happening than in what it means."

"By the time you're thirty-five or forty, you realize you've been acting on wrong suppositions all along," observes Sheila, a thirty-four-year-old account supervisor. "And by that point, it's a scary thing to come to grips with, because you realize the myths become a self-fulfilling prophecy." The failure of myth and expectation to predict reality has left women with a range of mixed emotions. "Success" is often less than meets the eye. And left behind in the unprecedented glamorization of corporate life and its rewards is an agenda of unfinished business. Unresolved dilemmas between their conditioning and their condition set up a series of no-win scenarios. Unarticulated questions about their identity at the very moment of their greatest success undercut the thrill of victory. Comment psychotherapists Celia Halas and Roberta Matteson, "If women fashion their lives according to myths, they find, even when they achieve their dreams, that their cups are not brimful and running over; they are, rather, sieve-bottomed and empty. Women lose *especially* when they win."[25]

How do women resolve the paradoxes set up by their own myths and expectations, and exacerbated by society's approbation? How do women escape what appears to be a seamless Möbius strip of infinite expectation and inevitable disappointment? Only by learning to recognize the conflicting pattern between mythic and corporate reality will women break the success and betrayal cycle. The first step in that recognition is an insight into how powerful illusions pervade every landing of their corporate experience.

CHAPTER 3

WOOED AND WON

ENTRY LEVEL–THE VIEW FROM BELOW

Today's adolescent women see work as self-defining, and they're simply projecting themselves into the next context of their lives after college. For this generation, that ideal context is work, not the baby in the high chair, which was what filled you with ecstasy in my generation.

Margaret Touborg
executive assistant to the president,
Radcliffe College

When women look back with us to the decision to enter corporate culture, strikingly similar patterns begin to emerge. Whether the women go on to great or only modest success, whether they come from happy or unhappy families, whether they graduate from same-sex or coed colleges, whether they start out filled with ambition or with none—their stories contain the wondrous, fairy tale–like elements on which women are nurtured. What happens to women in pursuit of their first corporate experience as they are wooed and won? Does the experience foreshadow the ambivalence of the rest of their corporate careers? How are women attracted to corporate cultures in the first place?

Almost without exception, women describe the pattern leading up to the decision as a curiously passive courtship. And the process of choosing a job as one of "falling into" a career, as in love. "When I was twenty-four, I had no idea I'd still be working now," says one forty-year-old cosmetics executive, "or that I'd want to be a manager—not that I wasn't capable. But I never thought of it. I knew I didn't want to be like my mother, but what I wanted to be I never knew. I still don't." They speak of getting lucky, of the impact of happenstance and accident on their lives: "I didn't particularly think I wanted to work for the rest of my life, but I needed to get a good job to support myself," said one corporate counsel. "I guess I veered toward the idea I would have a job, but I can't say it was any calculated decision." Yet they describe their childhood and adolescence as a time of ambition, as a decade of dreams of the future. Given the myths with which women are conditioned, what is it about the critical early years of college conditioning and career choice that make the corporation appear so attractive an option?

Conditioned by childhood role models and ambiguous parental signals, undermined by changing rules in college as well as by their own myths and expectations, women—despite their feminist or post-feminist orientation—become the unconscious victims of the corporation's siren song. Even the most dynamic women, while filling their résumés with "experience," are still waiting for the recruiter to woo. In another ten years, often sooner, they will wonder how they could have so gratefully awaited the corporate gentleman caller on their own front porch. How was it they allowed destiny to seize them, instead of the other way around? To understand the significant parallels between romantic courtship and women's headlong rush to embrace the new corporate relationship, one must begin at the beginning.

Our Parents, Ourselves

The mixed signals women receive from both parents often undermine the very independence modern parents attempt to foster in their daughters. As one woman recalls, "I was raised to believe I could have anything I wanted—but not to get it for myself. So it took me a long time to believe I could be anything I wanted to be." Or, as psychologist Maggie Scarf notes, the urge to "win" this struggle for separation from parents and to achieve an independent self appears to be the most urgent unfinished business of women about to embark on a career.[1] Ironically, even in the process of gaining autonomy from parents, women have internalized the messages that will bind them to a newer, more powerful corporate family.

In fact, the turn to corporate culture is in many ways a signal to parents and society, an acceptance of the mantle of self-reliance and responsibility on a "serious" proving ground. The decision has significant shock value to parents who have raised their daughters to believe that they can accomplish anything but should prepare to achieve nothing. Most successful women, contrary to what profiles and studies of corporate women show, have no successful role models in their fathers.[2] Even in the most solid father-daughter relationships, until recently fathers have had no idea of the explosion of possibilities ahead for their daughters. Admits former Phelps Dodge International president Russell Marks, Jr., candidly, "I have two girls, and I wanted them to have a link with me, and I thought it would be harder to project that link with girls. And it came to me only recently that when you think about it, there are now opportunities for them to be just as publicly prominent as men are. You couldn't do that with daughters earlier." Fathers seldom comprehend the degree of ambition or the importance to their daughters of making their own mark. So they prepare them in only the most cursory fashion for the exacting demands, choices, and discipline to come. Having led compartmentalized lives in which business was carefully segregated from family, how could fathers have known that one day their daughters would find business sexy?

Knowledge gleaned from a father's role model was as likely to be negative as positive. Several women played back a story similar to the one told by Dana, a thirty-two-year-old cosmetics executive. "I think I picked up a lot from my father's values. When I was growing up, most decisions were made for the sake of security. His career was important to him, but after thirty-five years of giving to his company, he got the shaft." Kelly, a decade younger than Dana, talks about the impact of her father's workaholism on her childhood: "I call my father at the office and he says, 'Who's this?' when I'm his only daughter. It's like he has to prove how hard work is. I never wanted to work that hard." No wonder that Kelly chose a career on the nonquantitive side of the corporation, a choice of which her lawyer-father disapproved: "My father wanted me to get an M.B.A.—actually, an M.B.A., J.D. I think he hopes this job is just a phase I'm going through. To him success is only business in his terms." For many women, corporate life becomes an opportunity to run away from their father's model—or to replay the scenario, somehow making it come out different this time.

In more than a few cases, the choice of a corporate career is an attempt to reach out toward common ground heretofore unexplored and unexperienced between father and daughter. Whether the father model resembles Walter Wriston or Willy Loman, two striking characteristics permeate the childhood of successful corporate women. First, as noted in Chapter 2, a disproportionate number of them come from single-female-head-of-household homes. The drive for separation from a negative role model fuels the urge to become independent—to be their own breadwinners. Many have retained that dream and are still subject to the Living-on-the-Edge Myth. They are driven not by strong example but by graphic failure—the quick Oedipal fall that Freud describes wherein women lose their illusions about an all-powerful father. In a frequent, unwitting, and unconscious transference, the daughter inherits all the drive of her father—together with all his doubts about her ability to compete.

Second, there is also a strikingly clear lack of communication between father and daughter of the tangible substance, responsibilities, products, or politics of the daily grind. The family is "sheltered" from all that, except in those few households in which fathers headed a family business. Janice, a thirty-four-year-old human resources executive with a leading energy company, recalls no substantive early career discussions because of her mother's strong belief that "Business is something men do, boring in its details. It was something not to be talked about at the dinner table. So I never heard about what my father did." This conspiracy of silence often contributes to the hazy, insubstantial expectations women bring to the career choice.[3] The silence creates a mystique, an aura of something taboo. The less substantial the details, the greater the allure. The corporate culture becomes a mysteriously magic place, a Secret Garden ripe for discovery. By contrast, while sons also grew up largely ignorant of the substance of their father's careers, role models for them were abundant. There was less choice involved; business was largely an automatic, unexamined option. Recalls one male manager, "When I was a little boy, I thought it would be neat to be a business tycoon. My father was a reasonably successful businessman. I think I assumed I'd be successful; there wasn't any choice." To which Sally, a cable television executive, adds, "Men grow up with the concept that they will go to work and that will be their life and that's the reality. By contrast, we've been raised with too many choices." For women of the pioneer generation, the information gap that arose from their childhood ignorance of "Daddy's work" became a crucial missing link in their ability to make knowledgeable choices about corporate life.

When today's middle-management women look back with us, it becomes obvious that if fathers were uncommunicative, mothers were not. In fact, they were frighteningly graphic in describing their frustration and helplessness. As a result, they articulated to their daughters glorified ambitions and Technicolor scenarios of "success." The message was clear: You, who have opportunities I could only dream about, you must not fail me now. But the modus operandi was vague. "What really changed things—you know, you look back on life and see key things—what was instrumental for me was my mother," says Denise, now issues manager with a large packaged goods conglomerate. "She had a way of putting things in front of me that might encourage me. When I was sixteen or seventeen, she read about an internship program for congressmen in the papers. And she gave it to me and I just tucked it away. I was convinced that if I just tried hard enough, I would succeed. My mother beat it into me that there is nothing you can't do." Fran is a director of strategic planning with a diversified defense contractor: "My mother had certain expectations for me. We all felt we had to go the extra mile to please her." Martha, a chemical company executive, recalls, "I was the daughter most like my mother, so I got more messages relative to the career. She wanted more for me—but I wasn't supposed to do better than she did."

Women choose alliances often based on which parent has invested more heavily in their future. In most cases, that parent is the mother. A bargain is struck: approval in exchange for performance. Even the most happily married mothers sent daughters that subliminal message. "I grew up with a mother who left aeronautical engineering to raise a family. I know definitely that I, as the oldest daughter, got the live-my-life-through-my-daughter routine, not in a competitive or negative sense. But I always felt I was doing the right thing in business, something she was not able to do," one bank vice president recalls. An insurance executive adds, "People in my family were expected to be self-supporting. Both my parents came from homes where money was an issue. There was no sense of 'Get married and someone will take care of you.' " No formal plan, no road map, just a tacit expectation from parents that daughters are smart enough to find the way. "My mother raised me to believe I could do anything I wanted. She worked at GM and Kraft, and I always recall her in business suits," says Beth, now a successful paper products executive. "Because my mother didn't have a lot of time to talk things out, I was raised on pithy sayings. And one of those sayings was 'Never say can't.' " When mothers worked, only to "retire" to home-making, their often conflicted decision aroused in a daughter the determination to finish mother's unfinished business. Robin, a former CPA and manager with a major forest products corporation recalls: "My mom worked as a secretary in an insurance office until I was born. I think she kind of liked it, because even now she'll let slip a little comment. She had this ancient fur coat I borrowed when I was pregnant, because it was the only thing that would fit around me. And my dad said, 'Oh, that was the first fur I bought your mother.' And she snapped, 'I bought it with my last paycheck from the insurance company.' That was thirty-two years ago! Occasionally little things like that slip out."

The single most striking signal women receive from their mothers is that the job is the gold standard of independence, and that an independently earned income is valuable. The majority of successful corporate women have hanging beside all the Anne Klein suits in their closets the skeletons of their parents' marriages and the corollary lessons of their mother's brush with dependence and helplessness. It is the single most frequent experience women cite when asked why they were determined to have a corporate career. Hillary is thirty-seven, a senior executive with an energy company: "I think it boils down to the fact that if my mother's marriage had been wonderfully happy I might have felt differently. But even at eight I could see she was dependent. I never wanted that and I still don't. I knew there was something very wrong with that power structure. Mother did everything right, everything she was supposed to do. She was attractive. Nice. Loyal. And the harder she tried, the worse her marriage became."

Seeing their mothers betrayed by the rules of an old game, women set out in search of a new one. At forty, Eve is an extremely successful executive with a national real estate firm: "I don't think I ever went to college to find the Doctor who was going to be the Answer. The most important thing to me was to be independent and to be able to make my own choices. I don't think it came from an intelligent decision; I think it came from an environmental decision. I saw my mother sacrifice certain things in order to become independent. It never occurred to me that marriage was the answer. It was the exact opposite. Because marriage certainly was not permanent. And I couldn't rely on it." The decision to "go corporate" is, as Eve observes, an intuitive decision rather than the result of conscious investigation. It is a decision arrived at out of fear of repeating a negative experience rather than out of embracing a positive one. Second, in a society of delayed marriages, women now routinely marry a career before (if ever) they marry a man. In essence, their first adult commitment is to a career as the sustainer-provider. The illusion of the stability and permanence of corporate life after the years of uncertainty in one's childhood is a strong lure. Women now make long-term corporate marriages in their very early twenties much as their mothers once chose spouses—without even acknowledging the root of the attraction or the long-term tenure of the decision. "Congratulations!" reads one new wave greeting card. "You've finally become the person your mother always wanted you to marry."

Over and over, even the latest corporate recruits corroborate the familiar story. Dina, a twenty-four-year-old public relations executive, is representative: "My mother did volunteer work until my parents got divorced, and then she had absolutely no idea what she'd do. She went into real estate, and I was able to observe her work—all the time she spent at it, the deals she made. . . . It was just my mother and me— I was closer to business in a way that my father never exposed me to because he was never around for me to observe." As a result, "I learned the value of money incredibly strongly. My mother was always pushing me—'If everything falls apart, you can go out and take care of yourself.'" Writes Louise Bernikow: "A daughter looking at her mother's life is looking at her own, shaping and fitting one life to suit the needs of another. Some have shaped monsters and some angels."[4] In a sense everyone lost, as women carried their mother's ambition to unquestioning extremes of corporate devotion. As Radcliffe College Assistant to the President Margaret Touborg observes: "Mothers have to learn to talk to their daughters and to give them a realistic picture of what mothering is all about. There was a whole generation of mothers in the fifties who could only share their unhappiness and suppression of self." No wonder, then, when it comes time to make professional choices, women find themselves on the brink of a career decision suddenly bereft, after all those years of admonition, of any concrete advice. No wonder they approach corporate culture with a combination of passivity and serendipity.

Where the Boys Are

College only adds to the confusion with which women approach their corporate commitment—a confusion which appears in today's newest corporate recruits as well as among its pioneers. Lori, a UCLA junior and business major comments, "I feel sometimes women have to sneak up the back way—to not visibly compete with men. I don't know why I feel that way—maybe grades, the competition in the classroom with men. It's a put-down, almost, if you do better than they do."

Despite the floodgates of corporate opportunity now open to women at the entry level, surprisingly little has fundamentally changed in the preemployment college years—those critical years when women should be shaping choices and options for themselves. While women paddle furiously just to stay afloat in a sea of career decisions immediately ahead, men sanguinely pursue options often laid out years earlier. Contemporary explanations of why women fail to respond to the challenge of "Where do I fit?" seem curiously simplistic. Psychologists Celia Halas and Roberta Matteson suggest that social pressure conditions women to "a crazy message that says that, although women must prepare for careers, they must not take the task too seriously. To do so would suggest they are not seriously interested in affiliation. To invest heavily in a career would jeopardize their chances for future relationships."[5] This generation is certainly not obsessed by marriage. Yet the conditioning concept that one's first career is femininity lingers on.

The last of the winter snows has barely congealed on the placement office steps as recruiters five years out of college make their way back to campus, searching out the best and the brightest, or at least the eager and most expectant. Suddenly it is spring, and the fever of corporate courtship hits hard among senior women. Talk of management trainee programs, mass letter-writing campaigns, and executive assistantships that are bound to lead to more fills the dining room. All the rambling discussion and uncertainty about what to do presages the first professional evaluation a woman will have to make: Where do I go from here? Today's lack of long-range planning is still evident, underscoring a pervasive ambivalence or uncertainty about the professional decade ahead. A twenty-three-year-old investment banker comments, "Senior year in college, nobody knew anything about what we wanted to do. We all tried to fool ourselves into thinking we did. But we didn't. I would pretend, but I really didn't know." Writes one Smith College senior, "I am trying to sort through my own thoughts about 'life after Smith.' At this point I am toying with the arenas of public relations, advertising, and journalism. Starting positions seem boring. I can see myself doing that now, but not forever. And that is scary." She is not alone. Observes Antonia Earnshaw, a researcher studying the changing trends in women's culture: "College women feel conflicted today. They're not as gung-ho about the job thing; they feel guilty because that's what they're supposed to want. They're coming to realize earlier than we did that you can't have it all. So they feel they have to protect themselves."

Such college-level ambivalence is all the more disturbing given women's self-described early sense of mastery over the environment: These are women who described their upbringing, in many cases, as having been aggressive, independent, even classically "masculine"—as most books have described the childhoods of "successful" managerial women. One bank vice president says, "I come from a family of three boys. It was an environment where I played and competed against boys all my life, climbing trees with them when I was eight years old, until my mother sent me to a convent school to learn decorum." Adds a senior-level oil company executive in her thirties, "As a child I honestly never liked dolls or played with them. When I was eight I made a vow to myself—and remember how old thirty seemed then—that I didn't want to get married until I was thirty. I wanted to work, to be independent."

By the end of the recruiting process much of that sense of mastery has been eroded. Why must so much energy be funneled away from career decision-making at the precise moment when those decisions come into such sharp male focus? Having successfully competed with men academically to this point, women enter college with a sense of academic superiority. Four years later, they leave, having learned that the rules of the game have changed.

At college, women experience a rule change that fundamentally alters the way they view male competition. Conditioned by circumstances to suppress much of their essential female self-esteem and mastery, they find that this rule change exacts new values and aspirations as the price of transition from college to corporate entry level. It dictates that women surrender the persona that has "worked" all through their adolescence, then assume an unfamiliar, androgynous personality in its place. Why do women start so strong and finish so weak? The explanation begins with the repression of that precious, intuitive, and very female part of themselves—the Authentic Voice—which is least reinforced and most obliterated by conditioning. It is women's artistic voice, shouted down by society's preference for quantification. It is women's intuitive insight, repressed in favor of documentation. Women quickly learn that although these qualities served them well in school, they are comparatively "cheap" commodities, quick fixes. The conditioning asserts that what comes easily to women is trivial, that what is "feminine" is unreliable and not to be taken seriously. Women, it is assumed, must give up that side of themselves and set out in pursuit of their quantitative, empirical selves. It is a search that often ends in an outright rejection of one self in favor of the other and culminates in the choice of corporate culture as the ultimate proof of that evolution.

Repression of the Authentic Voice leads to some laborious misfits between intuitive attraction or ability and the eventual career choice. "I wanted to use my degree to get an entry-level position that was 'responsible,' " recalls Amanda, whose corporate odyssey carried her from publishing to a prominent textile conglomerate to eventual corporate dropout and a new career as a stockbroker. "I felt that working with numbers was more responsible than just my little ideas. I don't know why. I guess it was because my little ideas were too easy. I knew them. I didn't know numbers." Says Lou Anne, a Chicago-based banker, "I was a French and religion major in college and saw myself more as a minister or in some sort of social service role—working with people, counseling them." Martha, the chemistry major who joined a *Fortune* 500 chemical conglomerate only to drop out in frustration fifteen years later, notes as a word of warning to other women: "All along I've had a struggle between my scientific and my artistic instincts. Science was highly regarded in my family; everything else was a gray, fuzzy area. I clearly wanted to make a mark, do something different. Being a woman in science was different. But I never had a burning interest in discovering why the grass was green or the sky was blue." For Martha, this early conflict foreshadowed the rocky road ahead.

The link between the suppression of this Authentic Voice and the sudden turn toward corporate culture seems inevitable. Greta chose a career in retailing and then financial services over one in interior design. Diana gravitated to banking: "I was looking forward to . . . something definite. One of the frustrations and the joys of creative work is that you don't have that clear path ahead of you—which is something that the corporation offers." What Diana unwittingly articulated was the ultimate lesson of the rule change: the need for external structure. Her interior, feminine judgment, so carefully nurtured through adolescence, is no longer reliable, having proven inferior, even obsolete, in getting women by in the male world. It must be traded in for some newer model. The suppression of the Authentic Voice is just a taste of compromises to come.

Another element underlying women's passive choice of a corporate career is ignorance: No one explains to women what college is *really* about. "In college, I took courses that would make me an 'interesting woman,' " one research director wryly admits. Women are socialized to continue the superior academic performance that brought them through a successful freshman year long after men have trained their sights on the larger game that lies beyond the campus. Women are the "grinds," the grade-grubbers from whom men borrow notes on the eve of the big exam. Yet men seldom educate women in return to the larger game they are pursuing beyond the campus while women are still buried in the book stalls. "I was the class of sixty-eight, finishing up on the fringe of the Vietnam era at college," recalls Anthony Morris, founder and president of his own business information systems company, "and one thing I recall at the University of Pennsylvania was that women got no preparation for what was to follow—none. It was as if they graduated and hit a wall. They were somehow dominant in the environment, but they never got tracked out." Fifteen years later, a new study confirms his perception that women's campus intellectual preoccupation is at odds with "the ethos of the institution." The study portends the troubling clash ahead between women's personal goals of self-fulfillment and achievement within organizations and the collective goals of the corporate culture.[6] The faculty often perceives the same ambivalence in women's motives at college. Recounts Diana, thirty-four, "I was at Cornell, and a professor asked, 'How many women in this room expect to meet their husbands at school?' I was the only one who didn't raise my hand. And everyone said, 'Oh, sure, Diana.' " Such ambivalent objectives —a schizoid confusion between conditioned feminine dependency and the quest for independent self-fulfillment—persist even today. One UCLA coed, class of 1986, casually estimated that approximately 30 percent of her classmates were there to find husbands, though few would admit it.

Ultimately, the college lesson assimilated by women who are now poised for a potential breakthrough into senior management was that they were for the first time explicitly in second place. Martha, one of only three female chemistry majors in her class in 1961, recalls, "I didn't take any seminars, only large survey courses, since I was a woman. Yet it was clear men felt threatened by me. I just kept trying to keep a low profile— even though I was top of my class. In those days we thought the real brilliance came from men; the women were just the drones." "It was very fashionable to leave the impression with boys that you were on the verge of flunking out," comments one senior financial officer of a *Fortune* 100 company. "Oh, we were trained well. And that stuff just doesn't come unglued. My husband says I'm still self-deprecating around men. Even now, when men meet me, they ask, 'Vice president? You mean of the whole thing?' "

Even today, the rules, amorphous to this point, become clear as the senior year recruiting process begins. Men are being groomed for leadership. Women are being groomed for some ambiguous, ill-defined destiny. Men are focused; women are playing catch-up in a game whose rules are unwritten or dimly understood. Says Tina, a 1984 graduate of Barnard College, "I suddenly felt inadequate. I took a writing class freshman year, and instead of competing aggressively and intellectually with men, I was taught to look for the feelings— the feminine stuff inside me—to achieve. Then I was criticized for being overly sensitive, 'flighty and insubstantial.' I think then I seriously began to realize that the way I had been trained to indulge in my feelings and femininity was not going to make me successful. I realized if I was going to compete in a man's world, there was a serious flaw in me."

Certainly women enter college more confidently now, with more role models than ever. But college is still a poor conditioning environment for future corporate success. At Harvard, women are not taking leadership roles in any campus political organizations, though the majority of the Democratic Club membership is female. The president of the Harvard Committee on Foreign Affairs reports only one female member—who joined because her boyfriend was active. Concludes a recent article on the subject, "Women often do not become more politically active out of fear of losing their femininity. . . . Their inclination to work unseen and unheard often leads them to do most of the tedious work. . . . Women may believe they are satisfied and fulfilled doing menial, follower's work because society has told them they should be."[7] One thing is certain. By the end of senior year, even the most directed, determined woman has picked up the rule change. The surrender to a dominant male culture and value system— is one no course teaches, no books prepare women for. Like Alice down the rabbit hole, women are pushed and hurried and prodded along faster than their capacity to assimilate and digest. "But what are the rules?" they ask. Like Alice, women learn soon enough to make them up as they go along. There is fearfully little time: they are late for a very important (corporate) date.

The consequences of the rule change and its attendant loss of the Authentic Voice are persistent and pervasive. Maggie Scarf admonishes—"This hard aspect of adolescence is something that so many people find hard to recall, to remember, to believe is really there. There's just so much envious glorification of this phase of life! Of the freedom, the physical beauty, of the potential and future possibilities that are the inheritance of the emerging adolescent."[8] Despite that, women all but erase their memories of the pain and uncertainty of this transition. Their learning from this period is imprisoned in a cell locked from the inside with no key available. They all tell the same bewildered story, but it takes ten years to sort out the choices made in haste at this landing.

Meanwhile, the energy it takes to make the leap to masculine rules and masculine culture distracts women from planning for the future. Women often busy themselves externalizing their drive to help others; men begin internalizing to help themselves. Women wait for career choices to come to them via experience; men create the experiences that provide them career choices. In an effort to regain a sense of mastery over their environment, women turn to a variety of service activities that consume time and energy which they might otherwise apply to planning for the future. One pioneer corporate mother said of her daughter, a college senior, "She had this huge campus 'thing' to run and she didn't sign up for interviews until it was over. And we sort of encouraged her to 'veg out' that spring and summer." Other college women, competing to accumulate more brownie points for the résumé, lose sight of the initial objective: "I got involved in a lot of charity work: Big Brother, Big Sister, a nursing home nearby. That kind of stuff made me community-conscious." Under the illusion that "packaging" makes them more attractive to the corporate culture, women still concentrate far more on the résumé than on analyzing instincts and listening to the Authentic Voice inside themselves when looking for guidance on next steps.

Surprisingly, graduates of supportive same-sex women's colleges—long considered "an atmosphere supportive to the assumption of responsibility"[9]—are today struggling with the same universal themes of ambivalence, success, amazonian expectations, and flagging ambition, despite their different college conditioning. Greta, an alumna of a women's college explains, "There's a definite sense for all those years that the girls aren't sitting back waiting for boys to be at the head of the class. It never occurred to us to step back. You learn to manage, to take charge and assert yourself." As long as women continue to compete only against other women, their success and bold self-confidence *are* safe. Yet there is a price to pay. Such experience merely postpones the encounter with the rule change until women enter the recruiting process or the corporate culture. One senior financial officer of a *Fortune* 500 company puts it bluntly: "It was a terrible shock coming out of that single-sex environment in which we were told there was no limit to what we could do. We were told that because they honestly didn't perceive any limits. And then we went out to look for a job in a male-dominated world. I think women today at co-ed colleges are more aware there is discrimination out there, and they expect it. Whereas a couple of months after women graduate from same-sex colleges today, they walk into my office, and they're astounded this sexist stuff still exists." Her analysis is echoed by many of today's graduates. Asserts Tina, recently graduated from Barnard: "Going to a women's college and having it pounded into me, 'You can do it, you can do it,' ironically just makes me feel there's something I have to fight against. The more I was told I had nothing to fear, the more it made me feel there was something to battle, that it *is* a man's world. It made me less sure of myself." Dina, a twenty-six-year-old Smith graduate, echoes the covert message instilled from freshman year on: "By God, you're going to kill the world, conquer anything, be a huge success. They taught us that nothing can stop you. I never realized what that pressure meant until a friend in our dorm got engaged senior year and was practically ostracized— as if she was ruining her chances for the rest of her life." Women's colleges may demand too much performance of women, coed schools too little. But the net effect is the same —a forced fit into corporate culture in order to prove something to themselves and to the world.

By senior year, the message is loud and clear: women must begin projecting to that fuzzy next dimension wherein lies their future "success." As soon as women begin that process of projection—still ill-at-ease with their new post–rule change personae—they recognize another reality: they begin to appreciate what men have been focusing on while women have unwittingly directed their energies at succeeding academically. Suddenly, they see in their relative lack of sharp focus and direction a direct contrast with the men around them. Said one Stanford M.B.A., "I never had a sense of all the opportunities available, all the ways you could structure your career. I had a sense that my male friends knew, but nobody ever told me how you got through the game, how you got from A to B. And by now, even if I knew, I don't have the confidence to make all the transitions and connections. The interview process at the end of school destroyed what was left of an already fragile ego."

After graduation, men enter the familiar domain of work, the realm of natural male superiority. Women are about to leave the realm of academia and gold stars—*their* natural domain of superiority. It is hard to remember how immediate those decisions loom, how overwhelming they are: "I was absolutely frantic when I was a senior. From the time I was a freshman, I was encouraged to attend all kinds of career-planning courses, to sign up for internships," says one recent graduate. "So if you're not absolutely sure of your career plans by the time May rolls around, you feel as if you've absolutely missed the boat. To your right and to your left are people who made all the right moves. And you're under intense pressure to match that." Women find themselves, despite all the internships and summer jobs, adrift in *terra incognita,* and their sense of drift is exacerbated by the perception that everyone else appears to be charging furiously forward. Observes a college junior: "I watch the kids in my house who are older than me and it is unbelievable. The seniors stop speaking to each other because they are going for the same company. The only companies that come on campus are the banks with their training programs and the competition for these is incredible. There's a lot of pressure, a lot of stress. You have a sense that if you don't do this, you are going to miss your opportunity." This fear of being the only one adrift creates its own self-fulfilling prophecy. Because they're so worried about making the wrong choice, women often end up doing exactly that. Under so much pressure, the entire process resembles the old-fashioned dance, where one rushes to fill one's corporate dance card. Who wants to be typed a wallflower?

Women who have been in the work force more than ten

years survived an even more frustrating quandary. With few or no role models available, simply developing the game plan became less a matter of luxuriating in options than a process of elimination. The decision to pursue a corporate career becomes, in essence, a decision against the two most frequently considered alternatives: teaching and law. This process of decision by elimination is crucial to understanding the eventual shotgun corporate marriage. "The jobs I knew about were secretaries, teachers, and nurses," recalls one corporate veteran. "And I knew I did not want to teach." The choice of a corporate career is a courageous leap into the unknown, a flouting of society's attitudes toward what socially correct satisfactions a woman should derive from a "career." Secretary, nurse, teacher—the woman as nurturer, an expectation reinforced by much parental cheerleading. "The message from my father was that if I failed in everything else I could go teach kids. The idea of a business career came from my mother," reports Becka, now a bank vice president in human resource development. Women who received *no* direction simply panicked and grabbed for the teaching formula as if it were an aspirin to cure a large career migraine. "When I was in college," says another, "it suddenly became important to start thinking, to have a career. I finally picked teaching. At that age everything suddenly started seeming more real. I didn't know what my prospects for getting married were at that point so I just thought I better think about something."

Choosing teaching, for the pioneer generation of corporate women, was in many ways a nonchoice, a means of postponing the ultimate redefinition of their lives from a traditional to a career role. Many women eventually outgrew that career crutch and went on to successful careers. Still, it is striking how many corporate women, even today, have as the first job on their résumé some form of teaching or guidance counseling. At the other extreme, almost all the younger corporate women we interviewed had considered and rejected law before turning to corporate life. Law, perceived as the gold standard of prestige and security, is also regarded as boring in its substance —a theme that surfaced again and again among women who rejected law for business. Corporate life is perceived as glamorous and mysterious in a way that the substance of law is not.[10]

How can women's career bewilderment be explained? Perhaps senior year, women finally face reality, surrendering the role of being unconditionally sheltered, treasured, and adored simply because they are *daughters*. "Boys are left to their own devices more than girls are," observes one male pharmaceuticals executive, "so we realize if we intend to get anything, we'll have to do it for ourselves." A nineteen-year-old male college student at the University of Chicago comments, "There's this one friend of the family who's always taking me aside and asking what I'm majoring in and is always giving me advice. He *never* does that with my sister. I think the assumption is still that she's going to get married." At this landing, women jealously realize that everything is in place for men to make, at least, an intelligent decision. Recalls Clark, a thirty-three-year-old group product manager in Los Angeles, "I started out driving limousines because I had no idea what I wanted to do. And a lot of the people I drove were interested in me. I was even offered jobs—like in *The Graduate*—they'd say 'Plastics!' And then, one day on the way to the airport, somebody did offer me a job that made sense. And I took it." Ted, an airline executive in his mid-thirties, referred to what he calls "an intuitive planning process going on at various junctures." Despite the uncertainty that often dogs men as well as women at this level, the decision, once made by them, is unencumbered by the multiple uncertainties that still govern women's choices.

Male peers, in turn, still perceive the career decision-making process to be optional for women, despite an economy where two incomes are not a luxury but a necessity. Even today, women's corporate decisions are often made against a backdrop of male backlash—an often unarticulated male resentment grounded in the belief that because a corporate career choice is "optional" for women, women do not experience the same ambition or need to achieve that men do. (Is it any wonder many in this generation, when asked how far they expected to rise, reluctantly admit they aren't shooting for the top spot? Says Lori, a UCLA junior, "I could go pretty far. But a combination of circumstances and something inside myself would probably keep me from the top.") The often unconscious male selfishness in sharing information, leads, or opinions leaves women primed for the last available alternative: the corporate recruiter. He—for it has almost always been a man—will save them. And his approval starts an ongoing search for male corporate approval as a means by which women evaluate their career success.

The Case of the
Charismatic Recruiter

One Shearson Lehman Brothers recruiter estimates the firm spends $7,000 going after each M.B.A.; an evening's entertainment can run as high as $1,500.[11] Allowing proportionately less money for college recruiting, the net impact is the same. Women, faced with such ardent corporate wooing, both in college and after, are vulnerable and confused. They are bewildered by the abandonment of parents, teachers, even friends who, at the critical moment, volunteer high expectations but little or no concrete advice. Or they are increasingly confronted with a seemingly infinite variety of options and opinions. Writes one Smith College senior, "Dad thinks I should look into the bank training program route, but I don't think that I qualify. I had an informational interview with someone who has worked on one line of yogurt exclusively for two years—ugh! The fashion industry isn't totally my dream, but supposedly the retail/buying programs that some of the companies offer are business-oriented and would fit the criterion of putting me into business." Dr. Carol Galligan explains the uniquely female pressure that makes women particularly vulnerable to corporate pitches: "Women react to their senior year as an experience of leaving that just doesn't hit men that way. My daughter cried her entire year at the thought of separation." Women, experiencing systems overload, start looking for a new attachment, another institution with which to bond.[12] Under the circumstances, women do not see the contemporary corporate recruiting process as a seduction. At the time, they are convinced they are full partners in the process—partners making informed, considered decisions.

They see their male peers signing up for the same interviews, "winning" via the same process. Fair enough. But ten or fifteen years into their careers, when men reassess the forces at work during that crucial process of attraction and connection, they do not see themselves in retrospect as the passive partners in the corporate *pas de deux*. Women overwhelmingly do.

In fact, women's descriptions of the first encounter with the corporate recruiter are couched in all the rhetoric and imagery of a new romance. "I adored the man I interviewed with," remembers Bonnie, a twenty-five-year-old bank portfolio analyst. "We had a tremendous rapport. It was definitely a mentor relationship: I was a little kid. And he was very patient with me, he educated me. I felt elation at getting the job." Recalls Claire, at thirty-five a former telecommunications executive, "I really liked the guy I talked to at the company. He was young, just a few years out of school, and someone I could definitely relate to. He made the job sound pretty good— though I must say at the time I was kind of wondering whether this was really the job for me." Once the gentleman caller has charmed his way past the front door, he changes roles, becoming James Mason in A *Star Is Born* or Leslie Howard in *Intermezzo*. The gifted protégée is required to make good to justify the mentor's faith in her. The protégée becomes an ego extension. In fact, the corporate recruiter's thrill—and reward—is in bagging the prey. That is his job du jour in his role as a contemporary Pied Piper, a corporate gigolo.

But the Wooed and Won syndrome doesn't end with college. Women of any age standing on the brink of their first corporate experience are susceptible. "When I finally ended up in the cosmetics industry, its *lure*—and that's exactly the right word—was an incredible salesman," says Dana, who was thirty at the time she was hired. "Consciously or unconsciously, he got my number like that," she says, snapping her fingers emphatically. "He picked up on all my strengths and weaknesses. He was impressed by the money I was earning consulting. But he knew you never have any power in consulting. And that's what he played on. He wooed me with promises of prestige and power. I thought I'd walk in the door and everything would be handed to me, completely forgetting I'd have to learn the business. He was the classic charismatic salesman who was going to make you a star. I didn't have to do a thing. It was 'I've recognized this incredible talent in you that not even your parents recognize.' And when you're honest with yourself afterward, you're embarrassed that you bought it."

The relative brevity and casualness of the interview process compared with the intensity women ascribe to it suggest a powerful case of transference at work—a subconscious search for approval after weathering the rule change of the recent past. Dr. Carol Galligan offers, "Because they were so loved, so highly thought of all their lives, women no longer trust the approval that comes from school or home. So they're incredibly vulnerable to external approval. Approval from the corporation becomes the *real* test [of self-worth]. And I find that appalling." That desire for the same unconditional approval, remembered from one's parents and peers, elevates the recruiting interview to a place of much greater prominence for women than it does for men. Coupled with the natural male-female tension absent in male-male interviews, a complex and long-lasting tissue of expectations is quickly woven, which snares women. "My mentor had come to Washington to talk me into the job since he knew I was hesitant," recalls Denise, now an executive with a large health care products company. "He was so buoyant and magnanimous, saying things like, 'Oh, come to New York and we'll drive you around and show you all types of places.' Nothing was impossible to him. He was thinking of big possibilities, and I was thinking small." The seduction can take place in an hour, a day, or a summer. One young banker described her indoctrination this way: "I had an eight-week summer internship, and the bank gave me the red carpet treatment. I would go out for three-hour lunches and I would walk by the poor trainees who had papers all over their desks. . . . So I thought, 'Hmm, banking isn't so bad after all. That might be the career for me," she recalls, chuckling. In the second reel of *Casablanca*, Humphrey Bogart tells Ingrid Bergman, "I've heard a lot of stories like yours. They're usually accompanied by the beat of a tinny piano downstairs. They start, 'Mister, I met a man.'" That man today is frequently the corporate recruiter. His big-picture recruiting preview builds trust and plays on dependency patterns that far outlive the recruiting experience in women's corporate life. From the very first exposure, women begin to assume a different kind of relationship with the corporation than their male counterparts do. Simply put, most men never develop a crush on a company.

Why do women? Maggie Scarf suggests that in adolescence, a normal sublimation of intense feelings for one's father is transferred into acceptable crushes on movie or rock stars. "If a woman does not feel good about herself, it makes sense to hitch her wagon to someone who does, hoping that the union will give her life value and meaning."[13] Today women are hitching themselves to a corporate wagon without thinking about the yoke. Is it possible that in the process of being weaned from parents, prospective female corporate candidates transfer their intensity not to rock stars but to recruiters, a managerial Mel Gibson, uncovering the heretofore hidden attributes of thousands of talented women? Chris, marketing director for a *Fortune* 100 information systems corporation, recalls, "I was recruited by men only. So they're the ones I feel very competitive with and whose opinions I value." Long after that first charismatic relationship dissolves, the melody lingers on, with women unconsciously trying to recapture at every level the initial rush of that first elation.

The final element of women's inadvertent, even capricious "decision" in favor of a life within the corporate walls involves chance encounter, another variation on the passive courtship already noted. Destiny takes a hand. One successful executive —a woman who manages hundreds of thousands of dollars' worth of marketing plans and sales projections—reminisces over the decision-making process that led to her first career choice:

"I was really floating around. I was born and raised in Minneapolis, and there were a lot of food companies in the area ... so I picked one and went to work at Pillsbury." She stayed five years. Becka, the tomboy turned banking executive, chose business only as the result of a freak accident: "My college roommate and I were going to become stewardesses for TWA, but I tore a ligament in my leg, thank God, and I stayed home to mend while she went on to flight training." Becka is currently a vice president in charge of human resource development for one of the nation's largest banks. Chris, self-described as "a classic of [her] generation," identifies the process by which she ended up at the nation's largest computer corporation: "Circumstances imposed themselves, as they always have in my career. One day, I got lost on my way to New York and stopped to ask directions. I saw these big blue letters, and I didn't even know what it was, but the first letter was I, and I figured that stood for International. And I spoke French, so I thought maybe they'd offer me a job. And that was the extent of my career planning—then, or ever, probably. It's always circumstances that have driven me." She stayed at IBM for seventeen years before dropping out to take a key marketing position with another large information-systems corporation. The common denominator in all these stories is the role serendipity plays in the career-choice process. Perhaps no one story is as illustrative of the mail-order corporate marriage as Beth's: "I was in Grand Central in a phone booth looking up the address of one big computer company, and the conglomerate I eventually went to work for was listed on the same page, so I figured, 'Why not send them a letter and a résumé, too?' I had never heard of them before, had no idea what they manufactured or that they were in the *Fortune* 100. In fact, I didn't even know what the *Fortune* 100 was!" She stayed twelve years, until a corporate reorganization forced a separation.

Because women have not really planned careers, they strike a bargain with themselves not to examine their choices too closely. Instead, women try to beat the system by joining it. Theirs becomes the new unexamined life. "Marry in haste;

repent at leisure," paraphrasing William Congreave, Mother used to say. In this, at least, Mother was right.

The Honeymoon Is Over

Ultimately, what is the allure of corporate life? The easy answer is that the largest proportion of organizations in America are corporations, and the largest presence in placement offices each spring is corporate. Corporations initiate the star search. But other motives are also at work. There is women's attraction to the prestige of the corporation, the security of attaching oneself to an organization that is large, stable, and autonomous. Corporations confer legitimacy, instant elevation from the rank of outsider—as women have always been in commercial life—to insider status conferred by affiliation. As Chris, a seventeen-year veteran of a large computer company puts it, "What was important from the beginning was that mine was a terribly well established company. It was an institution—and I belonged." To other women, the corporate lure is the proferring of instant mastery and responsibility. Peggy said yes on the spot to the first bank to make her an offer: "Whereas other banks suggested I should spend a few years in the trust department to get my head into finance, this was a real job that could lead to a career. I liked the people I talked with; I was on cloud nine." The sense of assuming egalitarian status on day one, without having to fight for it, is a potent lure after the sobering experience of the rule change. Finally, corporate life often represents the retiring of adolescent fantasies: "I thought you only had a certain amount of time after college to explore and be somewhat carefree or self-indulgent with your choices," explains Beth. "And that limited what you could do." For some, a career choice turns on joining a multinational company in the era of the expanding global marketplace, wherein the fantasy of travel can become a very real part of the job. "When I was young, I wanted to travel, and I just assumed I would have to work to do those things," says one twenty-four-year-old pragmatist.

There is the concomitant lure of Bright Lights, Big City—the idealized expectation of Making It in New York. As Kyle, a young systems engineer puts it, "To me, New York epitomizes the land of opportunity. You can be anything you want in New York City." New York becomes the symbolic catalyst for many women, even if only in their dreams. For many women, the corporation represents their Argonaut. For them, corporate life offers the best of all worlds: exploration, seemingly without risk.

For some, the first months of entry-level life provide a time of immense satisfaction with oneself in the context of this new environment. "They'd just redone the offices, and the environment was just so . . . beautiful," recalls one successful corporate vice president of day one on her job. "I couldn't believe I'd landed in such a great position. I'd had a hard time even finding a job—I was willing to take almost anything. The company not only paid my expenses to come for the interview, but they told me to come up the night before—and to bill them for that, too! 'Wow. The big arena,' I thought. They want me." Kyle admits, "There's a large element of status and prestige. When I have to explain what I do, it takes away some of the prestige. But I'm proud to say I work for IBM. Its training program gets a lot of prestige and respect. I'd have to say that's a relatively large element of the appeal of working here." Explains Heidi, a twenty-five-year-old M.B.A. and product manager, "We divide responsibilities, so I am pretty much in charge of the execution of everything going on with the brand. I have a budget; I have control of all the promotions that go on. I can do what I want except when it does something to the strategic positioning of the brand."

For many women, however, the substance of corporate life comes as a rude awakening. "At present I'm slowly learning to become a banker," writes one young management trainee. "It's a difficult task from both a technical and a personal point of view. No more studies, but instead long days of work (9:00 A.M. to 8:00 P.M.), little feedback, and then this new feeling of emptiness in my life in the sense that I can't really have any long-term plans. I can't even measure my progress as easily as I could during my student life when I received grades. And most of all, there is very little free time." Gayle's entry-level experience in consumer products proved equally disillusioning. "The first level of the job was very detail-oriented. I felt like I was going to school all the time rather than moving things ahead. I like things to be buttoned up, but mostly I like to see them go somewhere. But that's just the way the corporate system works." Gayle, who eventually dropped out of her company at the birth of her first child, is now pregnant with a second. Amanda describes her first day with a chemical conglomerate: "When they offered me a job in finance and my degree was in marketing, I thought it would 'broaden my experience.' I was taken into a vice president's office, which was cluttered with binders full of charts and numbers. I knew I wasn't going to like it. I knew it would be stultifying, and it was really the worst year I've ever worked. It was very unimaginative, very uncreative; everything was done by the book, and it was simple numbers-crunching." To many entry-level women who have been nourished on promises and high expectations, the style of a job promises more allure than the actual substance delivers.

The job not only fails to live up to its screen test, it turns out to be a flop. "I was a commercial loan officer, but I really didn't like commercial lending," says Faye. "Being the new kid, I tried to prospect for new business—but I hated it. And lending was by and large very dull, just maintaining accounts, though it was what I'd always thought I would do when I grew up." When reality clashes with fantasy, the seeds of disenchantment can be sown at a perilously early age.

Entry-level blues reflect something else: the undermining of the very self-esteem a corporate career is supposed to bolster. At the start of Chris' seventeen-year career with a computer giant, she was told, " 'No you can't be in sales. You just don't have the killer instinct.' They were always worried that customers would make passes at me and I wouldn't know what to do. But I've never, ever had a pass from a customer. Ever." Kyle, a recent trainee at the same company, says that she, too, had been shunted into a support function: "It was stressed by the company during orientation that the marketing rep had to have very good communications skills and that although he gets the visibility, he also takes the biggest risk in terms of salary. I didn't think I was prepared for all the responsibility I was told a marketing executive would have." Intimidation that begins at the entry-level keeps women locked into career paths long after they decipher the selection process of which they have been the victim.

For most women, the line-staff epiphany begins at the entry level, where intuitive choices channel women into staff jobs—and permanently cloister them in a managerial underclass unqualified for top management later. When line jobs call for a technical expertise entry-level women lack, staff jobs come to the "rescue." One former junior staff member in investor relations at a major Chicago-based conglomerate explains, "It was the easiest place to enter, and from a conservative management's point of view, it is an ideal position for a woman if she is competent because there is a lot of exposure to the top. Yet you have no power. I mean, it's like being the weather girl." While women seldom consciously acknowledge the impact of line-staff decisions at this first stage of their careers, the sublimated Authentic Voice is already at work. Peggy, one of the few senior staff women in a *Fortune* 500 agricultural conglomerate, described her early line experience: "The first place they sent me was Savannah—grain is loaded into elevators there. I was the only professional woman in an office of four. Early on I asked one of the men what would happen if an elevator exploded from all the dust, and he said, 'You won't have time to worry.' It was very tough. I didn't know anyone. I had nothing in common with the men. I was ostracized. After five months, I was transferred to a staff job."

Most companies willingly—and permanently—transfer women to staff jobs after the first brush with line responsibility at the entry level. In the process, women move from the potential for real access and power to only the illusion of it. And few companies make the entry-level line easy to tough out. "I knew from the first day that joining the financial trainee program had been a mistake," Dina, a twenty-five-year-old former banker told us. "I had felt so confident that I could do anything after graduating from Smith. By the end of my first day at the bank, I thought, 'What am I doing here?' The day of my final exam, I went to my boss and told him, 'Look, I'm not stellar at math. What are the other opportunities?' He didn't even try to talk me out of my self-doubt. The offer of a staff position forced me to decide whether banking was something I wanted to do. That first six months, I put on twenty-five pounds out of misery. I felt like a klutz. I was working till one or two A.M. just to make sure I completed the financial trainee program. It was the worst." Like so many women who are attracted by the style of a financial position because it is currently a sexy major with men, Dina had never questioned the substance of what she would be asked to do while showing up at work every day in her banker's gray flannel. The bank, in turn, responded to her crisis of identity by slotting her where corporations usually slot women with less than compelling certainty about their future: into a staff ghetto. The acute symptoms of the line-staff conflict suffered in later landings appear at the entry level as the early aches and pains of a potentially terminal corporate illness.

Unprecedented glamorization of corporate life, coupled with unprecedented pressure to enlist, has driven young women to often ill-considered choices. Unlike the pioneer corporate prodigies of the late sixties and seventies, the new generation of graduating women has big dreams, even bigger visions. One career development counselor at Duke University volunteers this observation: "A lot of women are so pre-professionally oriented—they just *know* they want to go into business or law—that we have to really work to get them to think of alternatives, to consider why they are pursuing what they are pursuing." Some 71 percent of freshmen surveyed by the American Council on Education and UCLA list "being very well off financially" as an "essential" or "very important" goal in life, exceeded in importance only by the desire to be an authority in one's field. (The number one reason stated for college attendance was to procure a better job.)[14] Comments one publishing executive, "Younger people really have a sense now that you have to package yourself, that every job you take on the way up has to indicate you have a grand passion for a career." Yet the substance of these visions is just as disturbingly hazy as the vision of their predecessors. "Students haven't made the connection between their aspirations and reality, that they will have to make compromises," suggests one campus counselor. Confirms Kelly, a young advertising trainee, "Of course, you've gotta be rich to afford a maid, maid's room, gourmet food ordered in—all the things that ease the tension in a working marriage." Yet women of this newest generation also have the most invested, and the most to lose, in the corporate sweepstakes.[15] Comments Radcliffe College's Margaret Touborg, "In the wake of education debts that can total up to $200,000 by the time they finish grad school, women are waking up to the new financial reality. Suddenly, they're saying when it comes to money, 'Nice girls do!' " Confirms one University of Chicago junior, "People on campus are saying, 'Well, let's see, I'll go for the statistics major or the business major because then I can get a good starting salary and can make it.' " The pattern is increasingly to collect an M.B.A. right out of college. Do not pass Go. Do not waste time deciding whether corporate life is right for you. Commit—to something.

Yet there are disturbingly familiar signs even among this generation of the disillusionment to come. One twenty-three-year-old woman writes to an urban magazine, "When I graduated . . . I aspired to be nothing less than a full-fledged yuppie . . . [with] a gold American Express card." After seeing her friends evolve from happy college students to "rigid, uncaring corporate puppets, neglecting their friends for twelve-hour workdays and the elusive promise of an end-of-the-year bonus. . . ."[16] She quit her job to become a teacher. Comments the author of one recent book on this latest generation in the workplace, "Raised by middle-class parents, educated during years that promised meaningful jobs, comfortable incomes, and satisfied lives, it is a generation struggling to cope with a shrunken economy and abruptly diminished expectations. Many rationalize working in fields they don't really like, and some, discouraged by the gap between reality and their expectations, end up refusing all adult commitments."[17]

The Wooed and Won landing foreshadows the uneasy alliance to come between woman and the corporation. Swept up in an overwhelming wave of ambition, anxious to fit any pattern but the traditional, women make the career decision as adolescents, seldom calculating the repercussions.[18] Under pressure to bond, to achieve economic security, and to test themselves on the corporate proving ground, women are forced to live with the choice they make in late adolescence—until they reassess years later and make the appropriate, often costly, midcourse corrections. Coupled with women's inherent values of loyalty and obligation, reality, though it appears to be reversible, proves to be anything but.[19]

Through all of the Wooed and Won landing runs the stream of ambivalence so characteristic of today's corporate women—the same stream destined to become a muddy river churning with dissatisfaction after women finish proving themselves to the corporation.

CHAPTER 4
PROVING UP

I just realized that if I really wanted anything I had to work to get it. I think somewhere in me I knew that there was no one who was going to give it to me.

Lois Wyse
President of Wyse Advertising

The Proving Up phase—proving up to oneself, to the corporation, to other corporate women, and to men—is the most exciting, energetic, and rewarding landing for women in the corporate life cycle. As women look back on this landing from a more mature perspective, each recalls her most positive corporate experiences. She receives a title of assistant vice president or manager. She garners a four-figure bonus. She takes business trips to Europe instead of Pittsburgh. Headhunters begin to call. Increasingly, a woman senses her untapped powers for accomplishment in the corporation, as handed down through performance appraisals and other corporate report cards. But Proving Up reflects more than moving lockstep up the corporate rungs of promotions, titles, higher salaries, greater responsibilities. While men go through a similar stage in their careers, we found women's experiences have their own distinct momentum. The dynamic involves each woman's attempt to affirm herself in what has been largely an uncharted Wild West for women: the management track in corporate America. And with few true trail scouts, women must depend on their own myths and expectations to guide them through the vast open territories.

Proving Up to Oneself

Long ago, Sigmund Freud asserted man's need for both love and work. Psychologists, sociologists, and others have since put forth numerous variations on this theme, and recently they have focused on women. In *Lifeprints*, for instance, Grace Baruch, Rosalind Barnett, and Caryl Rivers claim that women as well as men need the two components of well-being— "mastery" (self-esteem, sense of control, low levels of depression and anxiety) and "pleasure" (satisfaction, happiness, optimism). The authors posit that the depressed, frustrated, and frazzled housewife whom Betty Friedan identified in the early 1960s suffered from a lack of mastery, which "is tied to the doing and achieving part of life. But women have often been encouraged to downplay the importance of achievement and to concentrate solely on emotions and relationships." Baruch, Barnett, and Rivers contend that a woman can neglect neither mastery nor pleasure and that "a healthy life demands the integration of both aspects."[1]

These days, men and women seem equally driven, and especially at the Proving Up landing, women might neglect their relationships as much as and sometimes even more than their male peers do in their efforts to prove themselves. Asked why she is working, Lou Anne, a twenty-five-year-old assistant vice president at a midwestern bank comments: "I like people saying I have done a good job, being tested on the outside. I think if I ever just stayed home, the way I am going now, my confidence would just plummet. Because so much of how I feel now is brought about by the feedback I get from my job and the satisfaction I get. It's not the money that drives me at all, although I do want to be fairly compensated. It is the responsibility, the recognition." She is surprised to realize how high her aspirations have risen since the Wooed and Won landing, when she first entered business several years before. "When I started banking, I really had no aspirations. I was always afraid to have any, but as I have gained more confidence over the last two years, I have started seeing myself in higher positions. Now I can see myself as a senior vice president. And I would love to be the chairman someday. That is my goal."

Such an aggressive, goal-oriented approach has often been referred to as more "masculine" than "feminine." But are most women "just like men" in the Proving Up landing? Or do they have their own viewpoint and value system regarding mastery and achievement? Our interviews suggest they do. Because the mythology remains, for the most part, intact. Some myths that were most pronounced in Wooed and Won continue into the Proving Up landing. One of them is the myth of the Corporation as Lover. Meanwhile, other myths—Growth through Learning, Unlimited Potential, Meritocracy, Individual Recognition, Irreplaceability, and Living on the Edge—operate at their strongest. Only a few myths and expectations

—the Peaceable Kingdom and the Moral Universe—begin to fade ever so slightly and lose their luster.

In the Wooed and Won landing, the woman has not yet garnered a sense of mastery. She is still a "Corporate Learner," which Gail Sheehy distinguishes from a "Corporate Doer." In the corporate learner stage, Sheehy explains, the individual is "busy qualifying to join the professional tribe." His or her advancement depends on the energy, loyalty, leadership ability, and "willingness to jump whenever the company says move." The Corporate Doer, on the other hand, has greater responsibility and is "under the gun." Moreover, competition and politics enter the struggle for advancement, and "much depends on the coattails to which one is attached—and that person's fate."[2] The Proving Up landing as we define it falls somewhere between the Corporate Learner and Corporate Doer stages—and for this very reason it is the stage most savored by women in business. At this stage, women are gaining more responsibility, as they have mastered certain basic entry-level tasks, but they are not forced into a political Appomattox for control or power. In fact, while they are accumulating the trappings of power—titles, larger offices with windows, administrative assistants—they have really not yet assumed any ultimate power to direct corporate resources in any significant way. Nor are they burdened with the attending risks. At the Proving Up landing, in other words, women are still not key power brokers and are not yet as threatening to anyone as they will increasingly become as they approach higher landings. They don't have to play power politics—yet.

Thus the Proving Up stage is the most exhilarating and intoxicating for most women because it perfectly balances learning and growth with accomplishment and corporate approval. At the same time women are being tested and stimulated in their jobs, the corporation is often thundershowering its accolades upon them. Certainly there are exceptions, but the fact remains that as they progress up the corporate ladder, women—even those younger women who have the highest corporate aspirations—tend to view power as learning, or knowledge, or *self*-mastery, not mastery over others. This further confirms the Myth of Growth. As twenty-three-year-old Catherine, now working at a prestigious investment banking firm, says: " 'Power' is such a weird word. I like to be used as a resource. I like it when people call me with questions and need my expertise in something. That motivates me to learn more about a particular area so as to gain that expertise. That is a motivation for me: to learn about something."

A Chinese folktale centers on a man who had such a great passion for gold that he ran right to a gold dealer's stall and snatched some gold in full sight of the guards. After easily apprehending the man, a guard asked, "With so many people around, how did you expect to get away with it?" And the man replied, "When I took it I saw only the gold, not the people."[3] Similarly, corporate women see only their own individual goals. And in the Proving Up stage for women, the "gold" is learning, personal growth, and self-mastery. Which leads to the fundamental question of whether men and women are working for somewhat different reasons and rewards. A number of the women and men we interviewed suggest that women get the greatest gratification from simply doing the job well while men are more concerned about monetary rewards because, despite the increasingly mandatory second income, they are still viewed as the primary breadwinners. While this may be a valid distinction in some cases, many women in the Proving Up landing have to support themselves, too—and for some this is as heartfelt and important a struggle for survival as it was in *Alice Doesn't Live Here Anymore*, when Alice packed up her son and moved across the country in search of employment after her husband died.

Are women, as they prove up, working for different psychic rewards than men? Are they in fact working to *prove* something to themselves and others? A recent survey revealed that more women than men have "an inner need to do the very best" they can "regardless of pay" and that they seem to be more highly motivated than men. The survey also found that women were more interested in "psychic income" such as good working relationships and ethically sound tasks than in "money, power, and career prospects." It noted, too, that "women managers and professionals and those with high incomes are more likely than their male counterparts to say their jobs are challenging and let them learn new things."[4] Another survey of 800 women between the ages of eighteen and sixty-five found that, "in general, women placed more emphasis on the excitement or stimulation of a job than on actual financial success."[5] Why do women still hold fast to the Myth of Reward? Why, even for younger women who see the chairman's salary and office as somewhat closer than Saturn, is the big payoff a sense of growth and personal mastery? Because, unlike men who consider a job their birthright, women still need to prove to themselves they can be successful at the office. The recent progress women have made in the corporation is still not enough to overcome years of being conditioned to view themselves as the Avis rather than the Hertz of the world of commerce. Thus, for all their accomplishments, women must still struggle in the Proving Up stage to counteract their own self-doubts, to prove to themselves that those who succeeded before them weren't at best exceptional and at worst lucky flukes.

The Living-on-the-Edge Myth—a corporate version of test anxiety—continues to manifest itself even as women receive strong corporate approbation. Chris, a division manager at one of the largest telecommunications companies, remembers the Proving Up landing of her career: "Since college . . . I always felt I hadn't done enough, so I rode into each little race with something to prove. At IBM there was a man who had a tremendous influence on me—a man with an eighth grade education who always asked, 'When are you going to have babies?' And that's always been a tremendous influence on me—someone basically saying, 'No, you can't.' " Sheila, an account supervisor at a major national advertising agency says, "It's like I've been chosen; therefore, I must prove myself."

Unfortunately, women for the most part have internalized since their earliest years a patriarchal view of the world and their place in it. What they have *not* internalized, with rare exceptions, is a realistic image of the type of corporate or working woman they would like to be when they "grow up." But what about all the women now in executive positions who can finally serve as role models for other women? Don't they serve as *actual* models that others might emulate? Surprisingly few women have found older women in business whom they would choose as role models. Women still are sorting out the feminine ideal in business; they still have neither internal or external role models to guide them and offer them tacit assurance that they can—and will—succeed. Catherine, the twenty-three-year-old investment banker, says, "It is hard for us just coming out of college to realize what the ramifications of our choices are going to be, because there are so few ahead of us. . . . Men have so many people ahead of them, so many people to listen to, including fathers." Or as advertising executive Lauren remarks, "It's *Romancing the Stone*. Women grow up with fantasy heroines; men grow up with real heroes to emulate." As a result, most women choose to continue to ape men, regardless of the cost to their own "feminine" instincts or to their Authentic Voice. On the other hand, men not only have external models but throughout their childhood and adolescent years they have fostered within themselves an image of "heroes" against whom to measure themselves—or a "dream" of exciting possibilities in the adult world, as Daniel Levinson describes it.[6] Robert Penn Warren writes of a similar vision which he calls "the image," in his Pulitzer Prize winning novel, *All the King's Men*: "I got an image in my head that never got out. We see a great many things and remember a great many things, but that is different. We get very few of the true images in our heads of the kind I am talking about, the kind which become more and more vivid for us as if the passage of years did not obscure their reality but, year by year, drew off another veil to expose a meaning which we had only surmised at first."[7]

Corporate women have an image, too, but are having trouble drawing off the veil of myth and expectation that can obscure it. Whereas men's image is grounded in fact, women have depended on fiction—from Katharine Hepburn who found romance at the office in *Desk Set*, to Princess Daisy, who became an overnight business wunderkind. As a result, women have created glamorized larger-than-life images of success that are virtually impossible to prove up to and sustain. Today the impossible dream has been expanded into that of the corporate Amazon, an Olympian ideal who is at once a perfect wife, a perfect mother, and a perfect corporate executive, an ideal that's been exalted in articles, advertisements, and fiction. Living up to this basically unattainable ideal, and without the sense of direction and priorities that a more realistic inner ideal provides, women must still rely on proving themselves *externally*—and all challenges are welcome. "I'm constantly proving to myself how well I can get something done. I think that's because our center of evaluation has always been outside ourselves," explains Sheila, the advertising account supervisor.

This lack of direction is exacerbated by the fact that, as described in previous chapters, many women were treated as extensions of mothers, who wanted their daughters to live the "perfect" life they had not been able to live. Which is one reason why women focus on mastering each task at hand—making it "perfect"—rather than taking a longer view of their careers, setting priorities, weighing costs and benefits of various activities, and so on. In addition, because they have no clear images or broadly accepted bench-marks of success perpetuated from generation to generation, women can often be much more demanding of themselves to reach a yet firmly defined standard of perfection. They are constantly shooting at a moving target of accomplishment and success. Paul, an executive vice president of a national hotel group, distinguishes this from men's drive: "I wouldn't be surprised if a woman would try to be the brand manager at Frito Lay or a partner at Morgan Stanley faster than a male with the same personality would. If I were a woman, if I had that opportunity, I might feel I had to work for it just to prove something."

As a result of all these drives—the compulsion to learn, the conditioning to do forever and again the "perfect job," the groping for the ultimate achievement—women acquire after their first taste of mastery an almost addictive need to master yet another area of knowledge. It's as if they want to prove they can jump still higher over the corporate hurdles, a case of the old school game of High Water, Low Water gone amok. This is why a number of women move on to other challenges during the Proving Up landing just when they have been highly rewarded—when most men would sit tight and stick it out. In the words of Jill, who herself worked at three *Forbes* 500 corporations before she was thirty-five, "Men have their role and expectations more clearly laid out for them than women do, and as a result they may seem less restless than we do."

Sometimes, in this relentless quest for more learning, women leave one corporation for another when such a move would be least expected. Jill, for example, left one of the nation's leading food companies to take a job at another *Fortune* 500 company in the Midwest. "I had been there for seven years and could have stayed and become a VP. I had no doubts about that," she says. "But I kept thinking, 'Do I want to do this for the rest of my life?' And I didn't want to deal with that. So I left the corporation to prove myself elsewhere. I was searching for something more challenging." Meredith, thirty-five, remained at the same network broadcasting company but shocked top management when she requested to leave a more lucrative, less demanding union job for a non-union position with greater learning potential. "The manager, a new guy, sent around questionnaires to all employees asking people if they could have other jobs besides what they were doing, what would they be interested in," she remembers. "And I was the only union person who filled one out. He called me into his office; he couldn't believe it. I was so protected in the union, and I made a lot of money then, a lot of overtime. He couldn't imagine I would want to leave the security of the union. If I had a family or if I had to do it totally for the money, I might have been like them. But I was cocky enough at the time that I thought, 'Hell, I will get the money; I will just do it in a different route.' I felt that I had every opportunity to get ahead."

As women prove up, they are often swept up in the more

glamorous aspects of a corporate job. Women recall flying first-class to Rio, eating expense-account dinners, riding in limousines, and entertaining lavishly at glamorous events like the Indy 500. Radcliffe's Margaret Touborg observes that women can appear to be the nouveau riche of the corporate culture: "It's like going through the Gilded Age all over again. There's the introduction of flinging around a business card; like Commodore Vanderbilt, they're trying to announce, 'Hell, ain't I got power?'" Men more often take the trappings for granted. Meanwhile, few men have commonly assumed *they* will never be bored, and they usually have more rational, grounded aspirations. While most men start out with a greater sense of possibilities and higher goals, such as at least a shot at becoming chairman or president, they have also cultivated patience and a clearer understanding of the precise corporate tithes they must pay. Again, perhaps it is because they had a role model in their fathers. "Men were *brought up* to think they should be general managers when they grow up," says Gary Knisely, a partner in the executive recruiting firm of Johnson, Smith and Knisely, touching on this basic aspect of male "career planning." "Honest to God, their fathers told them they should be general managers. And men will make the necessary compromises to do so." Even today, when corporate loyalty is often considered as outdated as never buying on credit, and when younger men as well as women are corporate Gypsies, they usually move for somewhat different reasons than women. Men more often leave a company for a better opportunity for advancement, greater power, and increased external reward. Women still tend to focus on the learning aspects and the intellectual challenge—to "prove up."

However, when the corporation asks for ultimate proof of commitment—the external manifestation of proving up by making a company move to another town—women stall. They refuse to prove up, for very internalized reasons, a fact not lost on most corporations. There is still the expectation that women will choose love over work, as hotel group executive vice president Paul points out: "There is one big difference between men and women: no man has ever refused a promotion because he wants to stay with his wife or girlfriend, whereas four women have." Some younger women believe they will be able to work out the dilemma that dual careers pose to couples. Marla, a twenty-seven-year-old financial analyst at a Chicago-based conglomerate, says, "If it weren't for the fact that I wanted to stay here in Chicago another year with my fiancé, I would probably be going to an operating group. Corporate exposure has been good for me, but I really don't want to stay in it too long. It's the staffy side of it." She has it all planned out. "After he graduates from school next year, I want to be in a location where we can have the potential for two promotions and stay there four or five years," she said. "I've talked to my managers about this, and when I have gone through career planning sessions I have written that in. I have also told the vice president I report to. I think it will work."

But there's a lot more to the stall than women being caught between love and work. The staff-line distinction that begins relatively innocuously at the entry-level landing accelerates at the Proving Up landing as women continue to gravitate away from the more powerful line positions. Denise, a thirty-eight year-old director, now at a *Forbes* 100 pharmaceutical concern, recalls her Proving Up landing: "I once thought, 'Gee, if I wanted to get my M.B.A. and really get some line operations background, I know they would pay for me to get an M.B.A. So I interviewed with a sausage casing division in Chicago—I really wanted to give it a shot. And then I looked at myself and said, 'You really don't want to be a line manager. You like writing, talking, communicating. Face it.' And so I changed my mind." In hindsight she analyzes it: "I think women can be better team players because they are better at getting input from a variety of sources. They are better at staff jobs than at running a division, where they are subject to criticism for being this bitch woman who is just throwing her weight around. I never wanted to be accused of that." Matt, an assistant treasurer at a Chicago-based conglomerate, notes that the distinction between corporate staff positions and line jobs out in the field could often be compared to the difference between the more glamorous service industries and the old-line manufacturing companies. "At least for the first few steps of their career, women can pick their spots, more or less. They are more in demand, and we are not in a glamour industry like broadcasting or media," he says. "If she is sharp and well qualified, she can make it in basically a male world but in an environment of her choosing. Why should she take on unnecessary battles? She can see bank vice presidents who are female. Why should she move to Huntington, West Virginia, and sell plastic cartons?"

Men have traditionally been willing to transfer as operating managers to small towns in the sticks in order to move ahead. For a number of reasons it may be difficult for women to make these moves, but men have been raised in a culture that helps them accept that moving a couple of times—even to boring jobs in "boring" towns—will be part of the career track, notes corporate recruiter Gary Knisely. Matt, the assistant treasurer, put it another way: "Women are more mature when they start working than their male counterparts are. But they don't seem to have the fear of losing a job most men do. There is not the inborn provider instinct. And in many cases their expectations are too high and they are not willing to put up with the shit that in some cases you have to put up with to do your job." Men, because they are more likely to view their career over the long haul, consider the hassles as part of the politics of the organization. This involves putting up with sublimation of ego desires and sometimes even humiliation to win the game in the end. Maccoby's "gamesman," for instance, has a "toughness and shrewdness" that "is self-protective to reassure himself that he has not been totally emasculated by the corporation."[8]

Men's contemporary emphasis on gamesmanship reminds one of Willy Loman's contention in *Death of a Salesman* that "the man who makes an appearance in the business world, the man who creates personal interest, is the man who gets ahead." And even if they aren't "gamesmen," the shrewdest professionals—male or female—become quickly aware of the concept that *The Wall Street Journal* Deputy Managing Editor Paul Steiger refers to when he remarks, "There is something to be said for working smarter rather than working harder. Knowing what to delegate is more important than the number of tasks you can accomplish yourself by working a 100-hour week." Women, in their eagerness to prove themselves, often lose sight of that—and can more commonly regard paying dues as working *harder* for reward. Forget all the self-help books that supposedly have taught younger women in business the games their older sisters never had a chance to learn. For all their ecstatic sense of possibility, virtually every woman interviewed—including the most politically savvy younger women with the most grandiose dreams—believes at the Proving Up landing that growth and accomplishment in the corporation will occur primarily through extra hard work, trusting still in the Myth of Growth and the Myth of Individual Recognition. While they may be impatient, women are earnest. Rachel, a young midwestern lawyer speaks of a young paralegal assistant who looks at the other women in the department and says, "You guys are fools. You take all the responsibility and do it." Meanwhile, she says "the men all claim to need two new people under them to do the same job." However, it should be remembered, that "gamesmanship" is often not even an option for a woman at the Proving Up landing. To begin with, she is not even considered a bona fide member of the team for the first five years or so of her career. Women still have to spend so much effort proving they have a right to be there, to be accepted, that they rarely have time to map out a strategy.

A related problem is that the moral or judgmental voice continues to haunt women throughout the Proving Up landing. Catherine, the investment banker, comments: "I would much rather be recognized down the road for making a social contribution than being on the *Forbes* 400 list of the richest Americans." It is at this stage that women first begin to discover, however, that business usually does not have a personal or moral pulse and that victory often goes to the highest—or toughest—bidder. Angela, a thirty-five-year-old manager at a large defense corporation, contrasts her earlier government work to her corporate job: "In the government, you are working for 'the people.' And if you really don't want to do something you can always say, 'Hey, I work for the people,' and do it differently. That doesn't happen in the corporate world. You don't work for people, you work for the company. And you can't follow your own conscience; you have to make compromises."

It is also at the Proving Up landing that women's loyalty and longevity are first tested. And even at this stage, there is indeed a perception by many men and even some women themselves that they are just "playing work." Perhaps because the corporate world is so new, it is still not quite real to them. Perhaps mother's adage that "you never know what's around the corner"—maybe a man to "rescue" them from work—is lodged in the subconscious. The inner clock ticks on. Many women at the Proving Up landing are moving into their late twenties or early thirties, and fantasy figures of marriage and a family tug at their pin-striped jackets. Some members of the older generation never expected to work much past the Proving Up stage. Some more recent corporate arrivals may be pushing ahead in business only as a result of peer pressure, not out of an honest personal commitment. Whatever the reason, and despite economic changes that increasingly mandate two-income couples, few women—even the younger, most career-oriented—are resigned to the fact that they will *have* to work forever in the same incontrovertible way men do. They are subconsciously torpedoed by society's conditioning that work is somehow still "optional" for women. Jeff, a thirty-five-year-old male media company executive remarks: "I think women in general sublimate their career plans because they're waiting for someone to come along and take control of their lives." Is this just another sexist cliché? Despite all their frantic activity, women are still fundamentally *reacting*, not actively formulating long-term plans that fit their own individual needs and goals.

Women approach their careers like sprinters rather than marathon runners at the early landings, such as Proving Up. They tend to take each day as it comes, hurling all their physical and emotional energies into each task at hand without pacing themselves for the long haul—sacrificing evenings, weekends, vacation days with few, if any, second thoughts. Meanwhile, living on the edge discourages the plotting out of political stategies or long-term corporate career campaigns. Which is why most women speak of the Proving Up landing in sentences like these: "I was killing myself," "I was putting in sixteen-hour days and didn't have time to see many friends," "I was working like a dog." Hillary, a thirty-seven-year-old manager in one of America's five largest corporations remembers her early days in the company: "I looked up from my desk the first day at 4:45 and thought the day was half done. I saw all these people rushing for the door, and I honestly thought there was a fire. Except I noticed they all had their coats on and were carrying their briefcases." Usually, women recognize that they are working much harder than their male peers. Denise, who worked in government before entering a large conglomerate, comments: "I was never adequately compensated for all my efforts. I quit three times. Here I was, working like a dog, supporting this guy who got all the credit. I would go home to my parents and cry. But then I would have to say, 'I am learning by leaps and bounds.' "

At the Proving Up landing women sow the seeds of disenchantment as they gradually start to realize they are indeed proving something to themselves—but what are they proving? That they can work hard to master . . . something. Yet, for now, the Myth of Growth prevails. It is enough to carry most women through the Proving Up phase. That and the belief in the Myths of Individual Recognition, Meritocracy, and Rewards, that the corporation will eventually adequately recompense them for all the hard work and extra effort. And in the Proving Up landing, it usually does.

Proving Up to the Corporation

The period between the early 1970s and the early 1980s could be called the decade of Proving Up for women in the corporation. Women started leaping two and sometimes three steps at a time up the corporate ladder, often moving even faster than their male counterparts. In 1972, some 322,000 women were managers. By 1985 the figure had ballooned to 1.3 million.[9] Between 1972 and 1980, the number of female managers and administrators more than doubled, while the number of male managers increased by only 22 percent.[10] If women were storming corporations by sheer force of numbers, they were taking key strongholds with the help of a most powerful weapon: Title Seven of the Civil Rights Act of 1964, strengthened in 1972, which provided the basis for antidiscrimination policy. In response to this government directive, corporations began aggressively seeking out promising female candidates for promotion and advancement. "Tokenism" became the catchword of the day.

This tokenism further reinforced women's belief in the Myth of Unlimited Potential, underscoring their sense of being selected and recognized, of being exceptional. Often the women themselves weren't clear why they had been tapped for a particular promotion. Hillary, a thirty-seven-year-old manager at one of the world's largest energy multinationals, describes her first major promotion in the corporation: "I was jumped three grade levels, which generally doesn't happen. I was so surprised I did. I never thought the head of my group was that impressed with me. But I heard from my new supervisor that my old supervisor pushed me. It is still a mystery to me." Women have mixed emotions about such rapid advancement. These swift promotions reinforced in many of them the "lucky break" orientation they first experienced at the entry level, further leading women to believe that planning was neither necessary nor possible in the Proving Up period. This quick advancement might actually undercut women's sense of mastery, leading them to wonder, "What did I ever do to deserve this?"

On the other hand, such corporate approval reinforced the positive feedback women had experienced at home and in school. As we've noted, these women had often been virtually spoon-fed the Myth of the Meritocracy. Combining intelligence, talent, and hard work, they had always been at the top of the class and in the honor society. Why shouldn't such a pattern continue into their corporate careers? Because they were accustomed to success, women generally never really considered that *their own* personal advancement depended on the goodwill of an invisible Big Brother. Many women, especially in the seventies, weren't even aware of the government forces at work behind the scenes in their behalf. Molly, a thirty-three-year-old vice president at one of the nation's top financial institutions recalls: "It was just so easy. I never even realized at that time what was going on in Washington. All we knew about Washington was Nixon and Vietnam. We really didn't think about what was going on behind the scenes, that the government was forcing changes. We knew about civil rights, but we thought that had to do with black people. I was totally unaware it had anything to do with women." But as Alex, a male vice president at a broadcasting network, remarks, "Women who are enormously successful tend to be in positions created for them in the corporation and not in traditional positions it would have taken them longer to attain." Usually these positions are special staff positions, created in the more robust days of blossoming corporate staffs. Eventually, in later landings, the problem with these nontraditional career paths will be that there are often no established benchmarks against which to measure and evaluate women's specific contributions to the corporation.

Throughout their corporate advancement, women are somewhat aware of the discrepancy between their own rise and that of older male line managers in the company. Hillary, the energy company manager, says: "I had been with the company only two years, and I was in the executive dining room. And I'd look around that dining room, and most of the men had gray hair. They'd been with the company since they left college, and it took them twenty-two years to get to the executive level." She also decribed in detail what it was like to be the only executive woman at a special management seminar. "We were sitting around a table describing ourselves and how many years we'd been at the corporation. And I was the only one who had been there only a few years. And here I was at this management course where some of the men were about fifty years old and had been with the company for eighteen years and said they had been rewarded by being sent to this management seminar. And their expectation levels were very different from mine. They probably looked at me and thought, 'You haven't served your time and you got this promotion.' And I am sure a number of them who didn't know me thought I got this promotion because I was a woman." She and women like her recognize that their careers have been switched to fast forward. And because they actually *are* exceptionally intelligent, capable, and hardworking, they see their rapid advancement as a just and proper reward. The downside to it all, however, is that women in the Proving Up landing have begun to *expect* that such fast-track advancement—suspiciously reminiscent of the hare's rapid start over the tortoise but based on what appears to be a highly rational meritocracy—will continue to function throughout their careers, that the smartest, most hardworking people would continue to be rewarded. Jodie, a thirty-eight-year-old financial service company executive, says of her Proving Up landing: "Just about every promotion I had I was the first woman to be in that role. . . . It's definitely a pleasant feeling, and if you go for it and had that aspiration all along, you can't help but be satisfied."

At the same time, while women thrive on this feeling of being special, an underlying ambivalence begins to manifest itself at the Proving Up landing. On the one hand, women want to excel and be recognized for it. On the other hand, they have learned that the rewards in the Proving Up stage come as much from fitting in as from standing out. They want to become part of the male team and not be noticed as "that cute blonde in accounting with the great pair of legs." It's the old dilemma: women have always wanted to be judged as special, but *not* for being female. At least consciously, women at this landing try to deny that being female makes any difference, or if they believe it does, they rationalize that it is an advantage that makes up for male advantages they do not have. As an executive woman observes: "Women want to be singled out because they have already been singled out by gender, like

'Oh, there's our woman VP of marketing.' So maybe we try to make the most of it, to be singled out in positive terms: 'Yes, she is different, but she brings this to the party.' " Brenda, a thirty-three-year-old manager at a midwestern technology company, describes how her well-intentioned company sponsored a seminar aimed at figuring out practical ways to advance women. During the seminar, one of the male executives suggested that a strategic planning post, which happened to be filled by a woman at the time, become a permanent "woman's position." "I thought what an odd way to look at it," she muses. "If it is going to help women, okay. But to do that, to create this special spot for women just to get women into the department seemed pretty ludicrous." Lou Anne, the twenty-five-year-old midwestern banker, speaks of her previous job at another bank: "I always felt female there, which is a really strange feeling. . . . I always felt self-conscious of the way I looked, and I always felt I had special treatment. I would go out on calls, and they would say things like, 'Make sure you are going into a safe area.' I felt that they pointed out the fact I was female a lot." And Catherine, a twenty-three-year-old investment banker, notes: "There are always those meetings where you sit there and someone starts talking about women in business and all heads turn to you; you are the one female there. And I think that as long as that singling out goes on there is still that little bit of tension." She described a case in point: "Yesterday, a client was talking to me and the managing director from the other firm, and he said, 'Well, you guys will just work this problem out, right?' And the managing director said, 'You don't mean *guys* in a literal sense.' It was just sort of a useless comment, and it really singled me out. It separated me for that one moment."

The feeling of being special, of being singled out, starts to fuel a sense of isolation for women at the Proving Up landing, which will only accelerate as they progress up through the management ranks. This is particularly difficult for many female managers since, as mentioned in an earlier chapter, women seem more in need than men of the tie that binds, of a sense of connectedness. Jill, a female executive at a large electrical products corporation, recalls her previous experience as a director at a leading midwestern packaged goods company: "I'm not the kind of person who has to be the center of attention, but I felt so alone there. There was one other woman at work and she wasn't a close friend, but she was the only person I could talk to." Often the smallest details will reinforce this sense of isolation. Angela, a thirty-three-year-old defense company manager comments: "I walked into the physical everyone has to have before joining the company. They treated me very well, but I looked at the forms and there were questions about prostate problems and so on but nothing about breast cancer or any women's problems, you know." Women had pretty much the same experience in many industries, even those supposedly most ideal for women. Elaine, a forty-six-year-old vice president at a cosmetic company, says, "I once got a buyer's memo that began, 'Dear Men,' and I wrote back saying, 'Isn't this a little inappropriate?'" They do make you feel familiar and at home—*if* you're male."

This sense of isolation in turn underscores women's inclination to deny the Authentic Voice in favor of the corporate mimic. We were surprised over and over again by women who thought their experiences in the corporation were unique. This holds true with relationships with female peers outside their particular company. Sheila, a thirty-four-year-old account supervisor at an advertising agency comments: "The incredible work load creates a real sense of isolation outside the organization. You end up compartmentalizing, and because of the isolation, you've no chance to articulate to anyone else what you're going through, or talk out goals or plans, or see where tasks are leading."

Because women often have no one else to test the reality of their views against, they assume that their views must be unauthentic. Thus they adopt the values and viewpoints of the male culture because they have no outlet to discuss their own values—and because they have such a strong desire to fit in and "belong," to once again play the perfect, dutiful daughter according to the rules of the father corporation. "My experience has reinforced male attitudes toward work in me," comments a thirty-five-year-old paper company executive. "Since I've been surrounded by men all during my career I probably tend to think more like a man. Because my day consists of seminars, lunches, presentations—all with men. So my thought patterns have probably come to resemble theirs. And I've been successful thus far, so I must somehow unwittingly function in their sphere." This desire to gain recognition without calling attention to oneself—so one can fit in—results in an unconscious modus operandi that differs substantially from that of male peers. Many women have noted that men seek to parade their accomplishments before the world much more than women do within the corporation. As Adrian, an assistant vice president at a New York insurance company, says: "I am not constantly representing myself as having achieved a great deal or having done something special. But men seem to do that." The infamous male ego aside, women probably tout themselves much less than men do because, in the Proving Up stage, they don't *have to*. They automatically stand out by virtue of being female. Unlike men, they haven't had to strive to differentiate themselves early in their careers. Instead, women work hard to prove they can do the job, and they put far more energy into doing it well rather than shouting about it. Partly this is because, as Susan Brownmiller observes, it is still deemed unfeminine to exhalt in a personal victory. "Arms raised in a winners' salute, the ritualized climax of a prize fight, wrestling match or tennis championship is unladylike, to say the least. . . . More appropriate to femininity are the predictable tears of the new Miss America as she accepts her crown and scepter."[11] MasterCard's Joanne Black makes the distinction: "Men at their worst skew heavily to form; women at their worst go the opposite direction and concentrate on content only. Which is why they're not good at promoting themselves." In short, women have actually been quite conflicted not only by the need to feel special but also by their desire to not serve as a lightning rod for males. In a survey of 722 female executives, many women complained of always being "on display" or "in a fishbowl."[12] Thus, most women have tended to hunker down and do the job, faithful that some omniscient executive father figure on the forty-fourth floor will peer down through the corporate ranks and magically be aware of their exceptionally fine work—without any salesmanship on their own part.

However, the proliferating self-help books and articles have at least made women more aware of the need, when proving up to the corporation, to think more strategically about advertising their capabilities and accomplishments—even if it goes against their sensibilities and conditioning. It's a good thing, too, because with, as one male put it, "a zillion" other women around them, they are often no longer automatically special in the way women of previous generations were. Susan Brownmiller notes of the new, more competitive reality of the situation between women that in the 1980s "female competition for two scarce resources—men and jobs —is especially fierce."[13] And where are the richest mines for both scarce resources? In the corporation, of course.

Proving Up to Women

A female public relations executive once received a phone call from a younger job-seeker who had heard her speak before a major trade association and who requested a meeting to discuss career opportunities. The executive refused.

"Hey, but what about networking?" the job-seeker gasped. "Don't you believe in networking?"

"Listen," the executive retorted, "the Old Boy Network consists of people who've gone to school together and known each other for *years*. It isn't calling up people you don't know at all and asking them to drop everything to help you. No wonder the term has gotten such a bad name!" She curtly hung up.

"Networking" is indeed one of the tired buzzwords of the 1970s. It has been so overused and misused that it evokes ambivalence and even outright hostility from a lot of managerial women. And despite the pages and pages of magazine articles heralding newly formed bonds between women, the truth is that women are only now beginning to sort out their relationships with one another in the business world. Only in recent years have enough women entered enough businesses so that they are no longer isolated cases, working and relating primarily to males. With greater numbers has come both camaraderie and competition among women themselves. Some of the women interviewed have had their most constructive, supportive experiences with other corporate women who have reached out to help them and served as guides for the corporate climb. Still, there are plenty of corporate women who forget the importance of relationships and concentrate only on winning—an obvious denial of the innate "relatedness' at the core of a woman's being.

Perhaps being forced into such overt competition is so new for women that they don't know how to handle it. Or, as one observer notes, entering the rough-and-tumble corporate world taps women's competitive drive for power, revenge, and status —a sometimes voracious appetite so long denied to them as good little girls that its reemergence scares them.[14] In this, most women differ from men who have developed frameworks —sports being one of the most obvious ones—to channel their competitive and aggressive tendencies. This tendency may go back as far as prehistoric days, when men formed groups to hunt and formed hierarchies around leaders or groups of leaders. Not only did this establish a clear competitive order, but it also organized and managed violent drives and instincts.[15] Women, perhaps as a result of biological evolution or psychological development, usually perceive aggression as "a fracture of the human connection." Therefore, they have tended to try to prevent aggression rather than seek "rules to limit its extent. . . . Rule bound competitive achievement situations, which for women threaten the web of connection, for men provide a mode of connection that establishes clear boundaries and limits aggressions, and thus appears comparatively safe."[16]

This ambivalence and confusion about competition underscores the fact that the *external* experience of each successive generation of women in the work force has been significantly different. As a result, women of various generations hold significantly different views of life in the corporation—unlike men of different generations, who throughout recent history have washed into business in virtually identical waves and who share a common experience which unites them. For instance, while younger women at the Proving Up landing appreciate to some extent the inroads their older counterparts have made for them, they fault these older women for being too aggressive and abrasive—corporate Calamity Janes—and for shadowboxing for women's rights in the corporation. Holding fast to the Myth of Unlimited Potential and the Myth of Meritocracy, many women of the younger generation believe they will be the exception to the rule. Kelly, a young New York manager contends: "The difference between the older generations of women in business and mine is that they fight more. Maybe they have to fight more. But it seems they read women's issues into situations when those issues really aren't there." The younger achievers "aren't interested in meeting other female executives for purposes of networking."[17]

Some of the disdain with which certain members of the younger generation view their older counterparts was reflected in the comments of a twenty-six-year-old public relations woman: "One of the ironies is that most of the women in senior positions got there because they were in the right place at the right time. And they don't like other women around them because it takes away their glory." Most older women would beg to differ with at least the first half of her contention. Few would trivialize their experience as having been "in the right place at the right time." And many younger women look at the women who have succeeded and concede they don't at all relish the often gargantuan personal sacrifices such trailblazers have had to make and *continue* to make for their careers. "I have not found anybody high enough in an organization to be a role model," Heidi, a twenty-five-year-old product manager, asserts. "Someone who has done what I would hope to do: have a good personal and family life and also be successful at work." She explained: "The ones I have seen, if they are really being considered for the top spots, their whole life is work. They are in their middle to late thirties and single and workaholics. They are machines. And the funny thing is, even though they are closer to the top, everyone I know in the younger set is frightened by them. There is a tremendous bond among younger people who just don't want to be like that. In fact, the thing that might deter women from wanting to become CEO is that they see these workaholic, usually unmarried women as kind of freakish." That so very few women have been able to identify senior women they would choose to emulate is unfortunate and discouraging. Do women have to conform to the Corporate Amazon ideal to be suitable role models? Otherwise, will women continue to copy only male behavior instead of establishing identities that are powerful in their own right?

For their part, older or more experienced women, after their hard-fought battles, resent the younger generations for their "sense of entitlement." Hillary, a thirty-seven-year-old energy company manager, describes how she was discussing this sense of entitlement with a male contemporary. "He and I were talking and agreed that we'd noticed this generation just coming out of school has a "this-world-is-my-oyster attitude." Both concurred too many contemporary graduates of prestigious colleges and business schools enter corporations with presumptuous expectations of success. "And we agreed that when *we* came out of school, *our* attitude toward the corporation was 'Oh, please, let me show you what I can do!' We finally had to admit that there was a generation gap. These younger women are still too naive to realize how it is *really* going to be." Joanne Black, formerly senior vice president at American Express and now holding that same title at MasterCard International, agrees: "The women who forged the path took a lot of bruises along the way in behalf of the ingenue—and she's not grateful. She's often disrespectful as she competes with you, and that hurts." A forty-one-year-old executive says, "I think they are presumptuous when they come in, assuming the world has made more progress on women in business than it has. They're pretty heady. They've been lured and wooed. They don't feel like an oddity when they look around at all the other women. They have a confidence, a spirit of independence that women ten years ago didn't have."

Older women—and even some older men—believe that younger women will encounter some of the same difficulties as those who preceded them, and that the future will in fact be tougher for the younger generation, because they expect to be the Lee Iacoccas and Cliff Garvins of tomorrow, heading Chryslers and Exxons within several short decades. "A lot of women in their mid-twenties assume older women have won most of the battles, but it's not true. Their attitude is that older women have been the shock troops and have knocked off their first echelon of the enemy, and all they have to do is climb over the prone bodies," observes Dr. Frederick Hauser. "But I think what has happened in the corporate world is that younger men are even more resistant than their predecessors. So young women will be zapped two ways: by their higher expectations and by their male peers." Recruiter Gary Knisely concurs: "Maybe the women in their twenties believe they are entering a work force where they are going to have a clear path to the top. Well, if they do—if they presume there is no battle to fight—they are wrong. Coming in thinking they have a shot at the touchdown is no more realistic now than it was twenty years ago. And I think these women are going to be even more disappointed because they presume they can do it." Energy executive Hillary also agrees: "They don't know what it cost us to get where we are. They don't know all the crap we've had to put up with or what we have done to earn our promotions. They just see that we have it. They are coming in late in the game. But they will top out, too." She concedes: "They may get a little further than we, but I think it is a fallacy to think it won't take at least fifty years."

"Role model resentment"—either at *not* being deemed a role model or for being too much of one—is common among the senior generation. Marian, a thirty-seven-year-old Harvard M.B.A., now at a leading consulting firm comments: "One younger woman in the company told me she had no role models, and I said, 'Thanks a lot!' " On the other hand, Ricki, age forty, who had two children while working, complains: "I don't like being a role model for anybody. There's enough pressure to deal with all you have to deal with when you're pregnant. . . . It's a position I've been put in from time to time and I resent it like hell. I don't want somebody to copy the way I've done things. You get bored being the first this or first that—and so few people understand that." As the sole female in management, a woman may be called upon to train and advise every new junior woman. That, too, can become tedious, as can being a representative of the profession. "I am so sick and tired of talking to female friends of friends of friends of friends about getting into my field," exclaims one exasperated female public relations vice president. "It's gotten so bad I've considered opening my own personnel agency!" Younger and less experienced women are often surprised and resentful if older women don't perform the role of a Dear Abby or Ann Landers in the business world, dispensing helpful hints and executive do's and don'ts. One younger woman describes her disappointment upon arriving at a New York bank and eagerly phoning one of the women who had interviewed her. "She wouldn't have lunch with me, or even coffee. I think in her culture there just weren't a lot of mentors, and she was looking out for number one." It is true that many women expect more of their female supervisors and peers than men do. MasterCard's Joanne Black tells of a man who refused to tell a woman colleague she would not get a promotion, postponing it until Joanne finally intervened. "And when I told her, she got enraged," Joanne recalls. "She said, 'You above all should know better.' Men are little boys in these women's eyes. But as a woman, I am supposed to fix it. You're supposed to be the Mommy." Eleanor, a bank vice president agrees: "I can identify two young women who were very ambitious and had idealized me as a role model and wanted to monopolize my time to the exclusion of the rest of the staff. And when I had to put them gently to one side, I sensed some friction. I wasn't giving them what they wanted—all the 'tricks' I used to get where I am. I think young, ambitious women expect a successful older woman—thirty-five to fifty-five—to unlock all the secrets, so *they* can be there in five years rather than the fifteen years it took us." This frustration of one more extra burden foreshadows and fuels the burn-out many women executives experience at a later landing. As Joanne Black comments: "When it's just you and the board of directors, who do *you* talk to for advice? You do burn out. So there are times when I just go under cover."

The lack of support and the presence of strong competition reinforces the sense of isolation most women feel in their corporate careers. Sheila, a thirty-four-year-old advertising executive, says, "It's unacceptable to ask other women the taboo questions about whether they're unhappy in the corporation or what they're doing with their lives. Come to think of it, I don't have a lot of female friends in the industry. When I used to, I felt overwhelmed by their compulsive ambition. I guess I didn't want to get drawn any deeper into the corporate drive by another woman's ambition." However, despite the isolation and loneliness, a number of the older generation would admit that standing out as the sole woman in managements offers substantial psychic, if not monetary, income in the earlier landings such as Proving Up. And like the wicked witch in *Snow White* (who *is* the fairest of them all at corporate headquarters?), many women instinctively want to guard that special position. "The younger women are going to make it faster, and that's the subtext in these interviews with women who resent being pioneers," Sunny, a thirty-six-year-old general counsel at a leading West Coast financial company, explains. "I know women who feel put upon because they've bled so much and now they aren't going to be so special anymore. They're much less enthusiastic about bringing other women up." One bank executive reports, "There's really very little sense of fair play among women. How can there be, when everyone's striving to be Daddy's favorite daughter?" Being the sole, often the token, woman gives some women their greatest sense of achievement. The Myth of the Corporation as Lover or Family unconsciously plays into this attitude. Sunny, the general counsel, adds, "Think of it in the context of a family: the children who didn't get enough nurturing are not able to give much away. Similarly, these early women didn't get enough nurturing and can't give anything away."

Intergenerational battles, however, don't tell the whole

story of female relationships in the corporation. In a survey of 525 working women performed by Kane, Parsons & Associates, this ambivalence among women is evident. Women reportedly preferred male bosses by a margin of better than two to one. But 76 percent of the respondents working for women described their bosses as "fair" and "unbiased," or as "exceptionally understanding and supporting," compared with only 66 percent who said the same about their male bosses.[18] Why this odd discrepancy? Why do women sell each other out at critical landings in their careers? One reason may be that women are more tightly controlled by their mothers than boys and as a result do not want to be similarly mothered by women bosses.[19] Also probably operating unconsciously is the woman's sense that she can "get more out of" a male boss, just as she cajoled her father into special treatment as Daddy's little girl. She may also be harboring memories of Mommy receiving presents only at Daddy's whim. And after all, throughout history women have bonded with men, not with other women, to achieve power and prestige. These often unconscious feelings are reinforced by the fact that men usually are in stronger positions within the corporation and can dispense greater rewards—higher raises, promotions, and so forth—to the women who work for them. A thirty-five-year-old female jobseeker, formerly a manager of marketing and strategic planning at a leading forest products company, comments: "I'm increasingly concerned about being referred only to other women. I might end up doing myself a disservice talking only to women, because men are still the primary information conduits and can identify openings or create them."

Another more conscious fear for women is that if they band together with too many other women, they will be held in lower esteem and denigrated by the male power structure. Unfortunately, the fear of a "sorority house stigma" is definitely not unfounded, and its "frat house" counterpart does not bear the same taint. One woman put it this way: "I go into a meeting where there are only women in the room, and I immediately think, 'This is going to be a second-class meeting.' And it usually is." Many men even admit that once women enter or dominate an occupation, males tend to trivialize it. Michael Korda observes that men denigrate jobs and flee management committees as soon as women prove themselves capable of performing equally. "It is not that an act of sexual equality is taking place—far from it, the men who run the committee are simply abandoning it to women and replacing it with another more exclusive one."[20] In addition, as one financial services marketing director remarked, men often don't like working for women who seem to manage and champion other women. "If your staff is primarily female, and if you do have men, you risk being perceived as a mother hen vis-à-vis the women in your group, or as overly protective," she noted. "And then, you can't attract men. I've actually made a decision to put a man in a job no matter what."

Of course, women at the middle management level know that there will be fewer and fewer positions open as they move up. They become more turf conscious and less willing to help women behind them. As Andrea, a thirty-nine-year-old commodity company executive, puts it, "Women sense there's room for only a few women on the ladder, so you're fighting to be the token. Instead of fighting to expand the pie—which seems feminist and aggressive—you are fighting over it, saying, 'I'm the one who should be the only senior woman.' " Patrick, a fifty-one-year-old general manager at one of the nation's largest energy corporations, explains it this way: "The competition among women is much more personal—probably because there are fewer women there. Women recognize there are only so many opportunities for women. So it becomes a case of 'me against her' rather than 'me against the rest of the boys.' When going head to head, men also experience the more vicious personal competition. But for women, I think there is more of a conception that they are *always* going head to head." Not to mention the fact, as a twenty-four-year-old advertising woman remarks, that older women feel the burden of representing their sex to the corporation: "If she screws up, she thinks the whole female population will suffer. If a man makes a mistake, it's his own individual error. So if a woman supports you, it's taking a risk she can't afford because she's a woman."

At the Proving Up landing, most women would admit that they have little hope and even less energy and time for changing the patriarchal system on which corporate America is founded. Joining with or vigorously supporting other women strikes them as similar to taking on the weakest partner in a doubles tennis tournament in which the other players are men. "Why can't we show the kind of support for other women that men show each other?" and interviewees asks rhetorically. "Because we're so busy developing our own skills and aptitudes. We realize only one woman may be selected for the level beyond so we can't be overtly supportive toward one another. It becomes a self-destructive pattern." As a result, the simple truth is that usually the women who have progressed beyond the Proving Up landing and made it to the higher executive ranks have done so by playing by male rules and rejecting or sacrificing their more "feminine" aspects. They have succeeded, as we suggested earlier, by identifying with male role models and ideals. "We are perpetuating the myth of women as second class more than anyone else because the only way we know how to succeed is to become more like men," admits Chris, division manager of a telecommunications company. Reinforcing this impulse is the all too common phenomenon of women distancing themselves from feminism. One female financial journalist said that the opening comment by 90 percent of the businesswomen she interviewed was "I'm not a feminist." Chicago *Tribune* editor Carol Kleiman explained, "These women are not comfortable being woman-identified, so they're trying to tell me how much they like men."[21] Many of our interviews, particularly with younger women, began the same way. "Feminism just doesn't touch my life," declares twenty-four-year-old Kelly. Ironically, the more successful a woman feels, the more of a feminist she often acknowledges herself to be—explaining that, after she has passed through later landings, the corporation acts as a radicalizing catalyst. But at the Proving Up landing, most women deny any feminist affiliation for fear of being branded as man haters, bra burners, ball-busters, or simply as anti-male. Benjamin R. Barber, a professor of political science at Rutgers University describes it this way: "With equality itself, there was no intrinsic quarrel—but at what cost? . . . Women might wish to be free, but not of their womanhood. If accepting sisterhood meant abjuring womanhood—husbands, generativity, love, babies, nurturing—then they would do without sisters." This is one of the reasons many women have avoided aggressively seeking out and supporting female "clubs," or "networks."[22] So the sense of isolation increases, standing in contrast to many women's basic impulse to relate to and nurture others. The internal ambivalence results in ambivalence toward one another.

"When I first got into business, women were my enemy," Joanne Black concludes: "You got talked about in the most horrible way, got the most gossip. They almost wanted you to fail. I learned to combat it by being much more accessible than men might be." She adds the warning: "If you want to engage other women, you have to reach out and take some risks, knowing one day you might get it right between the shoulderblades. Let's face it, there is still a very good chance you might get a real Joan Crawford out there."

Proving Up to Men

During the 1950s, when a lot of the women now filling middle management ranks were growing up, one of the favorite television characters was Lucy Ricardo (Lucille Ball) in "I Love Lucy." And Lucy was indeed lovable—daffy, and creatively resourceful, yet ultimately dependent on her husband Ricky. Who doesn't remember her plaintive wail, "Rick-k-k-ky!" While that Lucy is a far cry from the professional woman of today, another Lucy character might be a rather apt representative of women in the Proving Up landing of their careers. She's Lucy of Charles Schulz's *Peanuts*—shrewd, wise, and insightful, as well as strong-willed and independent. From

Lucy to Lucy, women have indeed traveled a fair distance, but not without major shifts and strains in their relationships with men. Remember, it is Lucy who so often leaves Charlie Brown dazed, dazzled, or dejected.

Corporate women at the Proving Up landing have different relationships with a variety of men—top executives, immediate supervisors, and peers as well as husbands and "significant others." A lot of these relationships have to do with "proving" oneself to males. As Chris, a division manager at a major telecommunications corporation, says: "It's all about proving—to oneself mostly. But since I grew up thinking women were second-class citizens, it was important to benchmark myself against men."

And, of course, a key relationship is with the mentor. Subject to the earlier described myth, women of all ages refer to their mentor of the Proving Up landing with awe and almost reverence. These primarily mythic Pygmalians, dispense not only titles, promotions, and raises but also advice, self-confidence, and encouragement. The mentor can be the same charismatic figure mentioned in Wooed and Won, who attracted the woman to the job and the company in the first place. He now personifies corporate authority in terms of advancement and recognition and is often much older and quite senior—as such, usually a father figure. Denise, a thirty-eight-year-old executive at a major pharmaceutical company raptly describes her relationship during the Proving Up landing with a male senior vice president. "He just adored me. I never knew why. It was very clear from the beginning. He was crazy about me just the way my parents had been, but the amazing thing was he hadn't known me all those years like they had."

Mentors play their most important role in the advancement of women's careers in the Proving Up landing. A study by Kathy E. Kram, a psychologist at Boston University, confirms that the relationship between mentors and their managers does pass through specific stages as the managers advance. In the Proving Up landing, the relationship has entered what Kram calls the "cultivation stage," where "the junior person enjoys the guidance and protection of the mentor, who usually ensures that challenging, visible projects are assigned to increase the exposure of the younger manager. The mentor also benefits during this period from the personal satisfaction and the peer recognition received for developing the talents of a protégée." She adds that "during this phase, lasting between two and five years, the relationship peaks and is mutually beneficial and satisfying."[23] Men obviously have similar mentor relationships, but despite efforts by both men and women to the contrary, these relationships differ from the male-female alliances because of the sexual element. Even though the relationship doesn't usually take on a sexual character, a sexual undercurrent, however repressed, is virtually always present as we will discuss in more detail in the following chapter.

Some women try to avoid the sexual aspects by keeping the relationship squarely in the father-daughter realm. One woman remembers an older male executive who had taken it upon himself to help her earlier in her career, saying with more than a trace of wistfulness, "You know, I often feel like your daddy." She recalls, "On the one hand, I felt silly and juvenile and slightly belittled by his comment. On the other, I felt relieved and 'safe.' I thought, 'Phew, good, at least he's gotten *that* message.' I really didn't know any other way to treat him and still keep the relationship on an even keel." But making the mentor into a father figure has its own risks. Many women in corporate America, because of their need for bonding and connection, coupled with their own still shaky sense of confidence at the Proving Up landing, become attached to their mentors without recognizing their dependence. This unusually strong psychological dependency on a mentor, which men seldom experience, often subconsciously hampers women from breaking away and shooting for the next level. It can also undercut their sense of independence at the very moment the mentor relationship gives them the illusion of mastery. The mentor is dangerous in this way because, besides advising and encouraging his protégée, he should function like the horse trader in the folktale. A man had an excellent animal to sell but could attract no customers. So he went to the famous horse trader and asked him to walk around the horse three times, inspect it, and look back as he walked away. The trader did so, and the horse was sold for ten times what it was worth.[24] In other words, by recognizing merit in young women, mentors make others within the company—especially the women themselves—appreciate their merit as well.

As a result, the conflicting messages that these women have picked up in their childhood—to depend on a man but then to *not* depend on a man, as a result of their mothers' experiences —are crystallized in the mentor relationship. In fact, as Srully Blotnick contends, women who are unconsciously fleeing from depending on a man to fulfill them through a personal relationship "unwittingly made the switch from men to mentors. Instead of looking for a man with whom to structure a satisfying personal life, each began searching for a mentor who would help her further her professional life." Blotnick continues: "Although she was unaware of it, the line that separated these two categories in her mind was extremely thin and usually missing altogether."[25] These mentors can give women the desired affiliation and at the same time allow them a sense of their own mastery, of independence. Because the basic service the mentor provides is to recognize abilities that *already* exist. Call them mentors, white knights, or horse traders, these men more than anyone else reinforce the woman's sense of being chosen, of being special, and in doing so, they rekindle the Myth of Irreplaceability. It is a myth that, further encouraged at this landing, sets up women for the disillusionment and ultimate sense of betrayal that follow once they discover that this individual recognition is not institutional and is often a once-in-a-corporate-lifetime experience.

As for relationships with male peers in the Proving Up landing, they are superficially full of healthy goodwill and mutual respect. Very few women at this landing admit to or even recognize any displays of discrimination. Belief in the myths of the Peaceable Kingdom and the Androgynous Manager is strongest at the Wooed and Won and Proving Up landings. Especially the younger women, fresh out of egalitarian colleges, think that discrimination doesn't exist anymore, that it went out of fashion in the 1970s like the mini-skirt. But we have found that women of all generations tend to deny any discrimination in the Proving Up landing. In part, this is because women at this landing are usually being adequately rewarded for their efforts by the corporation. It is also because women want to believe that the world is fair, that the meritocracy of hard work, talent, and brains will prevail. And even when the world is not fair, women have been conditioned to put on a happy face, to refrain from whining or complaining. A cartoon appearing in a magazine article on women in business captures graphically their prevailing attitude at the Proving Up landing, portraying one working woman declaring emphatically to another, "I've never been discriminated against because I've always worked twice as hard as the men to keep up." Some observers suggest that because men dominate corporations, women initially suppress any notions of discrimination. In the effort to avoid conflict, women are very careful at this Proving Up stage to handle male egos gingerly and not appear too strident, unfeminine, or "difficult." Many women resemble Denise, the pharmaceutical corporation executive, who remembers the earlier years of her career: "I put myself down to get things done. I think subconsciously I knew that if I asserted myself too much it would hurt me. I knew I was a threat to males, but I played it down. If I was to win, to exist, I had to do that. But deep down inside, I knew I was better than they were."

Meanwhile, women must undergo not only testing but double-testing by males. Says one male executive recruiter: "Women have more to prove early on, that's for sure." Marla, a twenty-seven-year-old financial executive at a midwest conglomerate, whose first full-time job was as a line supervisor at an industrial plant, comments: "When I worked there I was amazed at how many of the men knew my life story, and I had never *told* them my life story. They want to know if you are qualified . . . they always have to make sure at least originally that you should be there. So there has always been a lot of testing at the beginning." She describes her work in the plant in more depth: "I think they first tried to scare me or intimidate me. We were working in a very hazardous area, and I had to learn how to run the chemical operation. And in the beginning I think they thought I would be too scared, that I wouldn't want to go up on top of the tanks or operate things. But I would climb tanks no matter how tall . . . so I think they really learned to respect me." In short, as Angela, the defense company manager evaluates it: "You have to compensate. You have to work harder. You have to prove yourself intellectually. And you have to prove you are tough."

Thus, even if women are not aware of any overt discrimination, they are already burdened with conflicting aims—to prove just how good they are so they will be allowed to become members of the team but at the same time not be *too* good, the old "playing dumb" deception again. These burdens, which men do not bear, can be their own form of discrimination. One recent psychological study revealed that a woman makes a special effort to convince her boss that she is competent whereas a male manager tries to reassure his boss that he is not competing for the same job and does not appear overly confident.[26] All these mixed messages women receive might cause them to feel once again like Alice down the rabbit hole, where they are never quite the right size. By following instructions and by drinking in male encouragement and challenge, they grow larger and larger and larger but then perhaps *too* large to fit in. Curiouser and curiouser. Yet because, like Alice, women want to stay in what they view at the Proving Up landing as an enchanted garden, they force themselves to ignore all the illogic and contradiction.

But the myth of the Peaceable Kingdom does start to fade, if only on a subconscious level. One important area where virtually every woman at the Proving Up landing recognizes clear discrimination is in salaries. As Pia, a twenty-four-year-old marketing assistant at a computer corporation, says, "At my corporation, where entry salaries are basically equal, I already see a difference in terms of raises. I have noticed that most of the women who have done what I have get about the same percentage, whereas the men at our level, who haven't done as well, have gotten larger increases. We aren't supposed to talk about it, so we aren't supposed to know. It is just that they think, 'Well, this guy has a family to support,' or something like that." Meanwhile, it is interesting to note that for all women's attempts to ignore any differentiation between themselves and their male counterparts, men are aware that the system remains inherently discriminatory despite all the gains women think they have made in the past decade. Jim, a twenty-eight-year-old assistant vice president at a leading West Coast bank, notes that "they [women] achieve titular success very fast, but not influence. Women ranked higher than me have to come to me—although technically they are senior, I dispense the goodies." Comments such as his suggest that many men feel they can sit back and indulgently enjoy women's advancement because they know it will not threaten their own power. Meredith, who worked at one of the major television networks and had been rapidly advanced, says, "I was low middle management at the time, and I was one of only two women. And I think the men were kind of intrigued. It was a novelty. Hey, here was this pretty blonde and they sort of had a 'go for it' attitude. They were supportive. I was totally unthreatening to them at that point."

In the past, more men than would probably admit it have wagered that women will soon get this ridiculous notion of having a career out of their system and go back to raising families where they belong. This attitude still persists. When asked what men of his generation thought of their female peers, Ben, a thirty-nine-year-old legal counsel for an energy multinational, confides, "Honestly? On the unconscious level, I think we're all thinking that she's either looking for a husband and family or, if she's already got them, that she's not really competing for the top job. But people of my generation would never come right out and say that." In some instances, it might be wishful thinking. Because as women have stayed and even prospered in the work force, more than a few men have started resisting their advances. In fact, as futures forecaster Steve Custer notes, "We're starting to see war in the backlash toward equal opportunity. Men are claiming *they're* discriminated against." Jeff, a thirty-five-year-old vice president at a New York media company, comments: "I think it's amazing how a majority of the population have come to think *they're* a minority. It's one of the great public relations coups of the century."

For women brought up on the myth of the Peaceable Kingdom, who cherish the notion that at least the younger men have been enlightened, it may be particularly disheartening to find that it is often these younger men who are the most resentful and difficult regarding women's progress. The broadcasting manager who received so much support from her male peers in one position got a very different reaction when she was promoted to a higher level. "I thought the men my age would be the most accepting," she says. "But it was actually the people my father's age who were the most helpful. The men in their twenties and thirties were the most resistant; they almost seemed to be trying to sabotage me. It wasn't open sabotage, but they would do just every little thing they could to break me down, to make me say, 'I don't want this anymore, forget it.' "

It is at the Proving Up landing that women are beginning to flex their muscles, and that threatens many men. As Maria, a financial analyst, says, "Seems like a lot of male bosses get paranoid when they find out you are really qualified. Sometimes I think they don't want you to be better than they are. I don't think they are necessarily as supportive, putting you under their wing, as they are toward some other male." A thirty-year-old "new male" executive, whose mother sits on the board of directors of a *Forbes* 500 corporation, confides, "My peers were raised by their fathers to be male chauvinist pigs." The shift in men's attitudes from the Wooed and Won landing reflects the shift from the beginnings of the women's movement to today, as women have proven their worth. One mid-thirties male executive puts it this way: "Years ago, there was this feeling women didn't know what they were doing— pat them on the head, nice girl, now let me take care of business. There was a lack of respect . . . there were without question a great number of men who really felt women had nothing to add in the professional sense." Today, however, as Subrata Chakravarty, senior editor at *Forbes* observes of many men in business, "Men aren't patronizing women now; they are much more wary. In the early stages of this thing, men would say things like 'What's a nice girl like you doing in a business like this?' They aren't doing that anymore. Now, they are scared; they are resentful. They are threatened."

At the same time, relationships with males outside the corporation often have a bearing on women's advancement within the corporation. Work has now become another way to meet and attract men. In fact, most single women now believe that if they are not working at some relatively exciting job, their peer group of men will be less interested in them. Yet the fear still remains that if they become *too* successful, they will turn men off. Contends twenty-three-year-old investment banker Catherine about her "enlightened" generation of male peers: "The guys my age aren't interested in a professional woman like me. They are more interested in younger women or women in more 'feminine' fields like magazines or design. They use women to build their egos. They have been taught if you want to feel great about yourself, go to a woman who doesn't make as much money as you and who is impressed with the job you have." An even more somber but common notion is that if "he" never comes along, one at least has one's job. A young male author puts the plight well when he writes that "this generation sees no clear future, no predictable path. The fact is that our parents, as they now reach the golden years they once looked forward to, are finding themselves trapped in unhappy marriages or divorced . . . we aren't going to make the same mistake they did. Alone, at least, we are safe—from pain, from dependency, from sexually transmitted diseases. Those who belong to no one but themselves can never be abandoned."[27]

In Charles Dickens's *Great Expectations*, Miss Havisham, who had been deeply disappointed by her lover, brings up her adopted daughter, Estella, to treat males with cruelty or indifference. As we've suggested, some women are corporate Estellas, living out their mothers' usually unconscious but often bitter resentment of men and the disappointment they've experienced by devoting their lives to men. A lot of working women today seem to be striving to enhance their independence at the Proving Up landing—and they neglect or deny their family life. Yet our interviews corroborate the fact that a supportive husband often helps a wife through the vicissitudes of Proving Up. Declares Carrie, a forty-year-old broadcasting executive: "My husband's a better feminist than I will ever be." She, like a number of the women interviewed, credits her husband for much of her success. Another thirty-five-year-old woman describes her husband's support in some detail: "I think through my husband I got motivated. I think I would have been content at a lower-level position, but he was the corporate type and in many ways my own mentor outside the company. He motivated me a lot, gave me a lot of direction, and helped me set goals for myself. Being honest, I doubt I would have ever reached the level I reached if I hadn't had him to say, 'Hey, you can do that. Why don't you talk to so and so about it? Don't get down about that. There are other job possibilities,' and so forth. He really kept me going. I owe him a lot for that." This woman went to work in the early seventies, just as the feminist movement was taking hold. Her husband's strong support also reflects the shift in how men view working wives. It has become its own kind of a status symbol—not to mention the extra income. "I remember those times I was making maybe triple overtime pay and I would be at parties with him, and he loved to say, 'You know, my wife makes more money than I do.'" But she adds, "He sort of thought that what I was doing was 'in,' but if that had gone on over a long period of time it would have killed him." This parallels the be-good-but-not-too-good syndrome women encounter at work. Most of the men we interviewed admitted that while they wanted a successful wife, she shouldn't be *too* successful—and preferably should not work in his profession.

Often home relations only mirror those at work, with all the tensions and strains. The complex and multidimensional relationships between men and women—and their success—begin showing some signs of friction at the Proving Up landing. And as women climb the executive ranks, all that keeps this growing friction between the sexes from erupting into overt warfare is a fragile truce, an Uneasy Peace.

CHAPTER 5
THE UNEASY PEACE

When men are thinking about women
in business, they're still thinking
out of the same frame of reference
they were raised with all their lives.

Russell Marks, Jr.
former president
Phelps Dodge International

I think at the heart of it all is the age-old battle of the sexes. All the dynamics of what's happening in the workplace are simple extrapolations of what women and men have had in their personal lives for years," Jeff a thirty-five-year-old media company executive, sums up the current relationship between men and women in the corporation. "You're supposed to transcend your personal hostility and bias on the job, but in doing so all you really do is add a ton of pressure to the situation. If you think a man can have a fight with his wife in the morning and then go to the office and not look at the female corporate counsel differently, you're crazy." Until the Proving Up stage, while men and women have held somewhat different expectations and attitudes, they have been treated equitably, for the most part, by the corporation. But as women climb the ranks, corporate discrimination accelerates, leading to seeds of disenchantment and, finally, to success and betrayal. Which is why it is most important to pause in the landings progression and ask a critical question: How far have women and men really come in relating to one another in the corporation? Because in the answer lies the key to women's corporate progress.

The common belief is that, because of upbringing and socialization, older managers, those in their fifties and sixties, are simply not used to working with women and will have a difficult time treating them equitably. More popular folklore is that men in their forties "can go either way"—be either generally supportive of women or raving chauvinists. And younger men, in their twenties and thirties, have taken off the gender-colored glasses of the past and view women with the full clarity of 1980s vision. Yet, despite the prevalence of women in the marketplace, male unease with women in the corporate culture is not passé. Far from it.

Sociologist Christopher Lasch notes that the sexual stereotypes of earlier days, such as the emotional incompetence of men or the brainlessness of women, created a handy contempt for the weaknesses of the other sex. While certainly a put-down to women, such stereotypes had the benefit of giving basic sexual antagonism a less direct and confrontational channel of expression. Today, Lasch says, "feminism has discredited the means by which it was possible to acknowledge sexual antagonism without raising it to the level of all-out warfare."[1] And all-out warfare between males and females often exists. The battlefield has simply shifted to the office.

A startling discrepancy exists between most men's intellectual acceptance of women and their unconscious emotional resistance. Men have accepted that many women are qualified, well-trained, competitive candidates for top jobs. Men have now had ample exposure to what women can present; women no longer confront this educational problem, as they did in the seventies. In the eighties, the challenge will be to close the emotional gap and somehow make corporate relationships between men and women as comfortable as possible despite sexual tensions. Antonia Earnshaw, a researcher at a large New York advertising agency who has been doing a study on the evolving male and female attitudes toward one another asserts: "There's more of a divide between the sexes today. Men don't believe they can satisfy women on any level, so they are pulling back, creating distance, even though they're paying service to ideas like sensitivity and 'the new man.'" Many younger men, particularly those middle managers in their thirties, mention that dealing with women is actually more difficult for them than for their counterparts in their fifties and sixties because they have been caught in the rule change between traditional upbringing and today's prevailing social norms. Futures forecaster Steven Custer, thirty-two, is optimistic that the gender gap will disappear in the future: "I think more and more men and women are becoming alike. But it takes time for change to manifest itself. It's like eating habits: we've grown up with attitudes and ideas about eating better, but we were raised with bad eating habits. We've grown up with the belief in equality between men and women, but we're caught in the paradox that we were shaped by role models of non-working women." Jon, a thirty-five-year-old pharmaceutical company manager who is married to an executive, says: "I think subtle discrimination is definitely there. We are prisoners of, or at least deeply shaped by, what we grew up with. And while that is not an excuse to act inappropriately, it is certainly a fact to be reckoned with. It is like staying to the right when you should keep to the left while you are driving in England. It is reflex."

Even a man as young and enlightened as nineteen-year-old University of Chicago student Terry admits, "To a certain extent, it seems that certain of these biases have been erased. But it is a tremendously difficult thing to do sometimes, and there is no assurance that it has happened even when you completely convince yourself that you have made the jump. These things have been in the culture for so long it is very difficult to change them." He considers his own experience: "My father never does any cooking or cleaning, but my mother works longer at the office than he does. Just looking at it from an equitable point of view, I figured out something wasn't fair here." Yet he describes many of his college peers: "Last year, I was in an all-male dorm at college, and some guys had what seemed to be almost a terrible fear of women. They watched a lot of television and were into a lot of heavy metal music which is *extremely* sexist." And even he, who is trying hard to mesh his intellectual attitudes with his emotional ones, concedes: "I encounter these things sometimes in myself. For instance, a couple of years ago when I was having a college interview, I assumed my interviewer would be male. But when I found out it was a woman, I immediately felt better and not as threatened. And I suddenly asked myself, 'What's going on here?' "

Several of the men we interviewed drew an analogy between women's rights and other minority rights. One Asian male describes the gap between liberal biases and reality: "I understand women and sympathize with them. But again, I have never been hurt competitively by a woman in business. The interesting time is when your liberal biases come up against hard reality and one or the other has to give. That's when you really find out how you react. And I don't know." While a number of observers compare women to blacks in the corporation, Malcolm Forbes, Jr., deputy publisher and presi-

dent of *Forbes* magazine, contends: "You have racial prejudices, but it is simply taboo to act on them in today's society.
On the sexual side, it may be taboo to acknowledge them, but
they are very deeply ingrained. You have a harder time breaking down sexual barriers than racial barriers in this country."

Both men and women today would try to deny that such
attitudes persists. Says Heidi, a twenty-five-year-old female
M.B.A. at an East Coast packaged goods company: "Anyone
who tries to be difficult with women is viewed as a creep today.
There is peer pressure for that now. Men who have gone to
business school with women would be hard-pressed to be
chauvinists." And a forty-year-old male manager at a pharmaceutical company protests, "I don't see myself as some keeper
of the flame, that it's a male institution versus a female institution." But while there may be some conscientious objectors,
that doesn't mean an underground war isn't raging. It simply
isn't trendy to declare oneself a chauvinist about either sex
these days. What's more, many women are afraid to speak up
for fear of being labeled paranoid. Yet, as one woman executive says, "A male friend of mine once told me if a woman
ever thinks a man forgets that she's a woman, she's crazy."
She added, "And it's either an unpleasant or a pleasant association for him. But it's there, and you are dealing with it—
whether you remind him of his mother or his first girlfriend.
And all the articles written about women in management
forget that." MasterCard International's Joanne Black agrees:
"My greatest role as a mentor is to tell a woman she's not
hysterical, not a misfit, that what's going on is really what's
going on."

Part of the problem, of course, is that there are still plenty
of wolves donning various outfits of wool. Maggie, a thirty-
three-year-old corporate lawyer, for instance, described a recent
incident: "A guy at my company used to keep spouting off
about women's rights. And then, when they chose the cheer-
leaders for the local basketball team, he laid the newspaper with
their pictures in it down on my desk and said, 'Why didn't you
try out for this?' I was slightly pissed off." Joanne Black explains the inherent contradiction between men's intellectual

and emotional reactions this way: "I've heard men say, 'I'm for women.' But it's a long way from the mouth to the feet, and they don't see it. Unconsciously everything you do is being analyzed, whereas your male counterpart is the fair-haired boy. Men don't realize how much their programming runs them." Her evaluation was reconfirmed by a recent study of students from three different graduate schools at three different intervals: 1975, 1978, and 1983. The findings indicate that, despite all the feminist gains of the past two decades, male graduate business students continue to respond much more negatively about women executives than do female graduate students.[2] The majority of men may honestly believe they are supportive of women who prove themselves capable, and they may truly try to treat their female colleagues equitably. But often what men believe consciously can conflict with their unconscious desires. And as Dr. Frederick Hauser explains: "A lot of men consciously mean it very sincerely. But we'd have to put a mantle of nobility on men to ask them to give up what we've had for a millennia. We're not that heroic."

It is doubtful anything close to a 180-degree change will occur soon. Jason, a thirty-year-old public relations executive, said, "It's maybe going to change—but not in our lifetime, I don't think. You are changing the entire structure of society. And that doesn't happen overnight. This is an evolution, not a revolution." And a forty-year-old male former head of strategic planning for a leading tire and rubber company division predicts: "In the short term, meaning the next twenty years, as the current group of people work their way through society, it is initially going to become more confrontational between men and women. And," he warns, "it will be more regressive in terms of where women go in business."

When women finally understand how large the gap remains between many men's willingness to accept them as executive peers and their actual ability to do so, the success and betrayal syndrome will seem virtually inevitable. In the words of Joseph Conrad, "Being a woman is a terribly difficult trade since it consists primarily of dealing with men"—an assertion the rest of this chapter will illuminate.

We Remember Mama

Much of the male attitude toward women in the corporation is conditioned by their ambivalence to women's second career as childbearer and their attitude toward their own childhood separation from their mothers. A number of psychologists contend that many men spend a good deal of their adult lives working through their relationship with that first nurturing—and alternately demanding—figure: their mother.[3] They postulate that a good part of the resentment men hold toward women arises from the fact that women spark ancient and ambivalent reminders of the boundless love and longing men felt for thier mothers and at the same time the fears and frustrations they feel about being dominated by a woman. Confirms Keith, a thirty-three-year-old director of a New Jersey conglomerate: "That's the ultimate fear—the reason why men have trouble with a woman, particularly a woman boss. It's like 'Hey, I've been through this already. I got out of this already. I don't want to be in this again.' " Antonia Earnshaw says of her research into male and female attitudes: "It's Oedipal—the need to separate from parents after spending the early part of their lives working for mother's approval. After saying, in essence, 'Stay away from me' as an adolescent, they don't want to have to go back to answering to Mom."

Why don't men and women generally have the same reaction to their fathers—usually viewed as the *ultimate* authority figure? Because in recent generations, the fathers have usually been absent, at work all day, and sons have looked increasingly to their mothers for support and discipline. Keith continues: "Daddy may be the ultimate power, like 'Wait till your father comes home.' But it is the nitty-gritty stuff that you deal with Mommy about every day. She is the authority figure on a daily basis. And that is what dealing with the nitty-gritty at work is —every day."

Then there's the male exhaltation of motherhood. Throughout history, from the thousands of ancient clay figures of pregnant women with pendulous breasts and bulging torsos to the refined and elegant Renaissance paintings of the Virgin and Child, men have celebrated the mystical quality of child-birth. However, in many of today's corporate men, it can manifest itself as an often critical and chastising attitude, which smacks of resentment and jealousy, toward women who choose not to have children or who "abandon" their children for work. As Susan Brownmiller notes, motherhood and ambition have been seen as opposing forces for thousands of years, and even today the most highly ranked and accomplished woman must proclaim her family as first priority.[4] Sums up Russell E. Marks, Jr., former president of Phelps Dodge International: "There are still a lot of men—even younger men—who believe that women should still be taking care of the home, that our culture is weakened when women care more about work than childbearing."

A number of women interviewed found male co-workers surprisingly interested in and concerned about their pregnancies or how they balanced children with careers. As one fortyish woman says of her pregnancy when she was a marketing director at an East Coast personal care products company: "When my daughter came along she was 'our' baby. I remember coming back after the amniocentesis, and my boss said to me, 'Well, what are we having? A boy or a girl?' . . . Everyone was very, very pleased for me, very excited. . . . It was as if they were partaking in this celebration of my femininity." But too often, men hold an ambivalence toward working mothers, personified in thirty-three-year-old corporate lawyer Maggie's experience. "I was working for a man who had a working wife and who really thought himself a modern man. He bragged about it all the time—how he had the great modern marriage and how supportive he was of his wife's career and how he took the kids to preschool, and so on." One day, Maggie got a call that her child had fallen at the school and hit her head and that she should see a doctor. She went to her boss and explained. "He said I could leave, but I got the distinct impression he was mad. Like 'You better rush back here so we can get this done, blah-blah-blah.'" Maggie went to pick up her daughter, found out she was all right, and returned to work as quickly as possible. "And when I got back to work, the guy—

who had really made a fuss about me leaving, who had made me feel this huge responsibility to the company—started yelling at me about my responsibility to my kid and how I should have stayed home with her. First he made me feel guilty about leaving work, and then he made me feel guilty about coming back and shirking my responsibility as a parent!" She adds, "By the way, his wife recently left him."

Perhaps more important, men's unconscious and still unresolved separation traumas from their mothers also get displaced onto the workplace. One male director declares, "You come out of your mother physically, and I don't think there is any way to underestimate that. I think that has a tremendous bearing on things." A number of psychologists have noted that little boys must distinguish themselves and separate from identifying with and emulating their mothers to a far greater extent than little girls. This separation can cause great anxiety and psychic trauma—and also rage, fear, and dread of women. These feelings are, of course, repressed, since little boys also love and depend on their mothers for many years. Some men feel so deprived and abandoned for having to relinquish their early connections to their mothers that they can develop an aggressive and hostile reaction—one that can last into and throughout adult years. Psychologist Lillian Rubin says, "When directed against women, it can be understood as a response to that early loss, and to the sense of betrayal that went with it."[5] Such attitudes force women to examine more closely the unconscious rage some men may bring into the corporate world. Christopher Lasch observes: "Whereas the resentment of women against men for the most part has solid roots in discrimination and sexual danger to which women are constantly exposed, the resentment of men against women, when men still control most of the power and wealth in society yet feel themselves threatened on every hand—intimidated, emasculated—appears deeply irrational and for that reason not likely to be appeased by changes in feminist tactics designed to reassure men that liberated women threaten no one."[6]

In fact, one male media company manager suggests that the unconscious guilt males feel as a result of their repressed hostilities toward women may be one reason for all the affirmative action programs of the past. "All the corporate bending over backwards to include women in things is an attempt to allay this sense of guilt about what's *really* going on. It's easier to create an affirmative action program than to go into therapy yourself and admit where all this hostility is coming from." He adds, "One caveat: This doesn't mean that people don't try to overcome this past, to the limit of their capability, particularly in our generation. But it's difficult to transcend something you're not that in touch with in the first place." Lasch paints an even gloomier picture: "When even Mom is a menace, there is not much that feminists can say to soften the sex war or to assure their adversaries that men and women will live happily together when it is over."[7]

The Sissy Syndrome

From their earliest childhood, men associate masculinity with segregation from and superiority to girls. These attitudes continue, however subterranean, into adult years. As Lois Wyse, president of Wyse Advertising notes, "Men are more threatened by the success of a woman than they are by that of a man. It is easier to go home and say to the little woman, 'Well, Joe, the guy I play golf with, got the job.' But what does he say when a *woman* gets the job?" A male executive vice president acknowledges the truth of her statement: "The cultural tide is still running that way. An awful lot of men still depend on their sexual role to establish their identity: they are better simply because they are men. And when a woman is smarter, more aggressive, more energetic—that not only threatens their professional life, it threatens their very identity." It's difficult for men to be overshadowed by women. One newspaper article notes that this is becoming a significant "crisis point" in an increasing number of marriages.[8] Not that there aren't a few Frank Butlers around who will go so far as to marry an Annie Oakley *after* she beats him in a shooting match. But, in general, even the younger, more enlightened husbands of management women put on the pressure when their wives and other women outdo them too often at work. Marla, a twenty-seven-year-old financial executive, says of her twenty-seven-year-old husband, also an M.B.A., "He wants me to get ahead. He is very supportive. But I think in a very competitive environment, if he had to compete against a woman directly and he felt they were both equally qualified and the woman got the job, he would feel the woman got the promotion because she was a woman. I think it is because of the way he was brought up." Most men would deny that they harbor such an attitude. But, as Joyce, thirty-four, at a midwestern conglomerate, says, "It would be a very terrible affront to a man if women moved more rapidly than he did. It wouldn't probably be something you'd hear about, though—they wouldn't ever admit it." One woman comments, "You know Freud wrote tomes and tomes on penis envy, and it was a big mistake. He got it backwards. We're the ones who get to have children. That fact gives women a certain stability and a lot of inner strength. For men, their job is their counterbalance, their big reason for being. So when women begin to develop skills and abilities in the workplace, enough to become their partners, we're threatening something terribly fundamental in terms of balance."

Heidi, the twenty-five-year-old product manager, muses, "I think things might have been a lot easier when two people did things that were so completely different they really couldn't be compared. Now that they can be compared, I am sure the male ego would affect things a bit. But you know, females can have pretty big egos, too." In many ways, it seems, however, that males have the harder adjustment. For one, they need to fight their dependency fears, which they have often soothed through accomplishment and advancement in the outside world. Psychiatrist Roger Gould describes this "magic balm of work," the "stroking" that serves as a stand-in for the strokings of a now distant, loving mother: "We pursue careers with enthusiasm because we accept the mythology of the work world that a man can become invincible with power, money, and status. The system preys on our narcissistic weakness—the so-called ego massage or 'stroking.' No one can pass up a promotion. The rewards of rank proclaim that the higher the rank, the bigger we are and presumably the less vulnerable we are. The implication is that we can become so big that when we 'get there,' we'll be totally invulnerable."[9]

But since men have always proven their masculinity by comparing favorably to women, when women gain greater power, whither masculinity? MasterCard International Senior Vice President Joanne Black speaks for a lot of corporate women when she comments: "I'm not a 'woman's libber,' but men feel a tremendous deep-seated resentment at having to deal with us. And I have a lot of compassion for them." She continues, "A male friend said, 'Listen, before all this happened, I knew I could be better than fifty percent of the population.' Men always could look down on women before. There was always someone they could feel superior to. And now they're only better than maybe ten percent. . . . From a self-esteem point of view, that's very threatening."

The Corporate Code

Because men feel increasingly threatened by successful women competing with them in the workplace, they've developed a conveniently critical double standard by which to judge female versus male behavior. We've all heard that a businessman is aggressive but a businesswoman is pushy, or that he's careful about detail, but she's picky, and so on. That's the corporate code at work. The code is definitely a masculine voice although women have learned to decipher it. But one wonders how far along men are in understanding the female voice, and incorporating it into the corporate code—especially as they persist in considering that voice inferior.

The ramifications of the different voices men and women bring to the corporation extend far beyond simple conversation, as Carol Gilligan's *In a Different Voice* attests. The fact that men and women talk about different things and express themselves in very different manners and styles is only one of the clearest manifestations of the schism. Studies show that men talk more often about music, current events, and sports, while women talk about more personal concerns such as relationships, family, and health. Also, men said they enjoyed their friendships primarily for their freedom, playfulness, and easy camaraderie; women valued friendships for the emotional support they provide.[10] A male corporate president confirms the difference between male and female conversational content. "I think men are different from women. Women get together and talk about their problems, and men *never* get together and talk about their problems," he asserted. "It is not macho for men to do that. Things that are properly in the guidelines of antitrust laws, business challenges, opportunities, and so on are the basic topics. But other than how well the kids are doing, they don't talk about personal things."

Other studies have also found a difference not only in content but also in the way men and women express themselves. Women use more questions and qualifiers and are prone to express their doubts and uncertainties. Mary Brown Parlee, a professor at City University of New York, has done studies on communications styles. She observes that "Once a stereotype of a particular group creeps into consciousness . . . it perpetuates itself by serving as a 'filter' for interpreting a wide range of actions unrelated to the conversational styles from which the stereotype originally evolved."[11] In other words, the corporate codes are continually reinforced by the perceptual gap between men and women. And it has become clear from interviews that the real problem is a *perceptual* gap between what women are saying and how men perceive or interpret what women say. Placing the onus of the responsibility on women to "toughen up" their communications ignores a fundamental issue: that in the corporate world men and women are often not speaking the same language.

Marilyn French writes that "technological language is a tongue from which emotion has been obliterated and is therefore appropriate to institutions that aim to obliterate emotion in their workers, especially those at the upper levels." She explains that it is primarily a male language that reflects the masculine approach to the world that things exist not to be experienced for their own sake but to achieve some linear goal. It is also an attempt to suggest "objectivity."[12] As we all know, men, at least superficially, believe that being emotional reflects a lack of clear thinking, confidence, and control. And, in turn, the majority of women in management have accepted as one of the basic corporate commandments, "Thou shalt not cry or express strong emotions on the job." After all, business is business. "A nervous woman is much more nerve-racking than a nervous man," remarks Angela, a defense corporation executive. But just how truly "unemotional" are men in corporations?

Some men themselves will admit to sometimes feeling the urge to cry, as Sam, a thirty-seven-year-old director of human resources at a West Coast media conglomerate, confesses. He describes how a high-level executive female, the head of one of the company's biggest divisions, was so relentlessly and ruthlessly questioned by a male lawyer that she burst into tears in front of all the other men present. As he tells it: "It was one of the longest moments of my life. Nobody knew quite what to do about it; they just kept staring at the walls. And she just reached into her purse and said, 'Oh, I will be all right.' And we resumed, but there was this air of things being a little uncomfortable." But, he adds, "We were talking about it afterwards, and we men all had to admit, 'Well, gee, there have been some times when *I* have felt that way, too!' You could really sense the empathy in the room although it was very unspoken and kind of awkward. But men are very uncomfortable about being so direct about how they react."

The presumed ability men have to mask and often deny their emotions has caused psychologists and sociologists to refer to them as well-oiled, perfectly functioning machines.[13] But when most candid, a number of men reveal themselves as corporate Tin Men who, in actuality, have big hearts. Sam, a human resources executive, confides: "A surprising number of business decisions are made on an emotional basis. But they are disguised as other things. You know, they dress it up like a pragmatic decision all the time." The difference is, obviously, that women express their emotions more often and in a greater variety of circumstances than men do, and they express them differently. A male executive vice president at a consulting firm notes: "Men learn to hide it. To take it out, often in somewhat perverted ways, like ulcers and heart attacks." He continued, "I don't see anything particularly wrong when people cry if they are upset. As long as they can get a hold of the problem and cope with it. I think it is at least less destructive to cry when you are upset than to go down and have six drinks in the bar. That isn't better, it is just more accepted. I would rather have somebody cry."

Media executive Jeff even suggests that women's more directly "emotional" approach in business settings helped keep men from being "self-destructive." "In a certain sense, it's like when children are all dressed up for Sunday school. Women in corporate cultures help contain certain male behavior that's inherently destructive. Whereas I think men don't mind being self-destructive in that environment with other men." Women do bring emotional overtones and evaluations to even the most competitive situations because, as a number of writers have suggested, they more easily form empathetic bonds with people. A number of men refer to themselves, in contrast, as "islands"—separate, isolated, and independent. Dan, a thirty-nine-year-old manager, says, "I envy women their ability to keep the tie that binds, to make connections. Man is a unit. Maybe he is functioning efficiently, but he's an island—and no man should be an island." He and other men also refer to the corporate environment as an island. Based on the previous comments, it sounds as if these "islands" men find themselves on are less akin to a South Sea paradise than to the one in William Golding's Lord of the Flies.

Moreover men often do believe that women have some sort of "emotional superiority," which will enable them to see through males, to expose them to their peers, their bosses, and to themselves for what they really are behind the macho facade. Like the Wizard of Oz, behind the powerful reputation, demeanor, and voice, a man often believes himself to be a drone merely pressing buttons and pulling levers. Before women executives came on the scene, the office was one place where men could hide behind their grandiose facades. The pretenses were supported by the established and accepted rituals and rules of the "game." But women, by crying or expressing other heartfelt emotions, break the accepted rituals and rules. As one woman writes: "Tears . . . in a woman should be welcome, not repressed. They wash away all falsity."[14] Perhaps washing away all falsity is exactly what men fear most in the carefully constructed and staged world they have often created at the office. Or, as many men as well as women have put it, women expose the emperor's glorious ribbons and trappings, his grandly protective uniform, for what it truly is.

This refusal to play by masculine rules points up another aspect of women's emotions—they are unpredictable. Men cannot control them. And this sets in motion men's unconscious fears, again often based on their experiences with their mothers, of women as unpredictable, unfathomable, inconstant. With more women now in the workplace, there is a greater variety of personal styles, values, and viewpoints, a profuse multiformity that can overwhelm and baffle men. Further, women often send confused, mixed signals. Jeff, the media executive, says, "It's difficult to draw generalizations in management. It's all caught up with what's happening between men and women, with the changes between what women wanted when the feminist movement first started and what they want today, with what women say they want versus what they really want. And men are sick of changing and adapting." Eve, forty, a construction company manager, agrees: "I think men have a tough time because there are many different kinds of women in business today. Whereas most men are much better at having the same idea about what it means to be there and how they should act. They know what is expected of them and they know how to behave." She adds, "And the tough thing is that men accept a lot of things in men they don't accept in women. It's a language they can pick up because they know what certain behavior means."

There is irony in the fact that while men resent emotion in women they increasingly value sensitivity, believing women pick up the nuances and provide intuitive insight into each particular situation at hand. Jon, the manager at a pharmaceutical concern, says, "I have learned a lot about organizational 'politics,' or interpersonal relations in a corporation, how to satisfy different constituencies and so on, from my female boss." Broward Craig, former president of St. Joe Minerals and now managing partner at Webster & Sheffield, a law firm in New York, has also found that women tend to be more sensitive to how a person is reacting to things. "Men are more interested in putting on their own show, putting across their own point of view, than in how the other person is reacting. The women I've known put more effort into understanding what the person on the other side of the table has in mind." Interestingly, Roy Rowan, *Fortune* writer and author of *The Intuitive Manager*, responded to the question "Are women managers more intuitive?" by saying, "No, I don't think they automatically are. I just think they need to cultivate their intuitive skills more because they are given less access to information in business than men are. They have to compensate through intuition for not being let in on what's actually going on."

Whatever the case, in a slow but steady ground swell, women are beginning to actively assert the value of their emotionality and sensitivity. "I don't know if I am just dumb as a stump or not, but I can't put on a mask and not show how I feel about things," declares Robin, a thirty-three-year-old manager at a Chicago corporation. Catherine, twenty-three, working at a prestigious investment banking house, proudly asserts: "There have been a couple of situations at work where I have cried. I felt it coming and I would sit there and debate about whether or not I should run to the bathroom and not get upset or whether I should go right ahead and talk through my tears. Which I have done a couple times. It makes the guys very uncomfortable, but I don't give a damn. Because if I had run away, I wouldn't have gotten my point across." And getting one's point across effectively in business is one area where men and women differ most significantly.

"Say Good Night, Gracie"

Many men in the corporation see women as the Gracie Allens of the world and themselves as the George Burnses. In the television series, "Burns and Allen," George's dry, laconic humor contrasted dramatically with wife Gracie's ditsy, voluble approach. It was always Gracie who babbled on endlessly and got involved in every bit and piece of her family's life while George watched it all with detached bemusement on his big television screen. In management men's minds, they, like George, see the big picture while women waste time and fool around with the small details.

Dan, a thirty-nine-year-old pharmaceutical executive is particularly critical of this trait in women. "As a manager, all I want is results and results alone. It unnerves me when I hear women talking about procedure. Don't tell me how you're going to do it, don't tell me who you have to talk to. The next thing you're supposed to say is 'And that's how I'll get to point B.'" He continues, "It's like she's giving me her recipe for wandering off into the wilderness. With men there's the goal. Some women know how to be concise enough not to drag my mind out into the underbrush." Clark, thirty-three, a group product manager at a California packaged goods company, describes how a female peer went way overboard on details: "There is no denying that she is a very bright woman, but it was almost a joke. She could tell you in the most minute detail everything about a brand. You'd ask her a statistic, and she'd have it to the fifth decimal point. But I said, 'You know, they could hire smart eighth graders to do what we do. The business runs, the product gets on the shelf, they are making it in the plant, it is being distributed. But what we are hired for is to *move* those businesses. And if you don't know where you are going, you aren't doing your job. You are not writing a paper, you are not taking a test on your brand.' " Yet few men realize that women tend to reinforce in detail what they feel they lack in credibility. And, as Jim, a twenty-eight-year-old banker, evaluates it, men's ability to focus on goals can often make them miss the mark. "I'm so goal-oriented, I can get to the point immediately. Women can read correctly, but they don't focus. They get involved in all the emotional aspects but can't narrow in on the point. On the other hand, men misread. They just get to the point, and often it's the wrong one, not the main issue, and they beat it to death. So you have these large discussions about 'policy' and 'territory.' "

Many women themselves agree they tend to overdo the details. Pam, thirty-five, a former paper company executive turned consultant, remarks: "I think men and women orient to things differently. They respond at a different level of aware-ness. It may not be relevant to what's being done, but it is a different kind of recognition factor. There needs to be a bal-ance." Why are women so ensnarled in details? It probably has a lot to do with perfectionism picked up from their mothers. And, as Carol Gilligan says, women tend to value the personal —that which is specific to each situation, the exception rather than the rule—when making judgments or decisions.[15] This detail-oriented approach, however, could be contrasted to what many view as woman's broader, more encompassing vision, a "diffuse awareness," in the words of one psychological writer: "Most children are born with, and many women retain, a dif-fuse awareness of the wholeness of nature, where everything is linked with everything else and they feel themselves to be part of an individual whole. Here lies the wisdom of artists, and the words and parables of prophets."[16] This view may be in fact supported by physical evidence that the human brain consists of two hemispheres—the left governs logic, analytical reasoning, and language, and the right governs the analysis of shapes and space—and that researchers have suggested female brains have more neural connections between the two, providing them with greater capacity to integrate the two halves.[17]

It seems women have the ability to do the broadest possible thinking, but they have been conditioned to devalue and
ignore this gift in search of more regimented, rule-bound
perfectionism. It is, once again, a denial or betrayal of the
Authentic Voice. Women's conditioning to emphasize the importance of details has been reinforced in business. One male
media executive describes a woman manager who worked for
him as the best manager he ever had, except for her tendency
to overexplain everything: "She'd go overboard, like a school-
teacher, to define every detail of what had to be done." This
executive had an interesting explanation for her detail delir-
ium: "I'd say it's a lack of exposure, not anything indigenous
to women's personalities that makes them so detail-oriented.
The way you learn to see the big picture is to be exposed to
senior management because that's how they think. And the
fact is that women don't get that exposure. They are always the
last aboard; they're never asked into senior-level meetings. If
this woman had had that exposure, I'd say that she'd learn as
fast as I did, if not faster." His comments make us wonder
how many women actually are too detail-oriented. Could this
be another convenient perception gap utilized by many corporate men to keep female peers in their place? In fact, a
number of female managers said they found that men talk out
of both sides of their mouths when it comes to "detail work."
Often male managers encourage their female subordinates to
delegate—but when they do, the men criticize them for not
caring enough about the details! As one executive says, "A
woman I work with came in seething the other day because
her new male boss was giving her very explicit instructions on
how he wanted something prepared. And she made it clear
that it wasn't necessary to that degree of detail, that she'd
have her staff do it, and he said, 'Never be afraid to get into
the details; you'll learn something.' And she said, 'For eight
years, I've suffered with a reputation for excessive detail. But
the minute I announce I don't want to do that, I get slapped
back down!' "

In addition, some men simply don't want to give women

credit for understanding the big picture. In part, this is because they themselves often view, or want to view, women as decorations, or details. One manager, for instance, warned her boss about the potential for a major labor problem at her company. He ignored her, and the company has since been cited by the Labor Department for violation of an important labor law. "And so, I am beginning to wonder if I am invisible," she muses. "They are doing so many things now that I advised them to do *years* ago. But I don't think they are listening. They just say, 'There, there, that's nice.'" Other times such male 'oversights' often reflect their unconscious fears that women will outdo them in the corporation. Former NBC president and CEO Herb Schlosser now Senior Adviser, Entertainment and Broadcasting at Wertheim & Co., notes: "I've seen men deprecate women because of a sense of their own inadequacies. If you're in a meeting for two hours and if a man shines, you could deprecate him for other reasons, but when it's a woman. . . ." In fact, a number of women describe a "conspiracy of silence" among the men they work with. The conspiracy tends to broaden as women reach the higher levels of the corporation. "You get an overall sense early in the game that they've done you a favor by allowing you to be part of the game," a financial institution executive says. "But if you take them on in the presence of other men, it's a rare man who will speak up—even if he supports you. He'll support you in silence."

Angela, a defense corporation manager, was once told in a meeting by a male co-worker, "Shut up, little girl, and I think you will learn something." She recalls that no other males spoke out on her behalf. "They all apologized to me later, but no one challenged him there," she said. "They would do it if a guy challenged a guy on some other grounds. That was very humiliating." The conspiracy of silence among men when women are in the line of fire is yet more evidence of how the old quid pro quo has vanished; neither men nor women support each other in the traditional ways. The courtly conventions of the corporations are giving way to more primitive impulses.

The Hairy-Chested
School of Management

In an effort to assert and reinforce their superiority—either consciously or unconsciously—many men have developed all kinds of methods to allow women to enter the corporate jungle of business but to prevent these management Janes from swinging on *their* vines. And despite the promise of the arrival of generations of "new men" in business, younger men are as likely to use such guerrilla tactics as older ones are. In fact, Dr. Frederick Hauser asserts they are even more so: "I think the young jungle fighters will be even more jungly against women—they will view them as real competition. Whereas older guys could accommodate women moving up because they would never feel personally threatened by them, most young men legitimately see their young women peers as more competitive with them than earlier generations of men did. Today's corporate studs see themselves competing for exactly the same rewards and money that women are." Malcolm Forbes, Jr., agrees: "Remember, you have all the baby boomers, all the young people, jockeying for position and power. The younger men are just as, if not more, competitive than any older executive. Human nature does not change."

Corporate women are vocal about the ways men accept them into management ranks but deny them any real power or control. For instance, a corner office is okay for a woman, and she should be happy with a title. But no one should report to her directly. Or if someone does, she should not have any authority over anyone's salary. Men will insist that they alone have access to a director or vice president of the corporation or sit in on key meetings and have input on major policy decisions. When men take business trips, they institute ad hoc seniority arrangements that put junior men in charge rather than more experienced senior women. Male managers direct women into the least powerful jobs—like writing letters to angry customers or shareholders or doing backup work for projects, not managing them. And of course women are rarely invited to lunch in huddles or to talk sports over drinks—a prerogative of the exclusive boys' clubs. Remarks Jason, a thirty-year-old public relations executive: "You know how homosexuals have come out of the closet? Well, boys' clubs have gone *into* the closet. It's not in vogue to be one of the guys. But I don't think that it has really changed." Moreover, women complain, men set up a number of Catch-22 situations. For example, they say, "Be feminine," but the minute women are "feminine," they aren't "businesslike" and "professional" enough. A variation on that well-worn theme: men denigrate women for not acting confident, but when women do act confident, men respond with resentment. Jim, a twenty-eight-year-old West Coast banker notes: "Let's disregard the reality of whether women could achieve the CEO title. I don't think *they think* they can do the job. Now, my former boss did. Her attitude was "Teach me and I can do it. I haven't run into anything I can't learn.' And men resented it. It threatened them that she thought she could do the job. That she *knew* she could do it and walked around showing she could." So what's the message? Andrea, a thirty-nine-year-old commodities executives, sums up the dilemma: "Guys make it to the top level by standing out, by demonstrating they're better, by manipulating, by competing. And women are told to bury all that so as not to threaten the men. You have to become Madame de Pompadour professionally—and that means you're the power *behind* the throne, not *on* it." When these contradictory pressures, first identified in Proving Up, relentlessly continue even as women gain seniority, they are one more key factor that forces women to consider whether the price of success is actually worth it.

The weapons of intimidation men use against women are often economic. Many women who have inherited money or who have married wealthy men might relate to a West Coast corporate counsel's observation: "It's a good thing for women to dress expensively, but men may resent it because it implies women have more control over their money than men do. One thing that irks men, unconsciously if not consciously, is their belief that women are incredibly free—especially if they're single—to lavish luxuries on themselves." Some men turn this economic power into a weapon by insisting that the woman is "not serious" about her career. Jim, the California banker, describes this approach: "There's one woman in the bank whose husband has his own company, and people comment—never in front of her—that she's not interested in getting ahead. She's internalized that, and so she never talks about getting ahead." Clark, a thirty-three-year-old marketing executive at a packaged goods company, recalls his interview with a younger female job-seeker from a well-to-do family: "I had a good interview with her, but I saw the pitfalls—that no one in the company will really believe she wants to work; she has that safety valve. She can always fall back on Daddy's money." This pin-money put-down, of course, rankles the women who are working as hard as any male in the corporation. "The only thing that really bothers me is that it's true that people assume my income doesn't matter to us, that it's extra money, which is still a hot button to me," says one senior vice president of a *Forbes* 500 corporation. "They'll say, 'Oh, you've got a husband on Wall Street. What do you need to worry about money for?' " Kristin, a twenty-eight-year-old sales representative at a leading paper company, echoes her sentiment: "They look at my husband and me and say I don't need the job. It isn't fair." There seems to be another version of the double standard at work here: women who have economic power of their own are often treated as if they are merely dabbling at business. Yet men rarely treat other men as if they don't really want or need to succeed, even those who have inherited money or married it. MasterCard's Joanne Black asks rhetorically, "What if you hired a millionaire's son—as a lot of companies do? Would you expect to pay him less?"

Men also try to assert their authority over women by outright bullying or intimidation. Anne, a thirty-four-year-old human resource executive, recalls such an incident when she was training a very high-level group of male managers. "I was leading a discussion with them, when one of them came out with 'Remember when you used to be my secretary?' It was

157

his way of asserting control again in a teacher-learner situation. So I just said, 'Yes, I do remember,' and went on." Monica, a thirty-four-year-old vice president at an international consulting firm, tells how, at the age of twenty-eight, she was the only woman in a meeting with the top executives of a client company. The chairman pushed an obscure plastic sculpture in front of her and challenged her, "Guess what this is?" Because of his taunting tone, she teased back: "If I guess, do I win a prize?" The chairman's smile became a scowl and he grumbled, "Yeah, you get to stay."

It's a basic battle of dominance and submission. For centuries, males have held the dominant position and are loath to give it up. Male dominance is still so much the norm in our society, according to television reviewer David Zurawik of *The Dallas Times Herald News Service*, that peversely depicting more dominant female leads is a key reason for the recent success of such television shows as "Hill Street Blues," "Who's the Boss," and "Moonlighting." The game of dominance and submission is built into the hierarchical structure of corporate America. It is stronger in "macho" businesses—the older industries that flourished in the first half of the century—than in the more matrix-oriented and often more "egalitarian" high-tech and service companies that have sprung up recently. Christine, forty-seven, who worked as a manager at one of the nation's largest steel companies before leaving to join a non-profit agency, spoke for most women when she expressed her distaste for the corporation's pseudo-military structure where men would salute the office—the dominant position—rather than the man himself: "I didn't like authority. I didn't like this whole thing about 'This is the boss.' But men accepted it beautifully; they thrived on it." Betty Lehan Harragan corroborates this phenomenon in *Games Mother Never Taught You*.[18]

Meanwhile, in all business endeavors, the relationship between warfare-competition and sex is strong. Grant, a forty-four-year-old executive vice president says, "I think there is sexual tension, albeit not always sexual *attraction*, present in every male-female relationship, and it is there in business, which depends so much on dominance and submission. It is critical in hierarchical organizations. It comes out in the form of competition—the relationship between competition or warfare and sex has always been very, very strong. . . . If you think about a takeover situation, it is a struggle for dominance. It is loaded with sexual terms. Think of all the sexual metaphors that are used among men." Observes one sociologist, "It is symptomatic of the underlying tenor of American life that vulgar terms for sexual intercourse also convey the sense of getting the better of someone, working him over, taking him in, imposing your will through guile, deception, or superior force."[19] Thus, it is not surprising that the battle of the sexes can be even more competitive in the boardroom, where competition reigns in any case, than it is in the bedroom. *Industry Week* reported that "Regardless of the circumstances, experts agree that it is generally an abuse of power, not passion, that is the basis for most instances of sexual harassment."[20]

The fundamental power struggle behind sexual relations is one reason male executives have an exceptionally hard time dealing with female supervisors who are involved in affairs with subordinates. As Grant notes: "It turns things the wrong way. It threatens the male dominance on which American business has always thrived, that is integral to being part of the club." Everyone knows sex between superiors and subordinates is bad business. But female supervisors sleeping with male subordinates is a much more heinous transgression in most male managers' minds. Why? Because men think women have yet another advantage in that domain.

The Morgan le Fay Factor

Since Eve, men have cast women as enchantresses. Today they might view a corporate woman as a modern-day Morgan le Fay, a contemporary counterpart to King Arthur's sister, who betrayed him by luring him to her enchanted isle of Avalon and emasculated him by stealing his most powerful weapon, the sword Excalibur. Even though the majority of relationships between men and women in the corporation are platonic, the concept of a corporate Morgan le Fay persists—and threatens men enough to keep women from reaching the top. "Men think you have enormous magical powers and they presume a woman knows she has these immense powers over them," comments a thirty-nine-year-old woman commodities executive. She warns: "And they expect her to handle these powers responsibly. If she doesn't, it's as bad in their minds as having an irresponsible boss on their hands." Even if they themselves are not attracted to a particular woman, many men fear women will have an advantage over them with *other* men in business, and they resent it. Rachel, a thirty-three-year-old legal counsel at a leading midwestern corporation, remarks: "I work with a guy and every time, for nine years, whenever I show up with a new dress he says, 'Who do you have a meeting with?' He is so paranoid. So now I just play on it. I was asked to give a speech I knew he kind of wanted to give and I said, 'Oh, I have to get a new dress for this.' They feel they are being taken advantage of, or that we have this advantage." Evan, a chief executive officer in his sixties, discusses this "advantage": "I'll tell you, on a day-to-day basis, I don't think there is any question that a woman has the upper hand. Assuming the man and woman are both equally educated, talented . . . whether it is wiles, cleverness, or competence, I think once she sets her mind on a goal, a man becomes very much like putty in her hand. I really do believe that." Or as a thirty-four-year-old television executive says, "We are conditioned not to refuse women anything."

Some corporate males perceive themselves to be vulnerable to women's use of imagined powers and are constantly on guard against them. Dan, the thirty-nine-year-old pharmaceutical executive, says: "I can pick up feminine wiles a mile away. And I resent it—I think someone's trying to work me over. Here I am busting my gut taking work home over the weekend and she's trying to get out of it with some story so she can have a free weekend. No way." Men fear they are too easily charmed. In fact, when he was asked to *define* femininity, Ted, a thirty-six-year-old assistant treasurer at a major financial institution, says: "It is, instead of trying to be aggressive and assertive, resorting to the classic feminine charms and doing even more, accomplishing even more through them." He added, "For instance, if someone from a bank called up and wanted to talk to me about some undifferentiated product that required personal service, all things being equal, I'd much rather be talking about it over lunch or dinner with an attractive woman than with another man."

Such male fears, albeit usually unconscious, are a fundamental reason why women are frustrated in their advancement within the corporation, a frustration that eventually leads to success and betrayal. Polls and surveys offer hard evidence that many men assume attractive women professionals advance through seductiveness, manipulation, and sexual availability, more than through honest effort and talent. Such attitudes discourage other male executives from promoting women— for fear they themselves will become a target of gossip.[21] The sad irony, however, is that many, if not most, women don't see themselves as particularly good-looking and certainly don't believe they have the powers men ascribe to them. Chris, now a division manager at a telecommunications company, tells of a personal case in point: "Earlier in my career, this fatherly type in his mid-fifties said to me, 'I can't tell you why people don't want to hire you, but I think it's because you're too pretty.' What cruel irony—I've spent my whole life feeling ugly, and now *this!*"

We heard case after frustrated case of how the more attractive, stylish woman with a personal flair lost out to the plainer, less feminine woman who focused on "fitting in" with the male culture. The corporation often deems such women the safe choice over the more attractive—and often more creative, charismatic, and magnetic—woman. In fact, just because a "glamorous" woman has these more dynamic qualities she becomes even more threatening to men. When asked why men often seem to promote the plain Janes, Dan, the pharmaceutical manager admits: "Maybe it's a subconscious current that the sexual possibility is gone. The male mind may be more open to what she's saying professionally." Or as Broward Craig says, "Good looks are a help. But if you are attractive, it makes people more nervous because the sexual element is always there." Hillary, a thirty-seven-year-old energy company executive, contends, "In the context of business, the more attractive and feminine one is the bigger the drawback, because men are confused by the signals. They know this is business and they are supposed to be relating to you as business and yet all this other clutter—like static on a radio—is happening." Hillary, herself an exceptionally attractive woman, has come up with three specific types of women who could progress in corporations without turning the static volume way up:

- *The Airline Hostess: "She is successful because men are more comfortable with the airline hostess persona. 'I am serving you. You are stronger than I am.' And it kind of lulls them into feeling that it is okay to accept her."*

- *The Fixer: "She is gregarious and spends almost one hundred percent of her time gathering gossip. She has an uncanny sense of how to use it. She is very extroverted and makes a lot of contacts and uses them shamelessly to gain influence and cut deals. The fixer isn't attractive, but she's dynamic, amusing, and has a very good political instinct."*

- *The Fireplug: "Men are comfortable with her because she talks in the blunt, very straightforward male vernacular, that often seems to women almost brusque. Men accept her as one of the boys, a team player, because she is not pretty and they don't have to relate to her as a woman, which takes a tremendous burden off of them. They don't have to worry about succeeding with her as men, impressing her that they are handsome or whatever. There is none of the hostile 'This is the kind of girl who always turned me down for dancing school and dates.' It is, in fact, 'She's the kind of girl I always turned down.' "*

But the sexual static, no matter who tells you otherwise, is always there, even if a man and woman are not especially attracted to each other. Jeff, the media company executive, confides: "Whether I like to admit it to myself or not, I find it impossible not to have some sexual reaction to every woman I talk to. To say you can look at a woman in the workplace and pretend that doesn't exist is bullshit." And while it's no surprise that certain women might experience difficulties with the opposite sex at the office, what is alarming is that virtually *every* woman interviewed had some sexual horror story to relate. One southern California executive describes how she was accosted by an important customer at a business party during her first day on a job and had to deflect his advances. She was concerned that a lot of people might get the wrong idea and think that she had encouraged him. "To clear my name, I told this male vice president in the company," she recounts. "I tried to make it a humorous thing, though—I didn't want to make too big a deal. . . . And he read that wrong. I found out later he went around telling everyone that I was *bragging!*" Men often band together in such instances. So do the corporations that men still dominate. It's simply less messy to blame indirectly the woman who attracts the man and to take no action against the man other than chastisement. The powerlessness women feel in the face of increasingly clear sexual double standards is yet another driving force in the success and betrayal dynamic as women progress through their corporate career landings.

Most important, sexual tensions or the fear of getting too close violates the comfort zone between men and women. Pharmaceutical executive Dan says: "It's too intimate. When you get men and women together, the factor of biology is always likely to be present. You can't get away from it. The two aspects conflict—the personal and the professional—and they can obsess you. I think it's difficult for a man not to react to a woman and vice versa. I don't think you can drive nature out of the business setting." Which is why, ironically, the very comfort zone—that impossible-to-define but critical area of informal management camaraderie—finally attained, sends men and women right into the danger zone.

Comfort Zone, Danger Zone

It's a paradox but true. On the one hand, both men and women say the reason why women aren't moving into top management is that men don't feel comfortable sharing basic management lifestyles. On the other, the more comfortable the relationship between men and women, the closer they move to the danger zone of sexual relations or at least rumors of them. A male executive vice president explains: "There is not that comfort level at the top. You are comfortable with people on that level only when you relax with them, not necessarily when you work with them. And for some people it is golf, for others it is poker, for others it is sitting around getting drunk. But you are asking men in their fifties and sixties to become comfortable with women in their thirties and forties in those settings without sexual tension. And, boy, that is pretty difficult." The sexual tension in every male-female relationship in the corporation is the fundamental reason men and women have not been able to turn the Uneasy Peace into a sure and certain alliance. The success and betrayal management women are finding in the corporate world stems largely from their relationships with executive men. All the other difficulties women confront in corporations reflect this basic dilemma.

Granted, some men are uncomfortable simply because they are not accustomed to women executives. Denise, who was the first woman to be chosen as assistant to the chairman of her company, describes the discomfort older males felt around her. "I was the first woman with an office on the executive floor. I was the first woman to walk into many policy meetings, and they didn't know what to do. It was stand up, sit down, take off my coat. . . ." She described her specific relationship with the chairman. "He really didn't know how to use me. In fact, when I first went into his office, he said, 'Frankly, I have never related to women as colleagues. I am used to them as daughters, wives, secretaries. But not colleagues. And I feel very uncomfortable.' And I told him I was sorry he felt that way and asked him to let me know what I could do to help him not feel uncomfortable. But he was very on edge." A lot of people would want to chalk up this unease to the age factor alone—that older men are simply not used to women in executive ranks. But anthropologist Lionel Tiger has postulated that some form of "male bonding" to the exclusion of women has gone on throughout history, reaching as far back as prehistoric days when men formed hunting groups. As a result, he theorizes that no matter how hard women try, they will never truly be accepted as full-fledged members of the powerful male clubs that have since evolved.[22] Whether one believes his thesis that it's all the result of biological imprinting or not, most of the male managers we interviewed—of virtually all ages, occupations, and levels of seniority—admitted that they were more comfortable with men. One thirty-five-year-old male vice president puts the prevailing sentiment most succinctly: "Men prefer being among themselves, where they can talk about tits and ass at the board meeting again. And any guy who says anything different is bullshitting you."

Of course, no matter how many try to deny it, a most basic reason for the discomfort between men and women remains the sexual static. Often, people are less concerned with what is actually happening than with how it looks to others in the company. Paul, a hotel company executive vice president remarks, "With men you can go out and have some beers, and there is no static. With women, you can still go out and have some beers, but there is this concern about what looks bad. For instance, one of our female managers knew I was married and that I wasn't interested in her that way, but she wouldn't meet me in her or my hotel suite. We had to meet out in the park." This people-might-talk mentality discourages men and women from asking each other to lunch, or drinks or to those occasions that cement relationships between people of the same sex and develop the "connectedness" women seek on the job. Both men and women are afraid that socializing will be misinterpreted. Not to mention the fact that older men at the office are usually married to women who don't work. Often a single working woman doesn't fit into their life patterns in the same way a male would. A woman manager says: "There is an irrational element. I think the wives still have an influence. If you are working till seven and eight at night with your boss, the wife would much rather have him working till seven or eight with a man." Rachel, the corporate counsel, agrees: "I work with a guy who for four years never invited me to the house. He hired a guy junior to me, and within one week this guy was invited to his house. And I have no relationship problems with this guy. I know his wife. He could have invited me to bring a date. But there is just *something* between men. They can talk about baseball together." Top executive men themselves admit the truth of this. One former vice chairman says, "In high executive positions, recognizing the ability of a woman to move in the fast world of commerce takes very understanding people. Saying that I am getting on a jet and going to London to negotiate for the next two weeks with an attractive woman in her thirties or forties takes an understanding wife—and, in the reverse situation—a trusting husband. These are personal relationships that are now being exposed for the very first time—of equals dealing with equals." He describes his own experiences: "When I was an executive, I was six times around the world in the company jet visiting locations. Four times I was gone by myself two months, and my wife had to be the good-heart at home. I was gone on another occasion when it involved the acquisition of a company in London. In my generation, it would have been very difficult for my wife to understand that my number one senior vice president or assistant was a very attractive woman working with me in day-to-day close proximity—in London or traveling around the world in a Gulf Stream. I think she would have been uncomfortable, and if she had been uncomfortable, I would have been. And people in the company might look askance, too."

As forty-six-year-old recruiter Marjorie comments: "Much to my chagrin, I've heard my husband talk about men and women who travel frequently together. And I've always wondered why people assume the woman is sleeping with the man. Just because he's a man? It drives me nuts!"

In regard to male-female relationships, several managers brought up Mary Cunningham's name. Former NBC President Herb Schlosser, says of the most written and talked about male-female corporate relationship in history: "The problem was the story was just so juicy for the press—the fast rise of someone so young, coupled with the sex overlay. And most men understood it all. I don't think that it set women back, but there were just elements about it that don't relate to a woman's competence. It was just too juicy a story. She became, forgive me, a sex object." The Cunningham experience will be with us for a while because, even if sexual implications are not suggested, few corporate executives really view a woman as "one of the boys" at that lofty level. If anything, such a woman is often viewed as a anomaly. As Ben, a thirty-eight-year-old energy company executive puts it, "Men are still very suspicious of a woman without a family, or a woman with a family who can live the same life-style as these men, constantly traveling." Recruiter Gary Knisely remarks that similar male suspicion could be sparked when a single woman, dedicated to her career, accepts a line position in an out-of-the-way place. "You get the sense that if you are female and single and going out to an assignment in the boondocks, people would think you might have your priorities out of whack. And can you imagine what the long-time married males in the club at the top would think about *that*?" Ben explains further: "If a woman is willing to go out with the guys to play golf, or sit around and get drunk, and yet not willing to have an affair, the men would have real questions about her. They're still making a value judgment on why she's not married with a family. And they would have the same questions about a single man. Yet what amazes me is that they have *no* questions about a man who essentially abandons his family to do all the things the corporate life demands."

While it may all sound like minor league minutia, traveling together, lunching, and playing golf on weekends is the stuff corporate relationships are often made of. For people to be comfortable sharing power together, often in high-stakes situations, they must be much more than professionally comfortable. Says Nancy Reynolds, former vice president of Bendix and now a partner in her own consulting firm, "There has to be a comfort zone at the top, which I don't think there is a lot of times between men and women. No matter how smart you are, how brilliant you are, if men don't feel at ease having you around, you can't enter the club. It has to be *more* than your skills and ability. It has to be a feeling of trust, of comfort, the language that is spoken during hours at a gym, in a bar, all those things." And the comfort zone–danger zone dilemma does affect how much critical exposure women—particularly those in middle management trying to move up —get to important top male executives. What eventually leads to the final stall-out behind women's success and betrayal in the corporation is an ultimate lack of comfort. And often at the highest management levels, where promotion is based less on actual abilities than on how comfortable other key executives are with you, men feel that women are invading their previously exclusive ranks within the professional context as well as in more informal settings outside it.

One male CEO describes the scene: "Hundreds of millions of dollars have been spent on places where men get together and enjoy one another's company. I can name five major corporations that have beautiful shooting lodges where men get together and without any improprieties visit, talk business, go out to duck blinds, shoot, come in, and play cards." He goes on to say: "And, God, I have fished in Canada and Alaska. I have played golf in Scotland. I have had great times. I could have had equally good times with women, but that just hasn't been the business syndrome." He does ask, however, "Are you comfortable about getting out in the middle of a duck blind, where you have to stay with your feet in water for eight hours?

Men can just walk out and take a leak in the middle of it. How comfortable are you with a strange woman? I would walk out with the CEO of any company if he is a man and take a leak, but I will be damned if I would do that with a woman." He admits to the disadvantages such exclusionary clubs create for executive women: "I play golf with executives from companies like Exxon and Time at least fourteen times a year. I learned in every game, not in terms of the deals we made, but in my feeling of being close to them. And we had a lot of business exchanges in the weeks that followed. But where do women have that opportunity?" Usually not on the golf course. And often not even within corporate walls.

A number of people even remarked that women executives are handicapped because too many decisions are still made in the men's room. "It's true. The great thing about the men's room," confirms one male, "is that sometimes it's the only time you get to see the top gun. It's the only time you get informal interaction—and women will *never* get that." Advertising executive Lois Wyse views the Big John syndrome as anything but a laughing matter: "Men and women will never be equal until a meeting can be recessed and women can come back from the ladies' room without the decision already having been made in the men's room. Or we need enough women in the ladies' room to be able to make the decision there. Because right now, there are too few of us to affect anything." A male executive recruiter even recalls a search three years ago where no female candidates could be hired because there was only one rest room on the executive floor. The company told the candidate, in essence, "We really like you and your credentials, but you can't go to the bathroom where all the executives are, so you just can't make it. We think you're really good material—but we just can't hire you."

The comfort zone–danger zone problem doesn't occur only at top levels of corporate life either. Male middle managers, too, are often extremely uncomfortable around women. Usually these are the managers with the least self-confidence. Jeff, the thirty-five-year-old executive at an East Coast media conglomerate, explains: "Middle managers are the most scared managers, the most insecure, so they overmanage people. . . . Take a late twenties to early thirties middle manager managing a less experienced employee and if you get somebody freaked out about his own status in life, he won't be as forgiving about anyone who strays from the kind of corporate demeanor in a way that will undercut his success." The lack of comfort among younger men can sometimes be exacerbated by their fear that female peers will lash out at them for not being more sensitive to feminist issues. "I don't think men are that comfortable with women, and that is because women's liberation has gone so far overboard that men are forced to watch every single word we say," says Jason, a thirty-year-old public relations executive. "We are not allowed to be ourselves. You can spend all your time worrying about whether or not you are going to offend a woman." Because many men are not truly comfortable with women, women can't be truly comfortable with men—often with the result that men criticize women for being uncertain of themselves, contending that a lack of confidence keeps them from being competent managers. Jim, a twenty-eight-year-old banker, says: "I've never met a managerial woman who was comfortable with herself, her job, her position, and her role. And I don't trust anyone who's not comfortable. I'd love to meet a woman as comfortable and down-to-earth as male senior managers. But women are so unsure of themselves that they mimic senior men and become tough guys or sweet-smile back-stabbers." Without realizing it, he has succinctly described the impossible double standards men continue to apply to women in business. Dr. Frederick Hauser analyzes the situation this way: "The question of why can't they be more like us is still a plaintive cry. It explains why women can't find mentors. It becomes all the more destructive every so often when a woman comes along who mimics masculine behavior. Do men embrace her for it? No. They reject it out of hand."

It's still the same old story: Women in corporations continue to be condemned as either emotional weaklings or tough broads. As Gloria Steinem says, "A man can be called ruthless if he bombs a country to oblivion. A woman can be called

ruthless if she puts you on hold."[23] The ongoing doublt standard illustrates the unresolved sexual tensions between men and
women that have been displaced to the corporation. And such
tensions may be the single greatest contributor to the growing
disenchantment women increasingly feel as they continue to
climb the corporate ranks.

CHAPTER 6
SEEDS OF DISENCHANTMENT

*I think there's no question but that
women are in for hard times to come.
There's an image being projected of
the way things are supposed to be.
But reality is nowhere close.*

Dr. Frederick Hauser
Director, Center for
Graduate Management Studies
Pace University

As women advance from the Proving Up level through the corporate ranks, their experiences increasingly diverge from those of men, thanks in no small part to the differences just outlined. Men, relatively unencumbered by the Myths of Individual Recognition, Irreplaceability, and Loyalty continue their race unabated. Women, by contrast, being to slow—and to question. While most men at this stage are busy congratulating themselves for a game well played, women are becoming conscious of the game itself and beginning to rethink how they want to play it, if at all. Nuance and vague inference, often self-generated, distinguish the Seeds of Disenchantment landing, from the overt dissatisfactions and often corporate-generated crises of the Success and Betrayal landing which follows.

When the first pangs of dissatisfaction occur, women wonder what's hit them. Explains Amanda, a textile industry dropout, "Suddenly there was this why-am-I-breaking-my-neck feeling. It was a very sad lesson to learn—that I didn't have to do my best because nobody really wanted me to pass a certain point. Nobody really cared." So unexpected, so subtle is the transition that neither women nor the corporation recognize the beginnings of a crisis at this landing. Like the first tremors of an earthquake, the first signs of disenchantment are so quiet and quick that they barely disturb the landscape. Ambitious women gradually discover a loss of interest in their corporate careers. Women, perpetually accused by co-workers of workaholism at the Proving Up landing, suddenly start hoarding their vacation days. What are the Seeds of Disenchantment all about? And where do they begin?

Having entrusted to serendipity the first ten years or so of a career, women begin to worry at this landing that fate has been in charge long enough. It is a sudden, uncalculated coming-to-terms. "I don't feel I ever made a conscious decision to stay here," Rachel, the successful midwest corporate counsel, says. "I've been here nine years, I'll be vested in ten, and it looks as if I'm here for the long run. But I'm not sure I ever dealt with the problem. I don't think I have made peace with myself, to be honest." Bonnie, a young bank portfolio manager, adds, "I never thought when I started that I'd be at the bank four years. I thought one year, max."

Since this time of reckoning paradoxically coincides with women's first significant recognition within the corporate structure, they are reluctant to share these rumblings of uncertainty with others. A case of "should-ism" sets in quickly, brought on by the urgency of time passing. "I always thought I should get my act together by the time I was thirty-five," says Rachel. "It's kind of a process I'm looking forward to—figuring out if this is really where I want to stay. Because I really will have to make a commitment. I will have to decide instead of just passing through time." Such random non-planning also typifies the next generation of corporate women at this landing. Just when the job has finally become a career, the career becomes just a job. Women who felt unable to confront the permanence of a twenty-year relationship with a spouse suddenly awaken ten years into a career to a realization that they are slightly less than halfway toward a corporate silver anniversary. As the apparent beneficiary of caprice and happy circumstance, the corporate woman is perversely out of control at the exact moment when the world seems to reward her for being so much in control. With the inevitability of taking charge and acceptance that one is still working at the age of thirty comes both more and less emphasis on the career. More worry, less dedication. "I can't say what it is that's changed my mind about corporate life," reveals Jill, a mid-thirties marketing executive for an appliance manufacturer. "But the attraction just isn't what it was when I was twenty-four. I have a different personality now. You get a little tired."

Never having made a permanent corporate choice to start with, or never having perceived it as permanent, women ascend the landings only to experience a bewildering lack of motivation to continue. Charged with substantive professional responsibility, women suddenly realize they *must* take charge. As they begin to question the unexpected price of such new responsibility, the Seeds of Disenchantment are sown. For men, the glittering prizes of their thirties—merit increases, bonuses tied to enhanced bottom-line performance, company cars, pension and life-insurance perks—constitute a boastful mid-career scorecard, an incentive to continue. For women, however, they represent the achievement of an end point, or at the very least a plateau from which to take stock. Having proven up to the corporation, their parents, their spouses, and themselves, women are surprised to find they have reached the economic comfort level that ten or fifteen years earlier seemed a remote dream. Attaining the comfort level is an achievement; maintaining it is a lifelong burden. The realization triggers a reevaluation of their continued dedication to the corporation.

If this landing catches women by surprise, it seems inevitable nonetheless, given the confluence of events that have set corporate women up for an inevitable fall: arrival at the gates of the middle-management ghetto; the fading pleasure of early rewards like travel and expense accounts; and the inability of corporations to increase the incentives for hanging in. Women gain a new sophistication about corporate loyalty in the wake of headhunter spiels and lengthy exposure to the vagaries of bureaucratic guerrilla warfare. In the firm resolve to take charge during this decade of decision, women hear the ironic echoes of myths gone by. There is the trepidation of time passing. The old brass ring of self-reliance. For women who come to such a realization, what shakes their confidence in those myths?

Myths Under Siege

However influenced by charismatic, even paternalistic recruiting practices, women soon perceive the high price of assigning parental responsibility to an inanimate company. Often at this level, the separation anxiety women experience in attempting to break away from the corporate "family" mirrors similar anxieties from an earlier time. "I truly believed that if I worked hard, I'd be rewarded, that I'd become a long-term employee, and that meant security, because, for me, this place is like a family," admits Sheila, an unmarried corporate advertising vice president in her mid-thirties. "Each assignment I've been put on has been a challenge—a difficult account that was ready to walk. And I think now, looking back, their attitude must have been 'What an asshole she is for taking on all of this and hanging in.' Whereas I perceived it as important for me to keep the 'family' together—which was my role in my own family. I was always the oil on troubled waters at home." Running to escape her own unsatisfactory family, she found herself the victim of another, equally unhappy family relationship—the one she created herself within the corporation. Reevaluating one's assumptions about the familial nature of most corporations is an unhappy, often painful necessity. And not because most companies still encourage the paternal conceit that they're just one happy family despite the mergers, acquisitions, massive layoffs, and purges of the early eighties. It is women themselves who admit, ten years into their careers, a need to cling to the long-held, if unconscious, belief that the corporation embraces, cares, forgives, and rewards like a family. "It's a dogged pursuit of recognition, acceptance, and resolution within the corporate family," says Sheila. "That's what we're all playing out in one form or another. But we're all still searching for that resolution—to be loved against all odds."

Indeed, with the greater psychic distancing from home engendered by titles and salaries most parents could only dream of, the physical distancing from roots, and the advancing age or death of parents bringing to an end an influential source of both drive and approval, women, especially single women, have almost no other family left to turn to. "The office itself was more like a family kind of place. A lot of the people who worked there had worked together at other places, so that reinforced the idea," says Claire, a former supervisor at one of the country's largest telecommunications companies. Yet of her boss at the middle-management level, she recalled, "It was the first situation where I had a boss who wasn't supportive. I didn't click with him at all." Claire's experience was borne out by Joyce's, half a continent away at a major midwestern manufacturing firm. "I don't feel I'm patronized where I am, which is very good. But sometimes I feel very cold. Everything can be so ultra-businesslike. There is just no personal interaction there. There can be no amenities." One young foreign banking executive succinctly sums up the corporate culture: "Along with the pin-striped suit goes the behavior. There can be no excesses whether of joy or of friendship." Correctly perceiving themselves as independent and successful survivors within the corporate structure, women are reluctant to probe the source of their sense of disappointment—the inherent conflict between the desire for professional self-sufficiency and the deeper psychic yearning for connectedness. At the Seeds of Disenchantment landing, women are forced to confront reality: independence has its price, and exacts as its due the myth of familial togetherness.

But rejecting the corporate family doesn't come cheap. The high price: loneliness. Isolation between women, first established in the Proving Up stage, accelerates, cutting across all industries and age ranges, as women find themselves competing against one another for a narrowing number of middle-management openings. Rejecting the myth of the corporate family, women can no longer afford to acquire new stepsisters. "Women can't be viewed as weak and vulnerable," cautions Bonnie, a global bank portfolio manager. "I would never share my doubts or worries about my career progress with another woman. Who knows a woman better than another woman? So there's a conflict between wanting to talk about it and knowing it's not in your interest to do so." As women become conscious of this, they speak wistfully and sometimes angrily of the demanding culture that fosters disconnectedness. "I don't have a network," admits Angela, public relations director of a predominantly male defense company. "I mean, how can you network with two or three people? And all of the other women are secretaries. It isn't surprising, but that's the way life is. So you come in and you are a strange animal," she concludes. Kristin, a successful paper products salesperson in her late twenties, didn't realize the hidden costs of such isolation within her company until midway into the job. "In fairness to my management, I have to say that they've tried to support me and help me along. But a lot of times I've felt lonely. There are no other women here to relate to. There's really no one, except my mother. She's the only one who can support what I'm going through."

Other myths also die hard: the Myths of Irreplaceability, Growth, and Individual Recognition. Disillusionment sets in as women realize the limitations of their role in and value to the organization, despite—or perhaps because of—their apparent success. Long before the corporation decides whether its women employees are excess baggage, women have read the wind and sensed in its changing direction the seeds of their own dissatisfaction. Their reaction to the change within themselves and to the shift in their expectations triggers women's new resentment. Fueled by the leap in self-esteem that accompanies the ten-year mark, women begin an honest reappraisal of their role within the corporate structure. "It wasn't that I was afraid of failure, but I always felt . . . extraneous," recalls Claire, the telephone company executive, describing her supervisory experiences after the newness of the Proving Up landing had faded. "One of the things that made me nervous was that *I* didn't do anything. My job was to get *other* people to do what they were supposed to do. But personally, I didn't do anything but fill out a report from time to time. I was getting along with people, and I always felt I did a good job communicating with them, but I just didn't feel I was really contributing to our output, and that scared me to death." Preoccupied with the Myths of Growth and Irreplaceability, women resent the corporation for not rewarding the growth they sense in themselves with a concurrent rise in status. "They would take my stuff and say, 'Thank you very much,' and I would never hear about it again. Every so often I would read in the paper that we had done something based on my ideas. I was a little computer. They would feed me information, and I would give them output," recalls Faye of her former job at a bank. Even after moving to a health care conglomerate and rising in seniority, she feels much of the same frustration: "My boss never considers promoting me or giving me a bigger job. Because he really sees women as worker bees. They stay at a certain level, and they do all the work, as useful as worker bees."

Women are caught at this point in a Catch-22 scenario. If they surrender the Myth of Irreplaceability, they perceive themselves to be eclipsed by men who are better self-promoters than women. Yet if women attempt to step in and broadcast their personal achievements, they are accused of lacking the vital component of team spirit. As the ante is raised for those few managerial positions at the top, women are advised to prove themselves more visibly, to separate themselves from the Proving Up stage and propel their careers into overdrive to compete with self-promoting men. Paradoxically, women are expected to cooperate in a destructive double standard that rewards men for being self-promoters but can often punish women who push to excel or stand out.

When women discover that their self-image as irreplace-able custodians of a project, a department, or an idea is at an opposite end of the corporate view, that they are just willing team players, frustration sets in. The longer they work, the more abstract the concept of success becomes: Writes one psychologist, "When people begin to realize that their per-formance will place them somewhere in the middle of the pack, they react with frustration, anger, depression, and panic. Because their previous experiences have left them psychologi-cally unprepared for an 'average' role, they are likely to per-ceive themselves, unrealistically, as second-rate losers."[1] Adds Dr. Carol Galligan of the Women's Institute, "Women imagine the effort to succeed to be so difficult that when they do succeed, they're amazed at how easy it was. And if it's that easy, they couldn't have done it. They think they must have fooled everyone." Such a shock of recognition often impels women further toward the imposter syndrome, a term coined by Dr. Pauline Ross Clance. She explains that such women, perenially top performers in adolescence, often have trouble in their career years, regardless of often important positions, accepting that they are only one among many exceptional people. "As a result, you're all too ready to dismiss your real talents and presume you're stupid if you aren't the very best."[2] The result is a subtle, often unconscious, resentment at the discrepancy between the way women view themselves and their accomplishments, and the "report card" the corporation issues—if it bothers to issue one at all.

The Seeds of Disenchantment landing forces women to confront the gap between their glamorous expectations of insistent and incipient challenge and the reality of bureau-cratized structure, which is repetitious, dulling, limited, and uncreative. Women soon learn the truth of Edna St. Vincent Millay's observation that, "It's not true that life is one damn thing after another. It's one damn thing over and over." Women are preoccupied at this landing with time, its hurried passage, and its unsatisfactory corporate content. "You get dulled; your mind just falls asleep," reports Hillary, a top manager at a leading energy company. "You get more and more specialized until you know everything about nothing. You end up next to these forty-eight-year-old guys who have completely lost their edge. To me, it's like being buried alive. I feel as if I'm being suffocated, that I'm too young to die."

With this growing awareness of finite time for great expec-tations, women come to realize in their thirties the precious-ness of remaining time—particularly if they plan a hiatus of any duration for childbearing. "We all still think of ourselves as young," comments Rachel, the thirty-three-year-old mid-western corporate counsel, speaking of the hurry-up phenome-non. "But this is the point at which people become presidents of colleges and companies and so on. *This is it.* Time is passing." With the force of immediacy comes an appreciation that they are powerless to change the repetition of corporate life to meet their increasingly restless need to grow and expand. Women read into their inability to engineer their own growth an all-too-obvious signal that despite their enhanced authority, they are not in control. "My biggest complaint about my job, I think, is that it's making my life pass too quickly. I'd like to have more control over my personal life," Rachel admits. Meanwhile, the corporate wheel turns, blissfully unaware of the frustration that is building inside women. Corporate de-mands on their time—demands often no more extravagant than in years past, when women gladly surrendered evenings and weekends in an effort to prove up to themselves or to the corporation—trigger retaliation, with time itself as the symbolic weapon. Women take an extra-long lunch hour, tack a shopping spree onto an afternoon client meeting, or just call in sick.

Women often liken corporate life from this level onward to a prison sentence. No surprise, then, that the obsession with time precipitates value judgments on male peers, whom women often regard as "lifers." Comments Heidi, a mid-twenties assistant brand manager, "I didn't expect to encounter so many people who were resigned to a certain status in life and within the organization. They just accepted that this was where they were going to be and what they were going to do for nine hours out of every day. And it might change only marginally from year to year. I guess I didn't expect things to be so . . . so *static*." Adds Angela, a defense industry manager ten years Heidi's senior: "I see others in the industry, and these guys are hacks. They've been in these jobs for twenty-five years, and they are just cocktail party types. But their companies don't demand a lot. I want to be with a company that does."

Predictably, nowhere is the resentment of corporate demands on one's time as vehement as among the newest generation of corporate managers. Schooled from the start in the art of "making it before thirty," they grow impatient even earlier and cast a critical eye on the time demands that previous generations accepted with grumbling reticence. Jenny is a college intern of twenty, but already she has heard the horror stories: "There's all that competition. How early can you get to work and how late can you stay? Can you be the big Yuppie and go, go, go? It's what people feel they have to do to get ahead. They can't just work from nine to five and put the right effort into it. It's not enough. If you want to go anywhere, you have to bend over backwards and do three times that amount of work."

That women see corporate time demands as an intrusion in a way men do not is also clear. Grant, a forty-four-year-old executive vice president in the service sector, seemed baffled when asked, "Why not do other things with your life?" He agrees with the need to keep growing: "If I stop, I'll get bored. And if I get bored, I'll die." But he considers the corporation his lifeline *to* that growth: "So much of my life is focused on the office. That is where I get all my pleasure in life. All the challenges are right there." Observes Leslie, twenty-four, a Chicago accountant with a Big Eight firm, "Men seem able to adapt to the lack of time at home because they've decided to make the firm their career. And if that's what it takes, that's what they're willing to do. Whereas women say, 'This is nuts!' "

The Heart of the Matter

At the Seeds of Disenchantment landing, women discover that the "fix" of early and rapid promotions, to which they became accustomed during the Proving Up landing, disappears. Promotion, when it comes, often appears to be too little too late. Wanting more—more titles, more recognition, more progress —women find themselves defeated by their own rising expectations. For women are on separate timetables within the corporation. Unknown to the company, they have struck a unilateral bargain for promotion and recognition that ignores and even attempts to beat the system. Women discover that their resentment of the demands on their time is actually implicit resentment at what the substance of their career has turned out to be. They were willing to accept the drudgery of entry-level assignments as long as they were proving up, but at the Seeds of Disenchantment landing women must accept the fact that the work will probably never become any more interesting or challenging than it already is. "I think most women from the fifties on had a very romantic view of life," says career counselor Nella Barkley, president of Crystal-Barkley Corporation, a career counseling service that specializes in midcareer changes. "They see themselves in some very chic outfit in an office with a view, directing scores of people. And when the reality dawns, they realize that the childhood dream they've never let go of is in the process of falling apart."

Once they remove the blinders they have worn through the Proving Up landing, women discover that work is not inherently interesting, that their concentration on the style of achieving has camouflaged what is often boring substance. In fact, disillusionment appears to be one of the best-kept secrets of corporate women in America today. And yet, every woman experiences it, thinking she is alone in her waning enthusiasm. "I must be honest; I am basically not that turned on by business," admits Robin, a former paper products executive. "I always wondered how people could be so interested in reading all about finance in *The Wall Street Journal*. I would force myself to read it, and I hated every minute of it. And the issues would pile up beside my desk, and I would think, 'You really should read those newspapers.' It was embarrassing to admit it then, but at this point I can say I am just not that interested."

The flame of disenchantment is further fanned by the growing resistance women themselves bring to line or technical responsibilities. The Myth of Growth and the surfacing of the Authentic Voice, with a dash of the Impostor Syndrome thrown in for good measure, combine to deprive women from deriving satisfaction out of the boring details of technical mastery. "Being a technical heavy isn't all it's cracked up to be," says Kyle, a twenty-four-year-old systems analyst. "There are people who live and breathe this one piece of software. But I just throw around the terminology, and I sometimes feel overwhelmed." Claire, the former telephone company executive, is blunt: "It was a very technical business, and I didn't give a hoot about that side. I didn't care about it or want to know it."

A certain intellectual snobbery and social arrogance may leave women indifferent or even hostile to the technical side of the business, perhaps because they fear a diminished self-esteem. Where a man is willing to build a career on the plant floor, most women aren't. Their attitude is typified by Marla, a twenty-seven-year-old black executive who switched from a line job in operations to a financial staff position when she changed companies. Marla explains, "Ours is an industrial company, primarily in diversified chemicals and automotive parts. They would have rewarded me for my technical background. In fact, a lot of companies offered a lot of opportunities for technical advancement, but when it got right down to it, I thought, 'What about the people I'd have to work with from day to day?' It had been a really good experience, but I decided that I really didn't want to be in manufacturing. I didn't necessarily respect plant managers." To two decades of corporate women nurtured on the hype of selective profiles in women's magazines, "work" continues to mean something glamorous, something that is celebrated more for its style than for its substance. Dr. Willard Gaylin, professor of psychiatry at Columbia University, and author of a recently-published book on women and gender-differences, observes, "Since the creative force behind the gender revolution was women, it isn't surprising that the expectation of what work meant was determined by a class of intellectual women, whose exposure was limited to a tiny percentage of the jobs out there. They envisioned work as creative—but in reality few of us do anything that rewarding anymore. Work does not bring pleasure. It brings in the money that buys pleasure—if you still have the energy."

In coming to grips with their own dissatisfaction, women also discover that their values often conflict with the morality of the rest of the corporate culture. Women at this level of seniority, like men, are expected to *lead* others in support of policies. Instead, they privately begin challenging the morality behind them. "My bosses came back from a meeting in Boca Raton where they were setting long-range goals," reports Trish. "They spent a whole weekend composing the mission statement, and it was one sentence: 'Win the people's confidence.' And I just can't reconcile that with the fact that they don't really care about the quality of product that's going out. I have a real problem reconciling their goals with reality." Worse, these very policies and programs are designed as motivational *tools*. "My direct boss, the department head, had this

186

big program called 'Prescription for Excellence,' " explains Claire, the telecommunications executive. "I tell you, I didn't know *what* it was. It meant *nothing* to me." Comments Marilyn French of the values-policy gap: "To continue to challenge it even privately comes to seem 'sinful,' willful, and self-indulgent. The higher ones rises in the structure, the less possible it becomes to entertain a separate standard, especially with men who identify with their work."[3] Women, too, are caught in an internal conflict between their inherent morality and the values they are asked, as managers, to promote.

At the Seeds of Disenchantment landing, women are forced to make a decision about how judgmental they intend to remain. "My new boss was stupid, lazy, and arrogant," recalls one female department head at a top industrial conglomerate, "and I'm the kind of person who, if I have no respect for you, you'll be able to tell. It was clear from the beginning that I thought he was a dolt. Just my tone of voice and facial expression gave me away." By contrast, admits Diana, a banker in international finance. "I think I went the other direction. The job forced me to. I'm amazed at how uninvolved with these people's problems I remained. I was wrenched with pity, but I stayed detached. And this is how I became a manager." When pressed, she adds, "I feel guilty that I didn't feel more involved. It is a benefit not to in business. But you have to make sure it doesn't carry over to home, or you end up tuning out on your husband, too." Developing calluses demands both time and dedication. Observes one woman advertising executive, veteran of umpteen "miracle breakthrough" promotions: "For years, it was easy for women to be judgmental when they were sitting on the sidelines. It was easy to be moral keepers of the flame when you told people what to do from home." Women who surmount this conflict emerge changed, even guilty, and often defensive about the moral compromises that must be made to work among men in a masculine culture.

Men, by contrast, project less of their value system on the corporation and bring less of a need to leave an individual stamp on the corporate landscape. They adjust far more flexibly to the notion that "Solid, hard-working mediocrity is far more valued in most institutions; it is easier to live with and far easier to intimidate."[4] They generally tolerate a more lenient standard of morality than do women, who predicate so much of their self-esteem on growth, contribution, and individual excellence. Comments Ken Auletta, author of *Greed and Glory on Wall Street,* "I recently had occasion to interview scores of investment bankers and asked them, 'What wouldn't you do to get business?' There was a long pause, like the Tin Man unrusting his brain, and several finally offered, 'Well, we wouldn't do business with the Mafia.'" Ben, a middle-management executive with an energy conglomerate, says of such "standards": responds, "What do men find out once they've prostituted themselves? If they don't get to the top, those people eventually become the company alcoholics, have affairs, or spend the rest of their corporate lives taking their repressed misery out on the people working under them." Men enter as pragmatists; women enter as romantics. Men enter a culture where the rules were made by men. So do women.

As women get a closer fix on corporate morality, they are forced to question other implicit assumptions about success—assumptions grounded in the Myths of Meritocracy, Unlimited Potential, and Reward. "Up until the time of this last jump, performance was what had always gotten me ahead. I am a performer, not a politician," comments Hillary, senior executive of the same energy conglomerate at which Ben works. "And it never occurred to me that if you perform, people will be difficult and actively try to sabotage you, or feel threatened by you. Somehow, now you become one of the predators," she concludes, reflecting on the painful evolution. "If anything, you're induced to try to keep the Myth of the Meritocracy alive long after you subconsciously know better," admits Sheila, an advertising account supervisor who blames the corporate system for women's inability to come to grips with a credibility gap between expectation and reality. To the post-feminist generation of women who believed that nothing was beyond their grasp, if only they willed themselves to succeed, the death of the Myth of Meritocracy is particularly demoralizing. Kyle, a systems engineer for a large computer company renowned for its employee training and motivation programs, betrays a sense of frustration as the Myth of the Meritocracy crumbles: "I don't think I've been given a whole lot of opportunity, and it bothers me. Some things drop in other people's laps. If they just show up at work, they get an award. I look at the people who get rewarded every year, and I want to be like them."

Luck and gamesmanship, first brought into sharp relief at this competitive level, belie the notion of a fair universe in which dedication is swapped for reward. Frustration breeds cynicism, as women take to the sidelines as observers, not participants, in the charades. Meredith, a former corporate network television manager who resigned out of boredom, corroborates that observation: "I don't know any other production manager who was more suited for the job than I was. I think that helped a lot, at least initially. But then politics came in and everyone started schmoozing with the boss, and I felt like one of the masses again. I felt I really lost ground there because I wasn't good at politicking—because I wasn't a guy."

By the Seeds of Disenchantment landing women learn to shed their previous idealism, identifying with Christopher Lasch's observation that contemporary man "advances through the corporate ranks not by serving the organization but by convincing his associates that he possesses the attributes of a 'winner.' "[5] Lasch makes almost no reference to women's role within the corporate environment. But few women could read such an assessment without a shudder of recognition. The gamesmen have proved right. In their quest for upward mobility, women can no longer duck politics as they have in the Wooed and Won and Proving Up landings. With too many qualified managers competing for too few slots, the spoils often go to the best politician—who is likely to be a man. With that realization comes another that is just as disillusioning: not only are women not being rewarded for playing the game; they are not even perceived as playing it. Observes Dr. Willard Gaylin, "Men don't question the game as long as they can be on the team. Whereas for women, making the team isn't enough. They want to see the end product of the game—whether it's affection, approval, or whatever. For women the game isn't an end in itself. For men, it is."

Clearly, women are now aware—as they were not ten years ago—of the role of politics in promotion. Yet, after talking to scores of successful women, we were left with the impression that a *conscious* rejection is at work. Women are not ignorant of the political system; they *choose* to remain outside it—to their own admitted detriment. "I see the games being played in staff meetings, and it's all I can do to keep from giggling," says Trish, a media executive. "I see the hurdles these people are jumping over, and I can't take it seriously anymore." Malaise sets in as women discover they can neither live with politics nor live without it. The system itself refuses to leave politics out. The more frantically they strive to be rewarded, the more women find themselves at war with their own ambitions, their own bright, early expectations.

Although many myths die as the Seeds of Disenchantment take root, one remains disturbingly intact: the Living-on-the-Edge Myth. Having climbed so far and having tested the power of independence, women find themselves enmeshed in a series of paradoxes. Attaining a modicum of financial security, they become both less motivated and more driven to maintain their life-style. Having proven their independence, they are more dependent than ever on the corporation for economic self-sufficiency. And having proven they are responsible, they incur more responsibility than ever before.

The spontaneity that characterizes women's initial choice of corporate life also reflects the impromptu style with which they approach their financial well-being. Unlike men who use money as a scorecard of their ambition—"I want to make a million by the time I'm forty"—women seldom analyze the relationship between salary and satisfaction. Notes Dr. Gaylin, "For men, money is power. Harry Helmsley once said, 'In my business, money is the way you know you've won.' For men, money is the chips." For women, money is the vehicle to pleasure or stability. As earlier noted, jobs that are interesting often take precedence over jobs that offer early economic security. Lacking concrete economic goals, women wake up ten years into a career to find that, despite themselves, they have attained no small measure of economic security. But this economic comfort also contains seeds of a growing disenchantment with their economic dependence. At thirty, one retailing executive sighs, "I never thought I'd have to worry. I always thought I'd be working just for the challenge. It's only recently I realize I need to work for the money—and boy, does that come as an unpleasant surprise!" In reality, women are victims, in part, of the law of rising expectations. Or, as one Parisian executive succinctly puts it, "I have the spirit of true independence—but not the means." It is in an effort to deny such economic dependency that women, after a particularly grueling corporate experience, will indulge in what market researcher Judith Langer refers to a "cash therapy. When a woman is up to her neck with pressure, there's a great relief in spending money."[6]

The uncertainty created in the wake of these paradoxes should provide a strong inducement to perform, to work hard, to keep climbing the ladder lest one fall off, despite the incipient seeds of discontent. Instead, women react by trying to deny the instability of this landing. With a cushion of economic freedom, they suddenly discover they possess what one executive called "fuck-you money."

But how much money is enough? These are women caught in what organizational psychologist Srully Blotnick identifies as "The Loop":

1. I need more money.
2. I deserve more money.
3. They aren't giving me more.
4. So I'll cut back on the amount of work I do.

As night follows day, one thought leads to the next in the sequence. The trouble here—and it's a major one

—is that isn't a line of thought. It's a circle, because four leads inevitably to:

5. Now I need money even more.[7]

What is particularly striking about Blotnick's loop is how closely it correlates with women's success-and-betrayal cycle. "I have a real fear that I'm living right at the edge," admits one female young banker. "There's a big difference between what I feel about my place in the company and the confidence I project. If they ever knew how important the title and prestige are to me compared to money . . ." Women's incessant perception of near-disaster prevents many from escaping the Living on the Edge Myth. By this landing, their real sense of financial responsibility—to their creature comforts, their husbands, their children—keeps them perpetually at the economic mercy of the corporation. "Guys know how to play the power game if they aren't getting enough money or influence. They'll bitch and moan, or pretend to quit. I don't know how to shadowbox," says a defense industry executive in her mid-thirties. "I don't want to play that bluff. Because if they said, 'Go ahead and leave,' I'd be crushed." Comments career counselor Nella Barkley, "Most women don't have negotiating skills. It's something they just don't do and aren't taught—probably because it has overtones of the biblical woman in the bazaar or something. Men are no more comfortable, but they've had more models to learn from and slip into it more gracefully."

Women caught in corporate economic patriarchy are often conflicted about negotiating for the power, status, or influence within the company their expectations of success would otherwise demand. Peggy, a senior commodities executive well-positioned as one of the few women in the company in line for a top spot, has cut her engines and is admittedly drifting within the company for the time being. "I *do* owe them a lot," she explains. "I shouldn't rock the boat. I've got a husband, who was out of work all during my pregnancy, starting a job in a whole new industry. I've always provided the stability, and I've been with this company eight years. My husband's more explosive, more likely to change. I've got to be the anchor." And at another company, she sighs, "I'd just have to prove myself all over again." Driven by economic pressure, women feel they have no means of escape from their disillusionment.

As a result, and spurred by a subconscious need to extract promises that meet their early expectations of glamorous advancement, women discover that—however inadequate to the task they may feel—they *must* negotiate. Pushing the corporation to the limit is a way of denying their precariousness. Often, the gauntlet thrown is an ultimatum: "Give me or I'll quit." Recalls Peggy of her latest corporate move, "I think they were preparing to move me to a staff sales position. I needed to outwit them. You play psychological games, trading for your position as you go along." Recognizing at this landing the limitations of their corporate satisfaction, women lash out in an attempt to satisfy immediate needs, to test power, to gain commitments for the future, and to deny the dissension. Negotiation becomes a weapon with which to strike back against the Myth of Irreplaceability and reassert a sense of self-esteem. "I had department goals, but I saw that my boss took all the credit," recalls one financial analyst with a national information company. "So I asked to have my own goals formally written down so that at the end of the year I could say, 'These are the things I have personally accomplished.'"

Other women find that the test of corporate wills coincides with a benchmark in their personal lives, one that forces them to rearrange their priorities. Maternity leave—a point in a woman's career where she has already begun to reassess her priorities—reveals the system is seldom as personally involved and sympathetic to her crisis as she has been to the corporation's. As a result, one well-placed mother-to-be described her maternity negotiation this way: "I cut a real nice deal, with the understanding that when I worked I would work full-time, but I would take periods between to be with my children."

Each time they go head to head in the process, women merely raise the ante—and postpone the ultimate confrontation to the next landing: Success and Betrayal. As Srully

Blotnick notes, "The amount of time and energy someone continually devotes to trying to beat the system is one of the key variables we've used over the years to assess how happily caught up that person is in his work."[8] At this landing, women are confronting two battles at once: the immediate negotiation at hand, and a realization of their own authentic, often baffling resentment at the corporation that previously commanded the zealous loyalty of the true believer. Confused, even frightened by the sudden intensity of hitherto repressed resentment, women seldom realize until that moment of negotiating clout just how angry they are. Years of denying the myths and expectations with which they entered take their toll. "Your first reevaluation, when it finally comes takes place under a very negative light," admits Sheila, the advertising account supervisor. "Why have I been a fool so long? Am I too old, and too security-conscious to do anything about what I discover? In the process, you discover men have given ultimatums years earlier. So you begin to rebel—to test."

For women, the test of wills is an inevitable side effect of the exhausting process of trying to climb the corporate ladder —and stay there. It is also an outlet for resentment that has built up during all those years of good girl behavior. Often, getting what they want simply prolongs women's sense of insecurity until the next test. As Sheila observes, "I was almost disappointed when I got the promotion I'd argued for, because losing it would have given me a good excuse to bail out. So the test isn't just of the corporation but of yourself as well." For if the corporation won't come through with the prize, women are provided an easy and honorable out, without having to take active responsibility for, or the first step toward, leaving. Underscoring Sheila's experience is the continuing thread of passivity—a passivity that began with the recruiting process on campus. Disenchanted, women wait to be rescued— to be wooed again. Notes psychologist Susan Schenkle, "While men are encouraged to tolerate discomfort in pursuit of a goal, women have been encouraged simply to endure. Many women are remarkable in their ability to accept, tolerate, put up with, or make the best of rotten situations."[9] Frustrated by the paradoxes of this level, but, unlike their response at the Success and Betrayal landing, women seldom act here. Instead, they *react*. "I sometimes wish I could be fired tomorrow so I could start a new career," comments Michelle, managing director of a multinational corporation's Paris office. Conflicted about what they really want, how far they want to advance, how long they want to continue working, how dependent they want to be on corporations, women respond to each negotiation with the exhilarating awareness of risk. Yet doing the high-wire act without the safety net, with the knowledge that the corporation can at any time call endgame, creates a complicated scenario, an outlet, even an elaborate rationalization for women's anger.

Ultimately at this landing negotiating eyeball to eyeball until somebody blinks is really a subconscious attempt to assert control over the environment. As psychotherapists Celia Halas and Roberta Matteson write, "The underlying issue in many dysfunctional alliances centers around a struggle for power . . . [and over] who will determine what the rules for the relationship will be. This struggle for power surfaces in obvious as well as subtle ways designed to achieve victory without acknowledgment that there is any discord at all."[10]

Breakaway Blues

In many remarkably familiar ways, the Seeds of Disenchantment landing parallels what Gail Sheehy refers to as the Breakaway passage of the twenties. It is all about separation—and, like separation anxiety, it is horrifying, challenging, and traumatic. One symbolic rite of passage is the dumping of the Myth of the Mentor—a coming of age that symbolizes the successful separation from the Proving Up landing of apprenticeship. As women assume leadership responsibility, they reluctantly shed the mentor like a used chrysalis. Jill, a senior marketing manager with a packaged goods background, had already changed jobs once within the industry before coming to a realization that she had outgrown her mentor's sphere of influence: "At that point I knew enough headhunters, and could put together a list of companies to move to. I was selective, but I made a very conscious decision to move out of packaged goods. The same boredom and lack of challenge I'd felt at my first company caught up with me at the second. On the other hand, my mentor tried to steer me toward packaged goods, to what I knew. He was a big believer in that. I sort of rebelled against him, and to this day he thinks I made a mistake." Jill is now the third-ranked woman in her new corporation.

At this landing, women develop a new realism about the limits to which male advice is applicable or productive, realizing they face very different odds and challenges from this level on than do their male peers. Much of a mentor's advice, examined in this new light, seems inadequate, even misleading. Jill agrees: "My mentor's second agenda was women in business and where they really stand. He said it's a fact of life that women have a tougher row to hoe in business. He thought I was getting too cocky. He'd moved around himself in business, so it wasn't that he worried about my staying and proving myself. But as he looked at my skills, the things he thought I was best at were the creative, intuitive aspects of marketing. And to him that meant packaged goods." Eventually, Gail Sheehy points out, the mentor becomes too much like a father for women's developmental good.[11] Mentors, in turn, finding in their protégées an ego extension of themselves, grow frustrated at the divergence of experience from their own at this level. Unable any longer to offer salient advice out of their own background, they attempt to protect women from the future—ironically, the last thing most women want at this stage, when they are trying out their managerial wings for the first time. More often than not, concludes Boston University psychologist Kathy E. Kram in her study of mentor relationships, "a mentor relationship ends with considerable ambivalence and anger, with both gratitude and resentment . . . much like a love relationship."[12]

As women become less dependent on male role models, they begin questioning sacrifices male-dominated culture has exacted. "I had been a product manager at the company for three or four years, and I was having to get tougher and tougher," says Ricki, now a part-time marketing consultant, "and I knew it. I saw what was happening to me. I was just becoming aware of my own femininity, and I was worried at the same time that I'd lose it. I looked around, and all the women in the company were forty; they looked fifty-five—they all looked shriveled—and I said, 'I don't want that for me.' It became a very conscious decision on my part to be feminine. And I decided as I got more confident—which was much more a function of living than of working—that not only was I not going to give up what was me, but that I would let more of what was me come through in my work life."

For some, realization will eventually lead to a discovery that the effort to "be me" conflicts with corporate reality; they will eventually drop out after the Success and Betrayal landing. Others will stay and reconcile both sides of their persona. But at the Seeds of Disenchantment landing begins a game of catch-up with feminine needs outside the corporation. The same women who experienced a thrill at corporate entertaining, at the trips to new places at company expense, come to recognize after years of it that they cannot stand the sight of the two-suiter with its nicks and scratches and sequence of destination tags. If they see one more shag-carpeted, leatherheadboarded Marriott guest suite, they'll scream. And all the frequent-flyer bonuses in the world can't make up for the most elusive rewards of all: time, and a connection to place and people to which women long to return.

"I think it is bizarre to unplug your refrigerator for weeks at a time because you are on the road all the time," says Rachel, an exasperated corporate counsel who longs for a regular schedule that would allow her to train for a triathalon. Marian, principal with a prestigious national consulting firm, describes the night she walked seven blocks through pitch dark in the rain in an unknown city, "and when I finally dragged into the hotel, they had lost my room reservation. I was shivering with cold and exhaustion, and I started to cry at the desk, right in front of the clerk. And I remember saying to myself, 'How can you do this? You're almost forty years old.' "

In the end, travel and relocation become a test of values: women's versus the corporation's. "I realized my value system was out of synch with the requirements to get ahead in the management of my manufacturing company," admits a former paper company executive, now a consultant. "You have to be willing to travel and relocate. The company has to come first. I respect the line people who had moved around—and moved up. But I didn't want to be transferred. And I realized I was going to turn into one of those people who weren't high on my value scale. So I left." Meanwhile, the few women who did make the sacrifice to relocate during the Proving Up landing discover at this point that the investment was hardly worth it. Jill, who moved to a remote Wisconsin hamlet to work for a major packaged goods manufacturer, found it so wearing that she stayed the minimum two years and then quit. "It wasn't as if I woke up one morning and decided the move wasn't right. I started to date someone in Chicago, and that became my escape. I had my disappointments at work, and so I ran away from it every weekend. It became an easy way not to have to deal with my career. And I began to hate the job more," she recalls. "I'd drive back to this sleepy little town through bad weather, blinding snowstorms. I got real tired of the three-hour drive to Chicago. I had fooled myself into believing I could tough it out. And I couldn't." Says one marketing executive with a large information systems conglomerate notorious for its move-or-die policy, "I began to personalize their resistance against promoting me unless I moved not as a lack of support on principle, but as a lack of support for me personally. Since then, I've come to recognize the incredible arrogance of most corporations."

Although women have traditionally asked for equal treatment early on, by this landing they now recognize real limitations in their flexibility to meet corporate expectations. During corporate negotiations many women now seek recognition of and commitment to their limited mobility. Even so, some women discover the corporation has conveniently forgotten that bargain and stubbornly insists on moving women around like pins on a gigantic imaginary battle map. "It was very clear before I was hired that I was not willing to leave Chicago," says Robin, former manager with a large industrial products manufacturer. "I was very clear. I told personnel that being a comptroller at one of our plants outside Chicago was impossible. But they reassured me that obviously our headquarters are here in Chicago, and we can clearly find a good career path for you here. No problem." Women eventually discover a dearth of available opportunities at corporate headquarters, however, and almost all are condemned to staff jobs by their immobility. There, they are in ferocious competition with other, equally urban-bound women, a dispiriting situation most corporations can do little to remedy. "At a certain level, if you want to get to the top, you have to recognize that all the opportunities are out in the field. So there is a group of very talented, very frustrated women at headquarters," Robin concludes.

Meanwhile, in examining their lack of interest in making further sacrifices for the company, women discover another startling change in values: they no longer want to become stars. "I wonder why I want to relax? I don't know how far back this feeling goes. Or why. But I sense I don't want to be outstanding. I give things a big push in the beginning, then I want to coast into a more balanced life. I know I have the ability, but not the tenacity or incentive to stick with things. I don't follow through," admits Peggy, now a part-time commodities executive with a one-year-old daughter. "Somehow, outstanding people don't seem happy. If you're not outstanding, you fit in more." Peggy is not alone. It is at the Seeds landing that women first begin to question their purpose within the corporate constellation. If their objective is not to become stars, women find themselves increasingly less commited than the competition around them, increasingly less dazzled by the proferred rewards of commitment. Unaware that most other women are going through this same passage, women gravitate toward "normalcy," convinced they are the only ones experiencing such a crisis of confidence.

At this point, women reach a crucial decision: to move ahead despite their doubts and the odds against succeeding, or to fall back and regroup. The women who choose the latter alternative often embrace another, newer myth—the Myth of More Education. Like the Myth of Ideal Industries, this myth is perpetrated by a surprisingly large, surprisingly consistent fraternity of well-meaning male mentors and advisers. "My husband pushed me into getting an M.B.A. He sort of shamed me into it, because the degree is like a union card. He already had a business degree and was looking at it from my perspective—as a means of proving I was serious about business," said one executive. For others, the M.B.A. becomes a test of faith demanded of a beloved protégée, a test most women are afraid to fail. "It's the only thing my mentor ever pounded the table about," recalls one young banker. " 'You *will* go to business school.' He made me promise before he left." Most women don't need a mentor to discern the credential writ large on the corporate wall. One paper company executive in her thirties asserts, "I interviewed for jobs and quickly realized that the people I was talking to wanted to put me in a back room somewhere at a metal desk. And everyone kept asking me if I had an M.B.A. When I went back to school and got one, suddenly I received offers that weren't there two years before." A banking executive maintains, "There is no question that a B-school degree has been vital in landing all the jobs I've had. Not that I needed the information, but I did need the credentials to be considered." A New York–based money manager adds, "I got my M.B.A. out of necessity. Although I had a clear perception of myself coming out of college, I realized businesses only wanted me as a typist. It was that clear-cut: be a secretary, or go back to school."

In assessing the importance of the M.B.A. in the career patterns of women it becomes evident that the substance of what they learned is far less important to industry than the fact that they pass some collective test of the female species. Men, assumed to be serious from the start, are given the benefit of the doubt when they apply for a corporate career.

Women—even in 1986—are not. Business school is an expensive credential, both economically and in terms of time lost, a costly reassurance to corporations that women are sincere. And perhaps the M.B.A. has become a means by which women test their own dedication to business. Says an independent marketing consultant, "My guard went up very fast at business school—to be as hard-driving and aggressive as the guys, I struggled." Unfortunately, the only thing business school ultimately proves is that women, like men, can make it through. The M.B.A. is not a rabbit's foot against the incursions of reality, topping out, disillusionment, or burn-out. In a sense, business school becomes an elaborate cop-out, both for women and for the corporations that hire them. In fact, like any school, it perpetuates the Myth of the Meritocracy, of absolute right and wrong answers, of rewards for skills mastered. Women who enter business school believing they are proving their ability to excel within the system are misled. Work is the *real* system.

One might argue, if anything, that M.B.A. holders are in for a harder fall. The best that can be said for the degree is that it pulls women up to the starting line and just through the gate. But not much more. "The M.B.A. used to be really pushed here, especially one from the top ten business schools —but not anymore," asserts one paper industry executive in her thirties. "I don't think our environment attracts or keeps young M.B.A.'s. It's not scintillating enough. They come in and move along, but not at a sufficiently fast pace. They get sidetracked or feel they took the wrong job." Adds the marketing director of a nationally known cosmetics conglomerate, "I would never hire an M.B.A. for marketing. The minute I see M.B.A., I throw the résumé in the trash can because their expectations are too high and their experience is usually irrelevant." (Both women, it should be noted, are M.B.A.'s themselves.) The opinion of most women M.B.A.'s is that business school is overrated. One consultant characterized it as "absolute bullshit, a lot of buzzwords and a diploma." Another referred to it as "a very expensive vocabulary lesson."

Business school, despite the reassuring meritocracy of the classroom—with its known rules, seldom lives up to billing. While some women find business school makes a strong, lasting contribution to their careers, most who return to corporate life newly armed with the M.B.A. eventually agree with this financial analyst: "At the time I was definitely interested in business. But going to the University of Chicago business school and learning about theories of finance and economics . . . somehow I haven't retained it, and I haven't been able to use it as well as I think I should. I guess I have a stereotype of the University of Chicago M.B.A., that they should be able to do all this hot analysis, high-powered stuff. And I sort of feel like, hmmm . . . how come I can't do these things?" And the Seeds of Disenchantment are sown anew.

If business school is in fact graduating impostors—women who believe they have "failed" business school despite their apparent success—what is the real value of business school, other than as a gratuitous credential? And, as important, if most women evince a preference for marketing over more analytical skills, as evidenced by the high concentration of women marketing majors, are business schools in fact building a professional ghetto in which entire generations of women will work? One large packaged goods recruiter admits he was having trouble recruiting men because the top ten women marketing majors in any class were invariably women. Another confides that a recent directive, "clearly off the corporate record," has been to get more men in here, even though three-quarters of marketing majors who show up for interviews are women. "We've got plenty of women in product management," the unspoken directive states. "Let's get more men." The ultimate issue is whether business school—the newest mandatory credential for women—poses yet another double standard, yet another hoop for women to jump through in attempting to pull even with men's presumed "serious" commitment to business. If so, business school performs for most women a disservice that far outweighs any positive educational value it might have.

And what of women who neither negotiate nor subscribe to the Myth of More Education? What happens to their careers as disenchantment sets in? For many women, the last stages of this landing are, though not perceived as such, a desperate attempt to cling to a few of the old myths, to revise them, to rationalize, to allow themselves to be talked into hanging in, hanging on, giving the corporation one more try. Radcliffe College's Margaret Touborg writes: "The shedding of illusion [becomes] a new kind of knowledge, and a rite of passage itself; one that require[s] willingness to relinquish the image and the ideal and [summon] the ability to incorporate the altered image into one's plans. Disillusionment thus becomes a kind of enlightenment."[13] Joy, a manager at a large aerospace corporation, claims she is working at the company only until her husband finishes medical school. "On the one hand, I sometimes feel, 'Gee, I can't wait for the next two years to be over so I can quit.' And then, on the other hand, I think, 'Thank God, at least I have another two years here.' "

Women may blame the job for exerting on them the pressure to leave. But the old inner timetable, that pressure cooker of achievement about to blow any minute, is often the real enemy as this landing comes to a close. "I'd been with the company for seven years," remembers Jill. "The new job offered a director of marketing title, different opportunities. And I thought it would renew me. It was kind of selfish, but one thing I learned was that large companies don't look out for the individual. The individual has to look out for the individual." Most women are only too willing to grasp for straws of encouragement, because at this level, there seems to be little alternative. "If I didn't work, I don't know what I'd do with myself all day," says Dina, a single, twenty-seven-year-old public relations executive. Still living in extremes, women perceive few alternatives to corporate life and many reasons to believe.

If all this is happening, why does this landing take both corporations and women themselves by surprise? Why is disenchantment such a private experience, unsuspected by and unshared with the world at large and with other women? One answer is that few women are willing to admit to potentially subversive doubts about the nature of success. Even fewer are willing to admit publicly that they are starving before its apparently bountiful table. "It's still a little bit like rape," suggests one cosmetics executive by way of explanation. "It's too private, taboo. Most of us are ashamed to share our feelings. So we're silent." Chris, an eighteen-year veteran of corporate life in two giant communications conglomerates, puts it this way: "I don't know how other women feel about it because I haven't talked about these issues much. That's characteristic of my era. It's not a subject that makes us happy, because there's no resolution. So we don't talk."

The Seeds of Disenchantment landing ultimately alerts corporate women to the end of an era. Nothing turns out to be what it seemed; all is illusion. Reluctantly, one by one, women relinquish the myths and expectations that bring them into corporate culture and take them successfully up through the entry-level ranks. "The more you buy it, the more the company feeds it to you until you just can't let go," cautions one corporate executive. "You come to believe your self-worth is nothing without the company. I have a self that's learned a lot," she concedes, "but there's still within me the machine that responds like Pavlov's dogs to the same old stimuli. I don't necessarily act on that part, but I'm aware of it." Yet confronting reality, when it means abandoning the myths— particularly the powerful Myth of the Loyal Retainer—leaves women aware of a new vulnerability. Often it is the first career setback that opens women's eyes to the unreliability of myth as a predictor of reality. "If I hadn't been let go when they reorganized top management," says Ricki, former marketing director of a large consumer products company, "I never would have had to question, 'Is this what I really want?' Up until then, I didn't have to confront any choices about what I was doing. It's not passivity. It's just that you don't take the time to think until something forces you to."

One executive recruiter observes that women at the middle-management level appear to be "self-destructing," crediting a combination of naiveté, poor career planning, and an unwillingness to focus on the teamwork and politics needed to boost managers to the next level. But there is another possible explanation. Myths die hard, and when they do, women are left with a spiritual vacuum, a void, and no oracle to fill it. Paul Zweig writes that the experience of inner emptiness is "the frightening feeling that on some level of existence I'm nobody, that my identity has collapsed and deep down, no one's there."[14] The real significance of the Seeds of Disenchantment landing is that it leaves women with drive in search of direction. Thus disillusioned, they attempt to steer their rudderless ships like some blinded Ulysses. Small wonder so many founder on the shoals of success.

CHAPTER 7
SUCCESS
AND CORPORATE
BETRAYAL

*A lot of women who are now graduating
from Harvard with M.B.A.'s are thinking
they can do anything. The question is,
will they be allowed to?*

Anne Wexler
Co-founder and Chairman
Wexler, Reynolds, Harrison, and Schule

Recently, *The Wall Street Journal* ran its first special section on corporate women. It began with an article titled "The Glass Ceiling," whose first sentence provided the most damaging indictment yet to the progress of women in corporate culture: "Look at the names and pictures in almost any corporate annual report. Or consider the silence when a male executive is asked to name the women who hold policy-making positions in his company. Notice how far women *haven't* come in corporate America."[1] Futurist John Naisbitt predicts that by the year 2001, "Although more women will be collecting paychecks, only a handful will be able to walk into the boardroom of a *Fortune* 500 company. A woman will be elected President before a woman is chief executive officer of IBM," despite the fact that one recent survey shows the demand for CEOs is actually up.[2] In separate interviews, former Carter administration Secretary of Commerce Juanita Kreps, and former Reagan White House director of personnel Pendleton James, agree.

Clearly, women aren't getting to the top. Their experience within the corporate culture as they top out, are frozen out, or slug it out for a few token slots is often perceived as betrayal at this landing. But does that betrayal really exist? Does corporate culture betray women the closer they get to the top?

Many interviews with a range of successful women suggest that for the answers to be appreciated, one must start with how women define success, and how their expectations differ from what is traditionally rewarded in corporate America. Recalls Claire, the former communications executive, "The company was looking for some very specific things. They were looking for people they thought were leaders, which I don't particularly think I am. I know it meant a lot to them that I had been rush chairman and president of my sorority. But I don't think I really ever had the aspirations they thought I did. I never really wanted to be president of anything. All I wanted was to do something I liked." Like Angela, a defense industry executive, many women define success on a comparatively emotional level: "I go back to my hometown, and I see that my contemporaries haven't moved. They admire me, and I'm sitting there saying, 'I just had to do that. If I hadn't I would have gone crazy.' I wonder whether a lot of things we do that make us seem heroic are just things we basically *have* to do." For most women, success is about what they have to do to satisfy themselves. Suggests one commodities executive, "I believe in this great quote, 'Happiness isn't a station you arrive it; it's a way of traveling.' Well, success is that, too—if you are always growing."

Threading through these accounts are myths and expectations with which women start corporate careers—creating perhaps a self-fulfilling prophecy of what success will be, of how women will know it when they've reached it, and most important, determining what's "wrong," or at least incomplete, when women attain it. As noted in Proving Up, women's definition of success, unlike men's, has little to do with money. The game is still independence, with money merely the means to the end. Money represents control over their environment; men take that control as a given. For men, economic security is merely the price of entry in a game where the real prize is power. Unaware of the attitudinal differences between male and female as they climb the corporate ladder, corporations misunderstand women's motivations and sense of reward at this pivotal landing: "My definition of success is being very, very happy doing what I'm doing, liking the people I work with, and having attained the right symbols—money, title—that represent having made it. They're my security, the proof that I'm not desperate. And, of course, I need to feel intellectually stretched," states one marketing executive. Confirms Diana, a thirty-four-year-old bank vice president, "You know, success isn't material gains. And it isn't power. But it is a combination of feeling good about what you do, confidence, and contribution. What you say is heard. People do something about it."

The deeper one probes, the more candidly women assess how their definitions of success differ from those of men. It becomes obvious that for women self-fulfillment (rather than money) and success are synonymous. "What drives me on is a lot of job satisfaction and self-esteem," admits Jodie, one of the most senior division managers in a large financial services corporation. "Title, if I'm honest about it, and prestige. Managing people. And making a *measurable* contribution to business," she emphasized. "But what's missing in all that— what differs from what men have—is that men are absolutely driven by money and power over people." Observes Hilary, senior manager of a large energy company, "There's something much more dictatorial and Machiavellian in men than in the drive for power you see in women. Men have more of a need to get to a level where their opinion won't be challenged."

Perhaps the most significant discovery is that despite unparalleled exposure and opportunity within the corporate world, for most women success still does not equal power. Most successful corporate women, no matter how highly placed, stubbornly cling to inherent *values*—those values buried years earlier with the Authentic Voice as the presumed price of entry into the corporate world. Such values emerge unaccountably intact through the corporate climb of even the most successful woman.

Women are further surprised at how unsuccessful they *feel*. The most senior woman executive at a large computer conglomerate, now in her fifties, states "The rest of the world looks at me and says, 'Boy, did she make it big! Why would she complain? She's got a big office, good title.' They don't see me relative to my male peers. They don't see that I've been left behind." What she really means is that the corporate world still sets terminal points for women's achievements, is willing to celebrate them on a relative scale. "That's pretty good—for a woman."

How successful have women really been? The answer lies in a complex amalgam of often inadvertent betrayal by the corporation, and the different agendas women bring to corporate life. When both coincide, inextricably linked as they are in a complex double helix, the outcome is as predictable as the inevitability of genetics itself.

Judging from the women we talked to, there is almost no woman in corporate America who has not experienced some variation on the theme of corporate betrayal. Yet for ten years, society has been hearing only the good news. Litigation—the only tangible form any accusation of corporate betrayal can take—is assumed to be the venue of only the truly neurotic, the truly desperate, the career suicides. Yet the number of both sexual harassment and job discrimination suits is steadily growing, according to the Equal Employment Opportunity Commission.[3] In betrayal, as in success, the vast majority of corporate women form a kind of underclass, a women's underground, reporting discrimination only for nonattribution—another aspect of their unwilling membership in the new silent majority.

At the root of this betrayal lies a perverse compliment: women are finally acknowledged at this level as a force to be reckoned with. By this landing, women represent a double threat to male managers—the emotional threat of their femininity as established in the Uneasy Peace, and the growing recognition that women who have arrived at this level represent a serious competitive challenge that can no longer be nobly brushed aside. Observes Dr. Frederick Hauser, "As men begin competing for fewer and fewer jobs, they're not going to stand aside and hold the door open for a woman. They'll beat her to the door and slam it in her face—as they would do with any man they were competing against." As a result, men attempt to reassert control by neutralizing women from competitor to dutiful daughter, a role women have long since outgrown. "The worst experience I've ever had was with a man about my age," reports Jill, now the number three woman at a major appliance corporation. "We were peers at one time, but he got a promotion sooner. His way of dealing with me was to order me around publicly and punish me like a child. I had been in the division longer than he had, and I knew more about the business, and he saw that as a clear threat." Women quickly learn that seniority confers no immunity from discrimination. Contrary to their expectations, there is no let-up in the pressure from the Proving Up landing. The shock of recognizing that betrayal is not personal but institutional often contributes to the ambivalence with which most women appraise their own success. Into it women expertly read, not discrimination, but something worse, something more insulting, more intimidating: *invisibility*.

When threatened, the male culture reacts as an institutional barrier—a closing of the male ranks. The sudden invocation of the corporate code of silence is unexpected at this landing, where women have cultivated many male managers as peers. "My male friends advised me not to say anything," said one computer company marketing executive when her boss retaliated for her sexual rebuffs by noticeably barring her from management meetings. "The fact that I wasn't compliant led to a code of silence on the part of men I'd previously thought of as friends." Another executive at a major midwestern conglomerate was told to solve a discrimination problem herself. "I didn't know how to handle it," she recalls. "But neither did they."

The most demoralizing effect of discrimination, in fact, often comes not in the personal face-offs that might be adroitly defused on the spot, but in overheard comments that are left to fester with no release or resolution. A woman, up for partner in a highly respected national consulting firm, overheard one senior male manager ask another, "Why do we need those cunts, anyway?" She comments: "We all know that the firm is probably thinking those things. But it's another thing to hear someone say it."

The closing of male ranks encourages women's silent participation in perpetuating the status quo. Martha, a chemical company executive, was dismissed during a messy EEOC lawsuit. She looks back, "In essence, I bought into the system. I accepted the goals the corporation set and made them mine, even knowing the corporate priorities." In accepting those goals, women form a tacit, unilateral bargain with the corporation. When the corporation eventually turns on them, it is not surprising that women interpret their failure as betrayal—in some cases, a betrayal they'd been set up for years before.

In such a war of attrition, nobody wins. Women are forced out, and the corporation loses talented, often dedicated people in whom they've invested years of training. "It's uphill," concedes one prominent woman in executive recruitment. "The other night, there was a dinner at the Racquet Club in New York to honor the women members of a prominent professional society. And only four members of the board of trustees showed, and those four only because they *had* to be there."

The Death of Myth

The decline of myths that began at the Seeds of Disenchantment landing comes to full fruition at this landing. Some die a longer death than others. The Myth of Ideal Industries, perpetuated largely by optimistic, well-meaning men to a receptive audience of women, is among the last to fall in a male culture. By this landing, it becomes obvious that so-called "good" industries for women are losing followers at a singularly high rate—if not as industry dropouts, certainly as disillusioned participants. There is no ideal.

"Cosmetics," trumpets one satisfied male executive over drinks. "Now there's an area where women have done well for decades." He's right; he's also wrong. The cosmetics industry has always provided a feminized model of the old Horatio Alger myth: "the young woman blessed by nature with extraordinary skin who parlays a face cream, her aunt's original recipe from the old country, into a vast, lucrative empire."[4] For a few—Estée Lauder and Helena Rubinstein among them —the myth succeeds. But are these women really proof of an ideal industry for women? Or rather of the growing realization among women in the world of business that to get anywhere, in any industry, you've got to start a company yourself? Mary Kay Ash, founder of Mary Kay cosmetics, dropped out after twenty-six years at a company that refused to entertain her merchandising and distribution ideas. Ash built the Mary Kay empire predicated on the individual talents and skills of women distributors, creating unique corporate rewards tailored to women's unique expectations of success. For most women, however, cosmetics remains a tough industry to crack from within. Dana, a six-figure training executive with a prestigious cosmetics house, found she was driven into unwilling rivalries with other women managers by a boss who believed such competition kept everyone sharper. "Remember," she says, "the cosmetics culture was developed by Charles Revson." Adds Elaine, a marketing director of another nationally known cosmetics company, "Despite the money, travel, and the fact that it's a business women can uniquely relate to, of the top ten people in this company, only one is a woman. No woman is up there really steering the ship."

And so it goes with the rest of the so-called women's industries. Advertising has yet to produce more than one or two women running a major agency she did not found herself— Charlotte Beers and Jane Maas are the only two exceptions. Mary Wells Lawrence, founder of Wells Rich Green, has proved that in this, as in so many industries, if you want control at the top, start the company yourself. Lois Wyse, co-founder and president of Wyse Advertising, concurs: "Women can become senior vice presidents, but they cannot make it to the top. There are few women running accounts, and the whole secret of moving up in advertising is how much business a person controls. Advertising has always been judged a good profession for women because it has always been considered a very nice thing for a girl to write or paint."

Former NBC president Herb Schlosser touts the broadcasting industry as a receptive environment for women. Yet the industry appears to have learned its lesson after Jane Cahill Pfeiffer. No woman yet runs a major broadcast group, let alone a network, although Mary Alice Williams holds significant management responsibility at Ted Turner's Cable News Network, as does Kay Koplovitz at USA Network. Yet one recent departee from a large cable operation is pessimistic. "The only reason a few women are doing well in cable is that it started as a new technology that wasn't paying well. So it attracted a lot of women who thought they could segue into higher positions." On a recent "Donahue" show, Jane Pauley said, "Can I say something cynical? When [cable] got started, they had two requirements: they wanted people who were really talented, and weren't terribly expensive. And that's a lesson. If you want talented people and can't pay top dollar, hire a woman. Because she's *used* to not being paid top dollar." On the same show, "Good Morning America" co-host Joan Lunden observed of the major networks, "Let's look at top management. The people really in power, the people really making the decisions [are men who] have been there twenty years." The movie business, too, is still better at putting women on the screen than on the management team, with the exception of Sherry Lansing's much-publicized but short-lived tenure as president of 20th Century Fox.

Retailing? "It's very entrepreneurial and if you're given a division to run, your job is to bring in the numbers, make your own deals. You're less likely to be dealing with a peer group setting you up to fail," says one former merchandise manager with a highly respected midwestern chain. "But, although women can be individually excellent, management is reluctant to move them up. They're simply overlooked at promotion time, although compared to their peers, they've excelled, even though it's such a quantifiable environment." The husband of a longtime store buyer who is himself a senior corporate executive in human resources, is even blunter: "Retailing takes women and uses them very effectively—to a point. The industry needs the sensitivities to the marketplace that women bring in at the buying level. But beyond that, women are not welcome. I was shocked at the discrimination and second-class treatment women get from these men who are actually utterly dependent on them."

Recently, men and women have found a new crusade: the service sector. "Are service jobs good jobs?" asks *Fortune*, which goes on to say that "Services have been the engine, chassis and body of the great American job machine, providing nearly 95 percent of the 25 million new jobs created since 1969."[5] In the past five years alone, nearly 82 percent of the new jobs created were in services.[6] Service industries, says the new myths, are more receptive to women because they transcend gritty but essential details like how a woman would fit in on the plant floor, or whether a woman is willing to move twenty-five times (telecommunications technology will take care of that). Matt, thirty-five, and assistant treasurer of a major chemical conglomerate, articulates the rationale for this brave new world: "As you get away from manufacturing into service functions, I don't think there's as much of an emphasis on sex and gender, probably because the businesses are newer. You don't associate a gender with computers or financial services as much as you do with swinging a hammer." Then, augmenting his case, he adds the argument designed to clinch the sale: "In my experience, women are fairly effective managers of others where it is not a shouting type of environment—like at a plant."

The myth of the service sector as sex-blind, even innocent, a clean slate on which women can write their own ticket, is a pervasive fantasy among young middle-management men, eager to vindicate the present in the glowing promise of the future. Yet both CEO's and statistics refute such optimism. "I think the impression that an industry is good or bad for women has a lot to do with the state of the economy at a given time," observes Russell E. Marks, Jr., former president of Phelps Dodge International. "When there's growth potential in an industry, as there is in the service sector now, it's said to offer better chances, because it's easier to say and do more for women, and because there's less competition for jobs. It's an illusion. It isn't really true that one industry or another is 'ideal for women.' " Confirms *Business Week*, "Women who have landed the bulk of the new service jobs should have benefited most from the boom in these industries, yet they have made little progress." Five of the ten largest growth areas identified by the Labor Department are "sex-segregated jobs," suggesting a fools' paradise where women are exploited at the clerical and lower managerial levels but will not be permitted to gate-crash to the top jobs. When *Working Woman* ran a survey of seventy-three top women qualified to run corporate America, it discovered three-quarters of them work in service companies and concluded, "a sign, perhaps, that women do well in sectors of the economy where opportunities are growing the fastest."[7] Yet of the seventy-three, broken down by title, only two are president and CEO, and the vast majority—approximately a third—are only vice presidents of their firms, many in ancillary staff functions such as personnel. One otherwise sympathetic male recruiter candidly admits, "I know most of those women, and they aren't even ready to run a division, let alone a corporation." By any objective measure, women are hardly poised to make the breakthrough to the top but for a Cunningham-esque stroke of extraordinary fortune.

Moreover, a clear majority of those cited work in the banking and financial services community, the "ideal" industry of the seventies, and one that aggressively recruited women throughout the decade. Banking is an industry in which much was promised but little rewarded. Articles glowingly report, "Women are making huge gains in [financial services] . . . where experts predict the first major female CEOs will appear," but they seem overly optimistic.[8] Wrote one investment banker recently in an anonymously circulated letter among her colleagues, "there are significantly fewer, as a percentage, women professionals than men, and even fewer vice presidents . . . compensation of the top women is a fraction of that of top men. No women are partners."[9] Given the huge numbers of women who have gravitated to the industry, the notion that women have risen appreciably higher or faster than women in other industries appears illusory. Despite the relative success of a very few women senior vice presidents, many women reported mixed experiences, and often brief careers in banking. "The research indicates that we can no longer think entirely in terms of numbers, imagining that if more and more women were to work as . . . bankers . . . institutions necessarily would change," writes Louise Bernikow in a summary of San Francisco psychologist Beth Milwid's findings. Bankers are the professional group the study finds most troubled by discrimination.[10] Furthermore, financial services reveals itself to be particularly vulnerable to consolidation, corporate takeover, and merger. Adds Russell Marks,

"Eight years ago financial services was being touted for women because the industry was hiring lots of *people*. And you can see that now, with the banking industry undergoing a period of consolidation, the competition for those jobs has increased. While there seemed to be a breadth of opportunity within the industry eight years ago, it's now shrinking, because the whole economy is shrinking."

By service sector, insist others, what we really mean is high-tech. The good news is that the big percentage gainers in the service sector, according to the Bureau of Labor Statistics, are high-paying jobs in technical and computer fields. The bad news is that recent studies suggest a rocky road ahead for women in high-tech industries as traditional math aversion has given way to computer aversion even among toddlers.[11] Service industries, goes the new conventional wisdom, will be not only high-tech but also high touch. Men logically extrapolate from this jargon that women, traditionally strong in touchie-feelie areas, can make real inroads here. Jill, senior marketing director with a fast-growing high-tech appliance company, disagreed. "I think that's a myth. My business and a lot of other high-tech industries are viewed as a man's world more than any other business *because* they involve computers, math, and engineering. In the industry in which I started out —food and packaged goods—there was at least a perception that women could play a relevant role. High-tech industries are global, and women are eons behind, internationally— especially in the Pacific Basin," adds Jill, the number three woman at her company. "Besides, the women's magazines always pinpoint the few women who have started their *own* businesses in the high-tech field, but they're few and far between." One of those few is Sandra Kurtzig, the thirty-nine-year-old founder and chairman of ASK Computer Systems, which she started on a $2,000 shoestring out of her apartment. Today the company has annual revenues of close to $80 million.

The Myth of Ideal Industries has as its own wholly owned subsidiary, the Myth of Ideal Companies. Searching for excellence, we interviewed women from firms consistently on the

Savvy Ten Best list and firms that men claim have a large number of senior-level female managers. We also interviewed women from several notable companies singled out in *In Search of Excellence*. At most of those "ideal" companies— listed among the top 500 American corporations—women are experiencing the same barriers other women face outside the pale of so-called progressive management. Certain highly touted "model" corporations, which congratulate themselves on their liberalism and employee satisfaction, might be surprised to find themselves included in this category. Just how excellent are these companies for women? An employee at one midwestern conglomerate frequently cited for its liberal day care and maternity leave policies said that of the roughly 3,000 employees in profit sharing only about 60 are women. Reminded of her company's reputation in the women's media and business press, Joyce comments, "It's just like any other company. There are very few women in upper positions. Most of the women who are doing well are in my division, and there aren't many of them. None of the women can figure out why we enjoy the reputation we do." Women at an "excellent" data systems company also confirmed that the image seen from the outside doesn't always match the reality for women inside: "I was the thirteenth-ranked woman there, but I never thought I got support," says Chris, a former marketing director, now with a competitor. "They were hiring a lot of women when I started in 1967, but with no commitment to follow through on their success, it seemed to me. I tried to get into sales, the most lucrative area of the company, and was told, 'No, you can't be in sales; you don't have the killer instinct.'" One of the world's largest financial services corporations boasts a high percentage of women with impressive titles and even more impressive credentials. Comments one former vice president, "Last week I was comparing notes with a woman colleague about women who had gone through bad times at our company—women at the senior VP or executive VP level—and some of them had had departments dismantled on them or the company had one by one knocked them off." She concludes that the safety of a "good" reputation vis-à-vis women allows management latitude to knock off the few women who threaten to beat down the doors of the executive suite. One can only conclude that the Myth of the Ideal Company often blinds women to the reality that no corporate environment, regardless of industry, is immune to the success and betrayal syndrome. In the life cycle of most women in almost any corporation, the degree of success is limited.

The Frozen Pipeline

There is no more persuasive proof of the limited life cycle of women in corporate America than the current disappointing record which most corporations earnestly promise will be corrected when the women "in the pipeline" reach maturity. Ann Barry, director of research at Handy Associates, notes, "The reason you don't see more women in senior management is age-related. Many of our clients do have senior women in the pipeline, but the job they're looking to fill indicates a gap they expect to be able to fill from within in five years." Most CEOs we spoke with, and many executive recruiters as well, believe the problem is confined to the present generation of leaders. In five or ten years, goes the rationale, women will "mature," like fine wines. Corroborates Korn/Ferry International Vice President Leonard Pfeiffer, "Women aren't really old enough yet. Someone who enters the corporate culture at twenty-five doesn't make president at thirty-five. She might make it at fifty-five." At that point, leaders will tumble out the senior end of the pipeline—a concept with which most women and many male managers currently in the pipeline vehemently disagree.

Many believe that the pipeline theory has become a convenient screen behind which to duck further responsibility for examining why women haven't done better already. It lets the corporation off the hook with minimal responsibility for a change in vision that incorporates *all* players into all levels in the corporate hierarchy. Argues one middle manager, "I think it's harder than ever for women, because the perception is now that we're accepted in the workplace, but I don't think that's a reality." According to Catalyst, a New York-based information bank and business resource specializing in women managers, "Only 8 of every 1000 employed women hold high-level executive, administrative or managerial jobs, and women occupy . . . 3 percent of the 16,000 seats on the boards of the thousand largest companies."[12] Those figures have not changed appreciably in the past five years despite women's apparent maturation in the corporate market. In the Harvard Business School's Advanced Management Program, only nine of the three hundred participants as recently as two years ago were women.[13] As management consultant Alice Sargeant observes, "Women have been valued as strong resources to be held in reserve, while men have taken direct charge."[14]

Most senior managers in a position to know also dispute the pipeline theory. As corporations cut back on resources in an increasingly aggressive economy, "I doubt the rate of progress women have achieved in getting access will be matched by ascent," says Juanita Kreps, an economist and herself one of the few women in the country holding multiple corporate board appointments. "What corporations and other institutions are able and willing to do in advancing women greatly influences all our destinies." Another prominent woman, at forty-four a senior financial executive of one of America's top companies, believes the pipeline concept will be illusory until corporations come to grips with the anomaly still posed by the nomination of the first woman to a senior post. She says, "Every job I ever held at my previous company was one no woman had ever held before. The way people carried on, you'd think the whole structure was going to collapse or melt away into a tiny puddle of butter or something if they put a woman there. People were rending their clothing over the decision." Although women have admittedly made gains in the wake of her ascent, she firmly believes the barriers haven't disappeared; they're just invisible. "I don't see a lot of progress. The barrier's rising very slowly, and there's just a handful of women above it. And it won't change unless the next generation demands it." MasterCard International's Joanne Black agrees:

"There's always a wall. The difference is, in some industries, you hit it right at the door. And younger women think the issue has gone away. Then they hit that wall, and they're unprepared for it."

Some executive recruiters are also skeptical about the pipeline promise. "Very few CEOs will listen to a woman on gut business issues," observes recruiter Gary Knisely. They don't think women see things the same way they do—for too long men and women have lived in very different business environments."

Preaching pipeline to the outside world, corporations often look outside to provide the quick fix their own pipelines have failed to provide. "I can't tell you the number of clients who come in and say, 'My God, if you could find me a female I'd be delighted,'" contends one partner in a prestigious New York recruiting firm. "But so many conservative values also come into play in the course of a search. So the pressure is really on the corporation's own internal system to bring along a woman on the inside." The search firm is elevated by hopeful clients to the deus ex machina that will provide fully formed senior managers where companies have been unable to grow them at home. "A lot of companies come to me because they have no women in the pipeline at the senior level," confirms Korn/Ferry's Leonard Pfeiffer, "but they're actively looking to bring in a senior woman as a role model for younger women—to demonstrate that women will be promoted and given responsibility in their company." How promoting from without the corporation will encourage women to believe in upward mobility from within remains to be seen.

At least one recruiter contradicts Pfeiffer's experience: "Remember, in the search business, safety is everything. Clients come to us because they want someone with experience. You don't come to a search firm to take a chance on a candidate. Theoretically, we should be agents of change—but we're not. If women fare well, it's only due to positions they held before they got to the search process." Demand vastly exceeds supply, as companies scramble to hire the few senior women presumably already vetted in *someone else's* executive suite, raiding the few companies progressive enough to have promoted women and depriving them of the talent they've nurtured. "We don't have a large female resource," admits one headhunter, "primarily because we are generally going to people who are already in established positions." Confirms executive recruiter Pen James, now head of his own executive recruiting firm, Pendleton James and Associates, "What really bothers me is that we all have the same inventory. Have you ever seen the list that Catalyst sends out? Eleven hundred names, thirty-three pages long. And as we started to sort through the names for those without conflicts, I say we should throw the list away and start identifying new women who have the capability. That's the role of the executive recruiter: to find that type of new woman."

Only 15 percent of most search firm's placements are women, most of those at the middle-management level. Cautions Pen James, "More women are moving into the work force. More women are going to move up the ladder. But more are also going to drop off." James, like other recruiters, foresees a certain inevitability to the progress: "We will unquestionably arrive at the point where women are just as accepted in the corporate halls as men," and he points out that more and more frequently the first candidate many executives suggest for an opening is a woman. He admits, however, that many indicators are still bleak. When a recent *Fortune* survey listed America's most wanted managers, not one woman made the team in any industry.[15] Comments Roy Rowan, a member of the magazine's board of editors, "I interviewed a dozen headhunters and asked for their top candidates, their best managers on the way up as potential CEOs in ten industries. And I think of one hundred fifty names, only five women at most were suggested—two of whom were said by other recruiters to be unqualified. I would always have to ask them specifically about women. It's absolutely clear that they don't think of women unless you prod them." Concedes Russell E. Marks, Jr., sympathetically, "The pipeline gets heavily blocked at a certain point for all managers. But the reason women get blocked specifically is that they don't come to mind. They're not a part of the network. And that will be the real battle for women—a network they will have to create for themselves among men."

Meanwhile, the internal process of corporate management selection has come under increased scrutiny from women senior enough to have observed the exclusionary way the game is played. Support proferred at prior levels suddenly and mysteriously dries up. "These men really supported you when you weren't at their level—until they realize you're promotable beyond them," attests Jodie, a senior vice president in a large financial services conglomerate. "It's not a lack of communication; there's plenty of that. But you get an overall feeling at this level of the game that they're doing you a favor by allowing you to be part of it. There's definitely a gang feeling to it, like a fraternity initiation. Because there are so few women in the environment, we call it the male mafioso."

Pen James calls it BOGSAT: Bunch of Guys Sitting around a Table.[16] "Sure BOGSAT exists," he confirms. "There is no pure, scientific method for selecting and promoting people. It's a bunch of guys sitting around a table making a decision. And they are going to sense which way the wind is blowing and usually go with the senior guy in the room." Admits former Equitable Life Assurance Society Chairman Coy Eklund candidly, "To some extent, BOGSAT is true. It will be a long time until women are at the top of corporations in equal numbers. You're still on a frontier." Russell Marks also believes that BOGSAT is at work: "How do women get to be part of the presence around the table? Either you're physically present yourself, or you've co-opted a man in your behalf." One male general manager in the energy industry adds, "You know, corporate America talks a lot about job evaluations and computerized systems in human resource development. But I was sitting in the office of one of our corporate board members the other day when he was on the phone with another very senior executive. They were bouncing names back and forth, with comments like, 'I don't know him. Oh, he's good.' These were names they were just picking out of a hat, people they knew who could fill a position. So it's almost impossible to get into those top spots if you aren't known personally by the highest-level executives." Comments Coy Eklund, "Most companies have difficulty evaluating who has long-range potential for jobs like CEO or president. The systems businesses use for gauging who should be on the fast track are, to say the least, imperfect." To which Alex, a black broadcasting executive in his early fifties, responds, "It's like a fraternity initiation. When you sit around the executive suite discussing senior management promotions, nobody says about a black or a woman, 'She's bright as hell, been with us X number of years, very talented.' Nobody will give her the nod. Whereas they'll take a risk on a white male and say, 'He'll either go with it or blow it.' Which is why you'll never find a female Brandon Tartikoff."

Most women firmly believe the solution lies with those women dedicated enough to hang in and kick the system regularly. But how? "You're viewed with a lot of displeasure if you try to take an active role in your career," sighs one former financial executive in the forest products industry. "A lot of men started in finance or accounting, but there was a little bird on their shoulder saying, 'Okay, the next move needs to be sales, and I will be sure you will get that.' No one is doing that for women. In fact, when my woman boss tried to negotiate a division move that would broaden her exposure, they just gave her a one-level promotion to continue in planning. There was almost total deafness to her attempts to say what she wanted to do and what she needed to broaden her management background." Men confirm that there's little women can do to pull themselves through the pipeline in the face of institutional resistance. "Men and women are on a different competitive ladder in most industries," affirms Alex, who believes women themselves are reluctant to accept the truth of his observation. "It's not accidental that most women in industrial corporations are in staff positions. It's also not accidental that in the corporations for which America is known—steel, autos—women are in minor staff functions where they don't call the shots. Examine it industry by industry and you'll see patterns."

The senior vice president of a large northwestern corporation forwarded a memo not long ago to the chairman of her company. The memo included the fact that an independent survey had shown their company to be the best in the industry for women. He returned it to her with a note scribbled at the bottom of the page, "If we're the best, everybody else must be rotten."

Double Standards

As women move up, they discover that success confers no immunity from the male/female double standard earlier established in the Uneasy Peace. Confirms one midwestern manager, "Management had just interviewed a whole crop of potential financial analysts. And about the men they'd say things like 'He's a real go-getter. He's really going to go far.' But when it came to the women, the comments were 'She's really aggressive; she's going to turn everyone off.' And my boss finally said, 'Do you guys hear what you're saying? It's as if there's this one hundred–point scale of appropriate style, and women have to be between forty-nine and fifty-one to be acceptable, but the men can be anywhere from ten to ninety.' It's unfair. It's unrealistic. Who is going to dance on a pinhead at fifty?" Adds Jodie, "Whenever I've sat in on an evaluation session, when it comes to the men, the discussion focuses on what they can do. But when it comes to the women, it focuses on what they *can't* do." *The Managerial Woman* observed ten years ago, "A bright young man is a 'comer' and even the less bright have to prove by their performance that they do not belong. . . . Women on the other hand . . . have to prove success, and on a continuous basis."[17] Since then, the double standard has developed some interesting contemporary twists—whereby some male managers feel free to indulge in nontraditional behavior as women often do not. A recent profile of mergers and acquisitions mogul Saul Steinberg, chairman of the $4.2 billion Reliance Group Holdings, reports that the forty-six-year-old financier walks his two young sons to school every morning, and sometimes arrives late to work because he stays home to play with the baby. "Steinberg makes a point of being home by six to help his younger children with their homework. And he likes to take the kids to the office."[18]

The discrepancies grow rather than diminish with women's ascent. "More than before you have CEOs with staff backgrounds," says a former paper company executive now in consulting. "But I think there is still a double standard. It's one thing for a man to take that leap from staff to line management, and another for a woman to do so." Replies another woman dryly, "Yes, there's always the hope that a man can *improve*." As a result of such double-standard performance pressure, women themselves begin to question the validity of their efforts in search of success. "I guess I don't have any sense of the corporate environment in any sort of oppressive way, yet I see all around me the telling fact that women just don't get anywhere," admits Rhoda, manager with a large media conglomerate that employs many women as the staff writers, "and I know that it has absolutely nothing to do with ability. I put the women at every level up against almost any man who is doing the same thing, and I see that the women are better." Of the costs such pressure exerts, Dr. Frederick Hauser comments, "Any smart woman has every right to believe she's as good as any guy, and is working harder and smarter, only to be told in true male sports syntax, 'You're okay for the scrub team or intramural sports, but when it comes to varsity, you're only good as a cheerleader.' As a result, I think you're going to see fantastically larger numbers of resentful women, with all kinds of implications for the corporation." Another senior manager feels strongly that "It's a failure on the part of management not to have kept these women. Were you and I to be joined right this minute by the president of the company, he'd say it's not a woman's issue. The real issue is camouflage, because of the high number of women with an important title but no staff. Senior management never picks up the subtleties of what a woman has to go through." Thirty years ago, Simone de Beauvoir wrote, "It takes only a little trouble to remind a woman of the hostility of the universe and the injustice of her lot."[19] No one could have prophesied the frustrations of the corporate double standard more accurately.

Slugging It Out For the Slot

Meanwhile, the double standard by which women's performance is evaluated has created a super-race of women managers, each extraordinarily talented and selected by a Darwinian process in which only the fittest survive. Inherently competitive (or they would have dropped off earlier), these few women find themselves in splendid isolation, slugging it out for the one or two token slots the corporation intends to award to a senior woman.[20] "When this present cycle of women in corporate culture first started," suggests Dr. Willard Gaylin, "there was hope that women would bring to the corporation the values they'd been conditioned with—pride, compassion, empathy. But those qualities don't have a great marketplace value on the floor of, say, the Chicago commodities exchange. The values of the woman who survives and finally makes it to the top bear very few distinctions from those of her male counterpart. That's why she's been promoted to that spot. Margaret Thatcher isn't very different from Ronald Reagan." To which Natalie, a self-professed technocrat and the highest-placed woman at a defense contracting firm, replies, "I have all kinds of mixed feelings; I'm the token woman, brought up through the ranks before EEO pressure. I was sure that after I entered, the floodgates would open for other women, but there hasn't been another senior manager for ten years."

A *token* woman's currency is devaluated. Having promoted her to such a highly visible position, the corporation milks the promotion for as long as possible, ironically keeping women pinned in the pipeline like insects under glass. "My old boss— a woman—is in a potentially powerful position," reports one oil company executive. "She's director of business development, an important title. And in that job, you could really start reshaping the company. But she just functions as a conduit for men." Women who have been doers all their lives can find life at the top confining. The few women in token slots at the point of a narrowing pyramid do not always represent the best of a promising entering class, but often, only the most durable—the ones most willing to allow as the price of success their transformation like corporate Galateas. It's a process most women spend a corporate lifetime trying to resist, for fear of being categorized as "dykes" in the word of one manager, for fear of being molded, says another. As an animal created by the corporation, retrained in speech, etiquette and politics, she is trotted out for the world to see—to the self-satisfied smiles of the male corporate world that created her. "We women are like aliens in the upper ranks of management," admits one Big Eight accounting industry executive. "With that alien status we carry all the trappings of being a curiosity."[21]

Most insidious over the long haul is the narrowing pyramid's impact on women's friendships and support systems. Forced into competition like greyhounds mindlessly chasing a mechanical rabbit around the track, women seldom connect. Male corporate culture often plays on or even promotes competition as an acceptable institutional weapon in the arsenal of management expertise. ABC correspondent Carole Simpson recalls, "I was surprised when I came to ABC that the women correspondents didn't talk. Everyone was so busy surviving and competing there was no sense of common problems. When we began to get together six years ago, we discovered we had common problems. No woman was in charge of a major beat in Washington. No woman was involved in top management. And we realized we wouldn't get anywhere until we organized." Laurel Cutler, vice chairman of the Leber Katz advertising agency in New York, observed recently, "There's a long history of women in advertising . . . [but] there was also a separate women's ladder—and one woman's promotion meant another woman falling off the ladder. It won't work until we're on the ladder together."[22]

The inverse corollary to the token woman is the noble experiment, the ultimate casualty of the corporate double standard. When one woman fails, all fail, and corporations can exempt the rest of the species from further competition. "EEOC created a problem for women, because women found themselves artificially in promoted jobs, where they *had* to fail through lack of experience," notes Leonard Pfeiffer of Korn/Ferry. "Then companies point the finger and say, 'Hey, we *did* promote a woman back in 1969 and it cost us five million dollars!' It put women three steps behind men, not even leaving them at parity within the corporation for a very long time." Confirms Handy Associates' Ann Barry, "We're seeing some women being overpromoted to positions before they're ready for them, sometimes to fill a vacuum and meet affirmative action standards. Then these women fail and it becomes a self-fulfilling prophecy." Every company has such an example in its recent past. Elaine describes a boss she had during a prior tenure with a rival cosmetics house: "She's extremely bright and emotionally unbalanced. She's one of those women about whom men say, 'See? We gave her a lot of power and it made her crazy.' When the fact is that she was probably crazy all along."

Many senior managers argue that the corporation perpetuates the self-fulfilling prophecy of failure by promoting the least objectionable alternative. Remarks one senior corporate woman, "Corporations unconsciously—and I do believe it's not conscious—promote innocuous women, the women who can't do the job, but who fit their predetermined concept of what 'womanly' is. Then, when she fails they turn around and say, 'See? We gave her a chance. She just can't do it.'" Ironically, at the very threshold of what the corporation perceives as a career breakthrough, women's determination to continue to perform at a higher standard often burns out. When the pressure of emblematic responsibility derails many successful women sooner or later, plenty of people stand around ready to point their fingers. "It's still a fact that there's an audience of men *and* women waiting for the successful women to make a false move," contends Jodie, senior woman manager at a financial services company. "So to the extent that you're not in full control at all moments, you lose. By the time they become aware a senior woman manager is discontent, is leaving, or has been fired, her departure is surrounded by a few 'facts'—that she 'wasn't doing so great'—and the party line is now in place," she continues. "Her dismissal is put in business terms that make it an isolated dismissal rather than the result of a series of compounded events that put her in an impossible performance position, or because decisions were made when she wasn't around."

Suggests ad agency president Lois Wyse, "Jane Cahill Pfeifer failed visibly, but she wasn't replaced by a woman. And that's the key. The key is that women have the right to fail without other women being punished for it." As one CEO agrees: "If women are going to be accepted as equal—to break the barrier—they're going to have to fail just as men do. And just as visibly." At the Success and Betrayal landing, women become skeptical about how many women will be given that chance. Notes Lois Wyse, "If a man fails, they say, 'Too bad. We had high hopes for him. Now let's put in Joe.' If a woman fails, they say, 'See? I told you a woman couldn't do that job.' " ABC-TV's Carole Simpson adds, "All we're talking about is keeping the door open."

Most managers—male and female—seem united on one point: The most lasting effect of very public failures, such as the Mary Cunningham debacle at Bendix, is that it makes management that much more reluctant to try the noble experiment again. Too often women's failure becomes institutionalized as gender failure. And the circumstances under which corporations are willing to take a risk on a woman too often coincide with a no-win situation. Under these conditions, observes Leonard Pfeiffer, "Women are still too often elevated under circumstances in which they have to fail. And society doesn't tolerate failure, or forget it easily, especially when there's still a double standard surrounding it." Smart women, unlike smart young men, do not have the prerogative of beating the system, even when the corporation appoints them to do just that.

The latest threat to senior management success for women comes from outside the corporation. As raider mania heats up with no end in sight, staffs are being forced to consolidate. Whole corporate families are undergoing divorces and forming new families in which the children of the previous marriage are unwanted stepchildren. The first casualties are usually the staff jobs to which women gravitate. One recent study by an outplacement firm suggested women are three times more likely to be candidates for outplacement at the middle-management level than men are.[23] David Charlson, managing partner of Chicago's Richards Consultants, Ltd., predicts that other "sure-fire bets for cuts" in any acquisition are accounting and public affairs—traditionally staffed by women. To which Nancy Reynolds, former Bendix vice president for corporate affairs, comments, "When it really gets down to the nitty-gritty, one or two men will make it. But only an unusual woman will be assimilated into the new environment."

Career counselor Nella Barkley, president of Crystal-Barkley Corporation, specialists in mid-career change, pinpoints the greatest hazard still ahead for women as corporations continue to consolidate: "What men don't realize is that there's a whole population of women who may not be able to even *survive* if the economic rug is pulled out from under them." As fewer and fewer management positions remain in the wake of a corporate raid, will the remaining slots go to the men who appear to need them more? In addition, women seem singularly vulnerable to the sudden corporate divorces that mergers represent, suggests Nancy Noonan Geffner, principal of Right Associates, an outplacement and consulting firm. "If we see a man and a woman in equal positions at $125,000, the woman who is placed out takes it much harder. She has a much tougher time coming to grips with it. Maybe it's the culture that expects women to be good girls about it. Maybe it's the way sports have conditioned men. They don't take it as hard because they know someone's going to lose.

Women are probably giving up more initially to get to those senior positions in the $80,000-plus range. So they seem less able to realize that at any stage of their careers, regardless of the commitment, they will get pulled out of the company just as any man would." Geffner points out that the isolation and the long hours finally take their toll during a merger when women discover they have no personal support systems to turn to. "You'd think they'd have loads of friends to fall back on, to see them through. But many women at this level have become so tied up in work that they sacrifice not only personal relationships—marriage, children, even sisters—but also networks of all kinds. There's simply no time for friends." Geffner contends that while men are perceived not to build friendships as easily as women do, few men sacrifice their networks to the job. They have a camaraderie at upper levels, where women are isolated, Geffner notes. "The good girl notion—that you must be the first in the office in the morning and the last one out at night—doesn't leave you much time for forming or pursuing friendships." And it guarantees no immunity from getting the ax.

Separate Timetables, Separate Agendas

How long can women reasonably be expected to tough it out, watching the pipeline bulge with other equally qualified women before it bursts? There is growing evidence among America's female corporate managers that the time for waiting has passed and that there is less and less time to be bought. Having willingly worked significantly harder than male counterparts during the Proving Up phase of their careers and having hung in through early disenchantment, women are now twice as impatient for recognition. Meanwhile, having driven themselves furiously, they find their acute sense of time passing coincides with a realization that there is little hope of reaching the top. "Women have a crisis in their thirties," observed one human resources director, herself a recent corporate dropout. "They realize they are going to be working a lot longer than they expected when they started out. And suddenly they start reassessing their careers." Comparing women's corporate experience to that of men, Jodie says, "A woman who's been working for twenty years looks at her status within the corporation, seeking an explanation where none exists—there simply isn't any relationship between advancement and performance, even though she's worked twice as hard. And she says, 'I'm god damn angry.'" Doubts and despair that don't afflict men until middle age, as part of the midlife crisis, hit women a full decade earlier. Yet it is at precisely this level that patience becomes a critical asset—an irony not lost on recruiter Ann Barry: "You have to be persistent in business. You can't give up. You have to prove you can be shot down, so the corporation will know you will be supportive even if you disagree. And you have to wait for the right time. Timing is everything."

The fear that their professional life has slowed to a standstill drives many women to an early reckoning with the corporation. Sometimes it is a collision of expectations with basic corporate culture: "I have seen some women leave because they couldn't move very quickly. They weren't discriminated against, but it's a fact of life here that people don't move," comments a defense industry manager. To which Coy Eklund, a former CEO with a progressive record on promoting women responds, "No matter who we are, if we're given the feeling that now our chance has come, we develop a certain sureness that each one of us, personally, should be experiencing a rapid advancement. In the old (all-male) work world, most men didn't make it to the top. And the truth is most women won't, either." Some women suggest that a few highly visible over-eager achievers are spoiling it for the rest, putting pressure on the system too early in their careers to realistically expect results. But sometimes impatience assumes the character of a carefully planned career strategy. "I think women who are going to make the jump from middle management to senior management have to do so before the baby. Otherwise, they're going to have to pay a lot of dues after they come back and try to make the jump that late," comments one male manager. For some women, each decade ticking off provokes a confrontation with the company: "I wanted my VP title when I turned thirty," recalls one banking executive. "I got it when I turned thirty-one, and I was really pissed off that another woman literally clawed her way to the top and got her title before I did. And I think I could have handled the new responsibilities a lot earlier."

In all this, there remains the lingering, even tantalizing question of whether any part of this betrayal cycle—especially the side of it that appears to be corporate-driven—differs from what men experience. Indeed, as Coy Eklund suggests, the pyramid narrows for men, too, at the top. "A male without determination," adds Herb Schlosser, "won't pierce the barrier either." Yet substantive interviews with men suggest that although they experience middle-management blues and career crisis, they are five to ten years behind women, and the nature of their crisis is very different. Observes Diana, a bank vice president in her mid-thirties, "I think men find out later than women that there is more to life. I think it is the blinders that men wear. They don't allow themselves to let too many forces in. They are able to compartmentalize a lot better. I think women know all along that there are other forces at work, other choices." Juanita Kreps insists, "there is that whole set of issues that are peculiar to women; there are habits and attitudes that dictate different patterns for women in the corporation. The impact of these differences may not be helpful to women's advancement in the next five years or so." Women enter corporate life expecting everything—and nothing. Almost all women—and most men—agree, however, that regardless of what betrayal men may experience at the hands of the corporation, historical role experience forces them to interpret their experiences differently and then downplay the conclusions: "A lot of men here are scared for their lives. They've got fancy houses in the suburbs, big overheads, tuitions, maybe an ex-wife to support," says one woman executive. "It's a matter of survival."

There are other differences in the special character of

women's corporate disillusionment. Women see the career as having exacted a price—a trade-off—in the caretaker role at home. For men conditioned to a career as their primary role and lifetime calling, no such trade-off exists. As Dr. Willard Gaylin observes, "Women were caught in the middle of a revolution in which they adopted in their childhood the values and standards and models of their mothers—models which are now thirty years old—that left a psychic imprint on them. Intellectually they want to feel one way but emotionally women are stuck responding to an alternative set of built-in values." For men, there are no alternatives to shooting for the top spot. For women, there are all too many.

Women are also more likely than men to have paced themselves on an accelerated timetable—both to prove their worth early to themselves and to the corporation as well as to gain seniority that will allow them to deal with the child-care option from a position of strength. After running such an accelerated race, women are more likely to feel despondent when, having perceived themselves to have given more, they do not get more in exchange. "Women have been sold a bill of goods that everything is going to be wonderful," states executive recruiter Gary Knisely. "Only to get there and realize, 'Is that all there is? Is that what I've been fighting for so long?' " Men, with ample role models, enter corporate life with a more realistic set of expectations. They are more likely to have accepted, intellectually if not emotionally, the limits of upward mobility. Women, with few role models and an agenda of feminist possibilities on their plates, have substituted imagination and the expectation that they are persisting in the fight on behalf of society and those women to come after. In the observation of Dr. Willard Gaylin, "Women, deprived for years of the opportunity for mastery and pleasure in a work situation, focused on career roles they were deprived of—which in turn made for an overromantization of the workplace." Those same qualities that fueled their rise will also let them down harder than the reality which, for men, is all around them in the form of older men who have failed to make the grade.

Disappointment for men, when it comes, arrives in the context of a male corporate culture. The game has been played by essentially familiar rules. The fight has been a clean fight. Women will never have the satisfaction of knowing whether the fight was clean or not. The rules appear to be made up or adjusted at the convenience of a male corporate culture. As women attempt to comply with those rules, they come to increasingly resent the sacrifice of their own feminine nature, feeling they have lost a war fought by unfamiliar rules on alien soil. Once a woman has topped out, work no longer fuels her self-esteem. Ultimately, the impact of corporate culture on most women as they rise through the ranks makes them feel confident about their success neither inside the corporation nor outside it. Observes Nella Barkley, "Women are opting out because childhood visions they carried around are so out of touch with reality. A woman usually leaves because she hasn't gotten to a certain position or the right psychological feedback. Men, on the other hand, have gotten that positive feedback all along the line."

CHAPTER 8
SUCCESS AND SELF-BETRAYAL

*The average woman is at war with
her own internalized ideals, the
price she pays for being caught in
a revolution of values.*

Dr. Willard Gaylin
Professor of Psychiatry
Columbia University

W hen work isn't going so well," sighs Molly, a mid-thirties midwestern bank vice president, "and you come to the end of a day. Or week. Or month. Or year. And you look back and ask, 'What the hell have I accomplished?' You realize you're putting two-thirds of your waking hours into the corporation, and you have to ask, 'Is it worth it?' And you usually come back with the answer: 'No.'"

It would be tantalizingly easy to lay blame for the limited life cycle of corporate women wholly at the feet of the corporation itself. And it might be popular to do so. But corporations aren't the only ones questioning women's role in their world. Women are reassessing, too. In countless interviews, women expressed ambivalence about their goals and roles in corporate America. As a result of their corporate experiences, women are opting out of the power game, betraying their own initial high expectations of success. Marilyn French comments, "What it costs to be a member of the power establishment is nothing less than everything in life that's worthwhile. You give up the ability to trust; the ability to sit in a room with someone you trust and are intimate with and have them tell you what they feel and think without being afraid of you. . . . You only have that one little life, so you go for where there's a lot of money and prestige, and you're absolutely miserable. What have you gained?"[1] "It's true that there's discrimination, and it's true that women are stuck in many areas," confirms former Bendix vice president Nancy Reynolds. "But I also think it is true that in some cases women *want* to be stuck. I mean success at the top is just not easy." Whether women want to be stuck or, more likely, reevaluate and discover they are stuck, they have failed in either case to find, in Sister Carrie's words, "the door to life's perfect enjoyment." Comments Hillary, a senior energy executive in her late thirties, recently remarried, "Ultimately, my goals are different than they were ten years ago. At this level, men measure themselves by their exterior trappings: 'How large is my office? How many Mercedes are there in the garage?' I choose at this point not to be measured by others. My life is very internal. My work is the way I express myself—

it's like a work of art. If the brushstrokes are all wrong, I can't be happy. I could have ten vice presidencies and still feel the painting stank."

While the discouraging lack of progress over the past ten years has taken a toll on women's aspirations, women are susceptible to their own self-limiting attitudes—here termed self-betrayal. Ten years of women's management books have identified self-limiting *behavior* on the part of women, and much of it has begun to disappear. The problem is no longer the style women bring to corporate life, but a deeper, inherent conflict with the substance. Self-betrayal relates to attitudes and values, the fundamental conflict between early expectations and corporate reality. That conflict forces a confrontation —successfully suppressed at earlier landings—between how women define success and what the corporation recognizes and rewards as success.[2] By the time they reach the Success and Self-Betrayal landing, women have achieved sufficient seniority, financial security, validation, and independence to afford the luxury of questioning for the first time in their corporate careers what it all *means*. "In some ways in business, I still feel like I'm playing it as a game, like playing house," says Molly. "And a lot of my friends feel very much the same way about it. In other words, there isn't that permanence about the career. And I don't know what happens when you wake up and you're sixty and still going at it the same way."

Success in today's corporate environment seldom spurs women on to greater goals, or fuels a desire to achieve more. Far from it. By the time success is finally bestowed, it no longer appears to justify the effort expended. The pressure of being forced to monitor one's success as if one were a spectator, nose pressed against the glass at one's own career, exerts a consistent, subtle pressure on women to limit their own expectations. "From the outside looking in, this job looks pretty good," admits a cosmetics executive in her forties. What women really mean when they talk about being perceived as successful from the outside looking in is not a perceptual gap but resentment at how quickly the world lets them off the hook. In this lexicon of success, well-meaning but misinformed peers are reduced to a we-they relationship. They can scarcely appreciate how much is yet to be achieved, how long the road ahead is, or that it may be too far to go. "My friends think I'm very successful. I'm not that successful," Chris, a senior marketing director in the computer industry, confesses. "I think I'd be farther ahead if I worked harder. I'm too talented for the level I work at. I don't blame that on the culture but on my own lack of initiative."

Success is measured relatively rather than absolutely. Says anchorwoman Connie Chung: "I think that women are not so quick, don't find it as easy, to declare their success as men do. Even if I worked twenty hours a day I would still feel guilty."[3] Adds corporate counsel Rachel, "Sometimes I don't think people are fundamentally unhappy with their jobs as much as they are unsure—because they're achievers and because they measure themselves by other's perceptions—that they are a success. And I don't think I've made peace with myself on that score, to be honest." Women can't win. When the media celebrates another's achievement, women enviously hope to read themselves in. Yet when the outside world celebrates one's own success, women invariably read themselves out. One successful human resources director in the banking industry shook her head over the female success paradox: "A lot of women at a certain level of success have high achievement goals—it speaks to the quality of women you're talking to— and overly high expectations they will never achieve."

Twenty years ago, the frustration at having been caught in a tender trap was directed at husband and children. Now women find frustration in the paradox of an equivalent career tender trap, which, like all marriages, turns out to be a great deal more work and commitment than they expected. Having proven to their satisfaction (if not the corporation's) what they can do, women feel suddenly free to make choices about how—and whether—to continue. "At that point I had been with the same company for ten years," says Meredith, a broadcast network production manager. "I got my ten-year pin and started saying, 'My God, I've been with the same company for so long.' " For a majority of women, success does not mean

243

enough, because it fails to measure up to earlier, romanticized fantasies. Admits Jodie, a financial services executive in her late thirties, "What goes through your mind is 'Gee, I've proved this to myself and to the world.' But more likely what you're saying is 'All right, I've made it. All my skills are in place. I don't have to work eighty hours a week. I can use staff to get more time for myself.' " In giving themselves permission to cut back, she warns, women begin sending out signals that undermine their own potential for future success. "It can be risky, because the company has rewarded you for hard work, and they can conclude you're letting up."

The paradox is that success turns out to demand more, not less vigilance. As Dr. Ethel Spector Person, Director of the Columbia University Center for Psychoanalytic Training and Research, reminds women, an early diet of movie stars and fairy tale princesses as role models promotes the notion that women will be rewarded for innate gifts rather than for skills acquired through practice.

Women see before them an endless corporate expectation spiral with only a hazy reward at the summit. Most, tired of having to overperform just to stay even, see the Success landing as a time to shed the good girl image—some without recognizing the costs of their actions, many more realizing the implications and accepting them. "Going through that whole process of proving yourself all over again didn't attract me," Molly confesses, adding, "I know it's very important in business, but at the same time I view it as stepping backward. If you finally establish yourself and feel comfortable with who you are and what you're doing, I don't like the idea of having to retrench to start anew." Women feel that once they have proven a point to society, the rest is meaningless repetition of the trick. "We're still looking to be loved against all odds," argues Sheila, the advertising agency vice president, of this landing. "But once the corporation starts to 'love' you back, you break relations right away."

The feeling sneaks up on them. The hardest—typically feminine—emotion to fight is guilt. "I work to support myself, for the prestige, the interest," says Joyce, a supervisor at a large midwestern manufacturer, "but it isn't a burning interest—which is terrible; I wish it were. I think that's a reaction to the fact that my life doesn't seem very balanced. I don't like to work weekends. I do sometimes, but I don't like it. It isn't worth the effort." Success as it turns out offers less rather than more freedom at a time when women are being pulled in more directions than ever. That paradox lies at the heart of self-betrayal. Women, trying to live their dreams from the start, carry the fantasy of work as self-fulfillment with them long beyond the point at which reality proves them wrong. When they finally recognize that such attitudes are self-defeating, women blame themselves for their choices all along the way.

The Wrong Side of the Tracks:
Staff versus Line

One paper company executive recalls, "All the executives would go around giving speeches about women in management. But it was hard to get women into operating jobs—women who are going to travel around to plywood plants and work their way up from the bottom." Women come to recognize at this landing that although they have perennially gravitated to and succeeded at staff positions, those early choices come back to torpedo them after the middle-management level. "Realistically line managers are promoted from line positions," comments executive recruiter Gary Knisely. Knisely admits that women who now find themselves trapped by those early choices were often victims of convenient corporate entrapment: "Back in the seventies corporations had to bring women in, and they thought, 'Well, we won't put her in manufacturing; let's put her in staff.' That's exactly where you *don't* draw the people who are going to run the company." Part of the problem is that staff jobs often are specially created niches with no promotion or performance precedents by which to measure or promote progress. In such jobs, performance becomes impossible to assess. And few men are willing to risk going out on a limb with a subjective evaluation of the transferability of such specialized skills when a woman is ready to come in from the cold. That said, however, women themselves are finally coming around to sheepish admission that staff jobs are more interesting and worth the trade-off of ineligibility for the top spot. "I'm interested in policy, in how to organize things," confesses Adrian, a thirty-six-year-old real-estate analyst with a major insurance company, "I finally realized the processes that lead to CEO don't interest me. Nor does doing deals. If I spend the rest of my career here, which is a possibility, then so be it. I'm not interested in those line jobs." At the peak of women's success, realization dawns with ironic clarity. In a staff position, they can comfortably pursue a career within the corporation without having to admit their own lack of interest or ambition in the corporate product, without guilt at a lessened desire for involvement.

Women are willing to settle for access, visibility, and recognition as the measure of success—shades of the Myths of Irreplaceability and Individual Recognition. For them, staff careers provide that consolation prize. "Staff work is frustrating, but it's a better position for someone like me who just wants to do a good job and be cooperative," says Rachel, the corporate counsel. "If you want line responsibility that leads to the top you have to just set your sights on one or two jobs you want, and you have to be very ruthlessly determined to get there." "I know staff positions are always an occupational hazard, and I suffer from a feeling of being off to the side," admits Denise, the issues manager of a New York conglomerate, "but I can go to the chairman from time to time. I've gotten attention from top management—in a crisis. I think the competition is rougher in line jobs. And staff just called on the skills that came most naturally to me." Where earlier in their careers women may have confused access with power, status with influence, they now understand and accept the distinctions. Many even welcome the limitations of a peripheral function to get off the fast track. Confirms Rachel, "So they aren't going to put me up for CEO? I'm not sure why anyone would want the headache unless its for ego or power."

Though some might make the same choices all over again for very familiar reasons, others might not. Some made those choices at a time when the only openings were staff jobs; for others, their growing ambition came as a comparative surprise. Either way, choices made in the hazy ambitions of fifteen years ago leave women ill-prepared to shoot for the top spot. Cautions Ann Barry of Handy Associates, "It's a reality that you are fairly trapped in your life by your career choices, and you've got to work very hard to get yourself out of that trap."

To a generation that spent the first ten years of their careers just sorting out the rules and their own ambivalence, that advice may come years too late. As women come to grips with that realization, their aversion to line jobs illuminates the separate, diverging tracks on which they are traveling within the corporation. "I just quit," declares Claire, a former tele-communications executive. "I realized I just didn't feel I could be the person they wanted me to be—this district-level manager. I'm not a workaholic, and there was really an aura about these people. They just worked all the time, and their careers were everything, and that was just *not me*. It's still not," she acknowledges, with no regrets at having dumped the corporate world for academia.

The Moral Voice

At the Seeds of Disenchantment landing, women's suspicions are just forming about the degree of moral compromise required of them. At the Success and Betrayal landing, however, women determine a course of action that permits them to finally resolve the conflict. Success affords most women a privileged view of corporate reality, stripped of all its limousine and corner-office glamour, with all its moral compromises hanging out. "The guys at the top become increasingly unsure as to what reality is. And finally they begin to think they are God. We've seen good evidence of the impact throughout the corporate culture," offers Hillary, a Seven Sisters energy executive. Women discover that despite the relative freedom to maneuver, the price of further success is their willingness to go along to get along. The higher they rise, the more enthusiastically they are expected to conform to the paternalistic morality of the company.

Observes Dr. Ethel Person, "Some of these women have been rewarded . . . for being 'sassy,' outspoken, and scrupulously honest, and to some degree, these very attributes, having helped distinguish them early in their careers, become an adaptation that is hard to discard." Says Rachel, "You don't want to tell the corporation that a proposal's not realistic, because then you are saying you can't do it. And corporations don't like to hear that. It's better to tell them you can do it. When they see that you can't do it, they frown, but at least you get one smile as opposed to two frowns. But I think that's basically wrong," she continues, "because, number one, it's wrong for the company, and number two, it lacks dignity. I mean, you really have to play by your own code."

The majority of corporate women assume that the prerogative of success is the right to influence and perhaps change the code by which they play. When they discover the corporation is rewarding only those who play by its own code, disappointment and a conflict of wills ensue, wearing even the strongest down. Most women would rather quit than fight. Comments Dr. Person, "Far from having defective superegos, as Freud suggests, some women feel the compulsion to speak truth to power, whatever the circumstances. Thus, a successful woman disagrees with her boss or mentor at an open meeting and is surprised at the ferocity of his response." Marilyn French points out that in the world of power and influence, loyalty to an institution consistently demands that the individual put the larger, more important entity before the self. "On these grounds it is also always *right*, and men are expected to accept its rightness even when they themselves are being punished by it, diminished or expelled from it."[4] Women come to believe, by this landing, the exact opposite: that the power and value of attaining success should be a new enfranchisement to say no.

Power Denial

The guys who have succeeded in my business really are ball-busters," says Rita, excoriating the values of corporate leadership in her West Coast company. "You really do have to be tough to get to the top. Maybe that's why I don't want to. Maybe that's even a feminine plus. Maybe we are big enough to say we don't need it." Why *do* so many women shrink from the top spot? Is it conditioning? Fear of success? Or the certain knowledge of failure? Or is the key to success a combination of factors infinitely more complex? Power denial, believes Mary Cunningham, "is rooted in a basic confusion about what real power is." Cunningham suggests that women, satisfied with "recognition, executive titles, generous salaries and streamlined reporting relationships . . . blur the line between manifestations of power and its source."[5] Confirms Ted, the fast-track assistant treasurer of a large financial institution: "It's the difference between the power of some big macho guy manager at U.S. Steel and some bright little consultant running around doing studies. Power is making an impact on resources and people. And the more direct the impact, the greater the power." And a male corporate counsel suggests, "The critical question will be whether women are put on key management in the real power centers or operating committees. I mean, you can be a principal and have no power at all."

The difference is, in part, the gap between access—what most women deem "success"—and impact. "The power of access," asserts Denise, issues manager for a large packaged goods conglomerate, "is definitely power of its own kind. If I have a strong feeling about something, it is listened to at the highest levels." Access, or the illusion of power, often gives women a specious sense of their own importance and critical contribution—or success: "A lot of times I am protecting the top men in the firm," says one public relations director at a major defense corporation. "A lot of these guys have a tremor in their voice when they talk to the press. And that is my power. Hell, that is great power. You're with them in a situation where they're scared, and you aren't." Yet even women who make the fine distinction are often willing to substitute influence for impact. Comments a successful bank vice president, "I think I'm powerful in the creativity of my ideas. I have influence with my ideas, and that's what I enjoy. But power in the institutional sense? No." Sums up executive recruiter Gary Knisely, "Women feel close to top management in staff positions, but they don't have any power. They're married to it."

Although power denial is related to the blurring line between power and influence, style and substance, access and ascent, it is more complex than the confusion and avoidance Knisely and others suggest. It has a lot to do with perceptual differences about the application of power, and with ambivalence. Women's Institute's Carol Galligan suggests it is the transforming possibilities of power—power as a means, rather than an end, that interests women, a basic difference in perception between corporate men and women. And while most women would agree with Nina, who volunteered that "if I were offered the presidency of Time, Inc., I'd take it," even the most senior women admitted that the responsibility for a vacuum at the top is partly traceable to the vacuum of ambition inside themselves.

So the real questions before women who appear to top out is "How far did we want to go, anyway? And why no further?" Why did the majority of successful, senior women interviewed at this landing agree that they were no longer shooting for CEO—and perhaps never had been? "You set up some barriers yourself," says Angela, public relations director for a large defense contractor. "You don't see any other women doing it, so you don't think you should go that way unless you have a burning desire to. And I don't." Is the lack of a "burning desire"—the vacuum found in so many successful women—simply conditioning? Or are successful women perhaps reading the tea leaves earlier in their career than men do, deciding a full decade earlier that the top spot is neither available nor worth enough of their energy? Having decided, do they intuitively adjust their sights accordingly?

Women may not be too dumb to love power, but just wise enough to assess the risks and hedge their bets. Having assessed the risk/reward ratio, and having found that it scarcely dovetails with their definition of success, they opt out of corporate life, often in plenty of time to start a second career. Since the male denouement occurs a decade later, most men will never have the luxury of such an opportunity—another characteristic difference between male and female disillusionment within the corporation.[6]

"I like my job, but it can be only one part of my life," suggests Joyce, a manager at a large midwestern conglomerate. "I just think of what I'd have to sacrifice, and I'm not willing to do it. And I think if other women feel as I do, maybe that's why we as a group will never progress that far. We just aren't willing to sacrifice that much." Sacrifices of time and energy are not the only costs women perceive as too high a price to pay for power. "It's such an essentially male culture," observes Hillary, the energy company executive, "and I lack a Y chromosome. And that's much more germane than the lack of an M.B.A. or any of the other folderol they give you. There are just too many ways to keep you out. They can't say, 'We just don't want you,' because thanks to the EEO laws, they're afraid to tell you the truth. So they tell me I can't get into planning unless I have a B.S. degree, when the only thing B.S. about it are the initials." The long conditioning to pick up the corporate signals finally sinks in, according to Hillary. "There will always be code words to keep women out. I promise you that no woman for the next fifty years is going to be CEO of a major corporation that she didn't inherit." She adds: "We have one woman here who has been tremendously successful, but she's had to warp herself unbelievably. She's actually a very thinking and sensitive woman, which is more the pity, yet in a work environment, she will be seen only with men at lunch, because it isn't powerful to be with other women. She cuts the women dead, plays up to the men, tells dirty jokes with the guys."

Even the leadership workshops designed to train women to think of themselves as presidential material may inadvertently backfire or undercut. One consultant recalls, "I went to a managerial training program once, and I was told I don't take the leadership role myself—that I'd rather be the power behind the throne."

Twenty years ago, Radcliffe College President Matina Horner first published her doctoral dissertation on women and the fear of success.[7] Since then, reality has borne out her theoretical supposition that women fear sacrificing their femininity as the inherent cost of assuming power. Watchful women have seen corporations promote and reward only the most man-tailored stereotypes of corporate success. Some psychologists have suggested, as a result, that the explanation for women's presumed fear of success shifts from a lack inside themselves to an external reality.[8] Comments Dr. Ethel Person, "This label, 'fear of success,' has become a catchword to describe all work inhibitions" when in reality, what women are fighting in fear of success is "the fear of deviance." Today, many women believe that their ambivalence about power and femininity is based not on Horner's thesis, but on the models of the few senior women the corporation has promoted above and around them. In essence, they charge, the corporate stereotype of the promotable top senior woman corroborates Horner's subjects' worst fears. "Most of the women who do well in the corporation have excessively male traits," confirms Rachel, corporate counsel to a conglomerate with a strong sprinkling of women managers. "The ones who are really recognized think and feel on the male model. They have the same ambition, the same drive, and they never mention their children."

From earlier discussions on male-female dynamics, it's clear that men are at best ambivalent about these new "Y Chromosome" women. Yet as long as the corporation perpetuates this stereotype as model behavior for women on the way up, they can expect more of the same. The corporation, in turn, loses a very talented cadre of women who opt out when they discover that the price of success is their own sense of self. "Women's feared punishment around the issue of success is *not* neurotic; it's true," advises Dr. Carol Galligan of the Women's Institute. "Women *are* punished for success as men are not. By that I mean that women decrease the number of interested men the more successful they become. The number of men who will tolerate a successful woman becomes severely limited, whereas men become more desirable the more successful they get." Such fears are barely a concern as women in their twenties throw themselves unambivalently into proving up in their careers, but those fears become the consuming occupation for many women in their thirties, a concentration exacerbated by both the ticking clock and the ominous articles warning of a shortage of men and a permanent spinster population linked to careers. "For career women married to their jobs," predicts one recent article, "the clock is ticking on marriage as well . . . at thirty-five, [the odds of marrying] are only 5.4 percent and at forty it's 1.3."[9] The same article quotes another estimate that 40 percent of college-educated women graduating today will be childless. Small wonder that the fear of success that corrolates with power ambivalence comes to ironic fruition at this landing. Concludes Dr. Galligan, "In the end, it's not that women unconsciously abjure power, but that the price of power is found to be too high. A woman finds herself punished over and over again."

Some women believe the behavioral stress companies exact of women goes above and beyond the managerial traits demanded of men. Starting with a broader hierarchy of needs, women's multiple choice agendas force them to back off the top spot. "It has so much to do with women's choices. Because to choose one thing is to renounce other things," comments Michelle, managing director of the French subsidiary of an American multinational. "I think about whether I really want to be a v.p. here, which generally doesn't happen until you're fifty," adds midwest manager Joyce, "and I realize that the people who make it spend three nights a week entertaining clients. Their life is so regimented, and they have to be careful whom they are seen with. I am not willing to make the sacrifices. I don't want to entertain clients every night of the week, and I don't want to spend my weekends at Lake Tahoe or wherever it is all good executives go to brainstorm. In and of itself, it isn't that fulfilling," she observes, explaining why she lacks the ambition to vie for a top position in the company. Kristin, a paper products executive in her late twenties, echoes the sentiment: "They would never consider me for management, no way, not in a million years, and I don't want it. I don't want to have to deal with guys who can be pretty obnoxious and aggressive. They'd make it tough for me to manage." Dr. Willard Gaylin says, "Women's inherent female values are fighting role models their intellect rejects. In the corporate culture, she feels guilty when she's not compassionate, at the lack of attachments to people, and—at the opposite extreme—when she's asked to get down, dirty and aggressive as a corporate raider. A man, by contrast, is raised with a consistent rule—to beat the shit out of the competition. He gets a sense of power, pride, and glory out of it as a man. A woman doesn't get a sense of power, pride, and glory as a woman from the same corporate exercise."

The next generation, coming out of a very different conditioning, is less ambivalent about power—or thinks it is. "It's not so much of a woman's thing with my generation," says Kelly, a twenty-four-year-old junior manager, "because I really think I could go all the way to the top. But I think I'd have to compromise too much. I'd have to convince myself that all this shit I work on is creative. At a certain point, you realize that the emperor has no clothes on, and you want to say, 'C'mon.' I could convince myself of the corporate line and play the game. But why should I spend my time doing it?" The strong ambition of younger women at the start of their careers is quickly curtailed as they are exposed to the realities of life closer to the top. The reluctance of the younger generation of managers to make the jump to top management has some senior women managers worried: "I've had to encourage women to accept their first promotion—many are happy doing just what they're doing now," says one defense industry engineer. At stake, believe most women, is a trade-off few will accept. And whether the trade-off is real or merely perceptual is beside the point to an entire generation of women convinced that power isn't the ultimate aphrodisiac. "I wouldn't give up what the women you see profiled in magazines have given up," states one manager flatly. "It's not worth it. I would rather have a balance in my life. And anyway, I don't think a woman could be CEO of my company for an *awfully* long time because the industry is so macho." One of the top three women at a major packaged goods conglomerate concurs: "If these women want to deny the other areas of their lives, they can. There's no free lunch. But I don't want that life for me. I want more. I don't want the ulcers, the heart attacks, the terrible competition. One of my main goals now is striking the right balance—having a good job and paying attention to my friends and family."

As a result of this argument, women are sending conflicting signals to the corporation. Outwardly they are still competing for the top spot, but inwardly they are troubled about the costs such dedication traditionally exacts. Women admit, as a result of such pressures, to seesawing ambition, once they have crossed the threshold of success. Women under pressure to make total commitments, find they cannot. As one psychologist explains, "Total commitments demand a reasonable expectation of success. When we lack confidence, total commitments seem absurd as well as impossible."[10] When things are going badly at home, women shift their priorities and energy back to their job and a drive for the top. The opposite is also true. As women simply drift with their ambivalence about starting families, they similarly drift in their own ambivalent commitment to power. As one executive notes, "Women who place a premium on preserving female values are in danger of being cornered into leaving corporate structures for occupations where power, specifically critical decision-making power, is not an issue. The moment has come, or is coming, when women executives will have to choose between professional survival and personal values."[11]

Different Agendas,
Different Rewards

The women I see want what men want and recognize that they don't necessarily have to give up being women to get it," asserts publisher Michael Korda.[12] Despite Korda's assertion, women's ambivalence about power is also deeply rooted in the different rewards women seek from success. For many, corporate rewards from power to private jets appear to be increasingly irrelevant. Finding that their definition of success consists largely of intangible, often emotional values, women conclude that there is an emotional vacuum, something missing in places of the heart, that no title or bonus can fulfill. Male managers who evaluate women's success according to the traditional male hierarchy of values that places power above all else fail to grasp why it isn't the sweetest reward of all for women.

What *do* women want?

Recognition. Affirmation. Growth. And the power that derives not from control, but from mastery. Traditional corporate rewards may motivate a banker of twenty-four: "There's a lot of pressure on me to want to make CEO; it allows the corporation to get the most out of me." They fail to stir the jaded veteran prone to introspection at thirty-four. "I have a sneaking suspicion that even if I did have the killer instinct," says Andrea, a commodities executive, "it's hopeless. Why use up years of your life in a battle you'll never be allowed to win?" In short, what women want is something different. They want to have their early myths and expectations answered, often by intangible or unconventional corporate rewards. The implicit danger is that as women start prizing flexible schedules or free time over traditional perks, that have appeased men for long hours, travel, and frequent moves, men will begin to confront long-suppressed desires of their own. "These men are giving up their families, their homes, their relationships with their kids," Denise, issues manager with a large consumer conglomerate, points out. "And I think women are smarter than that.

They don't get caught up in all that. At the same time, nobody gives away vice presidential titles and $100,000 salaries."

The Burned-out Case

For the majority of women who have experienced any degree of success in corporate America, this is the landing at which they are forced to come to grips with the parameters that so closely circumscribe success. What happens? For all but an unusually resilient few women, insight leads to corporate burn-out—a particularly female burn-out—and to a reconsideration of their place and goals within corporate life. Whether burn-out leads to a born-again corporate reconciliation or the constructive start of a new life outside the corporate context, it is a signal of the acceptance of limitations, the death of myth, and the restructuring of priorities.

Burn-out, at its mildest, comes as a kind of rueful regret at the personal sacrifices made on behalf of success. "Careers Leave Yuppies Too Pooped for Passion" reads the headline in one midwestern daily.[13] Alice Hennessey, senior vice president with Boise Cascade and one of the highest-placed women in the industry, compares the success syndrome to being in "a pressure cooker. I would really have loved to have had the time over the years to play tennis with friends, to learn to ski well, to read more books. I read a lot of book reviews, but I've read darn few books." But she concedes, "I wouldn't be doing it if I didn't love it." For every Alice Hennessey, however, there are many women for whom the stress of playing catch-up and the eventual realization of the Sisyphean task ahead leads to burn-out. "It was like being in the eye of a hurricane," explains Fran of her decision in her mid-thirties to leave her job as director of strategic planning for a large multinational conglomerate in favor of a job in investment banking. "The pressure was enormous, as was the pressure to be neutral. You don't do any of what I did lightly." Jill is the number three woman with a major appliance conglomerate and seems the quintessential corporate woman on the rise. Yet she is about to quit, explaining: "My values and attitudes have changed dramatically. Deep down, I've always had a desire to do something on my own. But it's difficult. You get locked into a career path, a comfortable salary. I've also gotten cynical about corporations. They're very cold, impersonal environments. And my fiancé is a developer in another city, and there's no way I'd do a commuter relationship now. I would have for the company at twenty-five, but not now. Which means I'll ultimately leave the company. I could only be happy there maybe another two years." Jill is just the kind of stand-out woman employee most corporations trot out for interviews and keep as rainy-day corporate currency in the bank of promotable possibilities "some time in the future." A successful woman who still feels like an outsider—having played the game consummately well and done everything "right" by her own company's assessment—testifies to the real gap between what women seek and the environment corporations offer. For such women, the need for connectedness persists; the melody of caring lingers on.

Chris is another top executive who's apparently made it as a division marketing director of a large telecommunications company. She is a woman to whom other women instinctively look as a role model. Yet Chris's inner turmoil belies her veneer of calm accomplishment: "We're in another shuffle now, and I just can't deal with it. I've just had the stuffing knocked out of me. I'm suffering from severe battle fatigue. I've had it happen before, but each new day used to bring its own new challenge, and winning *that* race meant new challenges, new excitement. I don't feel that anymore. I don't know what my future at work is. I see a major void."

Just how far does one have to dig to come up with these signs of woman's burn-out? Not very far. Long-suppressed doubts and disillusionment, disappointments and despair bubble to the surface, aching like an old wound. If women we barely knew chose to reveal themselves by these scenarios, we reasoned, what must the rest, all the other, typical middle-management women, feel? Is a critical mass of extraordinarily well trained but burned-out cases about to collect on the doorstep of corporate America?

"I hate it here," says Marian, a consulting firm principal on the eve of being made partner of a prestigious national firm —too little too late. "I've already made up my mind to leave; I don't want to live this way. This place is full of people who are insecure, negative, boring, and dangerous. Why should I spend my life in a negative environment?" Leaning across the cluttered surface of a desk piled high with vital studies and documents, she sweeps them all aside, gesturing at the adjacent offices, and adds, "These people think they're on top of the world, but they're merely the elite of a small slice of the world." Like many of the other women who complained of the symptoms of burn-out without naming the disease, she, too, suddenly sees the corporate rewards for which she so eagerly toiled losing focus and meaning. Dr. Herbert J. Freudenberger confirms the ironic nature of women's corporate burn-out: "Burn-out is usual among those very key people the corporation *doesn't* want to lose," he says. "The cost to the company of replacing those people is tremendous: thirty percent of the replacement's salary goes to the headhunter alone." He cites as classic causes of burn-out too-high or contradictory expectations on the part of the employee, promotion delays, non-delegated authority, role ambiguity, and loneliness—all key components of women's history within the corporation. In *Women's Burnout*, Freudenberger identifies a series of twelve stages women who are burning out undergo. Many are consistent with the myths and expectations women bring to success. They include the Compulsion to Prove, Intensity, Dismissal of Conflict and Needs, Distortion of Values, Heightened Denial, Disengagement, Emptiness, and Depression.[14]

At an extreme, women who fail to reconcile the gap between expectation and reality within the corporation risk becoming victims of a rage either turned inward against the self or directed outward at the corporation. "I think you're going to see fantastically larger numbers of resentful women with implications for the corporation," predicts Dr. Frederick

Hauser. "Just in business schools, half of the degree candidates are now women, and they will get to the middle management ranks in the millions. And with millions of women running up against the glass wall, you'll see a lot of subtle corporate sabotage, especially among younger women who are less passive than their mothers, more able to express aggression. And they will give corporate America a hard kick in the ass." Or they will aim their anger at themselves. "The sublimated Authentic Voice, as you call it, is a fantastically rich source of self-betrayal," comments Dr. Hauser. "Women have to do psychic surgery on themselves to 'be all I can be' within the corporation when doing so means being male. Of necessity, women are forced to betray themselves. And when women discover that what they achieved turns out not to be all they can be, but instead all that a guy can be, a fantastic sense of depression—anger turned inward—sets in. Women think, 'I did this to myself.' " Sandy, a human resources vice president, confirms this: "When you realize you're achieving the limit you can aspire to, and you have no balance, that's when you get depressed." At an extreme, a sense of failure in the midst of success can create a suicidal personality, testimony to the failure of expectation. One television producer committed suicide after a consolidation move that left her jobless after twenty years with the network. Elizabeth Clow Peer, *Newsweek*'s first woman foreign correspondent and first woman bureau chief, committed suicide thirteen months after having been fired without warning. "As July 31, 1984, the date of her final termination, drew near, she felt she could not live without her job, without a connection to her employer of the last twenty-six years. . . . For Liz Peer, who desperately needed that old sense of office family in her life, it was a disaster. . . . She had a West Side luxury co-op with a Rembrandt etching on the wall, a hundred bottles of vintage wine. . . . She had everything, in fact, but a job."[15] *New York* magazine recently reported on the suicide of a thirty-six-year-old *New York Times* reporter who covered the Jackson and Mondale campaigns before beginning a self-inflicted downward career spiral that lead to her death. "She was . . . a person torn all her life between conflicting desires . . . the desire to do well for the *Times* as a political reporter and to make herself happy in love." She complained about the intrusions of her demanding professional life into her personal life, and about the constant pressure to choose between those two lives. When she could no longer reconcile the two, her work began to slide. In the end, suggested a close friend, "She had been very successful . . . and was psychologically unprepared to be anything but successful."[16]

Marilyn French has already suggested the price men pay who "dedicate themselves utterly to their jobs in the hope that will bring them love, but discover that their effort has destroyed the affection they crave."[17] The success and betrayal syndrome should put to rest the antiquated but convenient notion that failure is somehow more traumatic for men than for women. In their twenties women are seduced into patterns that become irrevocable choices in their thirties—often forgoing romance and children as the price of corporate approval, only to hit a wall and discover the good men are all taken, the "career woman's disease," endometriosis, has rendered them infertile, and they are alone, in the end with their self-recrimination. Comments Dr. Hauser, "Harry Levinson has found that career women in their late thirties and forties are having fantastically depressive experiences. Many of them wake up after having put in time and years of dedication and effort, in effect saying, 'Is this what I gave up children for? Is this really the fuller, richer life I was promised?' They feel betrayed by the myth of the business world they believed in. And they are conscious of betrayal by the self, the heaviest of all burdens. It's bad enough if the corporation's to blame. But to accept that I screwed *myself* over . . . that I did it to myself?"

This depressive self-blame is consistent with what outplacement counselors have discovered in fundamental differences between the way men and women cope with betrayal by the corporation. "Women find it harder to accept that they've been fired or terminated after they've done documentably superior work," confirms Nancy Noonan Geffner, a principal of Right Associates, outplacement consultants. "Their initial reaction is incomprehension about how this could have happened. As opposed to men, women have a harder time separating cause from effect—and they blame themselves. Many are unable to accept outplacement help and counseling. They need to project the feeling they can do it all on their own, that they don't need help. There's a lot of resistance. Somehow, they feel that if you seek strategic help planning the next step, it's a sign of failure." Dr. Ethel Person adds, "The woman, who may already feel betrayed by the empty promises of a traditional marriage, is seduced into magical promises of liberation through work, again taking a passive stance. The outcome of this new hope is only too often a renewed sense of failure as she internalizes the blame for yet another disappointment." Self-doubt often leads to paralyzing passivity.

The ongoing legacy of passivity, first noted at the Wooed and Won landing, belies women's hectic upward mobility. Of one magazine's seventy-three women best qualified to lead American corporations, only one-third had experienced a job change.[18] According to a recent Korn/Ferry International survey, the average woman executive has worked for her present employer for thirteen years and has changed jobs only three times in her forty-six years.[19] Many, despite the incompleteness of their success, simply wait for the recruiter to call— as much the victims of their own ambivalence now as they were in college. Professional women discover their unexpected passivity surfacing at the apex of success; too many end up deferring action on their own behalf until burn-out has taken its toll. Write psychologists Celia Halas and Roberta Matteson, "Faced with a situation in which they cannot win, women tend to respond to the paradox of resolving conflict without facing the issues: First by *giving* up; second, by *shutting* up; and third, by *putting* up with inequities."[20] Confirms one telecommunications executive of her reluctance to abandon a seventeen-year commitment to a company, which was unprepared to promote her beyond her present job: "There was a large element of avoidance. I felt I wasn't going to something, but running away from something. I wasn't focusing on my career, and it takes a lot of energy to make a switch. I'm just sorry I didn't leave earlier."

Ricki, a former marketing director who was reorganized out of a job argues that, "It's not passivity. But you get caught up. I think that women get more engrossed in what they're doing—be it a marketing plan, a budget, a tracking study—and they don't take the time to think until something forces them to." Dr. Person suggests much of this passivity is tied to low self-esteem, a continuation, perhaps, of the insider-outsider motif by which women deride the degree of their personal success. She further notes that women predicate the potential for further success not on their own abilities but upon the continuation of key relations, in this case continued affiliation with the all-powerful, highly respected corporation: "She feels exaggerated anxieties at times of transition. She merges her goals with those of her boss, an associate or a company," a practice exacerbated by career wisdom that assures women it's impossible to get another job if they're not currently employed, however unhappily. Other women have come to terms with their reluctance to take command of their careers. They acknowledge passivity as a price they willingly pay, but like almost all the women we interviewed, they assume their own passivity is an exception to the rule. "When I'm really honest with myself," says Adrian, the thirty-six-year-old insurance company executive, "I'm not as directed as an achieving person should be. I tend to drift into things more than I should. Unlike a lot of people, I have a very poorly defined vision of what my future is likely to be. I don't seem able to get beyond the next five years at this company. And what I do see I see emotionally, not realistically." Many women accept their passivity as the key component of their own self-sabotage. "I was comparing notes with a woman colleague last week," said another senior manager in financial services, "and we noticed that when women started to hit the brick wall, and they lost their mentors and support systems, they began to lose their confidence in a way that men seem to camouflage better if it happens to them. Women get sloppy right at the moment when they can least afford it—when the world is scrutinizing them, wondering if they will make it. Now, they're exhausted. And why not? After all, they'd spent years building up the internal energy a high corporate position demands of a woman."

Kissing It Good-bye

You've heard of people calling in sick," writes novelist Tom Robbins. "But have you ever thought of calling in well? It'd go like this: You'd get the boss on the line and say, 'Listen, I've been sick ever since I started working here. But today I'm well and I won't be in anymore.' Call in well."[21] At the tail end of the Success and Betrayal landing, the sweet moment of surrender comes as a surprising, even gratifying form of liberation for those who regard leaving the corporation as the only way out of the cycle. "She's saying, 'I'm god damn angry I've been a casualty,' " articulates Jodie, vice president in financial services. "She's seeking out an explanation where none—no relationship to her performance—exists. She says, 'God damn it. I worked for twenty years. I'm an executive vice president making $120,000 a year. I've proved what I set out to do. I have two kids I haven't seen in years. Why not drop out?' " Women describe an almost epiphany-like revelation, a religious conversation likened to a born-again commitment to self. Finally, they are capable of separating themselves and their identity from the responsibilities and rewards of corporate life.

Like a number of women, Dana experienced her revelation literally overnight: "I dreamed I went into a shoestore that had all these gorgeous Italian shoes. And I took the boxes home and unpacked them, and they turned out to be filled with K-Mart shoes. And it took an enormous amount of effort for me to understand that it meant my career isn't all that it was cracked up to be. That power is an illusion—it takes men years of hard work and big compromises to get it. I'm not willing to make those compromises and see no reason to. There are other kinds of prestige." She now runs her own consulting firm and is in the process of writing her first book.

Claire finally resigned from a large telecommunications firm because, "even though I was making more money than anyone in my peer group, and the benefits were up the wazoo, I felt locked in. I didn't know what I wanted; I just wasn't prepared to sacrifice my way of life. I felt finally that the only thing keeping me in the corporation was the money and the benefits. But I really didn't like what I did. I mean, I wasn't able to sleep on Sunday nights, because I really hated going in." Michelle, managing director of the French subsidiary of a large U.S. firm, reads something inherently healthy and uniquely female in the act of women rejecting corporate culture and its demands: "I've always been directed toward the future, toward new possibilities. An old friend from my previous industry recently asked me about an article in one of the professional journals, and I said I no longer read those papers. I have turned that page. And I'm not sure he understood that. It's not restlessness, as men perceive it, but a need to continue to grow."

Having successfully negotiated the psychic separation, the actual surgical cut becomes not merely a celebration of the newfound self but a chance to act out fantasies. "I sent a memo to my boss and copies to the vp, chairman, and CEO," reported one Chicago-based corporate financial analyst. "It read, 'Re: Resignation.' And I had it hand-delivered, so everyone was forced to read it. Two hours later, my boss came in and smiled his shitty little smile and asked to talk about it." A week later, her resignation triggered a shouting match that ended with her calling him an S.O.B. "He just went nuts," she recalls with relish today.

Dana decided during a meeting that the time had come to quit. "My boss just sat there drinking coffee while he threw next year's budget at me and challenged me to cut out $250,000, and I thought, 'I've run my own business, I know money is real, and I don't have to play with your numbers, asshole.' So I called my lawyer, and told her I was quitting my

$100,000-a-year job, and she asked if I could handle it financially, and I said I could. I didn't even call my husband to tell him. My boss said I was hysterical and that I should give it ten days. I called my boss at home the next morning, timed to coincide with his morning jog, and said, 'I'm done.' Then I drank a lot of champagne, took a bubble bath, and ran around singing, 'School's Out Forever' for the rest of the day."

The need to resolve the discrepancy between what women expect of the corporation and of themselves and what they are asked to sacrifice in turn is what motivates most corporate dropouts. To some extent, this is also true of men who leave corporate life. And to the extent that men undergo midlife career crises, there are resemblances. But a man often experiences such a crisis from the inside out; seldom are outside societal pressures ganging up on him as much as his own inner doubts. "A man the same age is just hitting his stride, he has the glow of CEO in his eyes, he's making more money, and he has more stock options," comments Jodie on the gender differences in perception of betrayal. "And he's getting the financial fulfillment he needs. The woman executive is in crisis, saying, 'After all I've done for them . . .' " When women question success a decade earlier, their feelings are in no small part generated by constant doubts of the outside world waiting for her to prove herself—or to stub her toe. Nor do men begin their corporate careers by repressing their Authentic Voice. When women finally give vent to that voice, fifteen or more years into their careers, its lure to return to a life outside the corporate walls is one many heed. Says Lauren, a marketing director turned independent consultant, "I experienced a lot of jealousy as the most senior woman in the company, and meanwhile I couldn't conceive a child. I went through all kinds of fertility workups, and they couldn't find anything wrong. Finally, I went to see a psychologist, and we talked about work and about my anger and aggression toward the company. Six weeks later, I got pregnant. And then I quit. Someday maybe I'll go back. I didn't do this to escape corporate life but to gain my freedom."

But isn't it the same thing?

Responds Valerie, until recently vice president for human resources at a major media conglomerate, "You get to a point where you think, 'Hey, I've proven it; I've gotten as far as I ever want to get. I've made an impact. Now I want time to do what I want.' You begin to ask yourself, if you aren't working to make money, how would you spend your time?" The recognition of limits combined with financial autonomy constitutes a powerful incentive to cut the cord. All one needs is that extra little push from the company—as recruiter Gary Knisely confirms: "Maybe that option is forced on a woman by hearing, 'Sweetie, we want you to know that when you get to this level, you are not going to make it to general management. So I'll give you a little career advice. Think about doing something else. You have reached the highest level you are going to reach. So drop out.' " Is there a way out of that syndrome? "Not for another hundred years," believes Knisely.

The net effect of the growing disillusionment of women in corporate America is the loss of a generation of carefully trained and managed talent—the first assault wave to make it through the dense firepower of discrimination, self-sacrifice, and the unfamiliar terrain of male territory. Ironically, they will also become the first generation to opt out. Jill, the high-level appliance executive who gave herself two more years before dropping out, is sure she won't be back: "I don't think I want to ever reenter. I see myself doing something on my own or with my husband forever. I see my life as a little more predictable than it was when I was twenty-one years old. At this point, you become a little more honest about what you want. I don't find the corporate environment particularly challenging. And I'm not scared. I think I will find something else." Adds Claire, the former telecommunications executive now in academia, "I could try another corporation, but why bother? Those same people who promised me the world four years ago would promise it to me now, and I'm sorry, but if they couldn't give it to me then, why would this time be different?" Another corporate dropout, one of the first women partners in a Big Eight accounting firm, resigned suddenly after delivering her second child. A "How long can I take it?" mentality sets in, and women begin subconsciously ticking off the days: "Every day for the last two weeks I've just walked out of work at three o'clock and gone home," said one demoralized twenty-year veteran manager. "I feel remarkably uncompetitive." Sums up another executive succinctly, "I believed it was a no-win situation no matter what I did. So I cut my losses." Comments John Artise, director of career placement for Adelphi University, "Typically, plateaued managers begin to feel desperate, to think of themselves as failures, to fall prey to wanting out and feeling stuck for life. In those cases, plateauing begins to turn into the fatigue, bitterness and ague of fast-track fever."[22]

No matter how little women feel they have achieved in terms of relative corporate success, they will be leaving, despite their disillusionment, richer in rewards than the corporation was ever aware. "You know, I'll never really be letting go of my career success," asserts Carla, research director at a major national advertising agency, "because no one can ever take away what I've made for myself." Certain she will ultimately drop out at least long enough to raise a family, she adds, "I guess I need that feeling of being needed, or at least the illusion of it. I'd want children to give my life purpose, a reason to go on living. And a job will never do that."

As women come to grips with the realities and limits of corporate success, they discover an ironic ally: their fathers. Joanne Black of MasterCard International recalls that the period immediately following her departure from American Express was a time of particular closeness. "It was a lovely time. My father shared with me more deeply than he ever had some of the hurts he had had in business. And he felt he could do it then without discrediting himself. He was allowed to let go of some of those deep pains since I had shared the same experience." One young packaged goods manufacturer was surprised when her father responded to her corporate disillusionment by urging her to do something entrepreneurial. "He doesn't think I'll get the rewards I need from the corporation," she said. "And he has been with one for twenty years." She adds, "Women feel bad if they give up too soon. You feel if you're going to be part of the system, you can't be a quitter. So it helped me a lot when my father told me that." Dana's father even lent her money to get her new business off the ground after he was let go after thirty-five years with a large pharmaceutical company: "He understood the feeling that you can put your whole life into a company and what have you gained? I guess, growing up, I had always felt my father put the stamp of approval on security. My father's understanding since I left the corporation has been one of the great rewards of my life."

The Next Generation

I think a lot of younger women are troubled. They know by now they're really bucking a system," says a young product manager in her twenties. "And, especially if they want a family, they look at the women ahead of them and realize the fast track is over. They might reach senior management by seniority, but that is the only way they're going to do it. A lot of the women I know are starting to become really disenchanted." According to the *Wall Street Journal,* young executive women are less likely to be married than lower-ranking peers. Thirty-two percent are single. A large number [32 percent] don't plan to have children. "These women are the most likely of all those surveyed to feel that they have had to give up something to achieve success."[23]

Like all managerial revolutions that start at the top, there is an inevitable trickle-down effect when so many role-model women make the decision to leave. Observes one seasoned twenty-six-year-old public relations executive, "There are no role models at the top. It's nothing I can articulate—just a feeling I have about the limits here. We have a woman who just got promoted, and I think the men were all wondering, 'What does the boss see in her? Is she really that good?'" "There is no next job, no place to go—there are only one or two positions left to go for," asserts one senior cosmetics executive of the possibilities for young women managers. "By the time they're thirty-five, women have gone as far as they can go. Men can be sales force managers, women can only be the sales force. I'm glad I'm not competing with them," she says of today's younger, driven managers, "because they're gonna trip all over themselves. You see, up till now everything's been fine for them, because there was plenty of room at the bottom."

As word of what lies ahead begins to trickle down, women are hearing the message for the first time and refracting its complexities back at the work world in an ambivalent combination of drive and dread. One twenty-year-old business major at UCLA comments after a two-hour discussion about career options, "I could see becoming very comfortable in that kind of secure corporate environment, but I don't have a goal like the presidency of IBM in twenty years. I like to take risks, but not big ones. I hope I go all the way to the top. But I think I'd put restrictions on myself." Clear across the country at Smith College, twenty-year-old Jenny struggles with the same questions after three years of internships, counseling sessions, and summer jobs: "I don't know how I am going to sort out the conflicts. I have been watching people to see what they do—only there is no answer. There isn't even a pattern or a role model that offers an acceptable way to go about it." She automatically asserts her goal of the eventual CEO position, then contradicts herself a moment later with a more honest, more realistic assessment: "I don't know," she answers slowly. Tina, twenty-two, sums up the impressions of her generation: "I've really seen how people can become slaves to their work. Your ego becomes chained to the corporate ladder as well as your pocketbook. It can be very seductive."

Women who understand where reality diverges from myth, women who have lived the confluence of events that defines success in today's current corporate culture, stand on a unique and lonely promontory of recognition. The possibilities are no longer endless. But neither, any longer, are the responsibilities for fulfilling those dreams. Recognition of that trade-off is the first step on the road to developing new models, new solutions. Wrote Pearl Craigie well over eighty years ago in

The Dream and the Business: "A false success made by the good humor of outside influences is always peaceful; a real success made by the qualities of the thing itself is always a declaration of war." In the end, corporate women are still groping for that reconciliation in the war between their own innermost, uniquely female needs, newly acknowledged, and the path that will allow them fullest flower.

CHAPTER 9
THE PIVOT POINT

There's no permanent structure in this country. If it doesn't work one place, you go and structure something else.

Malcolm Forbes, Jr.
President and deputy editor-in-chief
Forbes magazine

After experiencing the corporate cycle of landings culminating in success and betrayal, a significant percentage of women reject the corporate way of life in many or all of its aspects. Explains Valerie, who left her vice presidency at a financial institution at this pivotal landing to pursue volunteer activities, "You get to be one of the top women, and other than moving laterally, there is no way to go. And you look at the situation and think, (a) 'I am probably never going to get close to the top,' and (b) 'I would probably not want to be there even if I could be.'" When asked why she didn't just move to a larger corporation at the same level but for more money, she protests: "It would be just more of the same. It really is no different at that point. So why not just drop out?" With the myths no longer fueling their desire to tough it out and forge ahead, a number of women start to wonder, like Alfie: "Decent clothes . . . a car, but what's it all about?"

At the Pivot Point landing, women begin to believe there *must* be something better. What's "better?" Most women we interviewed said that if they could afford to just chuck it all and do exactly what they'd like, they would continue working at *something*. Anything but this always demanding, sometimes demeaning, rigid and constricting, wearing and tearing, interesting at times but ultimately unfulfilling, corporate career. As Russell Marks muses: "I'm wondering when women will begin to talk about *separate* but equal. Women will begin to ask, 'Why do I want to compete against the blockage? Why not compete with men *in the marketplace* instead of within a corporate context?'" A number of women, indeed, are asking just that. At the same time, many are responding to the now loud and clear Authentic Voice and are deciding to pursue activities they finally realize will best reflect their true interests and values. Of course, when we asked the men, they declared with equal enthusiasm that they, too, would like to jump out of the corporate Cuisinart. Popular wisdom has it that societal pressures make it far more difficult for men to drop out and pursue other options and that they have far fewer acceptable alternatives. "A woman who decides to take a leave and never come back is not looked on as having failed. A man who drops out to start a water skiing school in the Bahamas is," says Korn/Ferry's Leonard Pfeiffer. Many women agree: "Their status is so dependent on their work," comments Sally, thirty, who recently dropped out of a media corporation to go back to school in psychology. "If a thirty-year-old man decided to go back to school, he'd be virtually undatable. He wouldn't be making money, and he wouldn't be 'tracked,'" she contends, using the slang phrase for on a career fast track.

When asked whether they would work if they inherited enough money to live comfortably, 80 percent of a national sample of men said they would. Most of our interviews with male managers reflected the same ethic.[1] As described in the preceding chapter, male attitudes differ from those of women when it comes to coping with frustrations within the corporate system—frustrations that often have somewhat dissimilar roots and that men often don't experience until later in their careers. "Women are opting out, or questioning the fit between themselves and the corporate environment at earlier points than men are," observes career counselor Nella Barkley. "It has a lot to do with childhood visions that are out of touch with reality. And with a womanly desire to be lured and a realization that 'I'm not getting what I bargained for in a big organization.'" Certainly a number of women's greater "options" will depend on a man making money—in other words a husband or boy-friend's earning power. But some executive women would assert they are more often forced into these other options. Like Amanda, who dropped out of a marketing job at a textile and chemicals corporation to become a financial planner: "A man gets frustrated later, during the midlife crisis, when he's hit the end of his talent rope, whereas a woman gets frustrated because she's at the end of her opportunity rope." The result, according to Amanda? "We talk a good story. We have fought so hard to get into careers. But I see people falling like flies." Not all of the women who are "falling like flies" are dropping out to raise children or to pursue avocations. There are dozens of alternatives to the conventional corporate career. Why can these women cut the corporate umbilical cord when their peers, often equally dissatisfied, cannot? Of course, the most obvious answer is financial ability. Some women have working husbands who support them. Others have socked their money away and are willing to take certain financial risks. Their peers who remain at the corporation may not be able to afford to escape. According to Ralph Keyes, traditional corporate careerists remain in frustrating jobs less out of fear of going broke and more because they are afraid of having to lower their standard of living: "On the surface, this is expressed as a reluctance to sacrifice eating in four-star restaurants and taking winter trips to Aspen. But at a deeper level it expresses a simple fear of risking any part of a life to which they have been accustomed."[2] Some women decide such risks do not outweigh the frustrations of staying, and so they choose to remain on the job. And some women who have made it to middle and upper middle management cling to frustrating jobs determined to make it work—like women who languish in unhappy marriages.

A study of graduate school alumni at M.I.T. identified five categories that suggest what a person is fundamentally seeking in a career. The results provide some insight into the type of people who stay in large corporations and those most likely to drop out. The anchor categories include (1) management competence, (2) technical competence, (3) security, (4) creativity, and (5) autonomy and independence.[3] Obviously, people who tend toward the last two categories are those most likely to drop out of corporate life.

But whatever their category or typology, many of the women interviewed who actually did leave their jobs brings to mind Janis Joplin's famous line, "Freedom's just another word for nothing left to lose." They find the frustration and discontent caused by the Success and Betrayal cycle so overwhelming that no risk looms too large. Their choice to leave seems to almost make itself. Amanda, now a financial planner, says: "There was no alternative. I don't think I could articulate how frustrated I was in the corporation. I was bound by bosses, bound by the system, bound by a lot of things over which I had no control. I just had to assume more risk in order to penetrate those bonds." Women such as Amanda for whom no amount of security, prestige, or peer approval is adequate recompense, respond by developing the drive and the vision to create new jobs for themselves even if it takes a long, concerted effort. Amanda, for example, took a battery of aptitude tests in order to identify the best alternative career path for herself. Often, it is much simpler. In the course of their corporate work some women discover a window of new opportunity. Suzanne, for example, dropped out of a corporation to be a private distributor once she saw she would have greater opportunities doing the same thing on her own. Grace left a large cosmetics company after she was asked to run a nonprofit organization.

How do these options compare to corporate life? Are these women glad they made the break? Why did they pursue these particular alternatives? Do the myths that women bring to corporate life persist outside the corporation? Are women any happier and more fulfilled because of the switch? What follows is a brief glimpse of life on the other side of the corporate fast track.

Small Is Beautiful

Women are starting their own businesses at a record clip. They now own nearly a quarter of the 13 million small businesses in the country, and that figure is growing at least three times faster for women than for men.[4] It's as if we'll become a divided nation of a handful of major megabuck corporations run by men and millions of smaller companies and service organizations headed by women. Jill, thirty-five, worked for three *Forbes* 500 corporations and now plans to drop out to form her own company. She predicts: "Women leaving corporations today will build a whole new generation of women-led businesses. And you will see small companies today that evolve into significant industries." Malcolm Forbes, Jr., agrees that the smaller companies women join today could be the giants of tomorrow. "The *Forbes* 500 never stays the same. The fact a business is small today doesn't mean it is going to be small twenty years from now. The American economy is always changing." Korn/Ferry's Leonard Pfeiffer was equally sanguine: "I think it's healthy that the corporation will lose a certain percentage of managers to entrepreneurial projects. Look, Steven Jobs started Apple and created all sorts of new markets for products and new jobs. And now there's a company that lots of other companies supply to. Eventually, women entrepreneurs can have that impact, too." A pleasing notion for many women who believe they might follow the model of fashion designer, Liz Claiborne, who built her own company up to sales of more than $556 million in 1985.[5]

A company of one's own is indeed the fantasy for a majority of the women we interviewed. Virtually every one of them had at least toyed with the idea of dropping out to start her own venture. Often that venture ranges far afield of what they are actually doing in their corporate jobs. The American Women's Economic Development organization (AWED) sponsored a contest in which people submitted ideas for small businesses. A surprising number of winning entries were from women who rejected pursuing businesses akin to their jobs in the "male" corporate domain to answer the long submerged Authentic Voice that called them to more "female" enterprises. For instance, a systems design programmer plans to open a beauty shop, a subcontractor has created a Travel Line Launderette (using a basket, pins, a line, and two suction cups), and a computer sales representative is marketing a book of recipes for tailgate parties.[6] "The entrepreneurial boom has been driven by women," comments Steven Solomon, author of *Small Business U.S.A.* "But no one's really noticed it. Why? Because most of the glamour is in the high-tech businesses, which are usually run by men. But they're only a tiny percentage of the actual small businesses that are out there." Women might be called the invisible entrepreneurs, running the hundreds of thousands of other enterprises like the ones suggested in the AWED contest. "Most of the jobs in this economy are in small entities, which is where many people are finding the most opportunities," says Malcolm Forbes, Jr. "So being in a big corporation is not the be-all and end-all. In the *Forbes* 500, the number of jobs has slipped by about 600,000 in the last ten to fifteen years."

But what exactly attracts women to the entrepreneurial mode? One could almost go down the line of the myths women bring to the corporate world and see how, at a later point in their careers, they now project these myths once again onto the small business option. Women apply the same myth of the family to this smaller environment, still seeking out connectedness and bonding on the job. Dr. Frederick Hauser puts it this way: "Women tend to create an entrepreneurship as a means of recreating the family as they see it, after disappointment in the 'corporate family.'" Jodie, who works at one of Wall Street's largest financial services concerns, also identifies the sense of family women expect from small businesses: "The company has lost a lot of senior women; they've found they're happier and more fulfilled in a smaller environment. Maybe it's that sense of family, maybe they're more manageable environments or maybe their skills are more readily recognized. When they walk in the door, they're already on the team. They don't have to spend ten years clawing their way into the boardroom." At the same time, a number of women expect a smaller company to afford them more time and flexibility—two sought after qualities for women attempting to balance a career and a family. Tina, a twenty-nine-year-old, who works at a New York media conglomerate, reflects this notion. She wants to start her own business because "I'd like to have control over my destiny. I tend to have an entrepreneurial streak in me. My personality is suited to growing businesses. I like to build them." Shades of the Myth of Irreplaceability?

In addition, most women believe that the Myths of Growth, Individual Recognition, and the Meritocracy can become realities in smaller companies or companies they start themselves. Angela, a corporate communications executive at a defense corporation, explains why she was pondering leaving her job to start her own business: "Over time, the corporation's methods of doing business are a constant irritation. Why put up with that? I look at some of the things I have done and know the monetary value is very high, and yet I see other people get the credit for them, and it irritates the hell out of me. I want *total* credit." Eve, who left a large construction corporation to go with a smaller firm, comments, "There is a lot of mediocrity in corporations, and I was dumbfounded when all the lateral moves came into being. I think a lot of corporations are trying to find a place to put all the extra M.B.A.'s. But that wouldn't be acceptable to me. Why not go out and do your own thing?" Thousands of women are considering—and many are doing—just that, including cosmetics mogul Mary Kay Ash who "for twenty-five years worked in a male corporate world that underpaid her, passed her over for promotions, and dismissed her suggestions with a patronizing, 'Oh, Mary Kay, you're thinking just like a woman.' 'I wanted to start a company where being a woman wasn't a liability,' she says today."[7] Counsels Lois Wyse, "If you want to run something, be an entrepreneur, because you are going to be stuck in a corporation. You won't make it to the top."

"The people without the politics" may be another way of pinpointing what many women dream of finding in smaller businesses. Jodie says of her goals: "I see myself moving to a smaller organization because the corporation, like many big companies, requires at a certain point that you manage the process, not the business. Now most of my time is spent on managing upward, managing power—and I'm just reacting to demands." For Jodie and the majority of women who dislike political maneuvering, this increasingly puts them at a distinct disadvantage. "The more time I have to spend managing the politics, the more I'll fail. It's not the best use of my skills. Yet I know I'm very versatile and I could rise to the top of a smaller organization." Beyond recognition lies the reward. By the time most women have arrived at the Pivot Point, a few approving taps on the head and verbal "attagirls" aren't going to cut it anymore. Many women have developed a more targeted approach to financial rewards outside the corporation. They take an attitude similar to that of Jill, the director who worked at three different *Forbes* 500 corporations and now plans to go into business with her fiancé: "I've learned 'Do for yourself instead of doing for somebody else.' I can take my skills outside, and the rewards will be much more significant than they are in an environment that automatically expects it." Or as a former paper company manager put it: "I think you come to a point in your career where you cross that line from merely stretching yourself in a career and you start to focus on the financial rewards. I think there comes a pivotal point in your career at which you cross that line." Members of today's somewhat more business-savvy younger generation are already looking ahead and predicting they won't stick with corporate life because of its limited rewards. In a poll of seventy student leaders from twenty-three business schools, nearly two-thirds said they envision starting their own companies sometime during their careers.[8] Asserts Heidi, the product manager: "I don't think corporations can really compensate people. If you are good, you can make a lot more money on the outside." Young executives' disenchantment is further reinforced by the often reported middle-management crunch, as fewer and fewer opportunities for advancement are available.

But are women stampeding to start computer software firms or their own mail-order muffin businesses? No, they are not—primarily because even though women have gained confidence during their years in a corporation, the fear of living on the edge is stronger than ever when it comes to severing bonds with the organization. Leaving the ultimate symbol of authority and protection strikes many women as similar to being orphaned, a terrible, almost Dickensian fate. In the words of Angela, the defense company manager: "One thing about your own business—you don't have all those departments to protect you. Like from lawsuits. We have a huge legal department at our corporation, and I think of the legal system as magic, it is so mysterious." She adds: "Starting my own business is frightening now. I don't know if I could sell myself. I need to have the security of 'Okay, this is what *they* want me to do.'" Unresolved dependency needs often reassert themselves at the

Pivot Point. Jessica Dee, president of Jessica Dee Communications, observes, "Women don't see that a career really depends on earning a salary from somebody else—that they're really dependent on a career for financial security and their identity." Besides this need for security, many women cling to the prestige that comes of being married to a well-known national corporation. As one medical products entrepreneur notes after dropping out of three *Forbes* 500 corporations: "There is a whole group of people who take on the persona of the corporation they work for—say, IBM or Mobil. And it makes them feel good about themselves to be able to go to a party and tell their friends, who then say, 'Oh, wow, you work *there*?' But if you work for a company nobody knows the name of—well, some people will feel downtrodden when none of their friends recognize the company they work for."

When women do set forth on their own, how does the entrepreneurial reality measure up to the fantasy? That feeling of bonding and family, for instance—does the smaller business provide it in ways the corporation cannot? According to the men and women interviewed, yes, if one joins a smaller, already existing company where there is less pomp and circumstance. In smaller companies, sheer survival, the basic need to stay afloat, often forces everyone to clutch to the same raft of Medusa. "We have such a perfectly run machine here that we would never consider hiring a person whose chemistry isn't good with the rest of the 'family.' We have total trust, complete loyalty; we back one another up, and we never have problems. We don't set two people up to compete against each other," says Nancy Reynolds, who left her position as vice president of Bendix to start her own twenty-person consulting firm. Moreover, the often charismatic and visionary individuals who create such companies can demand a much greater dedication and commitment. "This organization is a family," Jessica Dee volunteers. "The people who work with me identify with me."

For those who start their own companies, however, the experts warn that loneliness is part of the order of the day. In fact, Ralph Keyes lists the three worst risks of starting one's own business as the three "shuns": frustration, humiliation, and isolation. He, like the entrepreneurs interviewed, cites isolation as the single worst aspect of entrepreneurial life as compared with life inside the corporation.[9] This may be a particular problem for women who work at home—and many of them do exactly that. According to a Census Bureau survey, nearly half of all female-owned businesses in 1977 were operated from home,[10] and a study of 14,000 women found that 94 percent of those who work at home have no full-time employees and that the isolation was their greatest complaint.[11] Suzanne, who left a job in sales at a cosmetics corporation to become a sole distributor working out of her apartment, remarks: "I feel that I am out there on my own. I think one of the great things about working for a corporation is the contact. The only reason, in fact, that I wouldn't recommend leaving the corporation to start your own business is the isolation. You are out there interacting on a superficial basis with hundreds of people. But basically, you can really isolate yourself." This inability to share information, expertise, and concerns with large numbers of people was mentioned by many who own or work for smaller companies, as a key drawback.

What about politics? Obviously, if one owns a company, the concept of politics is moot. According to one media executive turned entrepreneur, "I don't like internal politics, kissing ass and that kind of stuff, and I had to do a lot of that in the corporation. Now people ask me, 'Isn't there a lot of stress in having your own business?' And I say, 'No, there is about half as much stress as I had in the corporation, because all I have to worry about is bringing in the business. I don't have to worry what some bozo thinks of me. And I don't have to write letters to cover myself. That's the kind of thing you have to worry about eight hours a day in a big company. I feel *much* less stressed now." Former Bendix vice president Nancy Reynolds describes the atmosphere at her firm: "In a small company people are so busy working their tails off that they don't spend much time gossiping or jockeying for position."

Almost everyone we spoke with mentioned that small companies function much more as meritocracies, that one could gain the individual recognition often not possible at big corporations. Steve, who worked at three *Forbes* 500 companies before starting his own anesthesiology firm, which now employs a number of women, explains why smaller companies were better for women managers: "I think the key is that in a small company, you are under a microscope or a magnifying glass. It is easy to see which people contribute and which don't. At the corporation it is so political. It is so difficult to really measure individual accomplishment and performance. That's why, of course, it has to degenerate into politics." He also asserts that women could obtain the monetary rewards and other compensation that were far more reflective of their performance than those earned in large corporations. "Corporations often don't reward you for your efforts and achievements—again because it is often difficult to define and measure. Also, most middle managers are insecure. They don't want to be fired, and so they don't take risks. Because there is no upside to it really—if you think about what's in it for them. They may get some recognition, but usually their boss gets it all and they get none. Whereas, in a small company, you are not at the level where your salary is limited to some range between 10 to 15 percent of your salary; you are not on some regimented Hay point system."

However, again we found that most women were working for somewhat different rewards than men were—in small as well as big companies. Suzanne voices this difference: "So many men don't understand this, but I felt that going into business on my own had very little to do with money. It is the challenge I like. There are days I go out and don't make a penny, but I don't count it that way. I went out on my own because I thought it would be a great opportunity to me as a business person. I had done it as an employee, and I knew I could manage on my own. And from there it just started growing." Contrast her need for growth to the attitude of Bruce, founder of an investment banking firm, after he left a major media conglomerate: "The main reason I am doing this is for the bucks." On the other hand, as might be expected, it was the growth for its own sake that motivated Suzanne.

"What motivated me was the challenge of the job. I am never bored. I think it is very gratifying." She adds: "There were difficult times—but they were overcome because money hasn't been my main motivator. If it had been, I might have thrown in the towel. But I just enjoy the challenge of it. I think if you can say that about what you are doing, it doesn't matter what you are doing." While certainly a number of women who run or work for smaller businesses need the income to support their families, a study of 468 women entrepreneurs revealed that the typical woman business owner is seeking independence, achievement, and satisfaction before money.[12]

Personal growth continues to be important for many women outside as well as inside the corporation. Some observers such as Coy Eklund, former chairman of Equitable Life, suggest corporations, with their greater number of job slots and "career paths" offer more opportunity for growth, "whereas you get into a little company and you find that there are not as many routes to the top. A large job pyramid offers far more opportunities than a small job pyramid." But others contend that small businesses provide greater growth opportunities since, with smaller staffs, women can often take on more varied responsibilities. As Steven Solomon notes: "Big companies can better afford than small businesses the luxury of hiring a greater proportion of the most conventionally desirable employees—middle-aged white males—to fill specialized job functions. Small companies' limited size and resources require that they seek talent at economical cost wherever it is available and that their employees wear several job hats at the same time." Eve, the construction company manager, says of her decision: "Here at the smaller company I work on twelve projects at a time. It is never dull. I can work twelve-hour day after twelve-hour day and not get bored. It is challenging. Whereas my corporate management was crummy; they were all chauvinists. It is tough when you run into that, and my instinct was to run and not fight it. Maybe I should have stayed and fought, but I think my own personal growth is more important than fighting some larger problem for the good of women in general." Dana started her own communications consulting firm, left it to join a large corporation, and later returned to consulting. She expresses a similar sentiment: "I have time to create my whole life. The only limits are the ones I set for myself. I am now one of the happiest people I know." Bruce, too, says that he thrives on the promise he has as an entrepreneur. "I see unlimited potential, and I certainly didn't see that in the corporation. I only wish I had more hours in the day because there is so much to do." But when asked if he sought to learn on the job, he responded, "Naw, I don't have that interest. The older I get, the less interested I am in learning about other industries. The only learning I like is the kind that helps me in my business."

Another myth, the Myth of Irreplaceability, of creating a new business that will continue in perpetuity, also operates differently for men and women entrepreneurs. Some studies have even suggested that male entrepreneurs often start businesses because they are uncomfortable under strong male authority figures. As a result of unresolved fears of their fathers, they seek an exclusive position in their own company much as they once wanted exclusive possession of their mothers.[13] A New York Times article observes that while four out of ten new businesses are begun by women, female entrepreneurs have been largely neglected by psychologists. And what sparse data exists on female entrepreneurs suggests it is situational pressures—such as the lack of opportunity in large corporations or the need to work while raising small children—that drive women to create their own businesses: "It is in the talents that lead to success that men and women seem to resemble each other most, while they may differ most in their psychological motives."[14] Women, as we have noted, tend to value the corporation as a protective father figure, yet feel frustrated that they can't replicate the "irreplaceable" roles of their mothers—whom they identified with rather than sought possession of. In the smaller companies, women can often find this sense of irreplaceability. Jessica Dee comments: "You're automatically a special person because you're president of your own firm, not someone else's employee." But, for whatever reasons, women often identify less with the companies they created, considering them offspring rather than ego extensions. "Here's this thing I've created, and now it has to feed me. But to feed me, the company has to grow and that may not be healthy for the organism," Jessica adds. One possible reason women aren't busy building empires may be because they work more for income than for wealth.[15] Of the small-business women who were polled in the 1977 census, about 58 percent collected less than $5,000 in annual receipts and only 8.9 percent collected more than $100,000 in annual receipts.[16] Three-quarters of all female businesses are small retail and service concerns, generally less profitable than larger sales segments such as manufacturing, construction, and transportation, of which female-run companies constitute only 10 percent.[17] In part, this may, as we have mentioned, reflect the Authentic Voice at work, as women gravitate toward more "feminine" pursuits. But it may also be because women are still hanging on to the Living-on-the-Edge mentality, because they want to get by rather than shine. Perhaps women simply don't think big. In fact, expanding the business, once it's off the ground, is especially hard for women. That's when the financial risks deepen—one has other pocketbooks to fill besides one's own. Meanwhile, it is harder for women to get financial support and backing from banks and other institutions. Although legislation may help end discriminatory practices, according to the Small Business Administration, SBA loans to women declined from 17 percent in 1980 to 10 percent in 1984, and the Small Business direct loan program may be phased out altogether.

Which brings us to some of the fundamental disadvantages of running or working in a small business. While there is, to some degree, greater flexibility, and you can progress without the fear of the IBM (I've been moved) syndrome, most of the interviewees refuted the notion that one had more control over one's destiny in a smaller company. In fact, the time demands are often much greater than those of a standard nine-to-five corporate job. As Jessica says, "Most women here are very much like me. They're in their early thirties and their job is their life. They're here twelve hours a day—partly because that's the nature of the job at their level and partly because they like it." Also, while the small-business environment may be less regimented, it can be just as demanding, even more so. And if one runs a small business with other employees, one has even less flexibility and room for maneuvering—especially when it comes to ultimate responsibility. "I can't just decide to quit my job tomorrow," Jessica continues. "Thirty people in this office are dependent on me. And legally I couldn't get out even if I wanted to. It's my signature on rental leases, equipment leases. That's frightening." It goes without saying that a company of one's own is a big commitment in terms of money, time, and responsibility.

In addition, Heather Evans, who left a high-powered job as a Wall Street investment banker to start an apparel firm, also points out that small ventures often attract people who are just as driven to succeed outside the corporation as within it. "I did gain more control over my hours," she admitted. "But I also sat deaf, blind, and dumb at social events while I totaled projected orders in my head and spent sleepless nights planning negotiations with the union. It seems that my strong achievement orientation drives me toward obsession *whenever* I have responsibility and opportunity—whether it's me or somebody else in control."[18]

Alice Hennessey, senior vice president of Boise Cascade, also makes the point that larger corporations can play a social role in society that smaller companies often cannot. "Small business is so geared toward making it that not a lot of time can be spent on social responsibilities. Whereas, a big organization often can make the time and provide the resources to think about responsible behavior and the role it plays in society."

Finally, most of the entrepreneurs interviewed said that going out on one's own was not for everybody—especially the fainthearted, when about only one in three new businesses is expected to survive five years. Patricia O'Toole writes that "Entering the entrepreneurial world, alas, will not save women from the disappointments of corporate life any more than entering corporate life saved them from the confines of housewifery."[19] Every entrepreneur we spoke with said confidence was the key characteristic that had made him or her successful. Despite such odds, every woman and man interviewed working in a smaller company also recommended small business as a particularly good option for women. Steve is owner of his own anesthesiology company which has spawned several women entrepreneurs who, having gained experience with him, have left to set up their own firms. He comments, "In general, I think small companies give women better opportunities. It is very difficult in large companies to make a major personal contribution and be rewarded for it. I think you can be financially rewarded better in smaller companies. Maybe not right at the beginning but over the long haul." Cosmetics entrepreneur Suzanne is personally pleased with her decision to go out on her own: "It is very gratifying to do something on your own. I feel I have made a contribution that is very much mine. I enjoy it. I really do." Paul, an executive vice president of a small hotel chain remarks: "The president of the company and I both view women as equal. There is a lot of opportunity here for women. But that may be because it is a small company." He adds: "One woman working for us has a Harvard M.B.A. and a lot of friends working at big corporations. And she thinks she is *much* happier in her first year on the job than they are on theirs." Former Bendix vice president Nancy Reynolds concludes enthusiastically: "Running your own firm is more fun than anything. We still represent Bendix—they are a client—so it is a great progression. *We love* our own business; we run the show here. I could never go back to the corporation."

Mesdames Richelieus

The consultant, according to television commentator Eric Sevareid, is any ordinary guy more than fifty miles from home. Robert Townsend, author of *Up the Organization*, has his own definition: "Consultants are people who borrow your watch and tell you what time it is, and then walk off with the watch." For all the cracks about consulting, the field—which covers everything from management, public relations, accounting, outplacement, and personal image—has become an alternative for women whose illusions about unlimited influence within the corporation have been replaced by a new corporate realism, a sense that more power might accrue from *outside* the system. After all, women often hold consulting jobs within the corporation in the legal, human resources, public relations, issues management, and other staff departments. "I am a counselor; I am not in a power position," notes Angela, thirty-four, a public relations manager at a leading West Coast defense corporation. "All my power lies in credibility." Credibility, expertise, the ability to maintain good human relations—the same qualities that help women excel in these corporate staff functions also help them succeed as consultants.

Since the specific skills many women develop in the corporate domain are marketable outside the corporation, many women trapped in the success and betrayal doldrums consider dropping out and using their expertise as consultants. *Expertise* is a key word here, as it harkens back to women's drive for personal mastery through learning. Consulting, in the words of one Harvard M.B.A., J.D., is "a sort of halfway house for those who style themselves as intellectuals but still want to be in business"—again, shades of women's traditional academic and intellectual involvement whereby, as in college, they test themselves *against* the system. In fact, a number of women consultants we spoke with had either been teachers or felt their jobs were a form of glorified teaching. "When I first came to New York, I thought, 'Oh, I'll have a career instead of teaching,'" reminisces Connie Steensma, founder and president of Accel Communications, an executive communications training business. "I started teaching at Marymount Manhattan. I love teaching. It's such a female thing, but I love it. At the same time, I started coaching executives on speaking and presentation skills on the side. And I said, 'My god, I'm good at this and there's money in it.' I landed a corporate contract at CBS at two thousand dollars, and within six months I was making six figures as a consultant."

Consulting also addresses the low boredom thresholds that

are a common complaint among women. Because of their need for growth and intellectual challenge, women embrace the seemingly endless variety of new clients and projects that spin through the doors of a consulting firm. Hillary speaks for many women: "Consulting provides great opportunity for variety. I've decided I'd like to work on a project basis. That's my thing. I like setting things up, problem solving, getting good people in and training them. And then I want to go on to something else. That is the best MO for me. And you couldn't do that in a corporation, even if you were on the fastest track imaginable." Amanda, a thirty-three-year-old financial consultant, left a marketing job at a *Fortune* 100 chemical and textile corporation. She says of consulting, "It is constantly new, and that makes it fresh."

Another advantage to consulting that particularly attracts women is the heightened opportunity to interact personally, to gain the sense of family and connectedness women often seek in their jobs. This results from the fact that most consulting firms are often much homier down-in-the-valley places than corporation green giants are. Pam, who left a *Fortune* 100 corporation to join a smaller executive compensation firm, notes: "I met the head of the firm and liked him and the other people, and he liked me and offered me a job that night, and I started that Monday. It was small. It has always stayed around eleven consultants, twenty people. It *felt* good." As consultants, women express personally their concern for helping others. And that makes them feel more successful, not subordinate, as they would be in a corporate job. Lois Appleby, vice president at Merrill Lynch, Pierce, Fenner & Smith, and one of its top women financial consultants, credits her success with the fact that "I have always looked upon my business as helping people, not selling business. That is what I enjoy more than anything. I see my job primarily as identifying needs—and then figuring out how to fill them."

In addition, the Myth of Individual Recognition might be valid in consulting since a woman can claim credit for the expertise and counsel she's able to offer on a wide variety of problems without being dependent on the good graces and gold stars of one specific organization. Consulting is one area where women gain expertise and where that expertise really pays off. Consulting marries women's unique need for growth with their search for public validation and recognition. Pam enthusiastically describes the benefits of her consulting job: "It's neat being a consultant and knowing the answer to a question because you ran the numbers on it. But it is even neater when you know it even if you haven't seen the numbers—you just *know* that it is the right thing. You have the expertise. You have judgment from cumulative experience. And I just love having the opportunity to exercise my better judgment." What's more, depending on the size and nature of the consulting firm, women might also avoid the plots and political intrigues often rampant in the larger corporate palaces. (As noted in early chapters, however, some of the large consulting firms might have the same drawbacks as largest corporations when it comes to politics.) As Pam adds: "I like it because it is entrepreneurial, it is challenging. I can have a lot of responsibility. But I progress against myself, not other people. I don't compete against other people."

The structure of a consulting firm is usually less hierarchical and entrenched than that of a large corporation. Says one public relations consultant: "Certain kinds of companies are run more as peer group organizations, like public relations firms, architectural firms, law firms, general professional service firms. It is very hard to manage them as a hierarchy, and they tend to be run so that the most junior member can work as a colleague with the most senior member. Everybody is as good as anybody else because anybody could come up with the right idea. Success for one person doesn't mean someone else's failure. One person's win doesn't mean someone else has lost. We can all win or lose simultaneously." According to Robin, who has worked at a Big Eight accounting firm and at one of the world's largest corporations, "There is much more opportunity for women at the accounting firm than in a corporation. People are more willing to accept women advancing in the professions than in business. You have the exact same qualifications as anybody else, and nobody can say you aren't as good as anyone else." Donna, who worked for a Big Eight accounting firm while she was pregnant, confirms the idea that women do encounter less direct discrimination if they keep up with the best of the boys. "I never ran into anyone who assumed because you were pregnant you didn't have a brain. I still got the same kind of work. So it worked out fine. I don't really think I encountered any chauvinism," she recalls. "But sometimes I think that is a factor of how you present yourself and what you have to say. I think if you said, 'I can't do that because I am pregnant' or 'I have to leave early today because I am a little tired,' you might encounter a different reaction."

Perhaps most advantageous for women, consulting offers third party status to express opinions freely and be listened to in a way that is "safe" for male corporate managers. While a woman doesn't threaten a male client's ultimate power in his own company, she can still support and guide him. Meanwhile, she, at least, gets recognition within her own organization for doing a good job for her client. "At the corporation, we used to joke with each other about 'Ours not to reason why, ours but to do or die,' whenever some foolish project was handed down from top management," another consultant, who had previously worked at a large national energy corporation, recalls. "All along the way, the middle managers who were afraid to speak out had given the project their blessing and we were stuck doing it—even if we knew it wasn't the shrewd choice. But as a consultant, I *can* tell clients when I think they are making a mistake. I figure that's why they hired me. They may not take my advice, but at least I have the opportunity to express my honest opinion." Or as Anne Wexler, former assistant to the president for public liaison in the Carter White House and now co-head, with Nancy Reynolds, of a Washington consulting firm, says: "A lot of our clients are men who work for major corporations. They respect what we do because we do something they aren't familiar with, or they feel they need help with. I have found as a consultant, that as you speak up and establish yourself as a contributor on whatever issue it is, then you are taken more seriously." Consultants are in fact often specifically hired to be the expert witness who comes forth and tells the truth. As consultants, women can freely express their moral voice and be rewarded rather than maligned for it. Paradoxically, the voice nobody wants to hear in the corporate wilderness becomes a highly paid oracle on the outside—a gratifying aspect of consulting that is not lost on women. "We will tell people when we start out on a project, 'You are the client, but we view the ultimate constituency we have to satisfy as the shareowner.' And we feel that we are answerable to the board of directors," Pam proclaims with pride. "And I really like my firm because we have always taken the high road. We have turned down jobs we don't think are right for us."

The final advantage of consulting is its flexibility. Since your resources are basically all in your head, you *can* take them with you. "If I wanted to take two years and go to Tahiti to write the Great American Novel, I might drop out of the work world for a while—for a couple of years, but not forever," remarks Amanda, a corporate marketing executive turned financial consultant. "But I am in a situation where I can come back. And I couldn't do that in a corporation."

On the other hand, people who work at some of the most prestigious and demanding management consulting jobs could be called the Ishmaels of business, always moving from one client port to the next. This constant travel, plus the long hours, is why Robin went the opposite direction and left a Big Eight accounting firm to go to a corporation. "It was mostly the lifestyle," she reflects. "There was a tremendous demand for overtime." Moreover, the individual nature of the assignments and the requirement to travel can discourage a sense of belonging to the larger whole, the sharing and exchange of information on a broad basis that the corporation at its best can offer. In the words of Marian, who is an associate at one of New York's top management consulting firms: "This is a place that attracts loners. There was a joke here for a while that if you played team sports or had belonged to a fraternity or sorority you wouldn't be hired here. It's not a friendly place."

Interestingly, some men regard a consulting position as less influential than a corporate one. When asked why he thought women weren't more powerful in business, Ted, an assistant treasurer at one of the nation's largest financial institutions, responds. "They subordinate themselves to clients. In a service organization, you give studies to the client and there is no telling once you drop it off with the client what will happen. You have no control over the implementation."

Still, most women consultants interviewed recommended it over their corporate experience and are glad they made the switch. When asked if she would ever go back to the corporation, Pam replies without hesitation: "No. Corporations call me all the time. I feel my little situation is so closely related to my values and my enjoyment. I can influence that world. I can have a big influence on the firm. I like that. It is hard to find a place as fairly set up."

Part-Time Persephones

It's a sign of the times; a megatrend that's on a roll. Like Persephone of Greek mythology, who spent half her time with her husband Hades and the other half with her mother Demeter, many women who eat the pomegranate of male-oriented business don't want to sacrifice that world for the more personal, "female" bonds of hearth and home—and vice versa. Which is why the professional part-time work force is gaining strong momentum—having expanded some 50 percent between 1972 and 1982. According to the Bureau of Labor, about 2.3 million people worked part time in managerial and professional specialty occupations in the first half of 1984, and the majority, 71 percent, were women.[20] A select group of large corporations such as Control Data, Illinois Bell, and numerous banks including First National Bank of Chicago and Ameri-Trust in Cleveland, as well as smaller, more innovative companies like Guest Quarters, the all-suite hotel group, have offered this option to women.[21]

Companies are considering part-time jobs to be good business in response to a number of fundamental shifts in industry and the economy. Helen Axel, program director of the Work and Family Information Center at the Conference Board, an independent business research organization based in New York, calls these shifts "the four D's": decentralization, diversification, deregulation, and downsizing to smaller, leaner staffs.[22] The appeal to the company is the ability to run, and compensate for, assignments on a project basis and to avoid paying fringe benefits. Some more progressive corporations, such as Equitable Life, have also developed part-time options because of a fundamental policy toward encouraging equal opportunity and the desire to accommodate women who make a strong contribution but who can't, for personal reasons, work full time. Says former chairman Coy Eklund: "We have a high level female executive who worked with us for a period of years on a part time basis when she had certain obligations at home that really impaired her ability to be here. We accommodated that because she was particularly valuable and we wanted to retain her."

Women join this part-time work force in order to stay competitive in their industry while they take time out for other endeavors. A survey found that 77 percent of 4,900 women changed to part-time work because of motherhood.[23] Donna, who has four children and has become a part-time accountant, acknowledged: "Working, for me, is like a hobby now. By the time I pay taxes and pay the housekeeper, I don't make any money. I work just to keep myself marketable and to fill my day." But more and more women are finding part-time work an attractive option, especially if they have children. Marcie, who works three days a week as a research director at a Madison Avenue ad agency, finds part-time work the perfect solution: "It allows me time to enjoy life with the baby. If you are home or on a park bench, you have time to explore ideas, because you're meeting other women whom you respect intellectually—and you do start talking as you don't at work. You're also talking about the same baby-related issues your mother did and you laugh, but you like it because you know it's temporary. It's part of this time in your life to care about Pampers and cleaner toilet bowls."

Ruth, a forty-one-year-old vice president at a major New York City bank, was an early recipient of the benefits of part-time work. "I arranged early in my pregnancy to work full-time from my home two days a week for the first two years, and then go to the office on a part-time schedule. At that point, the people I talked with were very supportive," she recalls. "In 1973 and 1974 the bank was very sensitive to women's issues. If they got sued for not promoting women, they could also show some positive proposals. And pregnancy was a positive, enjoyable experience. I was promoted to a vice president after my maternity leave. I suspect that kind of progress and leave arrangement would be harder to get now." Despite Ruth's skepticism, part-time employment has become so common that younger women are in fact planning their careers around that option. Says Leslie, a twenty-four-year-old Big Eight accountant: "I need to do something that isn't full-time especially when the children are younger. I don't plan on staying at the accounting firm all my life. I want to put in two more years and then start a financial planning firm for individuals, something I can do on a part-time basis."

Yet most major corporations do not offer part-time work, finding the mechanics of setting up a realistic and equitable system of rewards and benefits too difficult. Moreover, most would also insist that key jobs—especially key line jobs—requiring on-site management can't be done part-time or through job sharing. As a result, it's usually women in consulting, service, or sales jobs who find this alternative most plausible. Says Ricki, a part-time advertising executive: "I was able to swing this arrangement only because my clients love me and the agency knows I perform a valuable service for them." Pam, an executive compensation consultant, plans to follow the lead of another woman in her office who worked three days a week—two in the office and one at home. "What makes it work is the economics of the consulting field," she explained. "I am my own economic entity. I could be looked at as a profit center. Our pay system is set up so it is unlikely I wouldn't at least be in a break-even situation."

For the woman who can swing it, part-time work affords other advantages besides staying home with the kids. Banker Ruth has even started a pottery business on the side. She finds it provides a balance between different aspects of herself, offering a more personal, intimate channel for expressing her creativity. "The store represents the personal side of me. It's small, easy to understand. There's a simplicity to it, unlike the bureaucracy of the bank." Part-time positions also allow women to explore nonprofit opportunities. "I find myself doing a lot of volunteer work," says Marcie. "I'd rather do that than come back full-time—which is scary." And she touched on the idea that part-time can offer women a way to save face in a society that still forces them to feel inadequate without a job. "Anybody you run into these days immediately asks, 'And what do you do?' at cocktail parties. And there are all these bright, talented women who are incredibly defensive about being home even for a while. You notice them being belligerent or defiant about planning to return to work. You'd think it was only the men who ask, but it's other women, too. You notice women saying, 'Well, I used to be a lawyer'—phrasing things in the past tense. And they are not hypocritical, insecure women. But they're struggling for an acceptable answer."

On the other hand, a number of women have not taken the part-time option—because they believe part-time jobs won't be as stimulating as full-time work, and also because they are afraid they won't be taken seriously. "A lot of people at the bank wouldn't treat my career seriously because I'm not there full-time. They discount me because of that," claims Ruth. Notes Nancy S. Inui, president of Focus, a Washington State organization that concentrates on alternative work patterns: "Many employers feel that anyone who works less than forty hours a week is not committed to her job."[24] A *Business Week* article on part-timers reports: "Careers almost inevitably suffer when [women] curtail work schedules."[25] Thus, a number of women eschew the part-time alternative as being for lightweights only. "I would love to work three or four days a week, but I think very few people could have a good job and do that," Doris, a financial analyst at a leading oil equipment conglomerate contends. "I'm not a staffy type person," concurs Diana, a bank vice president who supervises a department of eighty people. "The kind of part-time jobs that are available are more 'gal Friday' oriented than otherwise." As former U.S. commerce secretary Juanita Kreps observes: "The technology increasingly allows women to work at home. But when I suggest to women that they may in their childbearing years want to spend some time at home and do either part-time work or do some work at home rather than at the office, they don't resonate well with the notion. Some seem to see that as a kind of cop-out."

Perhaps this fear of the stigma of copping out explains why some women make somewhat excessive demands on companies that are honestly trying to be flexible about part-time opportunities. Even more fundamental, however, it may be a woman's unconscious conflict between the early expectations of unlimited potential and a current frustration of having to compromise for family or other reasons at one of the key junctures in her career. This harks back to the brinksmanship negotiation of the Seeds of Disenchantment landing—a testing of the limits. Such a reaction, often manifesting itself as a highly conflicted hostility toward the boundaries of company flexibility, understandably throws most male managers off balance. Paul, a vice president at a hotel group, recounts: "Our office manager had a baby and wanted to work part-time. We said okay, but she told us, 'This is an insult, you cut my pay forty percent.' But we thought, 'Gee, we made up a job for you on no notice. You get paid for working at home.' She was just incensed, and I was flabbergasted because we thought we'd win points with her. But she had these expectations. She stayed with us, but said she was going to prove that there were jobs that paid more and had the same flexible hours. She hasn't found one yet."

Today, part-time work is still regarded as a somewhat socially unacceptable choice of life-style. Unfortunate, since part-time may not be for everybody, but it could be seriously considered not only by women but also by corporate decision-makers who could implement more innovative, flexible part-time systems for both men and women. As Rita, an insurance company vice president, says: "I think it is terrific. It is not a bad way to go, for men as well as women. The point is, if you are getting your job done and you produce—what difference does it make? If I can produce millions of dollars of business by working two hours a day, who cares?"

Mother Knows Best

You hear it more and more at lunch and in the ladies' room: "You know Susan, don't you? The vice president at Megalopocorp? Can you believe it, she just chucked her whole career to stay home with her new baby? And she says it's for good. God, she was the *last* person I thought would drop out." It's almost as if we've come full cycle. Betty Friedan sent women charging into the labor force, and now, less than twenty-five years later, some women are scurrying back to make the beds, shop for the groceries, eat peanut butter sandwiches with the children, and match the slipcover material—the chores that the generation before them struggled so hard to escape. In recent years, 55 percent of women who gave birth have chosen to stay home with the child for at least a year.[26] Right Associates principal Nancy Geffner analyzes it this way: "Not every woman can have a fabulous career *and* bring up two kids. Very few women have the energy for that. And if you're not getting the financial rewards from the company, or any other rewards, you start to ask yourself, 'What's in it for me?' And then you drop out."

In a society that often denigrates women who leave good jobs to stay home, a lot of otherwise organized corporate career women rather abashedly recount their decision to become full-time mothers as if it were the result of serendipity. Actually, this decision is usually the result of a collision between short corporate maternity leaves and a mother's desire to be with her baby longer than such leaves allow. The corporations become unwitting coconspirators in making temporary leaves permanent. Robin, thirty-three, who worked as a financial analyst at one of the country's largest corporations and whose husband provides a good example. After she became pregnant, she was undecided whether to return to work after the baby was born. "They put a very heavy pressure on me to declare early whether I intended to come back or not," Robin recalls. "And I had a lot of problems with that. My friends told me, 'You're crazy if you even imply you might not be coming back, even if you know for sure you aren't. You could be fired; you won't be promoted; you will be given garbage work for the next six months—all those things could happen.' So I did lots of soul searching and crying. And I really didn't know whether I would be coming back or not. I wanted to explore some possibilities, see if there was some flexibility about the length of time I could take to come back. I thought it was unlikely that I would come back in six weeks." She explored getting an extension to her leave only to find it would be an unacceptable "precedent." "They will give you political leaves if you are running for office or supporting a campaign, that kind of thing, but they don't want to set a precedent for maternity. And they didn't feel part-time was feasible. They did it once and it worked quite well. They did it again and it didn't. So they ceased doing it. At least, that is the legend. So I thought, well, I know I won't be ready in six weeks. Secondly, this is not like the greatest job in the world. I don't get a nice warm glow or a feeling that I am going someplace real fast in this company—and I'm not sure that it is worth making a lot of personal sacrifices for. So I decided to leave." Seeing their advancement thwarted regardless of whether they stay or go, women feel little incentive to stay.

Not that the decision is easy to make. "I did it obviously not without a lot of second thoughts and strange feelings about thinks like 'Is my mind going to turn to oatmeal?' I had a slight crisis the week before the six-week leave began. I started crying about something totally irrelevant and then realized it was really because I was about to close this door. Certainly I can get a job again. After I officially terminated, however, I knew it was never going to be as easy to look for a job." There's a postscript to Robin's story. "About three weeks after resigning, I received a call from an employee relations guru who wanted to tell me how sorry they were that I'd left and see if there was anything that could have been done to change the situation. I told him the immediate catalyst was the terrible leave policy, and we discussed the possibility of six months without pay or part-time work as a future alternative. Then I decided to let him have it about the underlying problems of women's lack of progress to important positions. He listened but seemed all too ready to excuse the company. He did sound frustrated that it had made little or no progress with women since about 1970." Several days later, a senior executive in the company called Robin to say that he'd be "delighted to see what might be available" for her whenever she was interested in returning. "It was a nice gesture," concludes Robin, "but why did they wait to give me positive feedback until I had quit?"

Ex-product manager Gayle left a large food company when her first child was born. She describes pressures similar to Robin's about deciding whether to stay or go: "I didn't know how it was going to work out. There was a time I really worried. I thought I maybe had chosen the wrong kind of career path because it was not an area where you could work flexibly. It is either one hundred percent or nothing; you can't work part-time." Looking back, however, she concedes, "Even when I was pregnant, I must have known deep down that I wanted to stay home. But I didn't let that surface to anyone else—and I probably didn't even let it surface to myself." Much like Robin, she backed into leaving. "I said to everyone, 'I don't know how this is going to change my life and what the demands will be like. So I am just going to wait and see and not make any decision.' And part of it was that I didn't want to think about those things. Especially in the first pregnancy, you feel very vulnerable. You think, is everything going to be all right? Will the baby be okay? So I didn't want to commit myself to anything in any way. I didn't want to build up in my mind that I would be home with the baby who would be fine and everything would be great—only to see it dashed if something catastrophic happened. I wanted to wait and see." Because of a complicated pregnancy, Gayle had to leave her job two months before she planned, and that's when the real decision was reached: "Being away from the office those couple of months and just doing nothing gave me a break. I didn't go right from a meeting to having a baby that night. I really had time to get away, disassociate, and get in touch with myself again in a different way. And I think that helped make everything a lot clearer. Because right after you have a baby your life is so upside down. You are crazy, your hormones are running around, everything is different. You are tired. Everything is happening at once. It isn't necessarily the clearest thinking time. So I had those couple of months to ease into it." Gayle is like many women who find the time away from the office gives them a new perspective and a chance to reassess their goals and their corporate commitment. "I don't think I made the decision based on any long-term thinking as much as on gut instinct," Gayle concludes. "I had been working very intensely, a lot of long hours right before that. So I went from that to suddenly having to be totally off my feet for a couple of months and doing nothing. So I don't think I was thinking as much as just easing down and getting in touch with my true feelings."

Because of the current peer and societal pressure to have a career, women often don't realize the full extent of their ambivalence toward their jobs until confronted with the alternative of their own baby. This acceptable cop-out from the corporate world allows women to let dependency needs surface. Carla, for example, describing her disappointment that she couldn't conceive, admits: "I was doubly frustrated. I thought it would be a great transition period—an excuse to quit that wouldn't disappoint me. I wouldn't be totally dependent on my husband—not me alone. The only way I could have justified that dependency was with a child."

At the same time, pregnancy frees women from frustrating career paths, as they realize after success and betrayal the limits of opportunity within the corporation as well as the limits of corporate rewards to truly satisfy them. In fact, a number of women contend babies can be used as an excuse to drop out for those who, consciously or unconsciously, always wanted to leave anyway. "I think we're also going to see a lot of women saying they believe that staying home is best for the kids, and then choosing to opt out of a career. And that excuse will be justification for them to say good-bye to the corporate world. After all, who's going to say, 'I wasn't wildly successful in the corporate world'? Who's going to admit that?" asks Cynthia, a top financial officer at a *Fortune* 100 corporation, who raised her daughter while working full-time. Others suggest that women finally hit a suitably prestigious corporate level but know they will only plateau from there. Adds a vice president of human resources at a leading New York City bank, "It's interesting that the women who drop out to have children do so after they get the vice president title. They are all competing to make it at the same time. A lot of women have babies and still stay on the job. If a woman drops out to have a baby, it is because she *wants* to drop out." An executive recruiter agrees: "I think you can put all that into the category of people who just say, 'Hey, why am I doing this?' Somebody who has decided, 'I am sick of all this crap and I am going to do something else. I am going to have a baby' or do volunteer work or whatever." Faye, a financial executive at a leading midwest company, sums up the sentiments of many: "To a certain extent, I think some of us who are leaving didn't have that wonderful a job situation in the first place. The baby was a convenient reason to get out."

For many women, motherhood forces an unanticipated yet critical rendezvous with their own evolving expectations of themselves—an enforced checkpoint at which they discover the driving values of their twenties and thirties of the Proving Up landing have disappeared. These values are replaced by the Seeds of Disenchantment and, finally, by betrayal, a void only motherhood fills. The media have called this sudden contagion "baby fever," accusing women of choosing babies less for love and more for a socially acceptable retreat from the knocks and grind of the business world.[27] Some women fear this accusation will hurt their progress in corporations, confirming the worst stereotype: that women have never really been in it for the long haul anyway. Faye, single and childless, voices a concern of many of her peers: "The problem I am seeing now is that women get to be thirty-three-years-old and they just drop out to have a family. And corporations have put ten years of training and expense into these women. And some of them are saying 'I just love changing diapers, and I have never had more fun than playing with these Fisher Price toys.' And if corporations get burned enough, they may close the door." As this trend accelerates, will corporations revert to the more stereotyped thinking about babies, and careers—thus creating their own self-fulfilling prophecies? Or will some of the more enlightened corporations try to adopt more flexible policies and procedures to give women greater incentive to stay? Operating in the corporate response, consciously or unconsciously, is the basic male ambivalence about working mothers, which we discussed in "Uneasy Peace." Robin recounts: "When everyone said, 'Well, what are you going to do now?' and I said, 'I am resigning today,' almost all of the men almost furtively said, 'I applaud your decision; I think it is a great thing.'" One wonders whether this male approval reflected wholehearted support, or rather envy, relief from competition, or comfort that their most fundamental sexist beliefs —including "motherhood is the most noble profession for women"—were confirmed. In contrast, Robin's female colleagues responded differently. "The only women who seemed to think it was a great idea were those in their fifties who had raised a family and dropped out and then came back to work. Other women were very unenthusiastic. I don't know whether most of the women thought I had betrayed them because I was doing what all men accuse women of doing or whether they were envious."

Yet almost every woman interviewed who has made the decision to stay home with her children is much happier and more fulfilled than when she left the corporation. "I can't imagine sitting at my desk doing what I was doing and caring about it now. I can't imagine that I would care that the company got its quarterly figures out on time. I think the things that were not ultimately fulfilling on the job would seem even less crucial now. Because there would be something I am weighing it against," Robin assesses it. For many women, the limits of corporate rewards are never more obvious than when stacked up against the rewards of motherhood. Asked if she missed her job, Meredith, a former broadcasting manager confesses, "No, I can't say that I do. But then, I am not the typical housewife either. I travel a lot with my husband on business trips. And I could never have the job I did and have the baby. But it is so exciting to watch a child grow and when you see that you think, God, here I was running around New York and all that seemed so crucial at the time. But this is what's really important, what makes life beautiful. Watching her pick up Cheerios for the first time with her two fingers and not with her fist. I can honestly say I have never enjoyed a job nearly as much as I enjoy the time I spend with my daughter." Contends Dr. Willard Gaylin, "If you analyze most work done in the workplace, you'll see that the character of that work is often not as interesting as the raising of children. And if parenting paid as much in salary and prestige in our society, you'd see a lot more people doing it."

For many women who have lived through the various career landings and experienced success and betrayal, motherhood becomes the real accomplishment, giving them the personal connection, growth, irreplaceability, and recognition they have longed for. "I never had any remorse about the decision. Which makes me wonder if maybe I wasn't as committed as I thought," Gayle muses. "Maybe I really didn't have that necessary drive or commitment. Anyway, I am just thrilled with my life; I'm surprised how thrilled I am. It was never my dream to just raise kids. But it just went so well for me. I like it so much. It has been really rewarding." The biggest rewards? "You are really dealing with people. It is a very human thing. Not that my job was just cold and all numbers. But it really wasn't a rewarding experience from a people standpoint. It could be rewarding because a product got out or a project you were working on took off—say you got an ad campaign going. Rewarding in those respects. But not on some deeper level that affects you or your life in some ways that counted." The ties that bind, the affiliations women seek, that's what motherhood continues to provide. Gayle also cites the much greater degree of flexibility motherhood offered: "I like the fact it is so unstructured whereas my life before had been so structured. And I felt very frustrated by the working world. At least five days a week you had to be someplace, wearing a certain kind of clothing, motivated in a certain way. School was not that way at all, and I loved being a student—being responsible for myself and my own time. And being home is a lot like that. I don't owe anyone anything by the close of business on a given day." Radcliffe College's Margaret Touborg makes a similar point: "The best kept secret about motherhood is not that it's boring, but that it provides a lot of time to just think. To read. To be creative. I don't want to minimize the responsibility. But a mother is as creative, as flexible as she wants to be. And what's more, you don't even need a wardrobe to do it! For three years, I walked around in my comfortable bathrobe and I loved it. It gives you a freedom, a paradoxically confining freedom. You can sit on the stairs and write plays with a four-year old."

There are some negatives, of course—uppermost on the list being the lack of adult contact and stimulation. "Before, if someone else didn't read the *New York Times* or the *Wall Street Journal* every day I would think, God, this person is just not informed. And now, thank heaven for the *New York Times* Week in Review," Meredith laughs. Another disadvantage is the loss of the second paycheck. Bureau of Labor statistics show that the average two-paycheck family earned $28,000 in 1981; the average income when only the husband worked came to only $20,500.[28] A third problem is the potential difficulties of reentry if money once again becomes a factor. A fourth is that many women who are used to supporting themselves find it hard to maintain their self-esteem after leaving their jobs. "When I stopped working, the men who were my husband's business associates treated me like an air-head," laments Ava, who dropped out of a successful career at a publishing company. "It was terribly degrading." She has since returned to work. A Harvard/Stanford alumni poll found almost half of the people surveyed thought women who stay at home with families are less respected than those who work.[29]

In spite of its drawbacks, however, most of the women we interviewed enjoy motherhood and don't seem compelled to run right back to the corporate race in order to save face. Robin, among others, has decided to use the time out for some serious evaluation of her life goals, to finally sit still and listen to her Authentic Voice: "I decided I wouldn't get neurotic about it until six months had gone by, and then I would see how I feel. But the feeling that I am not all that interested in business makes me think I need to do some serious reevaluation and perhaps consider things that I have always wanted to do. For example, I have always wanted to be a veterinarian, do things in health care or with children. Obviously I am not going back to school, but I may decide to do some financial and accounting work in a nonprofit institution, in the health-care field as opposed to business. And if after six months, I decide I still don't want to go back to work for a while, I may start seeking some volunteer activities." The pause that motherhood provides can precipitate the post-corporate woman into totally new ventures. Sandra Kurtzig, established her own highly successful computer company, Ask Computer Systems, as a new business after she left her job as a software marketing representative at General Electric to have her first child.

Meanwhile, working women are becoming less critical of those who drop out to raise children—and are no longer blaming them for jeopardizing the progress of all women within the corporation. Ricki, for example, says: "I sympathize with women who decide after they get a maternity leave they don't want to come back. And I think it's wrong for other women to put pressure on them to come back, to be role models." While Harvard economist David Bloom predicts that as many as 40 percent of college-educated career women born in the 1960s will be childless,[30] ironically, many of their predecessors in the corporation appear to be having second thoughts about their own decision to postpone or forgo children. Adrienne Hall, a California advertising executive and mother of four, asserts, "More women approaching forty are talking about having a child, realizing it's one of the few things in their lives that they can control."[31] Whether greater control is just a new myth disenchanted corporate women are now embracing remains to be seen. But, as Radcliffe's Margaret Touborg concludes: "As for those women who will bypass motherhood in favor of a career, there are a lot of good genes going to waste. My generation learned in having babies that a job is no substitute for parenting because it is not just a dependent but an *interdependent* relationship. Can all women say that about the nature of their careers? Will that realization cause a backlash of women who opt to stay home and raise children instead of working? And would it be a bad thing if it did?"

Career Switchers and Other Corporate Dropouts

"I'm not real happy with my job—a lack of motivation and interest in the work. I'm burned out. I think I need a complete change of subject," writes a thirty-four-old woman banker from Chicago. "It's confusing to feel like this after so long and such an investment—but that's life." One of the most highly regarded women in her field, she reflects a trend among successful women managers to make complete career switches at a time when many would judge them most successful.

Sally, who dropped out of a highly paid, prestigious job at a media corporation to study developmental psychology, is another case in point. Why did she do it? "I had been saying for years that there has to be a better way to earn a living than being beaten up and yelled at and pushed around and playing political games, spending most of the time stroking people and not enough time on myself," she explains. "I felt I was working sixteen-hour days, and for all I was putting into it, I wasn't getting much in return." The Myth of the Meritocracy. "All of us were basically being used. After all, anybody in the place could be replaced in twenty minutes." The Myth of Irreplaceability. "And while I am ambitious, I saw I was just not determined enough to do what I knew I had to do to get through the structure." Myths of Growth and Unlimited Potential. "Plus I was simply burning out. I drank too much, I ate too much." A trim Sally explains she's lost twenty pounds since she quit. "And it was easy!" After dropping out, she listened to her Authentic Voice—discarded, like so many other women's, back in college during the rule change. "I started thinking back on all my childhood dreams, all the things I really enjoyed. I realized I like intense, involving things. I realized what I was looking for in a job was a lot of personal involvement." Myth of the Family. "I also wanted flexibility and more control over my life," she adds. "And I also looked at what I was good at: intellectual stimulation, and reading people. I was always the office consultant for people when I was at work. And I had minored in psychology in college." She has applied to several graduate schools. Interestingly, the economics major that led her to the corporate world has been replaced by the once "secondary" interest.

Thus far, she has few misgivings about her decision, except for a few Living-on-the-Edge doubts. "I am periodically terrified of going back to school. I am afraid my brain is like a car that's been left out in the front yard for eight years and has started to rust out. Kick-starting it has been difficult." She grins. "And I do have some second thoughts. I am investing a lot of time and money. I will now have to work part-time. And there is the danger that once I get into school, I won't like it. On the other hand, what I learn will be a useful thing in business if I decide to go back. Little phrases keep going through my head, like 'You can type ninety words a minute, so you won't starve.'" She pauses and then notes, "You know, it's funny, you really don't need that much money when you don't work, I've found. You don't get pissed off in the middle of the day and spend five hundred dollars on a suit to try to feel better about things."

Valerie, forty, has also dropped out of a corporate job—but unlike the other women profiled, she had no small-business venture, baby, part-time or consulting job, or graduate school possibility lined up when she left. "I wanted some time of my own," she says of her decision to quit. "I had worked for twenty years, and that was enough." She has busied herself renovating a brownstone and serving on the boards of two charitable organizations, one of which approached her after she quit her job. "I just love it. I have never had any regrets. What is interesting is that all my friends are telling me how much younger I look," she smiles, mentioning she can now easily go to the gym three times a week.

But what about many women's feeling that by dropping out, they have somehow blown it, that they are now nobodies? Even Walter Wriston, former chairman of Citibank who retired recently after thirty-eight years with the company, has said, "When you retire from Citibank, you go from Who's Who to Who's that."[32] Such obscurity has been no problem for Valerie: "The only bad moment I ever had was when my husband and I went abroad and I had to fill out on a form what my occupation was. And I didn't know what to put down. I thought, 'I just *can't* put down housewife!' I think I put consultant instead." Valerie was the ombudsman for women's rights at a corporation during the late sixties and early seventies, and so she recognizes that fear of failure is a key issue for many women who have previously fought for women's rights but now are choosing to drop out: "It may be especially tough for women in their forties, the ones who got out of school in the mid-sixties in the forefront of the women's movement. We felt we had to push, we had to do something. We are the ones who filed the class action suits. And now, twenty years later, we say, 'Okay, we did it. Now we are just going to relax.' Are we feeling more guilt than somebody twenty years from now would? I don't know. And should we feel guilty that we didn't get any further?"

A friend of hers who also dropped out of an executive position has suggested that she and Valerie go into business together to advise women who drop out and feel uncomfortable and doubtful about it. While Valerie questions the commercial appeal of such a venture, she does see some validity in the basic concept: "I think there does need to be some kind of support network for these women who drop out and are thinking, 'Well, I want to enjoy myself now, but am I wrong in doing it?' It may be important for these women to talk to other women who don't feel guilty and to find out how they cope. That's what the whole consciousness-raising phenomenon was about years ago, and maybe these women need that again." Ironically, "networking" may be just as important for women who choose to *leave* the system as it is for those trying to advance within it.

Sally agrees that fighting the "failure" stigma was the greatest difficulty in her decision. "Working women have this idea that they're supposed to do all this and look wonderful and have a high-status job and fit into all those categories," she says. "And getting rid of that idea is very hard. You wonder, 'If I don't go the corporate route, what will my status be?' You want to do what the media tell you you should be doing. And the fact that you have to get up at five in the morning every day in order to do it is something that they just leave out." But she, like Valerie, has learned to make her own peace with her self-doubts going for the substance of her life over the style.

"When I was trying to decide what to do next, it really came down to how I honestly wanted to spend my days," she concludes. Valerie has an even more sanguine attitude—for men as well as women. "In a sense it is a shame if everyone drops out of the work force, because what else have we fought for? But I think if men had the option, or at least had to be as introspective and think through choices as women have all along, I think men might also choose to drop out. After all, it wouldn't hurt men to rethink the priority work holds in their lives."

313

The Pivot Point is a critical landing for women and requires hard thought and evaluation. A frantic rush into another career, interviews show, can often be no better than the frenzied yet rather directionless scurry of activity of the Wooed and Won landing. Since some of the dissatisfaction women have experienced in the corporate environment derives from their own misguided notions and unrealistic expectations, the least successful Pivot Point experience can result when a woman simply escapes from corporate life, neglecting to thoroughly analyze her options in terms of how they relate to her own individual needs and goals. She runs the risk of being misled by the very false hopes, misguided myths, and unrealistic expectations with which she entered the corporate world a decade or so earlier. Career counselor Nella Barkley, who has seen plenty of unsuccessful Pivot Point examples, tells of a woman client who immediately accepted a position as a president of a college "without having examined how she'd fit in, where she wanted to go from there, and what she wanted to accomplish with the remainder of her career years. She was repeating the same pattern that had gotten her into trouble the first time," she recalls. "And I said, 'Hey, wait a second, you can do irrevocable harm by removing yourself from the corporate arena.'" Barkley recommends that women take time to mull and muse over their situation after the burn-out most experience at the Success and Betrayal landing. "I told her, 'You need a rest and some space before you decide what you're going to do next.' She was totally exhausted and trying to make a decision in that state. . . . You could see the exhaustion written all over her." Clear thinking is definitely what's needed at the Pivot Point. Otherwise women may discover they are still disenchanted—in fact, they may be *more* disenchanted with the alternative they have chosen than they were with corporate life. Then there are all the women who drop out to raise children but eventually find they can't afford to stay home forever. Cynthia, a senior financial officer who raised her daughter—now fourteen—while working full-time remarks: "In all probability, even the women M.B.A.'s who drop out now to have kids will still need to come back into the system regardless of whether it changes later on." And Nancy Geffner suggests that among most women today the perception of dropping out is "different than the reality. In reality, you don't drop out of the system for twenty-five years, just for a couple of years till the kids are in nursery school."

What are the prospects for such women—or for those who have left the corporation to pursue other interests—if they decide to return to the corporate life? Opinions are mixed. Executive recruiter Gary Knisely of Johnson, Smith and Knisely warns: "I'd like to talk to women who leave and three years later decide to come back. I think, 'Good luck.' It will be very difficult to get back in. People distrust you, particularly those in the middle to upper middle level. They want somebody who is dedicated to the organization, not somebody who decided to leave several years ago. I am a fairly liberal person, but I would have a hard time with that." Women who pursue professional activities or part-time work stand a better shot at reentry; obviously those who take a lengthy time out for personal or family-related reasons will have a much harder time getting back in the game. Unfortunately, despite the arrival of the new flexible arrangements, most corporate tracks are still too rigid and specific to encourage extensive time out. "No question dropping out is going to hurt women in business," Grant, an executive vice president asserts. "That's why entrepreneurial firms are better for women. Law firms are easier, too. Those kind of places, absolutely. But if a woman wants to become president of GE, taking three or four years off is tough." Recruiter Ann Barry of Handy Associates agrees: "It's going to be *very* hard for women to reenter management if they drop out to raise children. Right now there's just a flood of people behind you out there. If you have a business ambition to get ahead—and that's not necessarily a good thing—then you have to face up to the fact that people who are successful haven't left for long."

Many people point to the obsolescence of one's skills base as the major barrier to reentry. Dr. Willard Gaylin contends: "Reentry is easier in blue-collar jobs. You can always give someone time off the assembly line. But if my daughter were to drop out of her law firm for five years to start a family, she probably couldn't reenter because the issues would have outpaced her." Malcolm Forbes, Jr., however, thinks differently: "If you have background in a profession, you can get back in even after a three-year hiatus. Sure, there's a lot of catching up to do, you miss a lot of nuance. But within three to four months you can be back up to speed." William Greenough, retired chairman of Teachers Insurance and Annuity Association, agrees: "We have a half-dozen officers who left us and came back. Each of them lost from two to six years of seniority. Yet they came back and did well. The job in coming back has to do with what's in your skills inventory." Jeane Kirkpatrick, while not a corporate executive, is an example of a woman who left the work world to raise her family and managed to come back strong. "Professional and intellectual high gear are not always the same thing. All the reading and writing I did in those years at home were very important for me," she says. "I learned a lot. I never dropped out intellectually."[33] And Leonard Pfeiffer of Korn/Ferry International made the point that the criterion for many corporations in a search is increasingly the long-term availability of the prospect. And sometimes, he said, "women are *more* attractive if they have gotten their family out of the way and there's less question of long-term availability."

If women do decide to leave corporate life at the Pivot Point, they will have to learn to be shrewd and practice strategic planning on their own behalf. "They'll have to be innovative. They'll have to find new and creative ways to reenter," predicts Rhoda Green, a New York-based psychological consultant to management. Some will have to chart five- and ten-year plans for the first time. Nella Barkley also thinks women will have to take an aggressive approach if they want to reenter: "After a careful search of the companies in her field, a woman should go in and propose her next job. We don't believe in résumés at our company. You go in and find your next job the way all business deals are made. You pursue interests through people you know, but you don't ask people to get you a job. You learn enough to know what you want to be, and you propose your job to management." Nancy Geffner agrees that women should cultivate and play on their strengths. "We found out that if the women who took off three to five years did something to improve themselves—and it doesn't have to be affiliated with a company, even taking a course to improve your French or working on a degree—that's responsible." Rather than acting too worried and defensive about dropping out, women should present their choice positively to management. "They sound apologetic about being home scrubbing baby bottles. Instead, they should make it clear that they *wanted* to be home with their children—something most employers would see as a positive comment."

While women who choose to cut corporate ties run some clear risks, they may ultimately manage their own careers much more creatively. Most older women now making these choices did not have the variety of options at entry level. Younger women do, and the smart ones are considering many of them before making a corporate commitment. While a conventional corporate career path may be the appropriate road for many women to travel, the Authentic Voice urges other women to broader possibilities, more personally fulfilling side tracks. Nancy Reynolds, who left a vice presidency at Bendix to start her own consulting firm, advises: "Women are often not courageous and flexible about their own careers. They have to be willing to take risks." Antoinette Ford, president of Overseas Development Corporation, agrees, "To women who want to switch careers, I'd say that we cannot afford to be afraid."[34] And statistics suggest that 70 to 80 percent of the people who attempt a career switch are successful and stick with the change.[35] The Pivot Point at its best proves that many women can create options for themselves and finally shrug off the passivity of earlier landings, taking command and control of their lives by moving outside the corporation.

For others, creating options remains a choice within the corporate context—one that yields different but equally ripe fruits.

CHAPTER 10
RECONCILABLE DIFFERENCES

*The only way male corporate culture
is going to shift is if men and
women can work synergistically.
It will integrate only if we hang
in long enough.*

Joanne Black
Senior vice president
MasterCard International

Most management women at the Reconcilable Differences landing could again be compared to Lewis Carroll's Alice in Wonderland, who, when the caterpillar asked her who she was, responded: "I—I hardly know, sir, just at present—at least I know who I *was* when I got up this morning, but I think I must have been changed several times since then." Similarly, female executives knew who they were when they started life in the corporate world, but they have changed since then as, one by one, the myths have been proved to be unsound. But who are they now? It's particularly hard to tell since, as the previous chapters have shown, executive women have been operating in—and trying to fit into—a world of contradictory, often counterproductive rules.

For all the women who, after experiencing success and betrayal, grab their life preservers and head for other shores, there are many more women who don't. "I think other women see the game, hate it, have fantasies of leaving . . . but all they are are fantasies," a thirty-five-year-old executive remarks. These management women who remain believe they can, or must, reconcile their differences with the corporation. Most stay in the same management positions for a variety of reasons, including a desire for financial and other forms of security, the simple burn-out and fatigue that can result in inertia, indecisiveness and indifference, the reluctance to prove up all over again, and a hard-edged evaluation of their alternatives. They reach the decision that the corporation, for all its faults, is still the best option, and this realization leads to a renewed burst of energy and commitment to the corporation. In doing so, these women accept the fact that ultimate success as measured by conventional male-dominated corporate standards will very likely elude them. And they recognize that complete fulfillment from the job alone will probably escape them. In short, they discover the limits of success. But, having done so, everything is not business as usual. Our interviews reveal that women who stay are grappling with different and sometimes even thornier issues than they were at earlier landings. Accepting that decision to stay constitutes their Pivot Point within the corporation, forcing adjustments in their views and values, their activities and goals—changes that can be as dramatic as those made by their counterparts who choose to pack their briefcases.

At the same time, readjusting doesn't mean simply forcing themselves to conform to the male corporate culture. As more women have experienced the various landings, they are now, for the first time, beginning to contemplate how they might change the *rules*—not *themselves*—in order to happily inhabit the corporate Wonderland. Many women find they are replacing the generalized male "rules" with personal concerns. When women first start working in the earlier landings of their career life cycles, they are usually unaware of how they will weary from chasing the golden orb of success as epitomized in the predominant male ideal or reward. When they learn instead that such rewards come only at the expense of personal, affiliative bonds, finally experiencing Success and Betrayal, the toad prince of a personal life returns to claim his due. This more personal approach, as Gilligan and others have contended, is at the heart of most women's relation to life.[1] "We are all very good at covering up our mainspring," one female writer asserted, "but I have yet to meet the woman who did not know in her heart that love is her main concern and that the secret of her success in any field was her personal love in the background."[2] She defines "love" as each woman's personal connection to what is most authentically important to her, and contends that even a career woman who seems to focus on work has some personal relationship as a stimulus— be it a lover or children whom she needs to earn for—although this connection may not always be obvious.

This concern for personal connections is also why women must resolve the inconsistencies, the myths of meritocracy, irreplaceability, and growth before they can get on with life inside the corporation. It is also why the moral voice is so strong. And it is why women more than men find it so much more difficult to balance a family and a personal life with work. Unlike many men, few women can disregard the tug of personal bonds, no matter how professionally successful they are. Not to mention the obvious fact that women must still struggle to integrate a broader range of responsibilities and interests—such as family and other "caretaking responsibilities"—earlier and to a much greater extent than most men. In part because of biology and family demands, in part because of psychology and inherent disposition, more women than men seem torn by the breadth of possibilities, rather than pinpointing single-minded goals, less willing to focus on work to the exclusion of love, money to the exclusion of growth and a variety of experiences, power to the exclusion of fulfillment. More than men, women strive at a relatively early point in their careers to achieve what Frank Lloyd Wright described as the difficult unity of inclusivity rather than the easy unity of exclusivity.[3] Substitute the word "success" for "unity"—a sense of integrity and wholeness might not be a bad definition for success—and you can see a fundamental difference between how the two sexes often approach their careers and their lives.

Women recognize at the Success and Betrayal landing how radically their concept of success differs from the male concept. Thus, reconciling differences requires much more than balancing competing corporate and personal demands. An even more critical battle is being waged—and the territory at stake is at the very center of a woman's being. The fundamental issue for those who choose to remain within the corporate culture is this: How do they obtain and maintain positions of power in a male-dominated system without compromising their sense of feminine values? It is this conflict, between women's basic nature and the predominantly male values of the world of work, that women are now experiencing. It is a conflict that women who remain in the corporation after the Success and Betrayal landing must resolve for themselves as well as for future generations of women in business.

How are the women who remain in the corporation trying to resolve this conflict? What are the specific issues they are grappling with, issues distinct from those at earlier landings? Who are the happiest with their choices? Who feel the most successful? Why did they stay within the corporation? What are the benefits? What are the costs? What are the compromises? Are the differences truly reconcilable?

Gold-Plated Handcuffs

Women who earn six-figure salaries—or those in the high five figures—must face the startling truth that even if they wanted to drop out they could not afford to do so without a drastic downshift in their life-style. The economic dependency that women begin to sense at the Seeds of Disenchantment landing becomes the *raison d'être* for many who remain within the corporation. One forty-year-old single commodities executive talks at length of the frustration and disillusionment a number of older women managers feel: "I've finally come to the realization that there's a huge gap between me and the $300,000-a-year male executive, not just physically, but materially. I'll never be him, or be his wife, with her spending power via him. All I am, all I'll ever be, is a middle-class drone. And I look at all those young women out there who have sacrificed their personal lives to be 'happy' working long hours at $40,000 a year, and I laugh at them—at their gullibility—until I realize I've only moved one notch above them, from a middle-class drone to an upper-middle-class drone. But I've achieved no permanent financial security, no real independence or freedom." Whereas women early on balanced their relatively slender financial income with other, psychic, forms of remuneration, and then at later landings blamed their negotiating skills for not yielding bountiful financial rewards, more senior executive women often realize that their life-style requires them to continue working even if they would rather drop out. They have enough money to live well, quite well, but not enough for the ultimate freedom, the ultimate security: the choice to stay at the corporation or walk away.

Thus, for every woman who has left to start her own designer boutique, there are just as many or more who are listing under the weight of bulging briefcases because of their biweekly paycheck. With single women heading nearly one in three households, compared to one in seven in 1950,[4] many women are more than ever dependent on their jobs, dependent in ways they never intended to be. For unlike men, who from their earliest years are taught to be bread-winners and to save for those rainy days and drizzly months, women—especially older single women brought up before the rules were scrambled —remain subconsciously waiting to be swept away to Park Avenue or Beverly Hills. Ironically, just when many women finally become financially successful and secure enough to relax and breathe a short sigh of relief, they suddenly realize that they may have to support themselves, if not happily, at least, ever after. It's something men have always reckoned with. For women it is a shocking realization. The romantic notions of economic independence grow old under the incessant pressure of economic reality.

A number of senior women in corporations are held captive by the golden handcuffs that have always bound men. But because they expected a very different reward, they have usually not planned adequately for their financial future. Meanwhile, women have avoided the riskier but often shrewder financial investments their male counterparts have made because they are expected to be the primary supporters of their families. Says one twenty-eight-year-old male bank executive: "Men are conditioned to assume risk to a point, before they take on family responsibility. But society does not accept women assuming risk." Especially financial risk. As we mentioned before, women work for income; men for wealth. At the same time, women have insisted on making their own way, to never be dependent on a man. Trained to believe they, unlike men, have the freedom to leave any time, women are struck full force with the realization that the spiral of expectations and new economic necessities have conspired to keep them in the corporate world long after the will to work has failed. Despite the conflict with other myths, with their own moral judgments, and with their own disenchantment, they are, for all the bravado about independence, trapped economically at the very moment they have been liberated psychologically from their dependence on the corporate family. As a result, they find themselves like Chris, forty years old and single: "There's tremendous pressure on me because of my age. I've just realized in the past year that I have fewer years ahead of me than I have behind me. I haven't saved any money. I haven't operated financially like a man." She continues, "There is a financial requirement that's kept families together over the centuries and that now will keep women in the work force. I can't drop out until I find something else." Says one thirty-eight-year-old marketing consultant, a separated mother of two on a three-day-a-week arrangement with her corporation: "I took a battery of tests that suggested what I'd be best at, and it would be doing something entrepreneurial. But I have a financial responsibility that doesn't allow me the flexibility to obtain it. I'm afraid to attempt it. And imagine the time it would take. It would be a full-time job just beating the bushes for new business." She feels trapped by her own economic necessities and, like other corporate pioneers hitting early middle age, disappointed in the exaggerated promises of the women's movement that first urged her into corporate life in the late sixties.

Married as well as single women feel the pressure. Diana, a successful vice president at one of New York's top banks and married to a partner in a large law firm, contends: "It really would be tough to quit. I really like my paycheck. Money is important to me—not the actual dollar figure as much as the life-style and what it says about me. I am a strong contributor, and I am self-confident. I can buy something I want to buy and I don't think about it. It would never occur to me to ask my husband's permission. I would just die. I think it would be the scariest feeling—but all of our mothers had to do that." The same fear and avoidance of dependency that drove many women into corporations is now keeping them there.

But the burden weighs heaviest, obviously, on single women. "I see women coming in close to having a nervous breakdown because there's suddenly a new economic responsibility that's been handed to women, and few people have come along to share the burden with them," counselor Nella

Barkley comments. "I think all the way around it was easier in an earlier era when women had an extended family to rely on." A case in point is Elaine, a senior executive at a cosmetic company: "I just bought a co-op and I'm right back where I started financially. I never, ever dreamed I'd have to worry about a place to live. That was part of the era I grew up in, and now I'm back there, and every other paycheck goes to the mortgage and maintenance, and I'm forty-six years old, a vice president, making over $100,000 a year. I think women are getting back to marrying for money and security. And I'm talking about *independent* women."

Whether such a return to conventional relationships occurs among older women as well as younger women just graduating from school remains to be seen. It may be difficult since, as one woman writer notes, "If you want to attract men . . . it no longer helps to be a bimbo with time on your hands. Upscale young men seem to go for the kind of woman who plays with a full deck of credit cards."[5] Ask Maggie, a general counsel married to a director at a major West Coast company, why she hasn't dropped out to take care of her daughter and she exclaims: "I *begged* my husband to let me do that! But he wouldn't let me. He said we needed the money." In a career study conducted in 1982, Diana Zuckerman notes that on a 100-point scale, freshmen and senior women ranked career as a higher priority than did men (84 percent versus 79 percent).[6] "It's definitely accepted among the men I go out with that a wife will work all the way through," says one young systems analyst, "and eighty to ninety percent of the men I work with are married to working wives." In fact, for all their insistence that every *other* husband's wife's job is "optional," we found that most men thought a job was "necessary" for *their* wives. "All the twenty-three-year-old men today want their wives to have an opportunity for self-expression," says Radcliffe's Margaret Touborg. "They want her to have her own salary and for both of them to be involved in raising the children. But this new male dependency on the female paycheck may force more changes than we've foreseen."

These women are the new breadwinners. The simple reality is that a significantly large number of corporate women shoulder a large part of, if not the entire, burden for supporting a household—a burden the corporation has yet to come to terms with. For it is obvious that the corporation still evaluates women's economic needs as discretionary. As women begin to appreciate the dilemma, the gap between their own financial reality and the delicate fantasy land in which the corporation has placed them, the pressure mounts. "The responsibilities that men gave up have come increasingly to rest with us," suggests sociologist Barbara Ehrenreich discussing this phenomenon in depth. "For women as a group, the future holds terrifying insecurity: We are increasingly dependent on our own resources, but in a society and economy that never intended to admit us as independent persons, much less as breadwinners for others."[7] The new breadwinners are here, and corporate America is sleeping through their arrival. Men and corporations perceive them as lucky women with disposable incomes, while such women remain unable to wean themselves away from the insidious effects of the Living-on-the-Edge Myth. Women can neither overcome the stereotype nor let the corporation know the full degree of their economic dependence. Saddled with the public's ironically inaccurate public perception of them, they are in too precarious a position to deal with it.

A surprising number of corporate women spoke of having to shoulder greater financial responsibility than their spouses or lovers. "I'm now involved with somebody, and I know I'm better in business than he is," says one English businesswoman, an expert in human resource training. "And now that he's starting his own business, I'm consciously talking less and less about my own competence in business. In fact, I try to hide it." She ruefully notes the irony of her comment, coming as it does from the granddaughter of a suffragette and a feminist herself. Trish, a manager at a media company remarks: "A friend of mine was here visiting, and we talked until six in the morning. We agreed we had both observed a very interesting phenomenon among women who were doing well in business and in two-career families. The women are going great guns, but the husbands start to slack off. We both thought that women were starting to assume *all* the responsibility while the husbands were puttering around. It harks back to the fifties, except now *we* are the husbands and *they* are the wives."

Other new breadwinners discover the psychic costs are high. "I'm the breadwinner," says a publishing executive. "My husband stays home. My friends ask, 'Why do you let him get away with it?' These are the same women who express outrage at any man who would dare say he lets his wife work." While she is generally satisfied and resents the implications that in the new economic model women must pay a price for role reversal, she admits, "When it's six A.M., and I'm hurrying to get ready for work . . . and he asks me to leave him money because he won't be able to get to the bank before his golf date and still have time to pick up his custom-made fishing rod—yes, I'm resentful. I feel, just for a moment, the rage of generations of men: 'Is this all he can think about, new ways to spend *my* money?' "[8] Some breadwinners see their incomes as opening windows of opportunity for husbands who formerly toiled for the corporation and have since dropped out. The altruistic principle of being able to free a loved one from the indignities of corporate life is a strong motivator for many women, who regard their new corporate earning power as a means of reconciling the deeply felt, uniquely female calling to nurture. "My husband was in book publishing for five or six years," says a bank vice president and mother of two sons, "but he was really interested in working on his photography, in pursuing an artistic career. In 1969, after we'd spent a year living on my salary, he quit. We banked his salary that last year so he'd be totally free to work."

Humorist Art Buchwald calls these new corporate spouses "latchkey husbands" and imagines a conversation with one of them, called Bronfman, who wears the key to his apartment around his neck so he won't lose it, and whose working wife leaves him milk and cookies in the icebox. "She's given me permission to bring a male friend home providing we don't mess up the house,"[9] explains Bronfman. Buchwald's satire notwithstanding, male perception has yet to catch up with female economic reality.

Raised with one set of rules, conflicted by advice from mothers—"Marry well, but never depend on a man, and get a job just in case"—women find themselves in a love-hate relationship with the new fiduciary responsibility. What is the allure of the new breadwinner role to so many corporate women? "I didn't want to quit," says one corporate research director who is the key breadwinner. "The knowledge that I could take care of myself, has made it easier for me to stay working. And what would the alternative have been? I didn't mind supporting Elliot. But I let him know it was *my* security, *my* house, *my* job, *my* prestige—not ours. If the situation had been reversed, I could never let him support me. But it was easy for me to do the supporting. You see, I knew after seeing my mother that there was no way I was ever going to become beholden to somebody. But the reverse situation put me in control. I call the shots."

Calling the shots, being in the driver's seat at home as well as at work, has become important to corporate women. But many have gotten a lot more control than they bargained for. Because whatever their marital status, a severe case of performance exhaustion often attacks women who have lasted through the Success and Betrayal cycle, and along with exhaustion, they experience panic and frustration—the feeling that they may be stuck, that there is no escape, that they can't just click their heels three times and be back home in cozy Kansas where their financial obligations will be taken care of. Not that men haven't always experienced the same burn-out, loss of purpose, exhaustion, ennui, and apathy. Men assert that they, too, would love to drop out but, unlike women, don't have the option. But, these days, many women don't really have the option either. And women, by dint of having to fight their way into business and then fight it out in business, understandably grow weary faster. Yet the women who are bound to the corporation with gold-plated handcuffs have no recourse but to remain where they are. "You get in a rut. Especially if you are running this race, it's very hard to drop out," sighs Chris, a forty-one-year-old telecommunications executive. Perhaps Lily Tomlin put it best: "The trouble with the rat race is that even if you win, you're still a rat."

Grow Old along with Me?

This rat race is most taxing and wearisome for older, more senior corporate women who must also contend with fears and anxieties of growing old in the corporation—perhaps not always gracefully. Corporate women have only just begun to grapple with this problem, since it is the first time large numbers of women in their forties and fifties are management executives. And, as we have noted, they can be locked into unhappy relationships with the corporation much as they previously clung to unhappy marriages—living out year after frustrated year afraid to trade the "security" for a chance for greater self-satisfaction. "I worry about being thirty-eight years old and being stuck at my company, about being the oldest woman in middle management. You look around and there are fewer and fewer older women here, except for the one or two with the green eye shades who have been here forever," says Jodie, voicing the concerns of a number of older executive women. Granted, men have always had to cope with thwarted ambitions while another clock—not the biological one but the corporate gold watch—ticks louder and louder. But women worry more about crow's feet and wrinkled brows than men do. "Even though it sounds old-fashioned now, women saw their powers originate in the capacity to attract men, and they still unconsciously think their power is tied to beauty," observes Dr. Willard Gaylin of Columbia University. "They've also been conditioned to be sensitive to the fact that menopause is an ending. So whereas many men feel they are just gaining their power at forty, most women feel they are losing theirs." The concerns of older workers may be a key reason why cosmetic "surgery for success in competitive, image-corporate America is on the rise. . . . Women say, 'In the past,

I just had to compete with men. Now, I am competing with a whole new generation of aggressive, youthful women,' " says John M. Goin, president of the Plastic Surgeons Society.[10]

At the same time, the psychological burdens that aging women bear also differ from those of men. While men who are arrested in their corporate progress—either through lack of promotion, early retirement, letting go, or being fired—might feel as if they have failed in their *expected* role, women are often experiencing the opposite phenomenon. Long singled out for her achievements, a woman can find herself suddenly shoved aside to make room for younger competitors. Meanwhile, although one fifty-six-year-old bank vice president insisted that her salt-and-pepper hair made everyone in middle management feel comfortable, more women would probably agree with Joanne Black: "When you get good, men don't want you around. They liked you better ten years younger and three levels lower." She adds: "Younger women are less threatening and more appealing to men, and it's a little bit scary. We're in for a very rude shock." In a rich analysis of women and aging, Barbara Walker notes that an older woman can threaten men because they view her, usually unconsciously, as a scolding mother figure.[11] Older, more experienced women are perceived as being able—and willing—to tell it like it is.

The outlook for older employees isn't cheerful for either sex. The unemployment rate for all executives over forty, male and female, is around 14 percent—virtually double the national average.[12] In addition, with tighter economic conditions, most corporations are not developing new options for the swelling population of older workers. Instead, they are taking the opposite route and cutting staffs—so much so that the Labor Department's most recent figures show the trend toward retirement accelerating. Why? Because the corporation views older workers as "obsolete," according to Alan Pifer, president emeritus of the Carnegie Corporation.[13] But again, such age discrimination may be worse for women because, as a thirty-nine-year-old male energy company executive noted, older female executive "empty nesters"—whose children have grown, who have earned M.B.A.'s—are ready to give their all to the corporations. Ironically, just when women strengthen their commitment to the corporation, the corporation often starts backing off. One female communications corporation vice president relates a case in point: "I got a résumé from a woman in her late forties who clearly had had good experience in our profession. I sent it to my boss with a note asking him if he knew any possibilities for her—and I meant in the industry in general, not just our company. And he sent it right back, having scribbled across the top of my note: 'She's *my* age. Good grief!' "

Most experts believe that greater acceptance of aging for both men and women will be reinforced by the graying of the baby boomers; by the year 2000, those over-fifty-years-old will account for the biggest bulge in the population growth.[14] Ann Barry of Handy Associates remarks: "The marketplace will continue to be the baby boomers, but the imagery will change. And maybe the youth syndrome will have less impact than before on management." Perhaps in not too many years, corporate golden girls will be prized as never before. We may yet get to the point where women over forty-five—other than starlets, media celebrities, and politicians such as Joan Collins, Barbara Walters, and Margaret Thatcher—will not be penalized for aging.

In the meantime, however, executive women are acknowledging that growing old gracefully in the corporation could certainly take more than just a jar of collagen and a few weeks at the Golden Door, that it may require hard choices, a personal commitment, and in some cases a facelift in the attitude of the male powers that be.

The Corporate Amazon

Coping with financial security and aging is only part of senior management women's portfolio of pressures. Ask anybody: What's the single biggest career conundrum ambitious women must face? And you'll probably get this answer: Balancing a career with a family and children. Countless books and articles have been written about the psychic and physical wear and tear that results from the schizophrenia most "superwomen" experience—an identity crisis Clark Kent and Lana Lang certainly never had to resolve. An evaluation of women's progress in the corporate world cannot ignore what happens to the women who *don't* drop out to have babies, either because they choose not to or because they can't afford to. Nor can it ignore the management mothers who return after dropping out for several years, still having to satisfy two very different masters. Surveys tell us that almost 18 million mothers, 55 percent of them with children under eighteen, work outside the home, almost two-fifths of them full-time.[15] Another poll indicates that working women are taking little time for maternity leave—a majority (69 percent) stayed on the job almost the entire nine months of pregnancy, and nearly a third returned to work in six weeks.[16]

In addition to the simple polls and statistics, there are studies that point to a far more complicated and difficult situation. A Rand study, for instance, reveals a decline in average earnings and job prestige after working women have their first child.[17] Juanita Kreps speaks not only from the expertise gained while sitting on the boards of directors of ten major companies such as Chrysler and Kodak, but from the first-hand experience of having put her own career on hold while she raised her children: "Women who have the same background as their male colleagues expect to progress at the same pace. That is really where the most serious problems arise. Such a pace will be very difficult until there are changes in our traditional views of work and home responsibilities." Even though many women quietly return to work, they must experience more interruptions in their career than men do. Census data show that 54 percent of working women have dropped out of the work force at least once for family-related reasons, including maternity leave, whereas only 1 percent of men have.[18] A study of Stanford University's business school 1974 class reveals that 12 percent of the women had been out of the work force for at least a year versus only 1 percent of the men.[19]

Even after women are back on the job, everyone generally agrees that despite supportive husbands, most women—as ever—have to shoulder the burden of the family, including great aunts and third cousins as well as children. Fred MacMurray's role in "My Three Sons" remains largely limited to single fathers and widowers. Decrying the celebration of the "new father," Jane Pauley says, "Garbage. . . . They get the rewards of being Daddy. . . . They get a second income from the wife who is working. . . . They don't feel the guilt. . . . They have it great."[20] Statistics show almost 60 percent of working wives do more than ten hours of housework a week while barely more than 20 percent of working men do.[21] It is often the husband who puts pressure on his wife to back off from her career ambitions and take time out to have a family. "The corporate women I know who are in their thirties are really having a tough time. Some of them just started new careers, getting out of business school in their late twenties and early thirties, and often, the husband wants a family," Heidi, a single twenty-five-year-old product manager says. "I had a friend at work whose husband really wanted her to have a baby. And she had a dream about having a baby and putting it in the filing cabinet at work and not being able to find it. She had put it under B for baby, but she couldn't find it and was hysterical."

And even if a woman *doesn't* take time off, she can be penalized by the attitude that still pervades many corporate corridors and conference rooms that a woman who chooses to have a family isn't really serious about her career. Is pregnancy becoming an unavoidable "misstep" for most women who choose to remain within the corporation, taking them off the fast track no matter how well they perform and prolonging the separate-timetable dilemma—in fact, often making it permanent? Is the system totally unforgiving? Rachel, a midwest corporate counsel, describes what she observes in her company: "A lot of the women in my department are having children and coming back, and God, they waited till they were thirty-three, but suddenly, having a baby places significant limits on their careers in the corporation. Let alone the burden it obviously places on mothers." Ricki, who raised her children while working as a manager at a leading beauty products company, poses a question: "Think about this. Does anybody on a job interview with a man ask him how long he intends to stay on the job? And yet every employer is worried about how long a woman will stay before she quits to have a kid. As if a man wouldn't leave for another job." Employers appear most concerned about the second child, perceiving, in the words of one executive woman, "one child is an indulgence, the second child is a second career." Again, it can all be in the eye of the male beholder. Diana, vice president of a New York bank, who just had her first child, retorted on behalf of many women when her boss asked if she planned to have a second child: "Walter, if I leave this place, it is going to be for *dollars* not *diapers!* Give me a break."

Much talk centers around whether a woman sacrifices her career or her family, yet it is the woman herself who bears the brunt of the sacrifice. Rhoda, who at forty is a manager of a media conglomerate and the mother of two teenagers, tells a story she had heard about a woman in a small southern town who had simply come apart from the pressure of living up to the superwoman image: "And one day this woman just kind of showed up on my friend's doorstep in New York City and said, 'I walked out on my husband and children. I just couldn't stand it. I had to get away.' And my friend was flabbergasted because this was supposed to be her stable, sensible friend." It is sad and frightening that women are still casualties to unrealistic societal pressures and the relentless competition of the workplace despite the growing recognition that the corporate Amazon is only a media-manufactured myth. Women are even forming clubs for "reformed" superwomen. To get women off the superwoman "treadmill," an outfit called Superwoman Anonymous celebrates the "joys of doing nothing for a full five minutes."[22]

Adding to the pressures on management mothers are female peers. They resent as discrimination any version of a bill of rights for women caught in the double bind of management and motherhood. At the same time, not all management women *want* the corporation to be involved in what they view as a highly personal choice—that of providing day care and other benefits for working mothers. Similarly, a number of the women as well as the men interviewed insist that—excluding political campaigns and other "acceptable" leaves of absence—very few men could take a year or two off without losing a good deal of momentum. In fact, some of the critics are other women who accuse management mothers of having children as a status symbol and an excuse to dodge responsibility. And it's true that certain women who have ridden the roller coaster of success and betrayal in the corporation may seek from a child what they now realize they won't get from a corporate career. Maggie, the woman who has raised a child and worked full time since she was twenty, warns women who entertain such a notion: "Just don't approach balancing a child and a career with starry-eyed romance. Because a lot of women I talk to today are now saying 'Oh, I want to be fulfilled,' and they think a child will do it." This reminds one of Pablo Picasso's cheap shot: "The best prescription for a discontented female is to have a child."

Here is the reality of management motherhood according to Maggie: "You always feel guilty. For instance, if you are at work and the kid is sick, you feel guilty. If you are home and the kid is sick, you feel guilty." She mentions an episode of "Cagney and Lacey" in which a mother told her son he had to stay home from school because he had a fever, and the son retorted that when his mother was *working* she would have *made* him go to school even if he had a temperature of 103 degrees. "And you do terrible things like that, you do," Maggie confesses. "You know your kid should stay home, but it just isn't convenient." She is now considering dropping out or working part-time—if her management will accept the notion. "I tried to hint around to my boss about that because we've sold the project my job was dependent on. And if I got pregnant again, I would really want to do it. But he keeps saying, 'No, you would be bored.' And it's very hard for me to say, 'No, I'll take it. I know the job would be boring and simple, but I am not an ambitious person.' You just can't say that to your boss." Maggie comes to an interesting conclusion: "I think he projected on to me all the traditional male values. I think that shows I have truly been successful, because he assumed I was just like him and all the other men, that I had the same ambitions."

As we have said before, many women—perhaps most of them—do *not* have the same goals as men—especially when it comes to juggling a job and a family. In fact, the happiest women we interviewed were often those women in management who continued to work but who had throttled back on their ambitions, slowing their pace to take time to enjoy their families. Diana observes that people meant a lot more to her than power since her son's birth. "I don't need to get a sense of power from the job anymore, but I get a sense of really doing something meaningful with other people. And that comes from having a baby, I think. The people aspect of the business is much more important to me than it ever was. I will not give up being with my son just for a power kick. I will give it up if I can balance it with good people interaction elsewhere."

Rhoda, the manager with two teenage children, provides a good case study of some of the trade-offs a management mother has to make—and the satisfactions she can have. After working on Wall Street, Rhoda dropped out to have her children but returned to work several years later. She hadn't planned on returning to work, but like a number of women, she eventually felt frustrated by too many soiled diapers and too few stimulating discussions. As a result of her previous experience, she landed a good job—albeit at a worldwide consulting firm rather than a corporation—with very little difficulty. "I've had younger women come to me and ask me, 'How do you do it—have children and the job?' In a way, I think I was very lucky. Because at the time I was about to go back to work, a good job dropped in my lap. . . . I don't think dropping out held me back." Not that reentry was entirely easy. "I was able to go through the day-to-day operations and fulfill the responsibilities. But I didn't have a sense for a long time that I was doing a good job, and my confidence level was quite low. Within time, though, I got positive feedback and my clients were very satisfied." She has since returned to a corporate environment and is now a manager at a *Forbes* 500 media conglomerate. Moreover, she says she is not on the fast track, but she feels personally satisfied with the balance she's managed to achieve. "Women are fearful that if they take three or four years off to have children they will never catch up, but I think my experience flies in the face of that—unless you are on a direct corporate track and plan to spend a long time in a particular company. In that case, you might take time out and come back later to find that your job is no longer there or some younger person has it. So maybe my experience isn't comparable. I did end up with responsible jobs, though. I won't say I have had it all, because that would be overstating it. But I have had a family and a satisfactory career." What about the children? "When I first went back to work, my younger child was about four years old, and I was worried about leaving her in child care. After several weeks, when time came for a conference, her teacher said to me: 'Your daughter is so proud of you, that you have a job.' And I could have hugged her, because I was feeling so guilty that I had walked out on my four-year-old child. But the whole thing was fine with her. She felt good about it."

Rhoda's experience, like that of many of the women we interviewed, supports the fundamental hope this particular landing holds out for women: that they can reconcile lowered expectations with reality—without letting go of the dream entirely—and achieve an inner peace more fulfilling than mere "success." As much of a compromise as working motherhood may be for women, the majority view the other alternative as much less acceptable. Elaine, a single, forty-four-year-old cosmetics company manager, poses the fundamental question: "I think there will be a lot of angry women when they discover they've passed up the biological time clock—and for what?"

How do executive women who remain at the corporation respond to the ambivalence that follows success and betrayal? How do they reconcile the sacrifices to their family, their friends and lovers, their outside interests without opting out like their peers did at the Pivot Point? What happens when the vitalizing myths must be cast aside, the expectations brutally lowered? What happens when the corporate mystique wears off?

At this point, a few women become even more driven, as if to suppress any fears and doubts about the path they have chosen. These women discard any balance between career and personal life; regardless of the circumstances, the inner compass loses its grounding and points only due north. These are the women media celebrate and the polls and surveys cite as working harder and putting job ahead of family and everything else. These are the women who invest so much time and energy in succeeding on male terms that they can deny virtually all of their feminine nature. Such women are thoughtlessly labeled as the corporate cranks, the boardroom bitches, the red queens who sentence before the verdict, the ones who give all other women a bad name. In reality, most corporate survivors defy such negative stereotypes.

Some women have "checked out," content to simply plug along for the biweekly pay check. They approach the job with a lifeless sense of duty. These more passive women are the quiet cubicled drones who are "leading lives of quiet desperation." A cosmetics executive tells us, "I have some friends who got passed over for promotion and realized that's it. They settled in five or six years ago and are making $50,000 and they don't want to be bothered anymore." But most management women have far too much vitality to settle for less than they want—the vitality that powered them to success. The select number of women who have managed to reach upper middle management ranks often have had an unusual amount of ambition and skills. Which is why many of those who do not drop out of corporate life are making their own separate peace with the corporation, accepting that their definition of success differs from the one adhered to by men and the media.

Women we interviewed in all industries told us that they are becoming their own boss now, echoing the "I've Gotta Be Me" sentiment. "I've broken those bonds of fidelity to an organization. What I have is fidelity to *me*. This is my job and I demand a lot," says Sunny, a senior vice president of a West Coast financial institution. And in interview after interview women told us they were fed up with channeling all their time and energy into playing the corporate game by conventional male rules.

One way women learn to cope and compromise, but at the same time assert themselves, is to simply cut back. Take the comments of Doris, a thirty-five-year-old married senior financial analyst at an international oil service equipment corporation: "I have readjusted my work schedule. When I was younger I put a lot of time in. Now I rarely work weekends. I take long lunch hours. I work hard when I work, but I am not killing myself. I am not working twelve hour days. People think I am doing an excellent job, I got a great review, and working twenty-five hours a day isn't going to get me any further. I am comfortable; I like what I am doing. I have other jobs I want to move on to. I have a nice life-style." As the glittering prizes start to lose their gleam, women begin to take their own small rewards instead of waiting for the corporation to bestow less meaningful ones.

In fact, an unheralded movement toward domesticity seems to be well under way. "People don't want to travel with an attaché case on long business trips anymore. More women are starting to think they want to put up jams or something in a sweet little domestic household," says one management woman. "As I began living on my own, I fell into a more domestic life-style with more domestic ambitions, despite myself," admits one post-feminist, ambushed by this new, mutant side of herself, "and all of a sudden it became an important goal to have a work life that could accommodate

341

a comfortable personal life-style." Says thirty-eight-year-old Marian, up for partnership this year in one of the country's most notoriously competitive consulting firms: "It's not a desire for domesticity in the sense that I don't want to be home cooking dinner every night. But I discovered I like to entertain on the weekends. I like to spend all day Saturday cooking. I don't like all the extra efforts I have to make here," she said, gesturing around the sweep of thick ring binders, sheaves of reports, and newspapers that obliterated her desktop and encroached on the credenza. "There are a lot of things I'd like to have now that I certainly didn't think of even five years ago."

Marilyn French outlines a century-old phenomenon—the attraction of a home-created life, which French refers to as "the cult of domesticity." She writes, "Today, the cult of domesticity is considered ludicrous; at the same time, many of its elements are being reevaluated . . . because in a world given over to power, struggle, and abstraction, it offers sensuous satisfaction, nutritive values, and relief."[23] To French's observation we would add ours that besides sensuous satisfaction it is tangible accomplishment, authorship, individual expression, and creativity—four all-too-rare characteristics in the corporate sector—that reward women who turn to domesticity as a relief from the increasing demands and unfulfilling values of the corporate rat race. In the words of Trish, the forty-year-old media company manager, "I've changed. At this point, I want to live a comfortable life, make money, have a life-style that at least gives me time to enjoy myself." Recently married, she added: "I like to go home. I like to talk to my husband, plant bulbs in the backyard, cook, all kinds of things. And sometimes just do nothing. And I really do have that clear separation now between work and what is not work." She also has discovered where true identity and self-esteem lie—inside herself.

Yet this doesn't mean women are any less ambitious than men, as so many chastise themselves for not living up to the models of success they think they see all around them. They are a far cry from Charlie McCarthy's philosophy: "Hard work never killed anybody, but why take a chance?" What such women often can't recognize is that they are just as demanding of themselves as they were before, and what they call a lack of ambition is often a broadening of their concerns and efforts over a much wider, more varied range of activities than annually declared management objectives or corporate strategic goals. We've already discussed how many women redirect their energies to their children and their families— and if balancing both isn't "ambitious," nothing is. Meanwhile, other women—like Adrian, the insurance company vice president—pursue their outside interests in cultural or volunteer activities. "I don't feel so committed to this organization that being a star has a lot of meaning to me. I'm more interested in having other opportunities outside open to me. I work to live; I don't live to work. I go to a lot of cultural productions. I take a lot of advantage of New York." The women we interviewed had varied outside interests: Brenda served on a state government advisory board; Monica was a board member of two arts groups and a community health organization; Melissa formed and directed a group of young professionals interested in foreign affairs; Hillary advised a political organization on fund raising; the list goes on and on. These ventures give women the sense of personal contribution a corporation job often cannot, at the same time fulfilling the continuing need for growth the job can no longer provide. Where in a corporation might some of these women get experience on a board of directors? Where in a corporation can a financial analyst develop the financial plan for the entire organization? Where in a corporation can a public relations officer also contribute significantly to a financial plan? Perhaps most important, such philanthropic endeavors provide a forum for each woman's moral voice, her need to serve others—a forum that the monetarily or transaction-oriented corporation cannot offer. And they feed women's new business expertise back into the system, giving new force to women's tradition of volunteerism and caring.

Having experienced the Success and Betrayal landing, management women are better able to step back from their jobs and see their own identity as separate and distinct. This inner-directed mentality is a pendulum swing from the Success and Betrayal landing. Denise, issues manager at a New York–based health care products company comments, "I would like to think I could chuck it all tomorrow and not miss it, but maybe I am fooling myself. But I think it is important to think that way often. In recent years, I've been telling myself that I am separate from my work, that I have an identity, value, interests, and meaning in my life outside of my job." Trish has made a similar reassessment: "I try to imagine if I were run over by a truck tomorrow and there would be some people at work who would miss me and would appreciate the things I had done well. But by and large, it would be no big deal. The people who are going to remember are the ones I spend time with; they are the ones who are going to care. And I will be damned if I am going to spend my whole life giving to an organization that two weeks later is going to say, 'Oh, yeah, I think I remember her. . . .' It is not that important anymore."

This distance and perspective give women the courage to speak out with their own moral voice when they truly are concerned about an issue. One professional woman puts it: "I've always been glad I had my CPA because I always wanted to live as if I could get a job other places—knowing that I am not dependent on any one corporation for my skills. I remember my father, a top executive, telling me he was always thankful he had his law degree because if he ever needed to he could tell them all to go to hell and go back and practice law in Illinois. I've always wanted to have that attitude, the sense that I can stand up for my beliefs and not be afraid of losing my job out of security." This sense of inner security, that one can "tell them all to go to hell," keeps women from wasting energy and emotion on small slights, yet gives them the strength of character, the tough, unyielding fiber, to go to the barricades for important issues.

It also gives the most senior women the confidence to struc-ture the job the way they'd like it to be—in terms of content rather than power or influence. Denise, for example, created her own job when a senior vice president asked her to write a description of a new position in a new business area—dealing with corporate issues involving outside constituencies—which she suggested he consider. She recalls: "I really worked on it. But I had this sort of what-the-hell attitude. I knew I could also be happy staying where I was. I did a good but rather feisty job on it. And he said, 'Do you want this job? This is it.'" Interestingly, what Denise created for herself was the role of the corporate moral voice: "My job is to say, 'Why are we doing this?' or 'Hey, no one has ever thought of that.' Everyone else in the corporation is so concentrated on defending his or her job rather than looking at it like an outsider. I have won some arguments with my boss." Having accepted she is unlikely to climb much higher on the corporate ladder, Denise has successfully stopped striving for male model positions with classic upward mobility in favor of a self-expressive, unconventional job she wouldn't have had either the expertise or the confidence to propose ten years earlier.

Leonard Pfeiffer, vice president of Korn/Ferry, thinks it is still easier for women to approach corporate ascent this way than men: "A woman can stay in corporate culture even if she's given up the brass ring more easily than a man can. If she really likes the money, the prestige, the travel, the mental stimulation, then even though she's topped out, even though she's accepted the fact that she won't become president, she can stay, and she has an excuse for settling in to a more relaxed ambition. But if a man acknowledges to his boss that he's happy where he is and he'd just as soon stop pushing, he's shot himself in the foot, because one of the strongest values in any corporate culture is upward mobility." But perhaps women's new approach will lessen the pressures on men as well, with the added benefit of improving relationships between the sexes.

Our interviews reveal that many women's new focus on personal relationships outside the office is not so much a comfort level as previous studies suggest.[24] Rather, it is an outgrowth of reaching a new landing of maturity and realism about corporate limits that enables women to lower their career expectations accordingly. Despite all the talk about the biological clock, women usually reach this level of realism because they have achieved some of the success they strove for, only to find it, in typical success and betrayal pattern, less fulfilling and less dependable, than she expected. At the same time, she has finally developed enough personal confidence so that she is no longer terrified of trusting and being somewhat dependent on a man.

Often women who did not or could not form relationships during the Proving Up landing are now able to revise their outlook and rearrange their priorities. Sandy, thirty-eight, a vice president of human resources, had a first marriage "where I didn't have someone at home who was supportive," but she describes her second marriage this way: "My husband comes home and sometimes he'll say, 'I have a situation at work you can help with.' What a terrific feeling! The sharing, the respect, the fact he seeks my professional opinion. And one of the interesting outcomes is that of the two of us, he is more balanced, and it's forced me to seek a better balance in my life between work and what's outside work." Other women who sacrificed relationships to corporate demands in previous landings experienced the same satisfactions. A number of them watched their first marriages founder under the drive to get ahead in business. Sunny, a thirty-eight-year-old general counsel at a West Coast financial concern, remembers her first marriage: "My husband wanted more of a home life. The lack of it made him unhappy—and made me unhappy. I felt I had this weight of guilt, like trying to fly with lead on my ankles." Today, she is involved with a lawyer who "has a voracious appetite for work." Jill, thirty-five, a director at a large appliance concern, has a similar tale of first marriage: "We were both right out of school, just getting going, and I was trying to get my M.B.A. at night, and we both worked so hard we suddenly became total strangers and lost communication. We were both suffering from tunnel vision." She's about to remarry and join her entrepreneur husband in launching a new business. In this landing, single women are also allowing themselves relationships they have never had before. "The past six years, I've been more open to relationships than I was in my twenties when I would never let relationships become too big a part of my life because of career and travel," admits Greta, a forty-year-old vice president of financial services. "Right now, I'm serious about a man who's sixty-five. He's a lawyer, so we don't compete. He's very strong and confident. The more successful I was, the more driven. It absolutely got in the way of my relationships when I was younger. But I've connected with this man in a lot of ways, and there are no hidden agendas."

The greater self-assurance and realistic acceptance that comes after experiencing the life cycle of landings also encourages women to acknowledge their relationship to other women. Once women understand the limitations of the corporate dynamic and reject the ethic of ruthless competition, they are able to support one another in ways they could not at the Proving Up and earlier career landings. By the time they reach the Reconcilable Differences landing, the most successful managerial women apply almost a "tough love" approach to junior women they are encouraging, truly trying to pass along the lessons *they* learned the hard way. "I have a lot of women working for me, and more than ever I'm a role model. I never felt like one at my previous company. And perhaps it's me—I'm confident now, self-assured," comments Jodie. "I think it's important for women to be honest with each other. I spend a lot of time with a woman who is competitively good and doesn't know it. She's going to work for men who want her to ease in by way of a field promotion, and I exploded in the meeting to decide about her promotion and said, 'She's head and shoulders above you guys.' They said, 'Well, Jessie herself said it would be a good idea to move her slowly.' And I said, 'Well, I'll unsay it.' Jessie ultimately decided to turn down that interim promotion, and I was so proud of her." Women like Jodie recognize they are doing no one any favors by trying to sabotage other women, that they are only augmenting a male culture that often unconsciously works against female bonds and disempowers all women. Moreover, women understand that the bonding and communication they desire often comes first and foremost with other members of their sex. Does a woman as successful as Boise Cascade senior vice president Alice Hennessey resent serving as a role model? "No, because I figure, look, I've got to pay my dues. I was very fortunate; I was there early in a company that was willing to give women responsibility when many others weren't. I think I have an obligation to pay that back. There aren't that many role models for women, and they do need them, and there are problems that are unique to women that they need to discuss with other women. And I know frankly how tough it was never to have that opportunity, because I really didn't. So it does take some time, but I really don't begrudge it."

A deputy managing director for an advertising agency in fact brings up the point that senior women gain as much from the younger women as the newcomers gain from them: "I'm not sure the people I mentor realize how important they are to me. People under you support you. They're the reason you come in to work." Such women, who won't let other women sell themselves short, are the true role models of today. On the other hand, more women, as they gain confidence as executives, are less rigid in their demands that *all* women have high-powered careers. As Roger L. Gould notes in *Transformations*, "As we demand higher levels of authority around us, we automatically become generative: we provide a model of a real person rather than a collection of roles. Our children and our juniors learn more about life from us."[25] Ironically, being a *real* person rather than a collection of roles makes women truly irreplaceable in ways no normal amount of striving toward being a model could achieve.

Reconcilable Differences

The happiest, most fulfilled women in corporations, "while not denying to themselves the male lessons of achievement that almost all of our literature and history can afford," are as Carolyn Heilbrun suggests, recognizing "the importance

of taking the examples to themselves as *women*, supporting
other women, identifying with them, and imagining the
achievement of women generally . . . without being coopted
as honorary members of a male club."[26] Now that they have
reached positions of some authority, successful women in
corporations have before them the seemingly simple yet
extraordinarily complex and arduous task of transforming the
lessons of male achievement patterns to fit their own new
models of success.

Most women who stay at the corporation are willing to
make the compromises those women who left at the Pivot
Point believe they cannot. Women who remain have come
to terms with how much power they want and how much
power they think they will ultimately get. They have learned
to stay motivated without making unacceptable sacrifices,
believing that change is possible to at least some extent
within the system. We found among the women we interviewed the most commonly cited benefits of sticking with a
corporate position—the Six P's. The first and least positive is
Peer Pressure. "If I didn't have a job now that was important
I would feel that I was lacking. I think it is very difficult to
be from my background and not be working, not have a job
that is important, not have a good job," Joyce, a manager at
a midwestern conglomerate, comments. The flip side of this
is Prestige—something that small businesses and consulting
firms often don't provide. Closely allied to Prestige is Pride.
In ways far more rewarding than those experienced at the
Proving Up landing, these management women have gained
confidence and a strong sense of personal achievement; they
know they are very good at what they do. "I'm in a much
better position here personally. I have a job I like and know
how to do, I have a comfortable amount of authority. I'm
proud of my position," comments Chris, a division director
at a telecommunications corporation. The fourth P is People.
"What I like most about my job is the interaction with
people," Molly, a bank vice president, says. Boise Cascade
senior vice president Alice Hennessey concurs: "I like being
with a lot of quality people, who have a tremendous range of

talents. I care very deeply about the people at Boise Cascade. There are so many of them that I really feel if I had a problem I could go to them and they would help me out—people at all levels of the company." Then there is also the sense of Participation, of involvement in important issues of the day. "I like dealing with topical issues, to open the paper and see things I am a part of. To be a participant in the issues of the day," comments Denise, head of issues management for a *Fortune* 100 pharmaceuticals concern. Insurance company vice president Rita says enthusiastically, "I don't think I will ever retire. I think I will continue working till my dying day. Work adds something. There is just too much to do. There is just so much fun in life. There is so much in this world that needs to be *done*."

Many of these same women have, however, refused to abandon their own individual, feminine standards within the corporation. But just how different are men and women in their approach to management? A majority of the men and women interviewed contend that there is no difference in male and female management styles, that one could never generalize. While this may reflect that the increasing numbers of women in business have had some impact on how business is conducted, as books on "participative management" and "intrapreneuring" and so on suggest, it may be because women, in their eagerness to fit in to the masculine environment, have denied the more feminine aspects of themselves—even *to* themselves. No wonder people tend to lump female corporate managers with male managers. After years of aping male management styles, it would naturally be difficult to see any difference. Also, it's hard for corporate male managers to see that women can be equally good and equally effective in obtaining the same strategic ends using different means.

In recent years, management books have put forth some general differences between male and female styles in business, contending the masculine model is more competitive, hierarchical, rational, and goal oriented, while the feminine approach is more cooperative, intuitive, and quality-oriented.[27]

At the same time, an increasing number of women are discarding the concept of "androgynous management"—as if women and men could fuse into one corporate being through some mystic alchemical process—viewing as artificial and idealistic. In fact, sociologists, psychologists, and educators who have analyzed androgyny are now distinguishing between mono-androgyny—an ideal person who combines characteristics attributed to both men and women equally—and polyandrogyny that advocates no single ideal but a variety of options including pure femininity and masculinity as well as any combination of the two.[28] Many women at the Reconcilable Differences landing seem to espouse the latter—that women be encouraged to make a personal choice as to the appropriate style to bring to the corporation and not try to fit the old definition of androgyny that usually meant "neutering" all of women's more feminine aspects.

In short, the most successful women who have remained within corporations are learning to speak with their own Authentic Voice and play by their own rules. These women are starting to expand what is "feminine" beyond what one thirty-five-year-old male defines as "what makes men more comfortable," realizing that in their quest to be "normal" they have unnecessarily constrained themselves. After all, the parameters of "normal" in most aspects of life, predominantly the world of commerce, have been circumscribed by men. The enormous but potentially exhilarating task that now confronts women in business is to create brand-new modes of being. And since women are integrating a broader range of experiences, these options are more complex and varied than the roles men have defined for themselves. This is one of the fundamental reasons why there have been so few true role models until now. It is also why today, as Carolyn Heilbrun asserts, "The major difficulty for women will be to hold in mind at the same moment the male model and its ultimate transformation to female uses. Women must learn to call whatever she is or does female. Ultimately there are no male role models; there are only models of selfhood from which woman chooses to learn."[29]

Making these choices could be particularly difficult for

the older women who had to battle the male system the hardest and have often buried their feminine nature. Such women, in the words of *Esquire* publisher Phillip Moffitt, have been "separated from some essential sense of themself and have suffered much displacement and disorientation."[30] Women fear that by asserting their true nature in business they run the risk, just as in personal relations, of being rejected out of hand. Tina, twenty-two, speaks of the cynicism members of the younger generation have regarding their ability to be themselves in the corporation. "I think women's lib hasn't been internalized by corporations to such a degree that women can be themselves without playacting to succeed. Success requires that we deny for at least a good twenty years our feminine impulses—or any admission that we have feelings or emotions." Despite the odds, some more experienced women are taking up the gauntlet—realizing, after the Success and Betrayal landing, that there really isn't that much to lose. They have seen "success" for what it is, and they recognize that the most fulfilling success is highly personal and that the only reliable power is personal power.

The women who stay in the corporate world realize they must assert some control over their lives. They finally shrug off the passivity of earlier landings and begin to make the long-overdue decisions on issues they refused to confront while bobbing along in the sea of male models through the earlier landings of their career. Denise, now thirty-eight, puts her finger on the answer when she speaks of wanting to make her own choices: "I want to choose, even if I choose not to choose. I want to make decisions in my life. My not having a baby today is different than it was three years ago. Then I really took a serious look at my life and asked myself, 'Do I really want to have a child? Could I deal with it outside marriage?' I didn't want to just sit back and have time pass me by. But I really looked at it and thought about it and chose not to. And I am happy with that choice. I think the only way to live life is to make those choices. I see it as the only way to get true satisfaction."

Making personal choices, those that express her own individual preferences, is what the most successful businesswomen are now striving to do, both on and off the job. In the past, women have often hesitated to choose, not wanting *themselves* to define who they were. For one thing, it was safer to hand their lives over to men and say, "*You* figure it out." And perhaps more important, making choices necessarily involves setting limitations—a particularly soiled word for a generation raised in an age of unlimited frontiers in space, who crossed continents many times before they reached adulthood, and whose dreams and visions of life were often fed by mass media that suggested anything was possible. Most women, as we have seen from the Wooed and Won landing on, want to keep their options open. And because, most recently, they have seemed to have more options than men, they have not made the hard choices men have felt compelled to make. Instead, after falling into careers, they drift, always waiting for the better bet, the perfect job, Prince Charming. Despite all the hard work and frantic activity, they don't confront the key issues.

But women who choose to stay in the corporation actively take charge of their lives and measure success by much more personal yardsticks than corporate rewards and status. Diana, a bank vice president who must balance a new baby with supervising a staff of eighty people, spoke for many management women: "I will consider myself successful if I really do get rid of extraneous things that are not relevant to me. It is a very personal way of looking at it but that to me would be success." By actively choosing the personal goals they wish to pursue, women can help fight the sense of isolation they so often feel. Such inner priorities help them seek out other women they wish to support. It results in the self-knowledge and self-confidence that Ruth, a forty-year-old bank vice president, expresses: "I'm just different. And I feel comfortable in that difference. And that can be encouraging to other women."

Women learn that the first prerogative of true success is the ability to reassert their femininity. Most successful women we interviewed have decided that trying to act like one of the guys is counterproductive. "If you try to do everything like a man—dress like a man, act like a man—my theory is that you are going to lose," Rachel, the midwest corporate counsel, observes. "I mean, I can't be as good a man as my brother. So why do I want to set myself up to fail? I might as well be who I am." Hillary agrees: "The thing is, you will do really well only at something that comes naturally to you. There is no way I am going to play a southern flower convincingly. No way. Or a stewardess, or a fireplug!"

Many in business protest that despite women's inroads, the corporation is still a man's world and women will continue to have to suppress any aspects of their character that don't fit into the prevailing male standards if they are to accede to positions of power or influence. And, after all, how many *men* can truly "be themselves" and be riotously successful in corporate life? But most women in middle and top management, having experienced the Success and Betrayal landing, harbor no false dreams about how far they will actually go in this or the next generation of management change. And having recognized that being one of the boys will *not* guarantee power and will require them to deny much of their most basic natures, a number of the most successful women are going out of their way to assert, appropriately, their feminine attributes. Media company manager Trish gets to the bottom line in many women's opinion when she observes that the effectiveness of a specific "masculine" or "feminine" style is all in the eye of the—often male—beholder anyhow: "We can try to become like men—and we may even become like men—but if men don't perceive us as the same, it doesn't make any difference. In the end, if they don't perceive you as such, so what? If they perceive you as the barefoot and pregnant woman, no matter what you do, they are going to see you that way. It doesn't make any difference what you are or how you act." As a result, she was no longer trying to be one of the guys. "I have stopped wearing man-tailored suits," she adds. "I save them for when I have to entertain the Japanese."

Dr. Jean Baker Miller puts forth the hope that if women have a humanizing impact on corporate life, it may be most strongly felt in the examples they set of redefining strength and weakness, success and failure: She postulates that men in our society have been conditioned to support the status quo and "encouraged from early on in their life to incorporate and to aim toward living up to the highest value of their society." And she contends: "While men are made to feel weak in many ways, women are made to feel weaker. But because they know weakness, women can cease being the carriers of weakness and become the developers of a different understanding of it and the appropriate paths out of it." Miller concludes: "Because when women perceive forms of strength based on their own life experience rather than believing they should have the qualities they attribute to men, they often find new definitions of strength."[31]

Women, by not playing by the male rules, bring to the game of success a whole new dimension. A number of men also recognize this. Michael Korda notes that not knowing what the rules are—or, more accurately at this level of sophistication, not *wanting* to know—can be very useful for women. And he observes that one of the main fears of men is that women won't abide by the rules.[32] Robin articulates her husband's view: "He thinks women tend to have a more realistic attitude about themselves than men do. Women are more likely to evaluate things and decide whether an action is worth the risk. He said they tend to be more balanced. They look at their whole lives and think, 'Is this taking too much of a toll? Is this really where I want to go as a balanced person?' Whereas a man is more likely to say, 'Yes, I will go where you send me, and work forty hours, and jump so high.'" Recruiter Gary Knisely agrees: "Maybe the world would be happier if a large portion of women realized they aren't going to get to the top. Because many men are reaching the same conclusion." Reassessment and reevaluation are becoming pervasive among men in corporate culture as well as among women. "Clearly by most broad definitions I have been successful in my adult life," writes the president of Neiman-Marcus. Describing how he is invited to dinner parties with well-known people, sits on several boards and provides well for his family, he nevertheless notes ". . . there are nights—many nights—when I am awakened by disturbing thoughts. . . . Images of a world not right. . . . They make me ask, in the face of a life dedicated to achievement: 'Is this all there is?' "[33]

Women who stay in the corporate world get the satisfaction that perhaps they are at last beginning to make an impact on the culture around them, that at least the tacit one-way bargain struck in earlier years is beginning to pay off in more of a balanced two-way relationship. Certainly, a number of women are still debating with themselves how lasting their corporate commitment will be, but those who have remained have chosen it as the best alternative. The choice is now a conscious one, based on mature, realistic criteria. The women who have chosen to stay have developed their own ladder of challenge and reward, separate and distinct from that of organizations as a whole. "For me, it is just the feeling that you have done as good a job as possible. But the thing is, who's measuring?" asks Molly, a bank vice president. "The only thing that counts is that *you* believe you have done something as well as you can. How *others* have measured it doesn't count." She has set realistic expectations that nourish and encourage rather than frustrate.

It is worth remembering Marilyn French's conclusion regarding the paradox that women are far more likely "to be coopted by institutional policy than to change it; they will either assimilate or be fired or quit."[34] She recognizes the pessimism of a generation of women who expected to influence America by exercising their power within the corporation, only to discover their own limitations and disenfranchisement—and that the bars that defined the parameters of their power are the very corporations themselves. Does this mean women are willing to sit by and let men continue to run the show? How far will women really go in leading American corporations? Do they really expect to change the fundamental power structure?

The most successful executive women in corporations have not been entirely assimilated or fired, nor quit. Instead, like Joanne Black, they see the corporation as an arena in which women can finally make their voices heard—for the good of women, men, and the corporation. "There just aren't enough entrepreneurial activities to create economic freedom for all women. There really is no alternative. There is for an individual, but none collectively unless we hang in," she contends. "I think what's missing in the world is the ability for men and women to communicate—it has importance. I like to stay open to the lessons men have to offer. I think what's at the issue is that we need to get a place for what I call 'authentic disagreement' as opposed to 'dominance/submission,' a model that has brought us to the point of nuclear war. Why can't a couple who are capable of producing a child get it together in the workplace?" Reaching "authentic disagreement" will require women to stop seeing themselves only as mediators and conciliators. And it will require men not to register and interpret women's disagreement as threatening the very foundation of their power but as an avenue of continued growth and enrichment for both the sexes.

Joanne Black, like a number of the women interviewed, suggests authentic engagement of differences between men and women in business can transcend corporate implications. Jeane Kirkpatrick expresses a similar sentiment: "I was the only woman in our history, I think, who ever sat in regularly at top-level foreign policy making meetings . . . and it matters a great deal. It's terribly important, maybe even to the future of the world, for women to take part in making the decisions that shape our destiny."[35] In the Preface to a recent edition of *The Feminine Mystique*, written twenty years after the book was first published, Betty Friedan says:

> . . . . Women may have to reach a point of critical mass in any institution to raise that different voice, and the institution may have to face its own critical crisis to hear it. It is not easy to question the mascu-

linism of a powerful and successful nation, until perhaps its most thoughtful men and women sense it may be coming too close to economic collapse or nuclear extinction for such questions not to be asked.[36]

This leads to a sixth basic reason for staying with the corporation: Pioneering. "I went through my bitter times, but I'm not bitter now. I look at it as pioneering," Joanne Black continues. "Like the pioneers of this country, the people who went west to open frontiers, the guys who went into space, I feel privileged to be a pioneer on this particular issue. There aren't many opportunities to be a pioneer these days. There are no more wagon trains." As ever, being a pioneer is not easy. Substantial personal and professional risk is often involved, as women who bring corporate injustices and conflicts out into the open are often branded as incendiaries and troublemakers. Losing the affiliation, the bonds with the corporation, for speaking out as an individual may be the most terrifying aspect of all for women. "Many companies don't want advocates," cautions executive recruiter Pen James, speaking of a fact of life in conservative companies. But he also counsels, "Women need to stay out of the adversarial role because that tends to alienate more than it attracts—but they do need to keep the pressure on."

There is an old saying: "The optimist is wrong as often as the pessimist. But he is far happier." Cynthia, a top corporate financial officer, is one of the optimists: "I was ambitious, but I had much lower aspirations early in my career. It wasn't until two years ago in this job that I could admit to myself that I eventually wanted to be CEO. It probably won't happen, but it's about time we started working on it." Like most of the highest-level women executives, she is far less sanguine than male counterparts that she'll see many female CEOs of America's largest corporations in her lifetime. But, also like the others, she sees herself as part of a process with far longer time lines. She understands and accepts her history, a history born of the collective imagination of her generation and all those who preceded and will follow it. As Joanne Black concludes:

"There are those of us who want to open up new possibilities for the human spirit. Doing so gets us in touch with new visions, and all visionaries know you'll take on resistance. To be bitter when I've taken on the responsibility for coping with resistance is contradictory. When the resistance was greater than I expected, when I was deeply hurt, the vision was the rope I used to pull myself out of the pit. When I was passed over for promotion or fired, that vision would get me back in the race."

Marilyn French is right: "To refuse to enter the establishment is to refuse even to try to change it from within and thus to accept the marginal position women have traditionally held. To refuse to enter American institutions may also be to doom oneself to poverty, and poverty is silent and invisible. It has no voice and no face."[37] At worst, "success" still represents for many women an ironic bounty of blessings, a tremendous risk incurred for an uncertain, often meaningless grab bag of rewards. But, at least at the beginning, it is often the only game in town. And in striking the unilateral bargain, women who choose to play the game defy that poverty of will and imagination. They abjure invisibility. Most important, they assume a face and a voice. Energy executive Hillary expresses the sentiments of many when she said, "It is like driving a wedge into a log. You have to keep driving it and driving it, and it moves very slowly. But finally the wedge goes all the way through and the log splits."

CHAPTER 11

LESSONS FROM
THE LANDINGS

*I think being authentic is what
it's all about. It's a lifelong
quest to discover who you are
and use that knowledge to yours
and others' advantage.*

Nella Barkley
President
Crystal-Barkley Corporation

Almost twenty-five years ago, Betty Friedan wrote of an image that trapped women in a cycle as relentlessly repetitive and sterile as their perma-press washing-machine cycles.[1] In recent times, we have experienced a momentous swing to a new corollary mystique and a new cycle that in many ways has been as fashioned and governed by men as was its quarter-century-old predecessor. This is the cycle of corporate success and betrayal.

This new, accepted image is fundamentally a conflict between the straitjacketed male definition of success and the unwillingness of even the most successful women to deny their authentically female expectations and values. In the words of one female writer: "For more than fifteen years we have blindly accepted income, title, and power as our gods, exchanged for home, hearth, and children, and we have fought to mold ourselves to resemble facsimiles of the men whose status in the professional world was a source of envy."[2] It is this restrictive, ill-fitting image that causes Chris, one of the highest-ranking women in one of the largest corporations in the world, to say: "I find the women's magazines depressing. It's like 'Can you top this?' on all the profiles they run. And I feel that I'm not doing so well after all." This conflict provokes MasterCard International's Joanne Black to remark: "I certainly would like somebody to tell the *truth* about what's going on. But I don't think all those books for women that gloss over reality with easy answers do that. So when women fail, they think it must be *them*."

Women have obtained a measure of the same status men have enjoyed only to discover it is not what they bargained for. It has been both much more and much less. The truth is that all the silence surrounding Dad's job at the dinner table didn't mean women were being barred from some enchanted kingdom—rather it was often just the opposite. As anthropologist Jules Henry has said, home for men was "a sanctuary where a part of every day they could forget their jobs."[3] Unfortunately, however, this silence, by its very mysteriousness, turned a job into an elusive lover onto which women could project their wildest hopes and dreams. Former St. Joe Mineral president Broward Craig notes: "For years, women have been hearing about the 'hidden valley' their husbands went to every day and came home from every night, and it raised some high expectations. And now they're finding the price people pay, the dead ends, the frustration. Surprise! Business is not all fun." For women, this discovery was just the beginning. The harsh reality of working in a corporation has disappointed and betrayed women, just as everyday living with the mysterious lover might. Even more, the corporate mystique as defined by men demand that women deny and neglect as much of their basic natures as the "feminine mystique" had. Can women break the cycle of success and betrayal? Are there lessons in the landings?

Lesson One: Women Should Recognize That the Life Cycle of Landings Exists and That Most Women Experience It

Many management women share the same corporate experience. They are not alone—far from it. More often than not, their own Authentic Voice is speaking a universal language. And one of the most fundamental common threads that ties women together is the set of myths and expectations they bring into the corporation. These myths and expectations are often misplaced or displaced in the corporate culture—and, as such, they fuel much of the self-betrayal women eventually experience. "Instead of women acknowledging reality, I see them pouring enormous amounts of energy into trying to fit their expectations into that reality," says career counselor Nella Barkley. "They spend hours and hours analyzing their success and why it hasn't lived up to expectations instead of recognizing the reality and deciding what they'd really like to be." Men, because they bring less baggage to the corporation, tend to make fewer emotional demands of it. And because of this lack of demands, men do not usually experience success and betrayal in the same way. Women should recognize they *do* bring an unconscious agenda into the corporation, and they should be aware that it will too often collide with the basic tenets and realities of corporate life.

Lesson Two: Women Should Accept That the Corporation Cannot Be Expected to Change to Fit Their Myths and Satisfy Their Expectations, Yearnings, and Needs

The Corporation as Lover and Family

Many corporate women as well as some men go wrong when they assign to the corporation responsibility for their own self-esteem and approval. By the end of the Success and Betrayal landing, experienced women no longer need to look for sanctions and confirmation outside themselves, whether from parent or patriarchal corporation. Dr. Carol Galligan, director of the Women's Institute, says of her daughter, a few short years into her career: "I am constantly responding to her statements that she wants to be appreciated on the job and I've said, 'That's work. That's what you get paid to do. If you want love, look to home. You can come home to get love and appreciation. *We* love you; *they* employ you.'" By contrast, Sally, a seasoned executive who recently dropped out of a corporation to go back to school remarks: "I think *people* care, but the *company* doesn't." Former Bendix vice president Nancy Reynolds observes, "I think you have to see the corporation as a whole, the big picture, and not get emotionally attached to a part of a company. I think those who have an innate ability to see the larger picture will do extremely well."

The Mentor

The task of dispelling the Myth of the Corporation as Lover is related to that of developing a more discerning approach to the Myth of the Mentor. While top-ranking men as well as women advise that a "rabbi" is beneficial and even crucial at times, many management women now are realizing that they run risks in a mentor relationship which differ from those that men face. Male mentors view their women protégées differently, and women, in their desire for connectedness and personal bonds, might give away their own strengths by becoming overly dependent on their mentors, especially in later career landings. Jon, a manager at a Chicago pharmaceutical corporation, explains how most males approach mentors: "My mentor has always been there to make sure I take the next step up the corporate ranks. But he has never been there to pick me up when I made a mistake. I champion my own cause. Fundamentally I believe you are an independent operator and you had better sell your stuff and yourself without depending on someone else to take care of you." Overreliance on a mentor can steer a management woman off her own best course. Grace, a cosmetic company executive, had this experience when she chose a job on her mentor's advice over another one she later realized would have been much more personally fulfilling. If she had it to do over again, she says, "I would look a lot harder at what I *wanted* to do as opposed to what I *ought* to do. I was not really following my own true lights. Because I thought to do that was naive. I didn't have confidence in my own vision. I should have listened to my instincts."

Living on the Edge

In listening to their instincts, women learn to upgrade their own perception of their value and contribution to the corporation. In fact, experienced management women often beseech other women to have confidence in themselves and accept their own strengths. Veteran female managers also urge other women to take risks as well as criticism, cultivating the kind of resiliency men have had to adopt. Remarks Dr. Carol Galligan: "You have to be able to persevere in the face of criticism within the corporation, and most women are destroyed by it." Nancy Reynolds advises: "I think women have to be willing to take risks and learn to take criticism and not sit around for weeks and agonize over things—not say, 'Oh, my God, this guy chewed me out. What did I do?' Maybe that guy gave you something you can use. Forget the criticism. *He's* forgotten it. Go on to the next step. Fall down; pick yourself up." Angela, an aerospace executive, suggests women should *act* confident even when they don't feel that way: "I have more confidence in someone who gives me that self-assurance act because I feel, 'Okay, I can give it to him, he'll handle it.' Whereas if you went to a doctor whose hands were shaking . . ." Corporate women should, in the words of cosmetics company founder Mary Kay Ash, "Fake it until you make it."[4]

Unlimited Potential, Meritocracy, Irreplaceability, and Individual Recognition

The women who've experienced the Success and Betrayal landing have also acquired some street smarts about the caprice and politics behind corporate advancements. They accept the rough-and-tumble truth that there is no such thing as a perfect meritocracy or unlimited potential. Even the CEO's potential is limited by his board and the stockholders. He can be fired or his company taken over, or both. The happiest corporate women finally learn that no one *always* puts on a perfect performance, no one is *always* applauded as a star, no one *always* fits the current image of success. The most disheartening moments in our interviews came when women suggested that they alone had failed and that other people had all the right answers. They never considered that there are no right answers, only individual contributions.

Nor are such individual contributions ever made in a vacuum. The savviest women no longer feel frustrated and guilty about things over which they have no control. They quickly see that politics and timing can play a much larger role in corporate advancement than merit. They are less hard on themselves, less demanding of themselves, and less disappointed when the corporation doesn't recognize them for their extra efforts. They can better weigh priorities and pace themselves so as at earlier landings such as Wooed and Won and Proving

Up to avoid burn-out later on. At the same time, while it's rare, if not impossible, to find a corporation that functions strictly as a meritocracy, women seem to have the best shot at the top when they focus their efforts on the bottom line and steer clear of staff jobs where individual contributions are hard to quantify, where politics can run amok, where personality can more easily triumph over performance. Heidi speaks of her previous experience on the staff of a large energy corporation: "They really didn't have a yardstick to measure you by, so they relied on things like seniority and how you managed the political network. If you don't have a profit-and-loss statement, you can't quantitatively measure your contributions." Jon, a Midwest pharmaceutical company manager, agrees that the most valued and least expendable managers are those who have a direct link to the bottom line: "You have to directly or indirectly translate your contribution into revenue production, either saving money or putting money into new areas where the company can make more money. New people coming into a business need to understand that revenue is the fundamental issue." Malcolm Forbes, Jr., sees this issue in an even broader perspective: "Alexander Hamilton said two hundred years ago that the coin doesn't care what your standing in the community is; it doesn't care what your background is. Money is money. Money is mobility."

Where are the best jobs for women, then? Women in sales jobs, while often unfairly put down for lacking prestige, commonly say they receive the recognition they deserve along with rewards commensurate with their accomplishments. "When I got into the business, selling was seen as a door-to-door job, not a very professional career," says Kristin, salesperson for a large forest products corporation. "But the image is improving, and there's a lot of opportunity for women in sales. I can do my own thing on my own timetable, take as much vacation as I want. Because numbers speak. If I produce, fine. If not, I'd be thrown out. I am happy where I am in basically an entrepreneurial position, where my success and accomplishments are measured in black and white." Amanda, who left a textile corporation to become a financial consultant, agrees: "I adore what I do now because my success is totally dependent on my efforts. The work is hard and it's scary, but it is great because I know I am good. It is up to me how much I will earn. And I know the sky's the limit because I'm the one in charge." Sales jobs are available in virtually every industry and in a wide range of professions. Says Lois Appleby, the first woman in Merrill Lynch to be a member as well as chairman of its advisory board to top management: "As far as women in sales are concerned, the limitations don't exist." That's in her own company—what about working with male clients? "I find the more sophisticated the client, the more willing they are to accept you," she remarks.

Other women who have worked in line jobs on Wall Street or in investment banking and money management firms around the country—those with the drive and stamina to take on everything from "gunslingers" to "Saturday Night Specials" —also find that performance reaps at least economic rewards, even if women are still not breaking through to top management positions in any great numbers. "The good thing about Wall Street is that whatever they start out thinking about you, the very fact that you can hold down your job means that you are performing," notes Hilliary, who once worked at a Wall Street investment banking house. "And if you perform, they don't care if you are purple and have three heads or what. As long as you are in some way directly making money, they couldn't care less. In fact, I find Wall Street the least chauvinistic environment because people are just too damn busy to cut other people's throats."

For other women who want more precise quantification of their accomplishments, one option might be to join a consulting firm, immediately transforming a staff function into a line job. Another possibility would be to switch to a smaller, more entrepreneurial company, or a smaller, more entrepreneurial, and independent division of a larger corporation, where there are fewer staff positions and therefore greater opportunity for individual contribution, recognition, and reward. "There is a lot more flexibility in a smaller company," says Heidi, contrasting her current job at a small division of a health-care company with the job she'd held at the energy corporation. "Plus, you are measured by how much you can build a business. I love being in a situation where I am being rewarded for performance." Nancy Reynolds recommends that women "go with a corporation and take a chance on living in some unattractive town for a couple years so they can learn the inside workings and eventually start their own business."

Meanwhile, those women who are simply happier with the *content* of staff jobs, who find the *substance* of these jobs so interesting they won't switch to line, must recognize and accept the fact they may very well never advance to the highest management ranks. They will have to work at educating management about the importance of their functions, and develop systems for quantifying their contributions. But some women in staff positions, such as corporate counsels, have found tremendous personal satisfaction in such jobs. And, as middle managements of larger corporations shrink, some observers predict the division between staff and line jobs will blur and women who advance along staff jobs will find themselves at fewer dead ends.

Growth and Reward

Experienced executive women are also learning to demand the monetary rewards due them while planning their finances over the long haul—recognizing they may end up as the sole or primary breadwinner of their household. They don't limit their ambitions to a job that looks "interesting." Rita, forty years old, divorced, and the sole supporter of her two children speaks from firsthand experience: "Women usually say money isn't important. Several years ago, I was on a volunteer board and we had to hire an executive director. And a guy on the board said, 'We can get a woman cheaper than a man,' and they *did* hire a woman for much less. As long as we say we aren't in it for the money, we are not going to get it. We've got to stop saying 'job satisfaction' and start saying 'money.'"

At the same time, the myth of growth often helps women adjust to the ceiling the majority of both men and women almost inevitably bump up against at some point in their careers. Because women value learning for its own sake more than men do, they often enjoy their jobs more than men do—especially in a time of diminishing opportunity for upward job mobility. "Much of the emphasis in the past has been on career progression, on where you expect to be in the future. We have got to stop talking about that, because it isn't an automatic up-up-up, lock-step promotion every two or three years. It really isn't," Alice Hennessey of Boise Cascade warns. "That's why we have to get much better at enriching existing jobs and making people feel they are growing even if they are not necessarily going on to a different job."

The Ideal Industry and the Peaceable Kingdom

Management women are becoming more realistic about their limited prospects in all industries, no longer believing it's easier to beat the system in one business area than another. As our interviews have confirmed, there are no ideal industries. In fact, "women's" industries might be less beneficial for women than the more "macho" ones where the differences between the way the sexes are viewed and valued are more overt and clear-cut and where women are still enough of a novelty that they can to some extent make their own exceptions to the rules. As Grace, a cosmetics company dropout, says, "In a male environment, I know when they're playing their games. It is when they play a phony game of 'Oh, we are all open'—when they really aren't—that it's tough. That led me right down the garden path."

Just as there are no ideal-industries, there are few, if any, Peaceable Kingdoms where all creatures great and small have learned to curb their primitive survival instincts. Says Ricki, a forty-year-old advertising executive, "You have to come into a corporation recognizing that you have to be better—that's a fact of life. And you have to realize all that defensiveness about being female is going to curtail your growth." Instead, both men and women said that women should defuse antagonisms as much as possible with humor. Keith, an executive at a New Jersey conglomerate, proffers this advice: "Most men are idiots, babies in a way, I think. I have more respect for women than men. If you are going to succeed in the business world you have to be resilient, and women have to be that much *more* resilient. They have to be able to take all the shit and deal with it and just keep going. It's unfortunate but true. And the first advice that comes to mind is that women should cultivate a sense of humor."

Another part of the resiliency is for women to choose their fights judiciously—to ask the corporation to change in a few concrete, specific ways and distinguish between tangible and emotional demands. Advertising executive Lois Wyse counsels, "Before you drop any bombs, be sure you've asked and answered these two questions to your satisfaction: 'What's the best thing that can happen if I win? And what is the worst thing that can happen if I lose?' " She concludes: "Sometimes it is better to lose this one battle so you can stay to fight another day."[5] Or as Alice Hennessey advises: "You can't get upset about everything. I pick where I want to dent the corporation very carefully." Urges Joanne Black, "Operate out of what is and inch toward what will be." Men agree that women gain the most credibility if they are judicious and level-headed in their demands. Former Phelps Dodge International president Russell E. Marks, Jr., comments: "One of the elements of the battle is for women to demonstrate they're just as rigorous thinkers, so if they wage the battle in terms that are perfectly understandable to men, they win two ways. They prove they can win—and they win by refuting the notion that they win men over by emotional manipulation."

Identifying the differences and antagonisms between men and women will *not* encourage a greater polarization between the sexes. In fact, it often will have just the opposite effect of enabling men and women to educate each other about their differences and help them understand and work more effectively together. Author and psychoanalyst Ann Belford Ulanov contends that "Opponents of images of sexual polarity fear that emphasis upon it will foster more divisions between men and women. On the contrary, perceptions of difference make experience of similarity possible." She adds, "Every effort to annihilate . . . sexual polarity amounts to little more than repressing it into the unconscious."[6] Moreover, if women do not recognize the differences, they can unwittingly speak one language and have it interpreted in quite another way, even when they are dealing with seemingly simple details. One senior woman speaks with savvy: "One of my daughters is getting married, and she wants to keep her name. And I am saying to her, 'Well, I can understand that, but I think it is important for you to understand how you will be judged in a whole bunch of circles if you do that. That is going to give a message you may not want to give. Do what you choose, but *understand it before you do.*' "

The Androgynous Manager

Knowledgable senior executives are recommending that the younger generation of managerial women wise up to the fact that they will always be regarded as women first and as managers second. They know the truth of the matter remains that a woman can wear all the bow-tied man-tailored blouses and read all the management texts she likes, but the first time she asserts herself in a business situation, she will trigger unconscious reactions with often unanticipated results. She may have obtained the same M.B.A., read the same management handbooks, and even aped the style of male managers, but she cannot become one of the boys.

In fact, older management women suggest that their younger counterparts might be better served by attending women's studies programs receiving renewed emphasis today at universities around the country, such as Duke, Yale, Princeton, and Rutgers.[7] Such courses offer realistic assessment of the particular issues women will have to confront in business, and they expose women to historical role models from which to develop new styles of leadership based on female patterns. Because unless they actively embrace their feminine nature, women run the risk of finding themselves betrayed at the middle-management level without understanding why. Since they have never regarded their femininity as a problem, they find it inconceivable that anyone else in the corporation has.

Both men and women interviewed urged women to accept and cultivate their own individual, feminine traits—warning them against modeling themselves after men. Phil, a Midwest treasurer, speaks for the majority: "The last advice I would give would be for women to act more like men, because I can't stand that. It is somehow sad because it says they are willing to turn into men. Women who have worked for me who have been the most successful are those who have been able to reconcile their femininity with their career aspirations."

The consensus is that the hairy-chested school of management will give way to a more humanistic style only if women assume responsibility for being the best *women* managers they can be. The values women often bring to that role—such as nurturing, a respect for the individual, task orientation, and reward-oriented management—can enhance the corporation by osmosis, even if those values are not currently stated goals of male management. At the same time, they also have helped some men recognize their own more "feminine" attributes, just as women have developed their "masculine" propensities in recent decades through their careers in business. "Some of my strongest aspects are female, and I wish women would be as feminine as they are." Jim, a twenty-eight-year-old banker, comments: "A woman will never be as good at being a man as a man can be. A woman we work with comes in after lunch smoking a cigar, she plays golf with the boys, and I want to say, 'Marcy, I don't respect you more for that, but less.'"

As greater numbers of women enter corporations, perhaps a wider range of behavior will be accepted, especially if each woman listens to her Authentic Voice. In fact, a groundswell seems to be occurring among top management women who contend that specifically "feminine" experiences, such as raising children, will actually enhance women's management skills. "Women who invest in developing their female skills will turn out to be better managers. And being a mother and wife are investments in their female selves. You don't get those qualities by being a smart-ass kid or an M.B.A.," insists Andrea, a commodities executive. "One thing that makes children valuable to a career woman is that they force her to deal with each child as an individual. My children certainly helped me learn to deal with people," Eleanor, a banker, asserts. "This is the coalition approach," agrees Nancy Reynolds. "I think that mothers who are settling fights with their kids learn how to say, 'Okay, we are going to sit down and I am not going to play favorites, but we are going to get to the root of things and work them out.'"

Lesson Three: Women Should Support One Another and Recognize Their Basic Bonds

In the words of Carolyn Heilbrun, "When successful women in every job and profession think of themselves as women rather than honorary males, their sympathy with other women will expand, too."[8] The token woman who bought her way into the male club, paying the dues of her denied womanhood, has helped all women by her mere presence in management circles. But the time has come for women to take the next step and help one another as *women*, recognizing they must support members of their own sex before they can expect to gain anything approaching the power or influence men in the corporation have obtained.

Networking is more than just a cynical and self-aggrandizing means of upward career mobility. Such connections can palliate corporate women's sense of profound insularity. By bringing women out of isolation, networks provide a sense of connectedness—to replace the disconnectedness between generations of women. In a network, older women can be honest about the difficulties they have faced while building a corporate career, without feeling embarrassed for not living up to the Corporate Amazon image, and without fear their candor will hurt their advancement. Through the network, younger women can learn to stop viewing older women as over-the-hill feminists and recognize they share some similar experiences, although the younger women may have advanced faster in the earlier landings of their careers.

Many enlightened men also urge women to help each other. Comments public relations executive Jason: "My only advice is for women to be good to other women. A woman who sees another woman as competition is saying, 'I have my job because I am a woman. I am a token.' " Meanwhile, executive women are starting to recognize the need to help other executive women, secretaries, and others, not only in terms of advancement, job enrichment, monetary rewards, and benefits, but also in terms of encouragement and emotional support. "Especially those in the lower socioeconomic scale—women who don't have money. They are trying to have more with no social structure in place to help or support them," notes Nella Barkley. "It is a very, very serious problem for low-income unskilled women," concurs Juanita Kreps. "They are the ones most in need of our support."

Being good to other women also means accepting and supporting one another's choices, whether they work or not. It means not criticizing other women for "fluffing out," a "term used by hard-nosed career-conscious women to describe less single-minded women who have allowed themselves to drift behind the career curve."[9] "I think if a woman decides to drop out of a job altogether—even if she is on the verge of becoming a vice president and decides to stay home with her new baby—she ought to do it," Juanita Kreps urges. "And it would probably be better if we could say to her, 'That's great!' " As a leading force in education who has long encouraged women to make the most of their talents and choose their own paths, Juanita Kreps understands the importance of opportunity for women—opportunity to make their own choices. Because, as Sheila, a corporate vice president, remarks, "For the next generations, I think there will continue to be no collective answers for women, only answers on an individual basis."

Lesson Four: Women Should Learn to Set Their Own Individual Goals. There is No Perfect Model.

I think women have very high expectations of themselves. I don't see anything wrong with that, but I think women have to be taught to make choices," admits Catherine, a twenty-three-year-old investment banker. "I don't think we are prepared to make those choices when we come out of college." Juanita Kreps agrees: "I talk with many young women not yet in their professions. And there isn't enough realism on the problems they will face in finding time to be everything." She defined the basic quandry modern women must face: "No job is going to satisfy a woman—or a man—altogether. The old way wasn't satisfactory either. The best compromise is probably a balancing of time and effort, and a recognition that not all things are possible."

But Rachel speaks for many women when she says, "It is very hard to identify exactly what it is you want. I can say what I am doing doesn't fulfill me totally. Well, what else would? I can't see anything in life that could give you it all." How much must women compromise? What should they compromise? Society continues to prize the conventional male corporate path as the most prestigious proving ground for women —but women can find few role models that fit their own individual circumstances. Diana, a vice president who just had her first child, says, "I think it is easier for men. It's like this guy I met in Russia a long time ago who asked me about our political system. 'Isn't having two parties confusing?' he asked. I told him it was a good idea because it gave people a choice. But he said, 'No, it's much easier here; the choice is made for you.' "

While women feel they have *too many* options today, they still tend to judge themselves against some unattainable image "out there" that society suggests. Annie Gottlieb wrote recently, "It's not only family expectations that can push us down a path that is wrong for us. Society always has a standard recipe for happiness—'a sort of shopping list,' one woman I know calls it. 'You're supposed to have this and this and this, and then you'll live happily ever after.' The trouble is, the recipe changes from decade to decade like fashion—and, like any fashion, it never suits everyone."[10] Juanita Kreps further observes: "Women today don't get much confirmation that if what they are doing is a bit unusual it isn't necessarily bad for them—in fact, it may be quite good. In the old days we found out very quickly; our peers would either confirm or condemn our choices. Today, women should learn to trust our own judgments a lot more than some of us do."

Management and career consultant Rhoda Green agrees: "You have to take a look inside yourself first. You have to think carefully about the contribution you really want to make." Women are learning that they must make some hard choices, that they must accept that for all their "unlimited potential," they can't do everything. They are recognizing they must stop falling into careers with blinders on, unquestioningly pursuing the standard, acceptable life-style choice of the moment—be it motherhood or management or a mixture of both. They are learning to accept that other people's choices are for other people and they are responsible for their own choices. Otherwise, as Boise Cascade's Alice Hennessey cautions, "You talk about disappointments. Most of the disappointments that women encounter come as a result of not doing a good enough job of thinking through and defining what they really want to do with their life and what price they are willing to pay."

Goal-oriented men are more skilled in setting up key terminal points on which to focus their efforts. Says one male executive vice president, "If I had any advice for women it would probably be about thinking strategically. How you do your job, how you get the help you need, how you develop the relationships with people who can help you on the job—sort of conceiving your life as a plan that needs to be completed. And how to act politically to get what you want without people resenting you for it. In short, the ability to think politically and strategically about your life." This includes financial planning, which, for women who must drop out of the work force for family reasons, often requires a special approach. One female senior manager draws an analogy with aging athletes: "You start thinking of yourself as a professional jock would. And you say, 'Hey, I'd better get a good salary so I can save a lot for the future.' " She's right, because women will never get off the economic treadmill until they confront, clear-eyed, the possibility they may indeed be the most significant and perhaps the sole breadwinner throughout their lives.

The most fulfilled women are not necessarily those who eschew a long-term professional commitment for fear it will reduce their "options," but rather those who take the approach chosen by Eleanor, who raised two children, returned to work, and became a bank vice president in her fifties: "My grandmother used to say 'Aim for the moon. If you don't get there, you're still better off than if you'd stayed on the ground.' And I always felt if you don't have a five-year plan you'll never get off the mark." Or Ricki, who raised two children while working. She notes, "All these choices are very healthy. They give you the freedom to create your own life, to make your own mistakes. That's the good part about being a pioneer." Career counselor Sharon Berman counsels women to regularly review their goals and take stock of their careers. This continual reassessment should help preclude the notion one will be trapped by one's own choices. "Even people who feel comfortable about their careers should stop once or twice a year to review their changing goals and motivations," she advises.[11]

Figuring out what one wants and setting flexible goals often requires hard analysis. Organization experts such as Ronni Eisenberg suggest specific procedures women might follow in order to ascertain their key objectives—such as listing goals as intricately as possible, setting up realistic time limits for attaining the goals, distinguishing short- from long-term goals, and setting priorities.[12] But sometimes it takes a more intuitive, gut approach to get in touch with one's Authentic Voice. Says one psychologist: "Sometimes it is helpful to notice which way our feet take us if we leave them to choose their own direction. When neither my thinking nor my heart will tell me clearly whether I should go to a certain place of importance, I personally notice whether I am putting on my shoes or hanging my coat in the cupboard."[13]

However one arrives at one's goals, it is important that they are one's *own* goals and that they provide a sense of *inner* security. "If you know what you want, you can get it. So I'm not recommending that women get good, secure jobs. I'm suggesting self-reliance," Judy Mapes, principal at Zehnder International, says, "Because a big institution won't take care of you. You've got to define self-sufficiency and think of what is going to make you self-sufficient." This means not waiting passively to be chosen by the corporation, or hoping that some top executive will notice your hard work. It requires taking the initiative and seeking out opportunities, looking ahead to specific jobs you might want and figuring out specific steps that will help you get them. Remarks Joyce, a manager at a midwestern corporation, "One thing I've learned is you have to look out for yourself. You have to figure out what you want to do and convince everyone to do it. I just want to take care of myself. My assumption is that it is easier for my boss if I stay in my job than if I want something else. So I better darn well talk about my goals."

Lesson Five: Women Should Develop Their Own Inner Core of Values That Will Sustain Them Precisely When the Male-Dominated Corporate Hierarchy May Dismiss Them

What if the corporation doesn't listen when a woman announces her goals? What if she receives no reward for obtaining them? As Ann Belford Ulanov states: "Women today must face the issue of their own authority."[14] The real sign of this authority is the ability to pursue goals without waiting for the corporate patriarchy's approving pat on the head. Management handbooks for women have been so busy explaining the proper way to handle a headhunter, negotiate a pay increase, and barter for a title that they may be missing a more important skill: how to develop an internal reward structure that will sustain a woman through the tortuous twists and difficult landings a professional career in the eighties entails.

The women managers who have experienced the Success and Betrayal landing have learned there is a fine line between persistence and rigidity. While it may be appropriate for men to adjust their value system to the external clues they receive, women do not always receive the same clues. If a woman responds to each signal from the corporate hierarchy and allows it to influence her plans, her values, and her management style, what will she have to cling to when that approval is ultimately withdrawn despite her best efforts to please?

Women are developing their own internal systems for determining when a bad job is really a bad job and should be evaluated and adjusted, and when another dynamic is at work. "All we have is what we are. And the only goals that are important to me are the ones I set for myself. Otherwise, it's not reality. We all live in our own reality. How can I only see myself as others see me?" Construction executive Eve poses that question and then responds: "To me success is achieving for yourself your own *individual goals* and having the respect of your contemporaries." Such women realize that the real test of a woman's successful adjustment to the corporate world does not come when she is recruited to a wonderful new job or promoted to the next level in the corporate hierarchy. It comes when she must reach inside herself to know she is good *even* if she is *not* recruited. Especially then. As long as women continue to measure their success by the same reward structure men use, they may find themselves consistently falling short, because in the current corporate work place there are few golden apples for women.

How do women, who have tried so hard and succeeded so well, learn to relax and follow their own natural instincts? The question is similar to one Betty Friedan asked several decades ago: "How can a woman see the whole truth within the bounds of her own life? How can she believe that voice inside herself, when it denies the conventional, accepted truths by which she has been living?"[15] Perhaps they might take note that the happiest women in business are those who focus on the substance of the job, not the style, on how it fits with their own specific needs and desires, not on how others view its worth. Nella Barkley advises, "If people can remember in their cumulative experience what they really enjoy doing and have enjoyed accomplishing—whether it's writing or whatever —if they can remember how good it felt to produce that, and if they attach that feeling to a product or service that can be identified, then they'd be much more fulfilled in a career." Marjorie spoke from her experience as an executive recruiter: "You need two barometers: Do you like the work you do? And are you enjoying your life? Because what the hell else are you here for? Making a zillion dollars isn't enough." Sunny, a thirty-seven-year-old corporate counsel, agrees: "If you're just working to prove to other people you can get a good title, it's finite. The trappings of success don't get you up at six A.M. year after year." But an honest assessment of what it will take to get yourself up that early year after year is exactly what's necessary for women who often must also balance their jobs with other demands.

Lesson Six: Each Woman Needs to Manage the Conflict between Her Professional and Personal Goals without Guilt or Apology. There are no Collective Solutions.

Wiser from the experience of success and betrayal, many women are finding that an individually tailored balance between the professional and personal spheres will bring them greater fulfillment over the long haul than an attempt to model themselves on male patterns of achievement and success. More draining and damaging for women than the actual demands made on them can be the sense of inadequacy they feel for not being perfect at everything they do. Never pausing to rest, let alone to smell the flowers, many women dart like hummingbirds from one project to the next without establishing priorities.

Women are starting to set limits and establish a balance between love and work. Books now admonish women to discover that "self realization comes from the achievement of both love and mastery."[16] Srully Blotnick contends that a woman can actually ruin her chances for success on the job if she strives to become a star and neglects her personal relationships in the process. Blotnick encourages a woman instead to "first fall in love, then take her personal life every bit as seriously as she does her career. Maybe more."[17] There may even be something to the notion that recent executive women have been trying to do it backwards, trying to achieve success professionally before seeking personal fulfillment. Nancy Geffner observes, "Men never had the idea they couldn't blend career and family. In women's lives, work goals are considered first and women attempt to fit personal goals around the work goals. I have two kids now in college, and I was the only woman who worked twenty years ago in the upper-middle-class suburb where we lived. But I established my *personal goals first*, and I worked around the work goals."

As women gain more self-confidence and free themselves from the Living-on-the-Edge myth and others, they once again put more of their energies into their personal as well as their professional goals. And they have the confidence to create their own unique blend of work and play. Ironically, stripped of its obsessive, perfectionistic tendencies, the juggling of both worlds, which can lead to the Corporate Amazon syndrome, seems also to lead to the greatest fulfillment for women.

While women, like men, must certainly sacrifice a good deal of their personal time and desires for corporate success, they should early on begin to develop their own individual gauge by which they can monitor the appropriate sacrifices they should make and are willing to make for their careers in order to avoid success and betrayal. And they should accept that this gauge is different for every woman. For instance, Chris, forty-one, one of the top women executives at a major telecommunications corporation, admits that she had put a career before a relationship. But it wasn't worth it: "I had a long holiday planned with someone who was very dear to me. I was offered a terrific new job, but I would have had to cancel the trip. I came to regret that decision. You need a job to eat. But personal relationships take time and energy and are what life's about." On the other hand, the women who honestly treasure their careers more than their "love life" should feel free to make that choice and not be viewed as "freaks." As Alice Hennessey comments: "You ask about balancing personal and business life. I think that is a *tough* question. Because just as men choose different balances in their lives, I think women do, too, and it comes down to what their individual definition of success is. For some women it is to have time for friendships and stay in good shape physically and have an active social life and an interesting career. That is their definition of success. For others it is doing awfully well in their careers and being willing to make sacrifices along the way. They don't feel unbalanced necessarily; it's just what's right for them."

Lesson Seven: Women Should Pace Themselves for the Long Haul

In determining the proper balance between work and play in their lives, women are starting to project out over a number of years in the job market, planning for the time when they may have to drop out. In retrospect, a number of the women interviewed suggested that their ferocious lunge into their careers in the early landings only fueled their later frustration and burn-out. Rachel, thirty-three, the corporate counsel says her advice to younger women just starting in business would be: to be determined, but not so intense. "I've had a *New Yorker* cartoon on my desk for the last fourteen years which pictures a bluebird sitting on a windowsill looking in at a little very old man in a rocking chair. And the bluebird is saying, 'Hi, Billy, I would have been here sooner, but I had other obligations.' It is the bluebird of happiness, and I keep thinking about it and telling myself not to get too wrapped up in the obligations," she explains. "So I would tell younger women to be self-confident and work hard—but to stop and smell the flowers. That's the only thing I didn't do that I regret."

Successful male managers said they would counsel women and other men similarly. Paul, an executive vice president at a hotel group, remarks: "I think having a balanced life gives you staying power, too. There are people who burn out at age forty-three. They try to climb the corporate ladder, and they get to a point and realize they aren't where they want to be, so they throw in the towel. Whereas my dad was assistant plant manager at forty-three, and that was because so many other guys his age gave up. They went through mid-life crisis and decided they weren't where they wanted to be, and they gave up all interest in their work. They had worked so hard that the fire was gone. Like him, I am hoping to have staying power. I don't need to be the youngest senior VP at IBM." Men, anticipating an uninterrupted career, often adjust their ambitions accordingly, and many are pleased with being named a vice president at forty. They don't feel an entire generation is on their backs to prove anything with an early title or responsibility. Men also seem to accept that not every player can be captain of the team. Especially in middle-management crunches, both men and women will have to lower expectations. Such a downshift will come more easily to women if they recognize the importance of pacing themselves for the long term.

Lesson Eight: Women Should View Their Career over a Total Life Cycle and Be Willing to Trade Off Various Aspects of Their Lives Sequentially

Betty Friedan long ago suggested women do not have to choose between marriage and a career; rather, it "merely takes a new life plan—in terms of one's whole life as a woman."[18] Perhaps more than anything else, biology will force women to accept the notion that their pattern of success can be *different* from men's. Women can develop their own timetables and yardsticks for achievement. A number of successful women have found that they were able to drop out and have children and still reenter the work force later and obtain interesting and challenging jobs. Bank vice president Eleanor comments: "The rewards are so great that it's worth it. I know I'd be further ahead sooner, and in a more important field perhaps, if I hadn't dropped out. But I wouldn't have traded the experience of having those kids."

Some younger women might protest that dropping out was a luxury of the good old days when women were more the exception than the rule in business, but most observers contend that this approach will not only unduly penalize women in their careers but will provide them more than counterbalancing rewards. Executive recruiter Judy Mapes puts it this way: "I think we *are* punished for taking time off to have children. But look what you get in return! And women don't look positively at that. I think women are getting too hung up on 'If I make this choice I'll get punished here, or, if I make that choice, I'll be punished there.' I interviewed a woman recently who was eight months pregnant with her second child, and we would have hired her in a minute if someone else hadn't gotten to her first."

Former U.N. ambassador and cabinet member Jeane Kirkpatrick says, in her entry in *Who's Who in America*: "My experience demonstrates to my satisfaction that it is both possible and feasible for women in our times to successfully combine traditional and professional roles, that it is not necessary to ape men's career patterns—starting early and keeping one's nose to a particular grindstone, but that, instead, one can do quite different things at different stages of life. All that is required is a little luck and a lot of hard work." Her sentiments are echoed by Juanita Kreps: "In terms of my own career, I feel the thing that I would do differently if I were doing it over again would be to spend more time with my children and be more relaxed about my job." She urges women to consider developing their own "individually tailored work-life cycle," distinct from the typical male version—one that can include dropping out for a few years for children or family concerns.

While she acknowledges that it can involve painful choices, she counsels women that a realistic acceptance of the trade-offs can make the individually tailored work and life cycle the most rewarding alternative for women. "I think many women today would find that if they took some time out, made their peace with a career development that did not necessarily match that of men and recognize that they may very well catch up later, it would enhance their careers, not impede them." Russell E. Marks, Jr., adds: "Maybe most women need to make career plans differently. Maybe they should plan to drop out and reenter. I think sequential careers are a good idea for women. Hell, I've worked in nine different industries in the course of my career."

Lesson Nine: Women Need to Make a Realistic Appraisal and Evaluation of the Sacrifices Required to Reach the Top Ranks of Management

Women must accept that few men reach the top, and those who do much make tremendous sacrifices. Executive recruiter Pen James speaks for many of the men and women we interviewed: "A lot of people will drop out because as you get higher up in that corporate world, it is a tougher job. You get assigned tougher and tougher projects. And some people— men *and* women—just don't want to do that. Their value systems aren't geared to keep hitting it every morning with everything they've got." Concludes Dr. Frederick Hauser, "The lesson is that we have to be as realistic as possible and demythologize corporate life as much as possible instead of allowing women to continue dreaming." For women who understand the trade-offs, the corporate experience can be easier. In the words of Jane Evans, who has been cited by executive recruiters and business journalists as one of the women most likely to be a CEO: "Until women can in large numbers say, 'My career is what I am and it comes first,' we are not going to crash the barriers that are keeping us out of

the executive suite and on the second string of the management team." Putting the career first requires taking a lot of
hard knocks and doing a lot of hard work, Nancy Reynolds
warns: "You pay your money and take your chance. Your
opponents are always going to gossip about you. Any time you
expose your head, whether in a corporation or in politics or
wherever, you've got to be willing to say, 'Okay, I am going to
take the heat that goes with this.' You can't run and say, 'Oh,
my God, why me? I am such a wonderful girl. I never said a
mean thing about anybody. I like everybody, I keep my nose
clean, why me?' "

Lesson Ten: Each Woman Should Recognize the Need to Keep Pushing for Her Own Rights and Those of Other Women in the Corporation

"I think you should have a high ambition or else you are going
to be like those older guys who are satisfied with the plateaus.
I think you should always be a bit irritated. Not fussy, but
irritated—because that is the only way to get ahead," advises
Angela, a thirty-five-year-old defense corporation executive.
MasterCard International's Joanne Black insists that women
should speak their own truth to the corporation, despite the
risks. "I have no illusions at all about how far women are from
the top," she acknowledges. But she urges other women:
"Don't be a pseudo man. Nobody gets ahead by fading into the
woodwork. The worst thing women can do is accommodate,"
she concludes. "Be a presence . . . the others who aren't get
more work and are put down far more, and abused more thoroughly than any wife ever has been." Like other management
women, she believes that women must accept their role in history and acknowledge the truth that, despite all the past advances, much remains to be accomplished in making the
workplace more equitable and humane.

Women need to speak out and assume leadership roles,
on behalf of both women and men in the corporation. In the

words of one male executive vice president, "There need to be women heroes. Italians have a hero—Lee Iacocca. There isn't that kind of a role model for women. They aren't head of the Business Roundtable, they aren't number two in the Chamber of Commerce. They aren't quoted all the time in *The Wall Street Journal*. And that is what is missing. It takes a long time, and some women are really high up—on lots of boards—but nobody has ever heard of most of them." Or, more accurately, only a handful of women are heard from in the media. Certainly, in many cases top women are not encouraged by their corporations to stand out. But this executive vice president thinks there is another factor at work: "A lot of women deliberately played their reputations down. They don't want to be examples; they don't want to be publicly acknowledged. I think they decided that the road to success is to be low profile. To be high profile means to be strident. None of those people ever really came out because they were afraid to be looked at as women's rights advocates—which is a mistake, because they can have a high profile on business issues that have nothing to do with gender issues." Executive recruiter Pen James also urges women to continue to apply pressure: "I take my hat off to the women's movement. I think they have done a phenomenal job in making corporate America aware of the vast resources and talent women have and in giving them recognition and opportunity. But I have noticed in the eighties that that pressure has started to diminish. And I think the eyes of corporate America are starting to hood over again."

Women should recognize that keeping the rights they've won—let alone further improving their position—requires constant vigilance. Marlo Thomas says that "Every single one of us is freer now than we were twenty years ago. But freer isn't the same as free. More fair isn't the same as just. If I know anything . . . it's that women cannot stop struggling for their rights any more than Americans can stop nurturing progress and defending democracy. You have to realize that there is no end to it. And once you learn that, you don't take anything for granted and you never lose hope for the future."[19]

All these lessons can help future generations of women entering the work force. But in the end, to break the cycle of success and betrayal, each woman must make her own decisions—and those decisions are far from easy. In the new frontier that continues to stretch out before women in the corporation each woman must fight to obtain *her own* personal version of success. And in obtaining it, enrich the chances for all women —and men—in and out of corporate life to find their own version as well.

"What is success?" multinational executive Michelle asks. "To be happy in life and to like life. To be, as the French say, happy in your own skin. I know people who aren't 'successful' but they look successful." Being "happy in one's own skin" may be one of the most difficult yet crucial challenges management women in the 1980s have before them. Because, in the final analysis, there are no easy and ultimate answers; there are only individual choices. There are no maps to follow; there are only inner compasses to trust. Looking back over her career, thirty-four-year-old Sheila observes: "I think one thing I've learned is there's no one happy resolution. There's no easy answer. It helps to know I'm not the only weird duck in a world where every other woman seems to have figured everything out. There is some solace in knowing it's being explored, that it's okay to search for solutions."

CHAPTER 12
LESSONS FOR
THE CORPORATION
WOMEN AND
THE FUTURE

*We must accept and live with the
sexual revolution and must give
full meaning to the notion that
there is total equality of opportunity within the corporation.*

Coy Eklund
Former Chairman
The Equitable Life
Assurance Society of
the United States

Throughout this book, we have stressed women managers' tendency to anthropomorphize the corporation. Yet, if the corporation is neither father, mother, lover, nor "betrayer," it is still organic—a thinking, feeling, responsive entity. As such, it is capable of evolution, if only it makes up its mind.

Clearly, the coming crisis of women in the corporate workplace is real, and growing. Now there is a new urgency. After scarcely two decades, is American business in danger of turning off a significant portion of women to the concept of a lifetime career in business? What can corporations do to prevent this crisis? After all, the corporation might argue, the crisis is a function of the female mind-set, not the responsibility of the workplace. Why change? And what can women do to make it worthwhile for companies to invest in the structural change that will ultimately provide the key to a resolution?

For the first time in history, women are beginning to reach a critical mass within the business community. According to futurist John Naisbitt, the balance of power is rapidly shifting in favor of women, making life for them "a new seller's market."[1] Women already outnumber men at 52 percent in the nation's colleges; at the elite business schools—Harvard, Yale, and Stanford—they constitute 50 percent of the student body. As of February, 1986, women professionals outnumbered men for the first time: the nation's pool of 13.8 million professional workers had 29,000 more women than men, according to the U.S. Bureau of Labor Statistics. The issue is no longer whether corporations will hire women but how many women they must hire to get the top graduates. If women will become the majority of the educated class within this century, even allowing for dropouts and marriage, can the corporation afford to ignore their special needs?

For years, women failed to call attention to these needs, to where they parted company with the corporation, for fear of calling attention to themselves. Now that they have reached a critical numerical presence and have gained some seniority within the corporation, they have begun to find a voice. Having recognized the limits of androgyny—and having come to realize that they will always be regarded as a breed apart—they are beginning to demand that positive distinctions be made in their behalf rather than against them. Yet the rewards that will become increasingly meaningful to women are not simply "women's issues." Flextime, flexible benefits, job enrichment in lieu of promotion—all these have surfaced before as androgynous concepts designed to improve the productivity and quality of corporate life and to reinvigorate the corporate structure. In many cases they are as attractive to men as to women.

What is different, and more urgent now, is the unambiguous link between the expectations of women and the rewards needed to keep them in the corporate game. What corporation can afford to ignore the opportunity for such positive evolution?

Lesson One: American Business Can't Afford to Alienate a Generation of Women

A quiet revolution of women managers is taking place in the workplace, slowly draining it of the best-educated, best-trained women ever to enter the workplace. This brain drain of female talent confirms our observations that an accelerating number of disillusioned, dispirited women are opting out of corporate culture scarcely ten years after opting in. Some leave to start their own entrepreneurial ventures. Most intend never to return. "It's ironic," comments Stanford University professor Myra Strober. "The problem of the 1970s was bringing women into the corporation. The problem of the 1980s is keeping them there."[2]

Can the corporation afford to lose these women? Demographic and psychographic evidence says no. According to one recent survey, only 58 percent of managers below the rank of

CEO said they were "reasonably confident that they will be with their present employers five years from now" versus 74 percent in 1970.[3] Despite the current glut of baby boom executives, a baby bust of managers is about to hit, creating a decade-long shortage of promotable male and female managers. Predicts *Fortune,* "Companies that have grown accustomed to choosing from the super-abundance of graduates are going to have to compete harder for the best of the lot—and pay them more." The conclusion? "Stock up on talent."[4] The threat is closer at hand than corporations now suspect. Management consultant Peter Drucker predicts that "Increasingly, it will be the job seeker who is the 'customer,' with job opportunities and job characteristics having to satisfy the job seeker."[5] One industrial publication warns: "[I]f companies allow their management ranks to be trimmed at random—by resentment—they risk losing their best performers and a good source of future top-management talent."[6]

Some managers already envision the cadre of exiting women some day providing real economic competition for their former employers. As a growing number of frustrated women leave their corporate jobs to start cottage-industry consulting firms whose hours, purposes, and rewards give them greater gratification, corporations may find it increasingly expensive to buy back at hourly supplier fees the expertise they previously had on call. "In an era of increased international competition where success depends more and more on the productive use of knowledge," suggests small business expert Steven Solomon, author of *Small Business U.S.A.,* "it's going to be more critical than ever not to lose women from key positions in the work force. A country can't afford to systematically exclude a large segment of talented individuals —in this case women—from exerting business influence and still hope to maximize its international competitiveness. Women have long been an important market for goods and services, and that market, influenced by the rise in the number of women holding jobs or going into business for themselves, is always changing. Corporations would certainly stand to gain from having the input of businesswomen in formulating marketing and other business plans."

If women entered corporations by accident, they will be leaving by design. And corporations will have to start paying well to keep them. Cautions Russell E. Marks, Jr., "There will always be a lot of women to fill the ranks of those who depart. However, there's a *but*—and that's the degree to which frustration grows. It's not difficult to imagine that frustration eventually coming to be felt throughout the nation. You risk creating an incredible reservoir of ill will, resentment, and destructive energies. So we *have* to worry about those problems and address them." Most women managers remain skeptical of the corporation's ability to halt the exodus of women managers without major structural improvements. Says Alice Hennessey, "If you're serious about bringing women along, you have to hire a bigger proportion at the bottom, because they will fall out one way or another. We lost four of our top women at Boise Cascade in the past few years—not because they didn't like Boise, but because they were very successful, quality people who had opportunities to do other things. So you are going to lose some. And you had better have a big fund to draw from." Ironically, the few corporations promoting women to senior management find such women are the first to be recruited by competing organizations—in essence, punishing progressive corporations for their liberal promotion policies. Adds another woman executive, "Under the pyramid structure we have now, it doesn't pay to think long term. Whoever is making decisions figures he won't be around long enough to reap the rewards, so why make long-term commitments?"

Some women managers worry that corporations are resting on the laurels of the late seventies. Most male managers from CEO down, however, appear to be skeptical about the progress so far. "I have been in the business world since 1962, and it has changed a lot," says executive recruiter Gary Knisely. "But on a scale of one to ten, we've only moved from one to three. There is a big difference between three and ten." Warns a senior-level male oil company executive in response: "I worry that the corporation won't adjust to the demands of frustrated, talented women. I think instead there will be a mass exodus of women from the corporation over time. Corporations don't change to keep people; they change only when absolutely necessary—when their very survival is threatened." To which Russell Marks responds: "I'm not convinced there should have to be a crisis to do that. I'm not convinced that crisis is the best way to motivate change." Increasingly, it is the men—CEOs, senior managers, and bright, younger executives who have worked side by side with talented women—who worry about the critical female managerial talent shortage ahead. Offers former AT&T chairman Charles Brown, "Removing the barriers that prevent women from realizing their potential is of critical importance for the stability, growth and competitive position of American business."[7]

Most managers contemplating the potential loss of managerial women are both more insistent on and more optimistic about corporate evolution. "We would be in deep shit without them," asserts one forty-four-year-old executive vice president, adding, "Business desperately needs as many bright people as it can get. Without its will or knowledge, business suddenly tapped a tremendous female reservoir of brains that doubled the existing pool of talent. If all that went away, you would find organizations tremendously impoverished." Comments C. H. Hardesty, Jr., chief executive officer of Purolator Courier and former vice chairman of Continental Oil: "What it says is that we are having to strain and break some practices that have grown up over the years. And any change takes time." Coy Eklund agrees change is seldom easy: "We'll have to learn how to manage these new situations. Like most new developments in this world, as we solve the crude problems, we end up creating more sophisticated, subtle, more difficult problems." For corporations committed to keeping women managers, productive change begins with an appreciation for and recognition of the different voice, attitudes, and expectations women bring to work.

Lesson Two: Companies in Search of
Excellence Can Begin by Capitalizing
on and Rewarding Their Own Natural
Resources—Managerial Women

It's interesting to discern how the *In Search of Excellence*
model companies—IBM, Coca-Cola, GE—treat women,"
mused Herb Schlosser recently. *In Search of Excellence* pre-
scribes incentives for "man waiting for motivation."[8] Its
solutions have revolutionized the way corporations think
about managing their human assets, and the role "right-brain
values" play in sensitizing corporations toward "excellence."
Managers of both sexes generally acknowledge that women
bring such qualities in abundance to the workplace. Writes
Marilyn Loden, "By my own definition, feminine leadership
differs from the traditional masculine approach in its preference for cooperation over competition; in its reliance on
intuition as well as rational thinking in problem-solving."[9]

Among the lessons for managers to absorb, according to
Thomas J. Peters and Robert H. Waterman, Jr., the authors
of *In Search of Excellence*, is productivity through people, accomplished through an appreciation of individual effort, recognition, encouragement of creativity, and individual initiative
in search of better products.[10] In short, all the values that
devolve from women's unique expectations at the threshold of
their careers have been rediscovered by corporations. Only now
such qualities are not called "feminine"; they are called "excellent." Finding themselves more at home with their femininity
in the rarefied middle- to upper-middle-management echelons,
women managers long to see their values filtered through the
corporation as legitimate leadership qualities. Most women
now confidently concede that there is a distinctly female style
of leadership and that such a style is not only legitimate but
highly productive as well. Feminine leadership, in short, is
coming out of the closet. This is the undiscovered, certainly
uncelebrated, and definitely unrewarded new excellence in the
post-androgynous workplace.

Eight years ago Alice Sargeant pointed out "the urgent

necessity of integrating masculine and feminine values, traits, and behaviors into ourselves and then slowly into organizational structures and processes."[11] Today, rather than an androgynous management style whose compromises threaten both sexes there is now talk afoot of a "bilingual" workplace, a concept coined by Susan E. Davis, the forty-three-year-old vice president of Chicago-based Harris Trust and Savings and organizer of the Committee of 200 top women in American business. "The successful manager of the 1980s will be the manager who is bilingual in both the men's culture and the women's culture."[12]

Lesson Three: Corporations Must
Evolve Structurally and Attitudinally

"Business *is* tough. It's not a benefactor," asserts executive recruiter Judy Mapes. "Corporations are not even aware they might be needed in that role. And even if they sense it, they shun it," she says. But as corporations move more and more toward the high-touch workplace of the future, two kinds of change will ultimately be required. One is attitudinal; the other is structural. Attitudinal changes can begin with a recognition by the corporation that women are on a separate timetable— both physiological and, even more important, psychological —that must be respected by corporations who want to keep them. Time, the cheap commodity of most women at the early landings of their careers, becomes their most precious asset from middle management on. Few are willing to continue to squander it as a mandatory loyalty test to the corporation. Most of the mystique of time and the woman, it turns out, is an anomolous form of fealty corporations have traditionally extracted from men. Eighty-seven percent of male managers polled by *The Wall Street Journal* put in fifty or more hours a week.[13] Asks psychiatrist Willard Gaylin, "*Why* do we have to work seventy to eighty hours a week? Especially when we have ample role models in this society of men forty to fifty who burned out in corporations and are left with no capacity for forming attachments or deriving pleasure?" For disenchanted corporate women, the misuse of their time is one of the most often discussed sticking points of their corporate resentment. Until the corporation legitimizes the notion that time expended is one but not the only measure of corporate "success," it will continue to lose women who become disillusioned with trying to cram too many life-styles into too few hours.

Increasingly, smaller companies and family-owned entrepreneurial ventures have capitalized on this frustration. Taking a long look at the new post-industrial economy, they, like Alvin Toffler, have concluded that the old needs for synchronized work schedules are often obsolete. It matters less when or where a job gets done than that the job simply gets done well: A "whole group of social and economic forces are converging to transfer the locus of work." According to Peter Tattle, vice-president of Ortho Pharmaceutical (Canada), Ltd., the question is not " 'How many can be permitted to work at home?' but rather, 'How many *have* to work in the office or factory. . . . Fully 75 percent [of employees] could work at home if we provided the necessary communications technology.' "[14] Toffler's suggestion that we turn homes into "smart" work stations with a minimal corporate investment in terminals and technology remains to be acted on in any appreciable numbers among the corporations whose managers we interviewed, though *Forbes* predicts there will be as many as 15 million telecommuters by 1990.[15] Yet, according to Weyerhauser Vice-President R. L. Siegal, "Working at home is consistent with our shift toward flexible hours. . . . The important thing is getting your job done. It's incidental to us where you do it."

The stability and security of a progressive corporation could theoretically attract women who are in the midst of flux and evolution after one or more marriages, childbearing, maturity, and retirement. "I've loved going to work every day," says one oil-company executive in human resources, "and I'd love to stay here for thirty years. I like working for a big organization. I know it's an 'out' thing, but I don't mind the security," she says, attributing much of the attitudinal difference between her and burned-out contemporaries at other companies to ample flexibility to come and go. The company also offered her liberal leave through a difficult pregnancy messengering work to her home. No wonder she says what any company would long to hear: "I love it here. It's great to be in a noncompetitive, supportive environment."

Another attitudinal change will be needed if corporations want to keep women managers: there must be a redefinition of loyalty. Women often measure it differently than corporations do. It is hard for women to be loyal team players in the face of decisions that offend their "different" voice. Jeane Kirkpatrick defends the accusation that she was not a team player by explaining, "I felt it was important for the President to . . . [hear me] raise questions, hear the interchange of opinion, and then make his decisions. I wasn't willing to join with other advisers to present one consensus recommendation."[16] A midwestern managerial woman added, "Corporations just want to hear the good news." That is why too many once-proud corporate giants have ended up like General Dynamics, caught with its hands in the federal till or, like A. H. Robbins, bankrupted by an excess of greed and a dearth of business ethics.

There needs to be an evolution in corporate notions of what makes women "loyal" company employees. Companies will have to encourage and reward the airing of divergent points of view and a different moral voice—a notion with which few contemporary corporations are comfortable. "To accept women as fully human means to accept 'feminine' values as human values appropriate to both sexes," writes Marilyn French. "To accept women politically means admitting their point of view to the halls of power and opening one's mind to sharing it."[17] Concerned university sociologists suggest that if professionals are to stay interested and productive, they need "a clearer sense that the large institutions most of them work for really contribute to the public good."[18] Already, there is ample evidence that younger managers concur. A recent *Forbes* survey of new M.B.A.'s revealed that a majority felt American businesses were not meeting their social responsibilities. Companies such as General Dynamics and Union Carbide showed up on their "least admired" list. Summed up one young M.B.A., "Now there is much more of a spoken concern about your contribution to society, about doing something worthwhile, about being part of the community."[19]

Another attitudinal shift is already in progress. The company move, a heretofore mandated loyalty test and prerequisite for success, has suddenly diminished in importance, according to Cris Collie, executive vice president of the Employee Relocation Council. He attributes the change to employees' increasingly vocal reluctance to move, and to the preponderance of dual career families. The move to a service economy and an upsurge in high-technology solutions such as teleconferencing and telemarketing have helped to take the pressure off the high-powered dual-career couple. Where relocation is still mandatory, necessity has forced a new sensitivity. Companies now routinely hire consultants to smooth the transition. "A third of our members have formal programs to address the spouse-employee issue. In many cases," says Collie, "nepotism rules are being dropped so a company can hire both husband and wife."[20] Corporate relocation experts such as PHH Group's subsidiary Homequity, for instance, offer special programs for "trailing spouses," advising women and men how to find jobs in the same city as their relocated spouses. Such support from corporations suggests a greater acceptance of the diminishing loyalty to corporate policy and the greater inner directedness of promising younger managers. If not, a homogenous corporate America will find itself in conflict with increased segmentation in its own workplace, inevitably leading to breakdown rather than breakthrough.

Lesson Four: The Best Run Companies Will Custom-Tailor Rewards to Keep a New Managerial Segment—Women

In today's competitive managerial marketplace, companies are going to have to rethink their reward strategies, matching the creativity of the individual with creative solutions that offer meaningful rewards. "Money, status, the outcomes of business are secondary to the act of creation," touts one recent management review.[21] Not surprisingly, that profile is consistent with the way most women define the satisfactions of career success: flexibility, creativity, the yearning for individualized, meaningful contribution, the desire to grow. Against these criteria, money alone proves a poor palliative. But are corporations flexible enough to meet the challenge of developing meaningful rewards for this growing "market segment" of the company? "[I]ncreasingly, the available work force is segmenting into a fairly large number of different markets, with considerable freedom for the individual to switch from one to another," advises Peter Drucker. "Increasingly, therefore, employers will have to learn that jobs are products that have to be designed for specific buyers and both marketed and sold to them. More and more we will need to have personnel policies that fit the person rather than bureaucratic convenience or tradition," Drucker continues, likening this transition period to a new reward structure to a "sea-change."[22] Almost alone among prominent male organizational consultants, he incorporates women into his plan for corporate revisionism as the vital resource they are becoming.

Notes a highly placed bank vice president and human resource executive, "The biggest problem we have is keeping good people who have always measured 'success' by their next move. We're all trying to beat the system." In an era of increasingly limited upward mobility where beating the system is an impossible dream, women particularly will look outside the corporation for rewards. Smaller companies, noticing an increase in the number of inner-directed managers of both sexes, are quick to offer such creative rewards. As a result, they are successfully wooing smart young managers away from the giant corporations. The Rockport Company, a Marlboro, Massachusetts, shoe manufacturer, for example, recently spent $15,000 to rent a twenty-room mansion in Newport, Rhode Island, which they renamed Camp Rockport. The 200 Rockport employees stay at the mansion, a dozen at a time, for two days of sports and shoptalk with the boss. The company had been growing so fast the owner feared he was falling out of touch with his employees: "We're trying to be a democratic company, one where people are just as important as the profits they make."[23] For women, meaningful nontraditional rewards might come in the form of flextime, leave policy, retraining, flexible benefits, and job enrichment. Smart companies have already begun offering a menu to choose from rather than standard benefits that have "always" worked for male managers. "It's amazing," confirms benefits consultant Dale Gifford, partner of Illinois-based Hewitt Associates, "what changes and cutbacks people will accept when they are given the ability to make some of their own choices at the same time."[24]

In addition to a holistic reward structure, managerial women have other important needs attitudinal change can satisfy:

- *Security: The Japanese have learned to provide security as a matter of course to keep all employees productive and feeling rewarded. This includes letting employees know where they stand, another practice at which the Japanese excel. The knowledge that there will continue to be a place for the successful woman in a corporation as she ages, as she surmounts the various landings in her professional life, and if she chooses time off, is key.*

- *Loyalty: Corporations may continue to profit from the unusual degree of loyalty many women bring to the corporate "family." But increasingly, younger women, noting the abuse of such loyalty—as reflected in lower salaries, slower promotions, more overtime demands, and insufficient psychic rewards—are learning to be less loyal. Women, for reasons we have already discussed, form the most natural potential constituency for long-term commitment, providing their loyalty is recognized and rewarded by structural changes that maximize their productivity and permit them to stay within the system.*

- *Individuality: The "star system" must return to corporate life. Women must be encouraged to express their individuality—in communications skills, in intuitive judgments that question linear assumptions, and in spontaneous behavior—without fearing such inherently "feminine" behavior will preclude them from the top jobs. Women work more productively when they are recognized and rewarded for the positive differences they bring to the workplace.*

While some of the change facing corporate America is attitudinal, many experts—managerial women and organizational consultants alike—agree that ultimately the challenge must be structural as well. What is at issue is more than just flexible leave time or benefits; it is the *symbolic* responsiveness of corporations, the corporate commitment to flexibility and change in turbulent times. The message from women is twofold: action on redesigning policy and longer-term corporate commitment to women's continued economic viability and vitality within the corporate managerial ranks. "What is urgently needed," comments Peter Drucker, "is a benefits policy that accepts the heterogeneity of the labor force in the period of population changes."[25] Among the large corporations that have already bought into a flexible benefits package of one sort or another are American Can and Procter & Gamble, which have added dependent care to their menu of optional benefits. Hewitt Associates' Christine Seltz estimates that eighty percent of all flexible benefit packages include a childcare option. Still, the biggest flexible benefits issues facing women managers, Seltz warns, are those of vesting and pension privileges among women managers who have to interrupt their careers for children. Women, unlike men, are likely to lose pension privileges as they drop out temporarily to have children. How can women accrue enough time to get benefits? The portability issue—the right to transfer accrued vesting years from a previous employer—is one Seltz suggests will force companies to the wall. But passage seems inevitable, despite the administrative nightmares of tracking women down years after they have left a company. "Flexible benefits," Seltz concludes, "are not a panacea. But they can help with a lot of issues." Innovative reward structures, however, don't come cheap to women. At Chemical Bank, for example, employees who elect extra benefits such as childcare get the costs taken from their paycheck.[26] Joanne Black recommends flexible benefits as "compensatory perks" in lieu of traditional but irrelevant male perks such as paid golf club memberships. Such perks, it is understood, are in addition to, not in lieu, of equal pay for equal work.

Lesson Five: Corporations Must Recognize That Maternity Leave Is Not Disability Leave

For the past twenty years, most of corporate America has been living on borrowed time. Now corporations, having accepted the initial charge to train this generation of women, are facing the fact that some of their women managers are becoming irreplaceable—just as their biological clock goes off. Because women managers have put off the decision to have children until the last possible moment to get maximum seniority under their belts, the fact of seniority makes leave twice as disruptive. The U.S. Health and Human Resources Department reports that the number of first births to women between the ages of thirty and thirty-four rose 83 percent between 1972 and 1980; the increase for women thirty-five to thirty-nine was 44 percent.[27] Companies are running out of time to gear up for a response. "You don't voluntarily lose key people," explains Cigna Corporation president Eugene Ricci about the decision to offer reduced working hours to one woman manager after the birth of her son. "Brains are hard to come by."[28] Corporate America is facing an unprecedented opportunity to experiment with the women managers of this decade by testing various innovative employment options on a segmented basis. Of these, maternity leave is persistently the hottest item. While some argue, as does Susan Deller Ross, director of the Georgetown Sex Discrimination Clinic, that "pregnancy classifications hurt other women and give employers disincentives to hire other pregnant women," most men and women are reluctantly coming to accept the limits of an androgynous corporate culture.[29]

"It's a fact of life that women become pregnant and bear children, and, thus, employers must provide unique benefits for women," wrote one respondent to a recent magazine survey on maternity leave.[30] "When women have children," confirms Russell E. Marks, Jr., "those women are taken out of the competition at precisely the point at which they're being tested in the race. So a problem is clearly the structure of our enterprise today." Adding to the pressure for corporations to keep pregnant managers happy are demographic and income shifts among an aging baby boom population—shifts that will begin to erase the current "new breadwinner" economic incentives for women to work through childbearing years. For a few women, as their husbands reach the senior-management level, dual incomes will increasingly become a luxury rather than a necessity.

The early 1980s dilemma—whether women should be singled out as a target for change—has fallen by the wayside as increasing numbers of key women managers leave the corporations to have and raise children. Our society glorifies motherhood without providing the appropriate institutions to back up its belief. Writes Jessie Bernard of this ambivalence: "Until we make up our minds, the technologies required to achieve our goals are secondary. . . . Do we want to encourage or discourage motherhood? Should we or should we not ease the mother's load? Should we or should we not encourage labor-force participation by mothers? . . . The answers still evade us."[31]

To the extent that institutions procrastinate on the issue facing the most talented, best-educated women in history, they contribute to the decline in quality mothering of the entire next generation. Too often, corporations inadvertently turn the issue of maternity leave from an objective policy decision into an emotional, judgmental loyalty test of women. Laments Rosalie Wolf of International Paper, one of only two women treasurers of a *Fortune* 500 industrial corporation: "Somewhere along the line, maternity leave got classified as equal to disability leave, sort of like being out with a broken leg. When it's healed, it's healed, and there's no recognition that there's now a child to deal with. These women are immediately pressured to be back working at the same level with no regard for the fatigue, the readjusted schedules, or anything else associated with postpartum changes." Women resent such loyalty tests and the concomitant pressure to declare their intentions even before they themselves have made up their minds.

Few companies can afford to signal mother-to-be managers that they are suddenly disposable. Some 80 percent of women in the work force are currently in their childbearing years. With 92 percent of the women respondents to one recent survey arguing that women should be guaranteed the same or comparable job after pregnancy leave, corporations ignore the issue at their own peril.[32] Three hundred lawsuits are pending in California alone over the issue of maternity leave. "The corporate response thus far has been, 'You want equality? It's your problem. We don't want to know about it,' " argues one of America's most senior corporate women. "Well, women today may be equal, but they are still different."

The answer, suggests a corporate veteran who is now a headhunter, is better counseling going into maternity leave. "Maybe companies shouldn't be forced to hold a position open," she argues. "That would give a woman more of a choice about when to come back. But she should be able to state her reservations about returning without repercussions." Maternity leave should become an essential part of human resource development, with the dual objective of keeping the leave as nondisruptive as possible to the corporation and keeping women in the company. In that connection, maternity leave should not be regarded as an aberration, and a woman manager's career potential should not be evaluated on how many times she requests leave and how many months it takes her to "get serious" about her career again.

Many women feel bitter that after years of loyal service, they are asked to bizarrely "prove" their loyalty in an emotionally complex, surprisingly unfamiliar personal arena in which the as yet unborn child is held hostage to future career advancement. Ironically, corporations may end up regressing to the self-fulfilling prophecy that women will be trained, just to have them drop out, unless they act quickly to institute new, responsive policies to avoid it. States former Commerce Secretary Juanita Kreps, "In many corporations, maternity leave is short. And I'm afraid that may encourage women to give up their jobs altogether."

Lesson Six: Corporations Need to Address Day Care and Assume Greater Responsibility for Taking Care of the Caretakers

Day care makes every corporation nervous. Individuals accept the need for it intellectually, but corporate America rejects it emotionally. The Conference Board's Dana Friedman suggests that this decade will be one in which corporations first appreciate the impact of working women and family issues on their bottom line: "We are in the transition phase of a tremendous social upheaval."[33] Married women with children under six constitute the fastest-growing segment of the work force. Yet currently only two thousand companies underwrite some form of day care. Resistance seems to linger over more than just the potential employer expense. Is resistance grounded in principle? Much is being asked of a corporation on behalf of one segment of the workplace that claims to be striving not for differentiation but for equality. Or is reluctance entrenched in the gap between old values and new behavior? The traditional compartmentalization of work and home can no longer be realistically enforced when economic necessity has put women in the work force and competence has kept them there.

It would be presumptuous to attempt to summarize in several pages the progress that has been made on day care so far. But it is worth pointing out connections perhaps heretofore ignored about women's expectations and need for non-traditional rewards and how day care might fit into a portfolio of corporate answers to gratify those needs.

Company policy grounded in surveys conducted as recently as five years ago may be woefully inadequate in telling corporations how employees feel about such issues as day care and flextime. In most companies, no long-range monitoring has been conducted to track attitudinal changes, a lapse that would be unthinkable in any other strategic planning function. Too often, surveys become the terminal point rather than the starting point of the day-care issue. Having conducted the obligatory poll, corporations breathe a sigh of relief when the marketplace momentarily shows no need for product to fill the potential niche.

In truth, companies face a difficult dilemma: the cost of on-premises day care can be high. And in the New York metropolitan area, which has the largest concentration of corporate headquarters in the country, the inefficient commuting system makes centralized day care on premises extremely inconvenient for women unable to bring their children to the office on overcrowded commuter trains. Outside New York, the pressure eases considerably. Procter & Gamble, Cigna Corp., Hoffmann–La Roche, Corning Glass, Campbell Soup, and Southland Corporation, among other companies, have invested in on-premises day care. Bill Greenough, retired chairman of Teachers Insurance and Annuity Association, assessed other aspects of the day-care dilemma from a purely financial perspective: "We studied the day-care issue and examined it in terms of feasibility and quality of services we could offer, and we found we had such a diversity of mothers that a centrally located facility would be of no use. And we didn't have enough pockets to handle the day-care issue from a logistical base. One of the problems in trying to provide on-premises day care is a whole set of public requirements that are difficult to meet and expensive to implement. For example, you're required to provide a full-time nurse in the facility, although we have a full-time health facility elsewhere in the building. So the very good efforts of government to make day care healthy . . . are good, they make sense, but they end up destroying the whole concept."

But in an era when the United States is struggling to stay competitive internationally, the greater cost may be in employee man-hours lost and in training people to replace women managers who cannot afford to work without day care. One Texas study found that a $30,000 investment in day care can save a company a total of $3 million in employee retraining, turnover, and lost work time.[34] Russell E. Marks, Jr. cites a first-hand example: When a new and expensive cable plant in Venezuela failed to motivate worker productivity, the company fired one of its three male shifts, replaced them with women, and installed on-premises day care. Absenteeism disappeared, and productivity soared so dramatically that the company replaced a second shift in the same manner. Concludes Marks, "Day care is important—a useful economic tool. There was a direct link between the day-care benefit offered and the enhanced productivity we got out of it." Southland Corporation agrees. A $200,000 child-care facility in its new headquarters building is expected to cut significantly into the $70,000 annual absenteeism rate. Campbell Soup Company in Camden, New Jersey, spends $175,000 a year subsidizing tuition in its day-care center. Big numbers? The combination of capital investment for the physical plant plus annual subsidies for qualified caretakers together amounts to less than the cost of producing three television commercials at current prices.

Employer response runs the gamut of ingenuity. Some offer vouchers—easiest to administer for the corporation because the onus of responsibility for finding qualified day care rests with the employee. The voucher system is most convenient for large, decentralized companies. Other corporations offer reimbursement on presentation of canceled checks, making day-care administration as simple as just another expense account reimbursement. Medium-sized companies will often contract out to a given facility. Big companies such as Honeywell and Kentucky Fried Chicken use their clout to negotiate discounts on day care similar to those that most businesses currently swing with rental car companies. The present discount is 10 percent but with more companies exerting leverage it is likely to grow. Finally, smaller companies are banding together in adopting "time-shared" economics to the costs of day care. In Sunnyvale, California, a group of high-tech companies pool their resources to offer employees a day-care collective where no one company had previously had enough mothers to justify the expense. Sums up Campbell Soup CEO Gordon McGovern, "This is a dollars and cents issue for us; it's part of running a business well."[35]

Pressure for change is rapidly spreading through women's networks, putting corporate reputations on the line. As women get closer to the parenthood decision, the pressure increases to find solutions. While a growing number of pacesetter companies such as IBM, AT&T, and Polaroid offer some kind of day-care assistance, at present, most CEOs regard day care as a problem outside the venue of business. "I'm not sure you are right in asking the enlightened company to provide day-care services," states one progressive CEO in the service sector. "I don't think the enlightened company is going to go out here and say, 'Look, we are going to put this on a satin pillowcase for you. But if you need to have this much extra time to make sure the children are okay, I will give it to you.' I think the company has to be tolerant of the mother as she makes her own way." The Conference Board's Dana Friedman points out that the Harvard Business School doesn't teach executives how to set up child-care centers, or how parenting pressures can affect business performance: "Many managers are fearful that by helping working mothers, they'll end up with babies in the boardroom." In this view, shared by many CEOs, enhanced productivity is "worth it" only up to a certain point. Is the corporation obliged to support all women or just an exemplary one or two managers? "A woman manager being compensated at $350,000 a year can damn well pay for her own baby-sitter," one CEO argues, sidestepping the obvious statistic that only a handful of $350,000-a-year executives are women, and of those, few are in the early childbearing years when day care is most necessary to avoid a disruptive work schedule. Day care or other corporate concessions evaluated on a case-by-case basis and doled out to the exception do not constitute policy.

Some CEOs reject the day-care issue because of implied value judgments they feel are attached to any endorsement of day care or surrogate parenting as a life-style: "One of the two spouses in a two-career marriage is going to have to give up the opportunity to be the top dog in the company if they're going to give enough time to the child," flatly states the former CEO of a large natural resource conglomerate. "I don't know that day care can substitute for somebody spending time with a child." IBM states it doesn't want to make "family decisions for our employees." But psychologist Willard Gaylin suggests that society has already outstripped corporate policy on this issue. Companies will be in the day care arena willingly or unwillingly. "Maybe as a society we'd better look at doing some genetic engineering to produce two times as many women as men to care for children while other women are working," he suggests facetiously. "Otherwise, where are all these women caretakers going to come from?" Warns Korn/Ferry's Leonard Pfeiffer, "The corporation should not and does not want to lose women after investing training in them. Unless we accept that women have the babies in this society and evolve with that reality, companies won't have any consumers for their products in twenty years." Within the next decade, children will not be the only dependents clamoring for a woman's care and time. According to *The Wall Street Journal*, aging parents, traditionally women's responsibility to care for, will be the next big dependency-care issue: "Often, caring for a parent results in cutting down on hours at work or even quitting jobs," as 28 percent of the survey respondents had already done. "The conflict between career and caretaking is likely to get worse as the population of elderly people continues to grow."[36]

Corporations may soon be forced to accelerate their day-care plans. If the corporation doesn't take the initiative in policy development, the government may do it for them. There is precedent abroad. In Belgium, full-time *creches* are operated by the government—day-care facilities that stay open until six or seven each evening—far more liberal coverage than most corporations would be inclined to offer. Such a government-sponsored program, if applied in the United States, would be a bureaucratic nightmare to administer, forcing corporations to add yet more benefits staff to an already overcrowded payroll. The money for such programs would probably come from corporate taxes in the wake of reduced federal subsidies for social welfare programs. The Alliance for Opportunity, "a program to help women turn the challenges of their personal and professional lives into opportunities," has already been founded by two leaders of the Republican National Committee with top White House political aide Edward J. Rollins. The President's Advisory Council on Private Sector Initiatives has sponsored a series of luncheons nationwide to lobby CEOs of the country's 750 largest corporations on child care. As a result of such pressure, new public and private sector initiatives are mushrooming. In California, companies including BankAmerica, Chevron, and Clorox have banded together with local governments in a $700,000 pilot program to train day-care workers. Meanwhile, aggressive day-care legislation has been introduced in both the House and the Senate by Republican Senator Alfonse D'Amato and Democratic Congressman Mario Biaggi to encourage on-premises day-care centers in the workplace by offering tax credits to corporations that do so.[37] And congressional day-care legislation has already been passed to the tune of $4 million annually.

Corporations that are tempted to dismiss such legislation as the wishful thinking of a minority should keep in mind that in a decade in which 92 percent of women surveyed favor day care in the workplace, legislation could become the political football of the late 1980s, kicked through Congress on a wave of political expedience.

Lesson Seven: Corporations Should Consider Part-Time Managerial Options As a Short-Term Solution That Will Help Them Keep Women Managers for the Long Term

Peter Drucker suggests that rights for part-time workers who are women may become the cause of the late eighties and early nineties,[38] much as women's rights were the cause of the seventies. Former Commerce Secretary Juanita Kreps points out that women who opt for part-time or flextime arrangements at the midpoint of their careers still have thirty productive, uninterrupted years ahead of them. Women managers now in their twenties talk of cyclical careers that embrace longer time frames than ever before. Yet corporations are doing little to address the issues implied in such long-term commitments.

It has been eight years since Alvin Toffler predicted the Third Wave of postindustrial change. In the wake of women's growing disillusionment with corporate life, many corporations might reexamine Toffler's prescriptions. His solutions for a postindustrial workplace seem particularly appropriate for the post-androgynous workplace as well. As recently as three years ago, a survey of a dozen U.S. cities did not turn up a single personnel policy on special arrangements for mothers.[39] Comments Juanita Kreps: "They no longer ask, 'Is she going to get married and drop out?' so we have turned that corner." But, she adds, "Corporations are not doing enough in two important areas that would help them hold talented women: flextime and part-time arrangements. Corporations shouldn't want to impede women's access to the good jobs, nor dampen their aspirations."

One of the greatest barriers to flextime or part-time arrangements is the pressure from other women and men who regard the flextime employee as somehow getting a free ride. "What about employee morale?" worry the members of the corporate human resource staff. Yet it is precisely when there is no stated policy on less-than-full-time employment that resentment arises. General Mills, for example, has a general policy of flexibility but no flextime policy, according to Patricia Anderson, manager of personnel services.[40] Clear part-time policy positions take the edge off charges of favoritism. Though resentment may still build up rules will be clear and policy consistent, proof that the system works on behalf of both full-time and part-time workers. Where there is no clear flextime policy, compensation is left to the imagination, performance equated to physical hours in the plant, and the notion of "value" of the part-time employee is up for grabs. One male publisher said, "We have one woman in the legal department who works three days a week. But she and her boss had to put up with a lot of flak to get her that kind of status. And, of course, you get off the fast track doing that."

Most manager mothers have reluctantly begun to accept the notion that they are on separate timetables, that promotion may take longer for them. Notes one bank division manager, "My promotion to vice president was up for five years before it happened because somewhere it was determined that part-time people couldn't become VPs. Then someone finally said, 'Forget the rules; let's get on to something else.' And I got the title." Women who have accepted the need for compromise expect the corporation to meet them halfway. Too often, they argue, co-workers forget that women have already been penalized by having their salary rescaled to reflect their part-time contribution. Often, they put in more unpaid overtime at home than full-time workers do. Promotion has to happen a different way, argues one West Coast broadcasting executive who has left the field to have her first child. "You can't just plug women into the male pattern. Childbirth is not even remotely androgynous." Some corporations are already beginning to plan for it. Warns the head of human resources for one of the country's largest, most-emulated banks, "The major financial services and consulting firms where women are beginning to make inroads will definitely have problems. Fifteen years out, we'll lose a substantial number of employees. We've already lost some of our best women. So we're looking at flextime and at electronic cottages for traders. It's difficult. You can't take a person in investment lending and start her doing interest rate swaps at home on a PC. It would be a disaster. But maybe she can continue to see clients twice a week."

Economics will drive the evolution toward integrating part-time work into mainstream policy. It will be more productive for companies to hire free-lancers than to spend money to train new employees. The advantages of such hiring are multifold. Companies pay for only the time they use; they pay no benefits. Compared to the present inefficiencies of full-time employment and the skyrocketing costs of benefits packages to full-time employees, part-time represents an attractive alternative for corporations managing in tough economic times. Suggests Alice Hennessey, "We are finding now that we're in a real cost-reduction tendency, as are most of our competitors, that it would be so much easier to do the kinds of things we are trying to do if it were accepted that people could take a step back, or take a lateral move, or go to work part-time."

Lesson Eight: Women Shouldn't be Punished for Reentry

With fewer and fewer managerial positions available, thanks to merger mania, corporations like CBS and AT&T are already encouraging early retirement to allow attrition of surplus talent they do not intend to replace. Women who opt for part-time work, request protracted maternity leave, or simply drop out until their children reach school age are presumed to have voluntarily removed themselves from career competition. "Corporations are going to be asking, 'What's her priority system? Where's her real commitment?' " suggests Dr. Frederick Hauser. "And they assume they can't count on that woman any longer, even though she may be a fantastic employee." Corporations and women differ on how long that assumption should hold. Women are willing to have a penalty called, but want to know how long they're expected to sit in the box before being allowed back on the ice. Right now most companies say forever. "It's not impossible to reenter," admits Leonard Pfeiffer. "But it wouldn't be easy. The critical question would be, 'What was she doing during those five years?' " To make exceptions, corporations rationalize, is to tell men who work through nonstop or women who have sacrificed the option to have children in favor of a career, that their contribution and the time they put in were not valued. "There's no incentive for a company to accommodate leaves," argues one male marketing division manager for an appliance manufacturer. "You can't hold a job open for two or five years. And if you hire a woman back and promote her, what if someone who's deserving doesn't get that job—someone who's worked here all along? I don't think companies have come to grips with the issue—and I don't think women have come to grips with it either." His argument is seconded by a personnel manager for a large New York bank: "Management has to be willing to repatriate women at the expense of some senior people. There will be a certain discomfort among people who stayed and worked. How would you feel if a woman came back and took a plum spot you'd been working for?"

Russell E. Marks, Jr., disputes such logic: "Traditionally in companies you bring in new people all the time to fill gaps in the pipeline and to keep existing people alert—to enliven the internal environment. And that's the best argument for reentering women. There is value to moving people in and out. You know, our society has always lauded mobility. A certain imposed mobility, like this, is a good thing. That's how we stay resilient in the face of social problems." One female network executive points out the double standard for men and women on the subject of reentry: "After all, men go off and work in the government, and they get hired right back into the system. And often they're hired into industries they've never worked in before." Some CEOs, willing to rehire after a leave of absence or a gap in employment experience, suggest the system does not work against the woman, but her equity among co-workers is at risk. One corporate president recounts the story of a mother who returned on reduced hours only to find that her peers were reluctant to delegate assignments to her.

Others voice concern about the ability of reentered women to keep their skills current. "The jobs are changing so dramatically," says one. "It would take months to catch someone up on the new products we're introducing." Argues *Forbes* deputy editor-in-chief Malcolm S. Forbes, Jr., "I don't buy that. That's a conceit of the priesthood—the concept that information is so voluminous that if you're not there all the time you can't possibly understand the industry. They build up that idea because it's threatening that somebody could drop out for three years and come back in and pick up where she left off. It's just a way of reducing the number of competitors among a bunch of baby boomers jockeying for position. One thing you discover in college is that even if you attended all the lectures and classes, you probably learn more under the gun than you do if you have all the time in the world." Futurist Steve Custer adds, "This is the first generation of workers in history who will be outdated by information several times in their careers. Where technology previously became obsolete at the same time a generation of workers turned over, it now outpaces worker turnover. Retraining or job changing will be necessary several times in a career whether you're a man or a woman."

A human resource director with one of the country's most emulated banks suggests some likely scenarios: "If you brought a woman back in a line job who was really smart, you could put her in as assistant to the EVP—a slot that requires strategic planning or marketing—and retool her skills,

419

test her mettle, and reposition her there. We've already created more planning and senior administration slots that give women more chances to reenter. Or you could tag-team her in a senior position with a manager who would be retiring soon. If she's a really good resource, she could begin to assume more and more of his responsibilities." But she admits to anticipating resistance from men in the pipeline who have been eyeing such slots for years. Hunter College president and former Carter administration cabinet officer Donna Shalala points out that a country that once took an entire generation of men back into the work force and retrained them after World War II should be able to do the same for women. Broward Craig disputes such analogies but is enthusiastic about the potential of reentered women within the corporation: "People who come back into the work force have usually made decisions that increase their enthusiasm for working, whereas you can have people who've worked straight through but have lost their enthusiasm, and are just putting in time." There is very little argument that most women can relearn the necessary skills—although some CEOs add a caveat that it is not up to corporations to retrain women but up to women to keep their skill current. The real enemy of reentering women lies in the signals, subtle and not so subtle, that trickle down from the top about the limited potential most corporations foresee for such women. Too often, argues Peter Drucker, the reentering woman "is put under a 'supervisor' who treats her like a moron who has never done anything on her own before, when what she needs is a teacher and an assistant. . . ."[41]

The specter of a corporate society prepared to punish or hold back talented women in whom they have invested years of training and development suggests there is more at work in corporate decisions than rational, objective assessments of the problems and opportunities ahead. Emotionalism rather than reality moves corporations to question whether a woman can assimilate the information required for reentry—when the same woman has already proven her learning curve once at the start of her successful career.

Columbia University Law School recently hired a woman dean, the first ever to hold such a post in the Ivy League. Barbara Aronstein Black had interrupted her career for nine years to raise three children. She believes her appointment is characteristic of a turnaround: "The message is not merely that a woman was appointed, but a woman who did what I did: who took on the traditional duties and obligations and joys of the woman's role, who traveled a terribly circuitous path back to the job that she had always wanted, whose work was not of the quantity that the more direct male path would have produced. . . . I do believe that where I am today has everything to do with the years that I spent hanging on to a career by my fingernails."[42]

Lesson Nine: Change Trickles
Down from the Top.
Wanted: A Few Good Men

Most managers, male and female, believe change can happen as soon as one good man at the top wills it to. Coy Eklund is adamant that unless equality is part of the personal agenda of corporate leaders, it will never make it to the corporate agenda. And the responsibility for making it happen cannot be delegated: "It is a fact with respect to any corporate policy that it be enunciated clearly from the top and that responsibility falls to the CEO as the acknowledged head and author of policy. Certainly equal opportunity for women and minorities is a fundamental expression of that policy." Those men able to separate emotional arguments from rational debate have the potential to guide corporate America toward the full flower of its investment in training and promoting women managers. While the sixty-eight-year-old chairman of one oil company reportedly explained of his company's all-male board of directors, "I had one lady in mind, but then she died," the CEO of the future agrees, like Home Box Office's Michael Fuchs, "I like the independence of powerful women."[43] There is no doubt in Pen James's mind of the value of change from the top: "If a major corporation has a woman EVP, that's going to be a clear message to everyone else that that is a possible path for them." Juanita Kreps believes change is bound up with a kind of corporate Catch-22: "I guess the question is whether we will see enough movement at the top until we get to a point where we have women more at the top."

"Some executives have devoted themselves to moving women up the ladder," comments Anne Wexler, "Coy Eklund made a point of it. But there has to be a conscious effort at the top." Argues one paper products company executive, speaking for most of the women interviewed, "One of our chairmen had as his goal a strong affirmative action program. As a result, his goals had be quantified in every department, and manager's bonuses depended on how well they fulfilled these affirmative action goals. When financial incentive is involved, it's amazing how you can motivate people." Comments Lois Wyse, "You need more than a thinking CEO who will say, 'I want to start moving women up. Let's start equalizing.' Then he gives this to his lieutenants who somehow or other get too busy doing something else. There are too many people who have to change the way they have always thought in order to make something really happen." Coy Eklund tied incentive compensation requirements to affirmative action goals. A women's rotating advisory panel met with the company president quarterly to discuss interests, aspirations and issues, and to monitor progress. Such commitment is echoed at Allied Corporation, where affirmative action goals are also tied to executive compensation. Allied president Alan Belzer, states one industry publication, doesn't take excuses. The company's human resources director adds, "Used to be that if a woman professional planned to get married or have a baby, we'd shrug our shoulders and write her off. [Now] we bend over backward to keep her around."[44] At Merck, Chairman John J. Horan insists women's progress be tracked on a specific timetable. As a result, since 1979, there has been a 40 percent growth in Merck's female managerial staff.[45]

The new-style CEO approaches women, like men, as valuable resources and recognizes flexibility as an important corporate strategy to keep them. Bill Greenough recalls running into a very capable, very pregnant employee who burst into tears one day as they were talking: "And I asked her, 'Was I insensitive in my comments? Please help me so I don't repeat the mistake.' And she told me the doctor had just informed her she was carrying triplets. She asked me what company policy was on a woman who would be staying away six years, until her children were in school. She had been reconstructing her life all the way back from the doctor—in a way a man will never have to—because up until that point she was planning to come right back to work. And I said to her, 'If we can work it out to your satisfaction, we will. And if not, let us call some of our competitors to see if they can fit you in.' " As a result of the consideration with which her case was treated, Greenough's company was able to keep her. She was motivated to return to work as soon as possible after the birth of her children—and is still there on a three-day-a-week schedule.

Seeing their own daughters in business seems to have opened the eyes of some CEOs to the degree of discrimination within their own companies. Comments Russell E. Marks, Jr., "Now there's an awareness on our part that women can't be shut off at a certain point." Adds Coy Eklund, "You don't ignore your daughter whom you not only love but respect." Another CEO says candidly, "Your daughter comes home and recounts the same stories you've heard about for years from the personnel guy, but now it's suddenly *your daughter*, damn it!" Additionally, as working wives accomplish changes within the ranks of their spouses, corporations will benefit from the insights these women can offer.

Finally, every CEO we spoke with applauded the intent— if not the execution—of government-sponsored affirmative action plans, and all of them believe that women's future advancement would be in peril without them. "I do think the EEOC was necessary," admits Broward Craig. "I don't think things happen fast enough in these discrimination areas unless the government takes the bull by the horns. Not everything about EEOC was good. But if everyone had been allowed to decide on a required skill level, women would never have had an adequate chance [at promotion]."

Other CEOs agree. "Do you need something [like EEOC] to take care of people and opportunities?" one asked rhetorically. "Absolutely. I believe government has a [necessary] role in EEOC and whoever says you don't need it is wrong. Because if we hadn't started it—however traumatizing it might have been—we would have done much less in business than we did." Like most progressive CEOs with whom we spoke, however, he adds that if government was right in setting the agenda, it was wrong in implementing it: "I don't want you telling me how to do it. But I do want you telling me it has to be done." Cautions Russell E. Marks, Jr., "I think EEOC was a very valuable impetus. But even if it had continued to be aggressive and enthusiastic, once men and women began moving up the ladder, its effect could never be as strong as it was at the entry level. At those middle- and upper-management levels, it's felt to be more intrusive the higher you move in the hierarchy. The battle will be fought a different way the higher up you move."

Lesson Ten: As Corporations Struggle to Attract and Hold a Diminishing Pool of Candidates in a Seller's Market, Today's Women Managers Represent a Valuable Actuarial Investment

As sixty no longer feels like sixty, as morale among older people remains high, corporations will confront a potential increase in the number of senior women managers reentering the work force and continuing to work long past the traditional retirement years. In fact, actuarial realities will favor the longevity of women over men in the workplace. Reports the *Wall Street Journal*: "[W]ith the baby-bust years producing smaller numbers of new young workers to replace the retiring baby boomers, there may be pressure on the boomers to stay on the job."[46] Malcolm Forbes, Jr., points to the number of senior citizens who now work at fast-food outlets, partly because of the low teenage population at present. Hewitt Associates' Howard Fine comments, "Business is going to need workers, and Social Security and other plans may have to be changed to encourage these people to stay on working."[47] A sizable number of baby boomers may never retire; Social Security will never be able to reimburse all those people.

A substantial cadre of empty-nesters, currently middle managers, may work long into the retirement years. They represent a better long-term actuarial risk than their male peers for the companies who invest in them. In fact, the government figures that a sixty-five-year-old man has an average of 14.5 [retirement] years to live, [but] a sixty-five-year-old woman has 18.6 years."[48] Most of these women will be primed, both psychologically and economically, to play their part. Those who have dropped out to raise a family will be fresher to the challenge, a scenario at least one CEO sees as promising: "I have known any number of men who were 'brain dead' on the job, because their heart wasn't in their work," suggests Broward Craig. "But people who come back into the work force usually have made decisions that increase their enthusiasm for working."

Lesson Eleven: Corporations Will Have to Implement Change to Stay Competitive in Bidding for the Services of the Next Generation

[If] the new M.B.A.'s remain members of the church of capitalism," notes *Forbes*, "they are fussy about its articles of faith." Only four of the recent M.B.A.'s sampled aspire to the CEO job. Nearly two-thirds expect to exit the corporation to start their own businesses, and 76 percent would move as often as every other year to advance their careers.[49] The nature of women's corporate disenchantment suggests that they may be motivated to move more often and sooner than men. Younger women bring not one but two differing sets of values—the values of a newer, more entrepreneurial generation and the values of their own post-feminist expectations and upbringing. Their values too often conflict with, rather than complement, those of today's corporate culture. Like many women managers in their twenties, a group recently interviewed in Chicago represents the post-modern attitude toward corporate life. Neither as loyal nor as patient as their older sisters, they are poised for change, even planning to precipitate it. "I need something that isn't full-time, especially when the children are younger—until my husband is a partner and the kids grow some," said one. "I like the idea of 'Well, I'll just quit,' and I think I can always get something else," another volunteered. A third woman told us, "You can get additional promotions by switching companies, and when you do the switching, take time off to travel in between." They express little of the fear of rocking the boat evinced by an older generation of women managers reluctant to press the corporation to their own advantage.

The lesson for corporations is clear: It will be significantly harder to attract and hold talented managers during the next decade. Half of them, demographics suggest, will be women. As such, they will be demanding more of the corporation on every front as their numerical superiority and egalitarian entry-level experiences increase their confidence and thus their willingness to assert their demands. And they will be monitoring corporate responsiveness more carefully than men ever have. Recent women M.B.A.'s are even more adamant: Says one thirty-year-old, "There is still much room for improvement in human relations, particularly in equal pay for women, day care, and participative management."[50] Women —with "more to prove early on," as one recruiter frankly admitted—are likely to be a more demanding, more skeptical audience than has ever confronted the corporation. Their cynicism about corporate flexibility is based on the lessons they learned from the present generation of women managers.

That generation, in the opinion of up-and-comers, has tolerated far more and made more sacrifices than this generation is willing to do. Radcliffe College's Margaret Touborg wonders, "What will we do with the idealism, with the visionary expectations of women who say, 'We'll take turns working while we raise the kids?' Is their sense of entitlement about the future in fact a reaction to a lack of options?"

"It's not as dramatic or as far-flung as it was in the sixties, but the romance of independence persists from that era," Steve Custer asserts. "More and more inner-directed people will come out of the closet as managers." And they will have the clout that comes with seniority. "The challenge remains with the corporations to motivate people and keep them effective," sums up one respected executive candidly, "because the strongest candidates for any job still come from within." In such a climate, women managers can no longer be regarded as expendable or disposable commodities.

Lesson Twelve: Corporations May Change to Accommodate "Women's Issues," But What Is Really at Issue Is a Structural Change to Maximize Human Potential in the Workplace

Few managers, male or female, underestimate the degree of corporate evolution necessary to bridge the gap between women's needs and what corporations are currently able to deliver. Women's concerns will most immediately fuel the workplace revolution.[51] Surprisingly, however, even male managers interviewed perceive the ultimate benefits of change as offering more than simple accommodation for women. These managers believe an enlightened sensitivity will replace the current atmosphere of benign neglect. Offered one male manager in his early forties, executive vice president of a large public relations concern, "I suppose I would say business has to be more of a meritocracy than it is. It really isn't now; it's still 'old boy.' It's really asking for a major cultural change for what is basically a white Anglo-Saxon–dominated culture." When he speaks of how corporate cultures may change, like other managers from entry level to CEO, he envisions change as holistic—psychological as well as structural. Day care, flextime, flexible benefits, important changes though they may be, are only half the answer to keeping women managers motivated. The other half of the answer—enlightened sensitivity and responsiveness to the cry for individuality, early recognition, corporate loyalty, and a moral voice in the conduct of business—is a change many men are also eager to see implemented.

Writes Adam Smith, "The only trouble with the business society is that it leaves behind those who are not buckobsessed, and has condescending contempt . . . for anyone not in the money chase. . . . If the discrepancy becomes too great, then we lose a sense of community, and gradually the majority become only spectators at the great feast."[52] The Harvard Business School now trains managers in a holistic view of career priorities. Professor Abraham Zaleznik teaches Social Psychology of Management, which emphasizes the impact of family life and values and "the tension between career goals and personal aspirations." Notes Zaleznik, "We have been abstracting *people* out of management as if they didn't exist. . . . The question is What kind of human beings are we producing by fostering this kind of experience?"[53] Change is in the wind.

"In my early years at Boise Cascade," notes senior vice president Alice Hennessey, "you were expected to leave early on Sunday afternoon for a business trip so you wouldn't spend time traveling on Monday, so you could get going in New York first thing Monday morning. It was wrapped up with a kind of pride. You know how much time we spend in airplanes and never travel during working hours. Well, that's nuts. It really downplays the value of the family. And I said to our chief executive officer, 'You know, if you keep doing this, you will cause everyone else to think this is expected.' It's taken time for that to change, but we don't do it anymore.

We travel a lot less on Sundays. That's a small thing, but it gives people a day with their families." Another woman manager, vice president with one of the country's largest insurance companies, tells of a corporate-supported women's network for middle managers. As a result of this "corporate commitment to equity," women discovered a great deal of encouragement from men to promote women. Now, she reports, "The support group makes a point of inviting men to its meetings—and some of them go."

This leads Alice Hennessey to suggest that corporate evolution be couched in human terms, that women can stimulate change that benefits male and female managers equally: "We encourage people at headquarters to take time off and go to their kids' Christmas programs. Years ago, it was okay for a guy to take off early to play golf, but he didn't take time out to go to the conference at school with his spouse to see how the kids were doing. We encourage that now." One divorced manager went so far as to suggest the typical holiday calendar be amended to include "parent days" off to address the realities of children's sick days, pediatric visits, or teacher consultations. "These are subtle things," concludes Hennessey, "but I think they are supportive of men *and* women." And of an inclusive rather than an exclusive corporate experience.[54] Few women, offered such benefits, are likely to look elsewhere for a better managerial job if the trade-off means losing such rewards.

And few men, offered such a choice, are likely to malign the company that gives them a break. The second stage of the women's movement, observes Betty Friedan, may actually be a genderless phenomenon evolving out of what women had previously thought of as "their" battle. "Where women seem to be moving out of the home to fulfill themselves in a men's world of work, men seem to be disentangling themselves from definition by success in the work world and shifting toward a new definition of themselves in the family and other new dimensions of self-fulfillment"[55]—an observation confirmed by our interviews with sympathetic male managers. Dr.

Willard Gaylin suggests, "If the system is to work, the role of men within it must change, as well as the role of women. Because now we're prepared to let a woman enter the corporate world, but not prepared to let a man leave."

Paternity leave, laughed off previously as a "Mr. Mom" phenomenon, is gaining respectability. Over one-third of corporations nationwide offer some type of paternity leave. Sweden, in fact, offers nine months of fully paid parental leave to both mother and father.[56] Among those companies offering lengthy leave is Procter & Gamble, whose spokeswoman says, "We wouldn't [offer] that if we thought it was disruptive." Their parental leave is six months. Suggests Nancy Reynolds, whose prestigious Washington public relations firm insists that fathers take paternity leave, "You know what the result has been? They don't want to leave our firm. They work ten times as hard. Wives are part of our team when we need them to be. When we need their husbands to work evenings and weekends, they do it without any compunction. We see to it here that people do not neglect their families. And what we get in return is unbelievable, incredible people who not only work for us and never quit, but a lot of people who want to come to work for us." Representative Patricia Schroeder of Colorado has already introduced into Congress a bill for a mandatory eighteen weeks of unpaid leave for all parents. Christopher Dodd of Connecticut has sponsored a similar bill in the Senate. Says Schroeder in defense of the bill, "Both mothers and fathers understand that the workplace *must* change to meet the needs of the work force." Women managers corroborate this. Says one: "Women won't reach the top until there is more equal parenting. There are now some fantastic male managers out there, but unless we come to grips with all of this as a society, it won't work."

Gender-blind leave policies force "women's issues" out of the disability column and into the human resources arena where policy can best be generated and adapted. This is one issue on which managerial women are likely to keep the pressure on: "I think somehow over time in business, it has to become acceptable to take a lateral move or to take a step back or a little time out for men and women. It can't be put just in the guise of a 'woman's issue,' " argues Alice Hennessey. "A lot of men would be perfectly content to do that if it were considered acceptable. It's still unusual, but if you could get to the point that it was okay in general, it would be so much easier to accommodate the needs of women in business."

By the same token, although male managers malign paternity leave as quick derailment off the fast track, secretly many appreciate that paternity leave represents the element of choice—options—a heretofore unknown phenomenon in the corporate culture of the organization man. Women can and will be the engine driving positive and long-due policy changes that adapt to these new managerial realities. Suggests one woman executive, "I don't think there's anything mutually exclusive about being supportive of people *and* making a profit."

In fact, in an era of limited upward mobility, the rewards will have to shift away from single-minded devotion to promotions to the idea of making work more palatable. The old corporate fruits of competition and upward mobility may no longer define the standards by which people succeed. As these challenges affect men, they, too, will begin reevaluating their priorities, making corporations more responsive to change influenced by female values as well. Men, in short, have begun to accept emotionally what the corporate culture is as yet unable to assimilate intellectually. In the future, the challenge will be to close that gap within the corporate culture in an effort to lure women and keep them motivated.

Until they do, top managerial spots awarded on the basis of competition and macho values will continue to demand the ultimate sacrifice from women. Women will still be asked to limit their expectations coming in if they expect to answer their own Authentic Voice. And when they do, most will automatically self-select out of the competition for the most powerful jobs in corporate America. As long as the corporation continues to mirror male values and attitudes toward women, no significant results can be gained by policy changes alone. Structural change must reflect attitudinal change—a "win-win" scenario for women and the corporation. That philosophy would eliminate either/or choices in favor of inclusive, mutually beneficial choices. Such choices in turn would maximize the potential of the most heavily recruited generation of women ever to cross the corporate threshold. With choices, with flexibility, with real opportunity for multidimensional success, women and the corporation can merge their futures on parallel, rather than on diverging tracks.

NOTES

Chapter 1

1. Leah Garchik, Letter to the Editor, *Vogue*, January 1986, p. 24.
2. "Women Face Job Bias, Experts Say," *New York Times*, November 25, 1984.
3. "More and More, She's the Boss," *Time*, December 2, 1985.
4. *Wall Street Journal*, January 21, 1986.
5. Kathleen Hendrix, "Women Executives: Is It a Doll or Bear Market?" *Los Angeles Times*, reprinted Fall 1985.
6. "How Executives Get on Boards," *Working Woman*, August 1985, p. 26; Kathleen Hendrix, "Women Executives: Is It a Doll or Bear Market?" *Los Angeles Times*, reprinted Fall 1985.
7. "You've Come A Long Way, Baby—But Not As Far As You Thought," *Business Week*, October 1, 1984, p. 126.
8. Helen Gurley Brown, "Step Into My Parlor," *Cosmopolitan*, March 1985, p. 16.
9. Connell Cowan and Melvyn Kinder, *Smart Women, Foolish Choices: Finding the Right Men and Avoiding the Wrong Ones* (New York: Clarkson N. Potter, 1985), p. 12.
10. "Executive Women Find It Difficult to Balance Demands of Job, Home," *Wall Street Journal*, October 26, 1984.
11. Betty Friedan, *The Feminine Mystique* (New York: Laurel Books, 1983).
12. Barbara Ehrenreich and Dierdre English, *For Her Own Good: 150 Years of Experts' Advice to Women* (Garden City, N.Y.: Anchor Doubleday, 1978), p. 259.
13. Helen Gurley Brown, *Sex and the Single Girl* (New York: Pocket Books, 1963), pp. 3-4.
14. Barbara Ehrenreich, "Strategies of the Corporate Woman: What Feminism Has Learned at the Office," *New Republic*, January 27, 1986, p. 29.
15. John A. Byrne, "No Time to Waste on Nonsense," *Forbes*, May 6, 1985, p. 114. Another financial industry publication explained women's silence on the downside of success this way: "[The] fact that Wall Street's women

are so handsomely compensated acts as a 'golden muzzle.' As one woman
banker concedes, 'It's awfully hard to feel sorry for someone who makes
$250,000 a year.' " Beth McGoldrick and Gregory Miller, "Wall Street
Women: You've Come a Short Way, Baby," *Institutional Investor*, June
1985, p. 85.

16. TRB, "The Incredible Dr. Hammer," *New Republic*, January 20, 1986,
p. 4.

Chapter 2

1. "As children, young girls identify with the fairy tales they read. . . .
Although [the] characters have humble beginnings, they are rescued,
through no efforts of their own, and led to a happy life."—Celia Halas
and Roberta Matteson, *I've Done So Well—Why Do I Feel So Bad?
Conflicts in the Female Experience and What Women Can Do about
Them* (New York: Macmillan, 1978), p. 29.

2. Gail Sheehy, *Passages: Predictable Crises of Adult Life* (New York:
Bantam, 1977), p. 125.

3. "The Successful Woman," *Forbes*, January 28, 1985, p. 9.

4. Warren Susman, *Culture As History: The Transformation of America in
the Twentieth Century* (New York: Pantheon Books, 1984), p. 9.

5. Quoted in Suzanne McNear, "The Heroine Complex," *Cosmopolitan*,
February 1984, p. 213.

6. Celia Halas and Roberta Matteson, *I've Done So Well—Why Do I Feel
So Bad?* (New York: Macmillan, 1978), p. 34.

7. Michael Maccoby, *The Gamesman: The New Corporate Leaders* (New
York: Simon & Schuster, 1976), p. 100.

8. Mary Cunningham, "Power Steering," *Harper's Bazaar*, September 1985,
p. 234.

9. Quoted in Sam Hull, "Having It All in the Eighties," *Duke: A Magazine
for Alumni and Friends*, 1985.

10. Paula Bernstein, *Family Ties, Corporate Bonds* (Garden City, N.Y.:
Doubleday, 1985), pp. 10–12.

11. In our discussions with corporate women, a necessary tension appears to
exist among women who are a contradictory amalgam of ambitious independence and generic interdependence. "Illuminating life as a web rather
than a succession of relationships, women portray autonomy rather than
attachment as the illusory and dangerous quest," writes Carol Gilligan in
In a Different Voice: Psychological Theory and Women's Development
(Cambridge, Mass.: Harvard University Press, 1982), p. 48.

12. Commented Elyse Wakerman, author of *Father Loss*, recently on "Today,"
"The need for control—to be the dumper, not the dumpee, is actually a
need to overcome paternal rejection. Simultaneously, women are looking
for someone to take responsibility for you as a father never did." With
women now marrying the corporation in their early twenties, it is not
surprising that women are visiting these same patterns on their relationship
with the corporation—conflicted about their dependency on even so im-
mutable an organization as an entire corporate culture.

13. Statistics excerpted from a survey of 300 top women executives at the Graduate School of Management at UCLA sponsored by Korn/Ferry International published in "Publisher's Note: Women at the Top," by Valerie Free, *Marketing Communications*, Fall 1985.
14. Megan Marshall, *The Cost of Loving: Women and Their Fear of Intimacy* (New York: Putnam, 1984), quoted in *Second Century Radcliffe News*, February 1985.
15. Halas and Matteson, *I've Done So Well*, p. 12.
16. Carol Gilligan, *Different Voice*, p. 49.
17. "Boy Babies Still Come First," *Self*, January 1985, p. 20.
18. Carmela Maresca, *Careers in Marketing: A Woman's Guide* (Prentice-Hall, 1983), quoted in *Marketing Communications*, October 1983.
19. "Learning How to Play the Corporate Power Game," *Business Week*, August 26, 1985, p. 54.
20. In *In a Different Voice*, Carol Gilligan provides a particularly useful discussion of women's "injunction to care," p. 100.
21. Alice G. Sargeant, *The Androgynous Manager*, AMACOM (The American Management Association), New York, 1983, p. 147.
22. Carol Gilligan, *Different Voice*, p. 100.
23. In the University of Texas study cited earlier in this chapter, women subjects who describe themselves as "more independent, achievement-oriented, and self-confident" also see themselves as more "intuitive, compassionate, and empathetic and less inclined to use power" than their male peers.
24. From Lily Tomlin's one-woman play, *The Search for Signs of Intelligent Life in the Universe*, by Jane Wagner.
25. Halas and Matteson, *I've Done So Well*, pp. 185, 204.

Chapter 3

1. Maggie Scarf, *Unfinished Business: Pressure Points in the Lives of Women* (Garden City, N.Y.: Doubleday, 1980), p. 103.
2. Profiles of successful father-daughter role model relationships include Linda M. Watkins, "Executive Fathers Prepare Their Daughters for Corporate Life," *Wall Street Journal*, October 28, 1985, p. 25. In a recent University of Texas survey, fifty successful women named their fathers as primary role models—"The Successful Woman," *Forbes*, January 28, 1985.
3. Even today most children claim to understand the substance of their father's employment, but when pressed, they cannot supply the details. Ninety-one percent of executive children surveyed by the *Wall Street Journal* and the Gallup Organization claimed "very good" or "somewhat good" understanding of what their fathers do to earn family income. But the actual number prepared to supply specific details fell short. Only thirty-six percent reported their fathers frequently talked about work at home, many claiming lack of interest in the details. Cynthia Crossen, "Kids of Top Executives Are Crazy about Dad—Especially His Money," *Wall Street Journal*, March 9, 1985.

4. Louise Bernikow, *Among Women* (New York: Harmony Books, 1980), p. 67.
5. Celia Halas and Roberta Matteson, *I've Done So Well—Why Do I Feel So Bad?* (New York: Macmillan, 1978), p. 84.
6. New studies link intellectual achievement at college to an inability to focus on career choices and a tendency to engage instead in volunteer or service activities and those that promise academic recognition. These students tend more frequently to be women—a clear link between gender and intellectual involvement on campus. The four-year study of four hundred randomly selected Stanford University students appears in Fred M. Hechinger, "College Students: Little Change Found," *New York Times*, February 4, 1986.
7. Katherine Jones, "How Many Women Are Club Presidents on Campus?," *Radcliffe Quarterly*, March 1985, p. 15.
8. Scarf, *Unfinished Business*, p. 21.
9. Quoted in Julie Wilson, "The Five Sisters: The Case for Women's Colleges," *Town & Country*, June 1983, p. 124. Confirms Mount Holyoke President Elizabeth Kennan in the same article, "We have a commitment to empower women to succeed."
10. Women describe law school as an option tried and rejected like an ill-fitting dress before the big dance: "I thought the likely thing when I graduated was to become a lawyer. I took the Law Boards and became a paralegal for three years. And after two, I realized I didn't want it. So I thought, 'Aha. I'll go to business school,' " said one young associate now with a national accounting firm.
11. Karen Springen, "M.B.A.: No Cheap Date," *Manhattan Inc.*, July 1985, p. 10.
12. Halas and Matteson, *I've Done So Well*, p. 52.
13. Scarf, *Unfinished Business*, p. 40.
14. "What Do Today's Freshmen Want from Life? To Be 'Very Well-Off,' " *Washington Post*, national weekly ed., January 28, 1985, p. 38.
15. A survey of the class of 1983 at Radcliffe College, conducted one year after graduation, suggests that the major career concerns revolve not around advancement but around the ability to juggle career and family. In general, "these women are optimistic about their future professional lives. They are confident about their ability to succeed in their chosen careers . . . they are, however, clearly apprehensive at the prospect of being able to combine successfully the career they have selected with the kind of family life they are also planning." Beth Frost, "Class of 1983: Optimism about the Future," *Second Century Radcliffe News*, April 1985. Confirms one Duke University career development counselor, "Whereas men assume they will have both career and family, today's college women feel they are being torn apart."
16. Robin Lichtenfeld, Letter to the Editor, *New York*, August 5, 1985.
17. From an advertisement for Susan Litwin, *The Postponed Generation: Why American Youth Are Growing Up Later* (New York: William Morrow, 1986).
18. Maggie Scarf writes of this adolescent experience: "Career goals . . . can be taken up with deadly earnestness, invested with overwhelming signifi-

cance—and cast aside in boredom within the space of months, even weeks. . . . Reality itself isn't at this phase of life a hard-and-fast thing; it feels, somehow, reversible." Many women soon find just the opposite to be true—*Unfinished Business*, p. 26.

19. Gail Sheehy, *Passages: Predictable Crises of Adult Life* (New York: Bantam, 1977): "People who slip into ready-made form without much self-examination are likely to find themselves locked in. . . . Although the choices of our twenties are not irrevocable, they do set in motion a Life Pattern" (p. 40).

Chapter 4

1. Grace Baruch, Roslind Barnett, and Caryl Rivers, *Lifeprints: New Patterns of Love and Work for Today's Women* (New York: McGraw-Hill, 1983), pp. 18, 20.

2. Gail Sheehy, *Pathfinders* (New York: Bantam, 1982), p. 34.

3. Moss Roberts, ed., *Chinese Fairy Tales and Fantasies* (New York: Pantheon, 1979), p. 55.

4. Julia Kagan, "Survey of Work in the 1980s and 1990s," *Working Woman*, April 1983.

5. *Glamour*, January 1986.

6. Daniel Levinson, with Charlotte N. Darrow, Edward B. Klein, Maria H. Levinson, and Barton McKee, *The Seasons of a Man's Life* (New York: Ballantine, 1978), p. 91.

7. Robert Penn Warren, *All The King's Men* (New York: Bantam, 1971), p. 118.

8. Michael Maccoby, *The Gamesman* (New York: Simon & Schuster, 1976), p. 115.

9. Amy Gluckman, "Women Clash: Older Workers vs. Younger Boss," *Wall Street Journal*, February 19, 1985.

10. Benjamin J. Forbes and James E. Percy, "Rising to the Top: Executive Women in 1983 and Beyond," *Business Horizons*, September-October 1983.

11. Susan Brownmiller, *Femininity* (New York: Fawcett, 1984), p. 212.

12. Cited in Helen Rogan, "Top Executives Find Path to Power is Strewn with Hurdles," *Wall Street Journal*, October 25, 1984.

13. Susan Brownmiller, *Femininity*, p. 17.

14. Roger L. Gould, *Transformations: Growth and Change in Adult Life* (New York: Simon & Schuster, 1978), p. 259.

15. Lionel Tiger, *Men in Groups* (New York: Random House, 1969), p. 33.

16. Carol Gilligan, *In a Different Voice: Psychological Theory and Women's Development* (Cambridge, Mass.: Harvard University Press, 1982), p. 44.

17. Helen Rogan, "Achievements and Ambition Typify Younger Executives," *Wall Street Journal*, October 25, 1984.

18. Carol Hymowitz, "Male Workers and Female Bosses Are Confronting Hard Challenges," *Wall Street Journal*, July 16, 1984.

19. Harry Levinson, *Executive Stress* (New York: New American Library, 1975), p. 179.

20. Michael Korda, *Power!* (New York: Ballantine, 1975), p. 256.

21. Quoted in Letty Cottin Pogrebin, ed., by Nancy Newhouse, *Hers: Through Women's Eyes* (New York: Villard Books, 1985), p. 49.
22. Benjamin R. Barber, "Beyond the Feminine Mystique," *New Republic*, July 11, 1983.
23. Kathy Kram, *Academy of Science Journal*, Vol. 26, No. 4; reprinted in Carol Austin Bridgewater, "The Phases of Mentorship," *Psychology Today*, June 1984.
24. Roberts, *Chinese Fairy Tales*, p. 60.
25. Srully Blotnick, *Otherwise Engaged: The Private Lives of Successful Career Women* (New York: Facts on File, 1985), pp. 243, 248.
26. Study by Robert Rosenthal and Nicole Steckler cited in *Psychology Today*, July 1984.
27. David Leavitt, "The New Lost Generation," *Esquire*, May 1985.

Chapter 5

1. Christopher Lasch, *The Culture of Narcissism: American Life in an Age of Diminishing Expectations* (New York: Warner Books, 1979), p. 331.
2. Robert E. Gould, "Why Can't a (Working) Woman Be More Like a Man," *Working Woman*, April 1985.
3. Lillian Rubin, *Intimate Strangers: Men and Women Together* (New York: Harper & Row, 1983), p. 57; Carol Klein, *Mothers and Sons* (Boston: Houghton Mifflin, 1984), p. 51.
4. Susan Brownmiller, *Femininity* (New York: Fawcett, 1984), p. 228.
5. Rubin, *Intimate Strangers*, pp. 56–57.
6. Lasch, *Narcissism*, p. 347.
7. *Ibid.*
8. Andree Brooks, "When a Wife Is Achiever," *New York Times*, April 29, 1985.
9. Roger L. Gould, *Transformations: Growth and Change in Adult Life* (New York: Simon & Schuster, 1978), pp. 237–38.
10. For more on the language of the sexes see Brownmiller, *Femininity*, pp. 105–26; Mary Brown Parlee, "Getting a Word in Sex-Wise," *Across the Board*, September 1984; Mark A. Sherman and Adelaide Haas, "Man to Man, Woman to Woman," *Psychology Today*, June 1984; John Pfeiffer, "Girl Talk–Boy Talk," *Science 85*, February 1985.
11. Mary Brown Parlee, "Getting a Word in Sex-Wise," *Across the Board*, September 1984.
12. Marilyn French, *Beyond Power* (New York: Simon & Schuster, 1985), p. 450.
13. Herb Goldberg, *The New Male-Female Relationship* (New York: New American Library, 1983), pp. 3–27; Daniel Levinson, with Charlotte N. Darrow, Edward B. Klein, Maria H. Levinson and Barton McKee, *The Seasons of a Man's Life* (New York: Ballantine Books, 1978), p. 233.
14. Irene Claremont de Castillejo, *Knowing Woman: A Feminine Psychology* (New York: Harper & Row, 1974), p. 20.
15. Carol Gilligan, *In a Different Voice: Psychological Theory and Women's Development* (Cambridge, Mass.: Harvard University Press, 1982), p. 159.
16. Claremont de Castillejo, *Knowing Woman*, p. 15.

---

17. Doreen Kimura, "Male Brain, Female Brain: The Hidden Difference," *Psychology Today*, November 1985.
18. Betty Lehan Harragan, *Games Mother Never Taught You: Corporate Gamesmanship for Women* (New York: Warner Books, 1977), pp. 50–51.
19. Lasch, *Narcissism*, p. 128.
20. Paul G. Engel, "Sexual Harassment," *Industry Week*, June 24, 1985.
21. A study by Madeline Heilman and Melanie Stopeck, reported in the *Wall Street Journal*, May 21, 1985, by Cathy Trost, "Labor Letter," noted that "good looks have negative consequences" for executive women and that "the success of attractive women was attributed more often to reasons other than skill" while the ascent of both plain and good-looking men was credited to ability. Nancy Baker, *The Beauty Trap*, also cites a study by Lita L. Schwartz and Florence W. Kaslow (New York: Franklin Watts, 1984), pp. 51–53.
22. Lionel Tiger, *Men in Groups* (New York: Random House, 1969), pp. 75–87.
23. Quoted in "Swap the Old Lady for a New Woman," *New Woman*, October 1985.

Chapter 6

1. David Burns, "The Perfectionist's Script for Self-Defeat," *Psychology Today*, November 1980, p. 37.
2. Pauline Ross Clance, "The Imposter Phenomenon," *New Woman*, July 1985, p. 42.
3. Marilyn French, *Beyond Power* (New York: Summit Books, 1985), p. 323.
4. *Ibid.*, p. 311.
5. Christopher Lasch, *The Culture of Narcissism: American Life in an Age of Diminishing Expectations* (New York: Warner Books, 1979), p. 120.
6. Quoted in Elaine Louie, "A Few of Their Favorite Things," *Working Woman*, December 1984, p. 102.
7. Srully Blotnick, *The Corporate Steeplechase: Predictable Crises in a Business Career* (New York: Facts on File, 1984).
8. *Ibid.*, p. 55.
9. Susan Schenkle, *Giving Away Success: Why Women Get Stuck And What to Do About It* (New York: McGraw-Hill, 1984), p. 47.
10. Celia Halas and Roberta Matteson, *I've Done So Well—Why Do I Feel So Bad? Conflicts in the Female Experience and What Women Can Do about Them* (New York: Macmillan, 1978), p. 152.
11. Gail Sheehy, *Passages: Predictable Crises of Adult Life* (New York: Bantam, 1977), pp. 38, 190.
12. Kathy Kram, *Academy of Management Journal*, Vol. 26, No. 4; rpt. in Carol Austin Bridgewater, "The Phases of Mentorship," *Psychology Today*, June 1984.
13. Margaret Touborg, "How Work Works: Profession as Meaning," paper presented to the Harvard Graduate School of Education, May 16, 1983, p. 8.
14. Paul Zweig, *Three Journeys* (New York: Basic Books, 1976), pp. 149–150.

Chapter 7

1. Carol Hymowitz and Timothy D. Schellhardt, "The Glass Ceiling: Why Women Can't Seem to Break the Invisible Barrier that Blocks them from the Top Jobs," *Wall Street Journal*, March 24, 1986, section 4, p. 1.
2. "The Year 2001," *Ladies' Home Journal*, January 1986, p. 33.
3. Latest statistics available show a steady increase in the number of complaints filed, up from 4,272 in 1981 to 5,566 in 1983. "Sexual Harassment: Victims Talk, Management Listens," *Industry Week*, June 24, 1985, p. 57. See also Robert Pear, "Agency Cities Statistical Evidence in Lawsuits on Job Discrimination," *New York Times*, November 13, 1985.
4. Susan Brownmiller, *Femininity* (New York: Fawcett, 1984), p. 161.
5. Richard I. Kirkland, Jr., *Fortune*, June 10, 1985, p. 38.
6. "The False Paradise of a Service Economy," *Business Week*, March 3, 1986.
7. Basia Hellwig, "The Breakthrough Generation: Seventy-three Women Ready to Run Corporate America," *Working Woman*, April 1985, p. 99.
8. Shirley James Longshore and Donna P. Conley, "Women to Watch," *Ladies' Home Journal*, November 1984, p. 143.
9. Beth McGoldrick and Gregory Miller, "Wall Street Women: You've Come A Short Way, Baby," *Institutional Investor*, June 1985, p. 85.
10. Louise Bernikow, "We're Dancing as Fast as We Can," *Savvy*, April 1984, p. 44.
11. The computer gender gap is corroborated by statistics showing that only one-third of students enrolled in computer classes are female. Summer computer camps sign up three boys for every girl. A North Carolina firm, Computers for Girls, is developing software specifically targeted toward girls. And the University of California at Berkeley has begun a three-hour course, Equals, to train teachers in helping girls overcome computer aversion.
12. "Women Face Job Bias, Experts Say," *New York Times*, November 25, 1984.
13. Liz Roman Gallese, "Women's Long March to the Top," *Best of Business*, September 1985.
14. Alice Sargeant, *The Androgynous Manager*, AMACOM (American Management Association): New York, 1983, p. 25.
15. Roy Rowan, "America's Most Wanted Managers," *Fortune*, February 3, 1986, p. 18.
16. Fred Barnes, "Who's in Charge?" *The Washingtonian*, August 1983, p. 126. He notes that the acronym was coined by Dan Fenn, personnel chief for President John F. Kennedy.
17. Margaret Hennig and Anne Jardim, *The Managerial Woman* (New York: Pocket Books/Simon & Schuster, 1976), p. 37.
18. Hope Lampert, "Saul Steinberg Steps Out," *Manhattan, Inc.*, October 1985, p. 100.
19. Simone de Beauvoir, *The Second Sex* (New York: Vintage Books, 1974), p. 676.

20. Rosabeth Moss Kanter first explored the phenomenon of women's isolation in token positions in *Men and Women of the Corporation* (New York: Basic Books, 1977), pp. 226–227.
21. Susan Sudman quoted in "Women of the Corporation 1985: Breaking through to the Top," *Working Woman*, April 1985, p. 99.
22. Barbara Lippert, "Laurel Cutler on Power and Women in Business," *Adweek*, January 7, 1985.
23. Eaton-Swaine Associates study cited by Jane Evans in speech to New York Women in Communications, December 1983.

Chapter 8

1. Marilyn French, "Currents: Women on Top," WNET/13 Program No. 201.
2. Dr. Ethel Spector Person, director of the Columbia University Center for Psychoanalytic Training and Research, notes of this level, "Women increasingly seek [psychoanalytic] treatment explicitly as an aid in their search for autonomy and self-realization, the vehicle of which they believe to be professional and creative achievement." These and all of Dr. Person's comments which follow are excerpted by permission from her article, "Women Working: Fears of Failure, Deviance and Success," *Journal of the American Academy of Psychoanalysis*, Vol. 10, No. 1.
3. "Connie Chung: Anchored at Last," *Harper's Bazaar*, October 1985, p. 218.
4. Marilyn French, *Beyond Power* (New York: Summit Books, 1985), p. 316.
5. Mary Cunningham, "Power Steering," *Harper's Bazaar*, October 1985.
6. Auren Uris and John J. Tarrant, "The Win Lose Decade," *Savvy*, December 1984, p. 44. Contains a good explanation of traditional catch-40's career crisis.
7. Matina Horner, "Toward an Understanding of Achievement-Related Conflicts in Women," *Journal of Social Issues*, Vol. 28 (1972). In this study the same hypothetical case concerning a career conflict on the part of the subject was given to both men and women. The test group was asked to furnish the outcome. When the group was told the subject was male, the conflicts were resolved conventionally. When the subject was renamed Anne, 62 percent of the women put forward a series of negative assumptions about the presumed cost of success.
8. J. M. Bardwick, *In Transition: How Feminism, Sexual Liberation, and the Search for Self-fulfillment Have Altered our Lives* (New York: Holt, Rinehart & Winston, 1979).
9. Paul Clancy, "Clock Ticking on Marriage and Family," *USA Today*, February 28, 1986.
10. Susan Schenkel, *Giving Away Success: Why Women Get Stuck and What To Do about It* (New York: McGraw-Hill, 1984), p. 98.
11. "Lady in a Man's World," *Vogue*, August 1983.
12. "Currents: Women on Top," WNET/13, Program No. 201.
13. *Chicago Tribune*, May 26, 1985, section 2, p. 6.

14. Herbert Freudenberger and Gail North, *Women's Burnout: How to Spot It, How to Reverse It, & How to Prevent It* (Garden City, N.Y.: Doubleday, 1985).
15. Gwenda Blair, "The Heart of the Matter," *Manhattan, Inc.*, October 1984, p. 72.
16. David Blum, "A Loss of Balance: Fay Joyce's Fall From Grace," *New York*, January 13, 1986, p. 32.
17. French, *Beyond Power*, p. 328.
18. Basia Hellwig, "The Breakthrough Generation: Seventy-three Women Ready to Run Corporate America," *Working Woman*, April 1985, p. 99.
19. "Women at the Top," *Marketing Communications*, July 1985, p. 3.
20. Celia Halas and Roberta Matteson, *I've Done So Well—Why Do I Feel So Bad? Conflicts in the Female Experience and What Women Can Do about Them* (New York: Macmillan, 1978), p. 140.
21. Tom Robbins, *Even Cowgirls Get the Blues* (New York: Bantam, 1981), p. 280.
22. Judy Linscott, "What You Can Do If Fast-Track Fever Burns You Out," *Working Woman*, February 1985, p. 25.
23. "Achievement and Ambition Typify Younger Executives," *Wall Street Journal*, October 25, 1984.

Chapter 9

1. Harry Levinson, *Executive Stress* (New York: New American Library, 1975), p. 20.
2. Ralph Keyes, *Chancing It: Why We Take Risks* (Boston: Little, Brown, 1985), p. 208.
3. Anne McKay Thompson and Marcia Donnan Wood, *Management Strategies for Women, or Now That I'm Boss, How Do I Run This Place?* (New York: Simon & Schuster, 1980), p. 227.
4. Jill Bettner and Christine Donahue, "Now They're Not Laughing," *Forbes*, November 21, 1983, p. 116.
5. Patricia O'Toole, "The Outside Route to the Top," *Working Woman*, November 1985; Liz Claiborne annual report, 12/28/85, p. 15.
6. *New Woman*, October 1985.
7. Kristin McMurran, *People*, July 29, 1985, p. 58.
8. *Forbes*, June 3, 1985.
9. Keyes, *Chancing It*, p. 200.
10. Joann S. Lublin, "Running a Firm from Home Gives Women Greater Flexibility," *Wall Street Journal*, December 31, 1984.
11. Gerri Hirshey, "How Women Feel about Working at Home," *Family Circle*, November 5, 1985, p. 72.
12. Robert Hisrich and Candida Brush, *The Woman Entrepreneur: Starting, Financing and Managing a Successful New Business* (New York: Lexington Books, 1986), pp. 14–15.
13. Levinson, *Stress*, p. 46.
14. Daniel Goleman, "The Psyche of the Entrepreneur, *New York Times Magazine*, February 2, 1986, p. 32.

15. Bettner and Donahue, "Now They're Not Laughing," p. 118.
16. Lublin, "Running a Firm."
17. Marlys Harris, "The Lure of Owning Your Own Business," *Cosmopolitan*, November 1985, p. 377.
18. Heather Evans, "The Plight of the 'Corporate Nun,' " *Working Woman*, November 1984.
19. O'Toole, "The Outside Route to the Top."
20. Laurel Sorenson, "How to Work Part-Time," *Working Woman*, November 1984, pp. 144–47.
21. Molly McKaughan and Julia Kagan, "Taking the Motherhood Plunge," *Working Woman*, February 1986, p. 70.
22. Sorenson, "Part-Time."
23. Quoted in Sorenson, "Part-Time."
24. Quoted in "The Three-Day Work Week—Making it Work," *Working Woman*, June 1985.
25. "Companies Start to Meet Executive Mothers Halfway," *Business Week*, October 17, 1983.
26. Ellen Sherman, "Separate Passages," *Ladies' Home Journal*, October 1985, p. 121.
27. Leslie Bennetts, "Baby Fever," *Vogue*, August 1985, p. 325.
28. Doris Byron Fuller, "Working Women Reshaping the Economy," *Los Angeles Times*, September 12, 1984.
29. *Harvard* magazine, March–April 1986.
30. Paul Clancy, "Clock Ticking on Marriage and Family," *USA Today*, February 28, 1986.
31. *Ibid.*
32. Quoted in "Voices," *Working Woman*, August 1985.
33. Quoted in Christa Worthington, "Jeane De Provence," *W* magazine, September 20–27, 1985, pp. 18–22.
34. Quoted in Lorraine Davis, "Between Us," *Vogue*, January 1986.
35. Walter Kiechel, "Starting Over," *Fortune*, April 2, 1984.

Chapter 10

1. Carol Gilligan, *In a Different Voice, Psychological Theory and Women's Development* (Cambridge, Mass.: Harvard University Press, 1982), p. 159.
2. Irene Claremont de Castillejo, *Knowing Woman, A Feminine Psychology* (New York: Harper & Row, 1974), pp. 154–55.
3. Frank Lloyd Wright, *Writings and Buildings* (New York: World Publishing, 1972), pp. 79, 292–96. Frank Lloyd Wright talks of the need for a "harmony of the whole" in architecture where "diverse functions cause diverse masses to occur," and he says that "holding all this diversity together in a preconceived direction is really no light matter."
4. Daphne Spain and Suzanne M. Bianchi, "How Women Have Changed," *American Demographics*, May 1983.
5. Barbara Ehrenreich, "Hers," *New York Times*, February 21, 1985.
6. Diana Zuckerman, "Career Life and Goals of Freshmen and Seniors," *Radcliffe Quarterly*, September 1982.

7. Barbara Ehrenreich, *The Hearts of Men: American Dreams and the Flight from Commitment* (Garden City, N.Y.: Anchor Doubleday, 1983), p. 175.

8. Luci Koizumi, "I'm the Breadwinner, My Husband Stays Home," *Glamour*, December 1985, p. 102.

9. Art Buchwald, "The Latchkey Husband," *International Herald Tribune*, December 11, 1984, p. 20.

10. Dianna Solis, "Plastic Surgery Wooing Patients Hoping to Move up the Career Ladder," *Wall Street Journal*, August 6, 1985.

11. Barbara G. Walker, *The Crone: Woman of Age, Wisdom, and Power* (New York: Harper & Row, 1985), p. 66.

12. Dorothy J. Gaiter, "Helping the Over-Forty Find Jobs," *New York Times*, July 23, 1984.

13. Quoted in Elliot Carlson, "Longer Work Life? A Look at the Future of Retirement," *Modern Maturity*, June–July 1985.

14. Joan Berger, " 'The New Old': Where the Economic Action Is," *Business Week*, November 25, 1985.

15. Kim Brown, "Do Working Mothers Cheat Their Kids?" *Redbook*, April 1985.

16. "Working Mother Survey Results in Surprises," *Working Mother Market Report*, November 1983. (Meanwhile, a government study by Lois M. Verbugge and Jennifer H. Madans shows that busy management women who combine an outside job with marriage tend to be healthier than those who are either unmarried or not employed outside the home—"Multiple Roles Called Healthy," *New York Times*, February 21, 1985.)

17. Cathy Trost, "Labor Letter," *Wall Street Journal*, June 18, 1985.

18. Karen Tumulty, "Wage Gap: Women Still the Second Sex," *Los Angeles Times*, September 13, 1984.

19. Liz Gallese, "Women's Long March to the Top," *Best of Business*, September 1985.

20. Maryann Bucknum Brinley, "Jane Pauley: The Frustrations of a Working Mother," *McCall's*, November 1984.

21. "Uncommon Facts and Figures that Capture the Changing Roles and Rules of Women's Lives at the Close of 1984," *Glamour*, December 1984.

22. George Dullea, "Enough Is Enough for Ex-Superwoman," *New York Times*, November 15, 1985.

23. Marilyn French, *Beyond Power* (New York: Simon & Schuster, 1985), p. 315.

24. Margaret Hennig and Anne Jardim, *The Managerial Woman* (New York: Pocket Books, 1977), p. 180.

25. Roger L. Gould, M.D., *Transformations: Growth and Change in Adult Life* (New York: Simon & Schuster, 1978), p. 245.

26. Carolyn G. Heilbrun, *Reinventing Womanhood* (New York: Norton, 1979), p. 32.

27. Marilyn Loden, *Feminine Leadership or How to Succeed in Business without Being One of the Boys* (New York: Times Books, 1985), pp. 26, 63.

28. Joyce Trebilcot, "Two Forms of Androgynism," in Mary Vetterling-Braggin, ed., *"Femininity," "Masculinity," and "Androgyny"* (Totowa, N.J.: Littlefield, Adams, 1982), pp. 161–69.
29. Heilbrun, *Reinventing*, p. 140.
30. Phillip Moffitt, "Dancing and Dazzling," *Esquire*, August 1985, p. 19.
31. Jean Baker Miller, *Toward a New Psychology of Women* (Boston: Beacon Press, 1976), p. 3.
32. Michael Korda, *Power!* (New York: Ballantine, 1975), p. 285.
33. David Dworkin, "A Question of Happiness," *New York Times Magazine*, March 17, 1985.
24. French, *Beyond Power*, p. 469.
35. Quoted in "Jeane De Provence," Christa Worthington, W magazine, September 20–27, 1985, pp. 18–22.
36. Betty Friedan, *The Feminine Mystique* (New York: Laurel Books, 1984), pp. xxv–xxvi.
37. French, *Beyond Power*, p. 469.

Chapter 11

1. Betty Friedan, *The Feminine Mystique* (New York: Laurel Books, 1983), p. 34.
2. Hilary Cosell, *Woman on a Seesaw: The Ups and Downs of Making It* (New York: Putnam, 1985), p. 17.
3. Quoted in Betty Friedan, *The Second Stage* (New York: Summit Books, 1981), p. 151.
4. Quoted in Kristin McMurran, "Mary Kay Ash," *People*, July 29, 1985.
5. Lois Wyse, *The Six Figure Woman And How to Be One* (New York: Fawcett, 1983), p. 177.
6. Ann Belford Ulanov, *Receiving Woman: Studies in the Psychology and Theology of the Feminine* (Philadelphia, Pa.: Westminster Press, 1981), pp. 66, 40.
7. About half of four-year colleges and universities around the country now offer women's studies. In 1986, Duke University became the first college to develop a National Council for Women's Studies to advise the program including women in executive positions in business and corporations.
8. Carolyn G. Heilbrun, *Reinventing Womanhood* (New York: Norton, 1979), p. 98.
9. Ron Rosenbaum, "The Frantic Screaming Voice of the Rich and Famous," *Manhattan, Inc.*, January 1986, quotes a *New York Times* report.
10. Annie Gottlieb, "When Having It All Isn't Enough," *McCall's*, January 1986.
11. Quoted in Marcia Stamell, "Is Your Job Meeting Your Needs?" *Working Woman*, June 1985.
12. Ronni Eisenberg, "10 Steps to Take Control of Your Life," *Glamour*, January 1986.
13. Irene Claremont de Castillejo, *Knowing Woman* (New York: Putnam, 1973), p. 140.

14. Ann Belford Ulanov, *Receiving Woman: Studies in the Psychology and Theology of the Feminine* (Philadelphia, Pa.: Westminster Press, 1981), p. 115.
15. Friedan, *Mystique*, p. 31.
16. Connell Cowan and Melvyn Kinder, *Smart Women, Foolish Choices: Finding the Right Men and Avoiding the Wrong Ones* (New York: Clarkson N. Potter, 1985), p. 13.
17. Srully Blotnick, *Otherwise Engaged: The Private Lives of Successful Career Women* (New York: Facts on File, 1985), p. 242.
18. Friedan, *Mystique*, p. 342.
19. Quoted in "Marlo Thomas," Susan Dworkin, *Ladies' Home Journal*, November 1984, p. 32.

Chapter 12

1. John Naisbitt and the Naisbitt Group, *The Year Ahead 1986: Ten Powerful Trends that will Shape Your Future"* (New York: Warner Books, 1985), p. 50.
2. Quoted in Susan Fraker, "Why Women Aren't Getting to the Top," *Fortune*, April 16, 1984, p. 45.
3. Perry Pascarella, "Malcontent Managers: Will They Retard the Recovery?," *Industry Week*, January 23, 1984, p. 32.
4. Monci Jo Williams, "The Baby Bust Hits the Job Market," *Fortune*, May 27, 1985, p. 122.
5. Peter Drucker, "A Growing Mismatch of Jobs and Job Seekers," *Wall Street Journal*, March 26, 1985.
6. Pascarella, "Malcontent Managers," p. 33.
7. Quoted in "More and More, She's the Boss," *Time*, December 2, 1985, p. 66.
8. Thomas J. Peters and Robert H. Waterman, Jr., *In Search of Excellence: Lessons from America's Best-Run Companies* (New York: Harper & Row, 1982), p. 55.
9. Marilyn Loden, "A Machismo That Drives Women Out," *New York Times*, February 9, 1986.
10. Quoted in "Who's Excellent Now?" *Business Week*, November 5, 1984, p. 77.
11. Alice Sargeant, *The Androgynous Manager*, AMACOM (American Management Association), New York, 1983, p. 190.
12. Quoted in "Entrepreneurial Spirit Often Begins at Home," *USA Today*, May 9, 1985, p. 11A.
13. Cynthia Crossen, "Kids of Top Executives Are Crazy about Dad—Especially His Money," *Wall Street Journal*, March 19, 1985.
14. Alvin Toffler, *The Third Wave* (New York: Bantam, 1981), pp. 195–98.
15. "Knit One, Purl Two," *Forbes*, December 3, 1984. According to *Forbes*, there are presently only twenty to thirty thousand telecommuters. Legal restrictions on cottage industries constitute the largest institutional roadblock to progress right now.
16. Quoted in "Jeane De Provence," Christa Worthington, *W* magazine, September 20–27, 1985, pp. 18–22.

17. Marilyn French, *Beyond Power* (New York: Simon & Schuster, 1985), p. 487.
18. Robert N. Bellahm, Richard Madsen, William M. Sullivan, Ann Swidler, and Steven M. Tipton, *Habits of the Heart: Individualism and Commitment in American Life* (Berkeley: University of California Press, 1985), p. 288.
19. John A. Byrne, "Some Thoughts from the Best and Brightest M.B.A.'s," *Forbes*, June 3, 1985.
20. "As Businesses Try to Ease the Pain of Moving," *U.S. News & World Report*, Special report. Fall 1985.
21. Marsha Sinetar, "SMR Forum: Entrepreneurs, Chaos, and Creativity—Can Creative People Really Survive Large Company Structure?" *Sloan Management Review*, Winter 1985, p. 57.
22. Peter F. Drucker, *Managing in Turbulent Times* (New York: Harper & Row, 1980), p. 121.
23. "Croquet on Company Time," *Time*, September 2, 1985. The owner of Rockport Company, who dreamed up the notion of Camp Rockport, is Bruce Katz.
24. Ellen Wojahn, "Beyond the Fringes: How Smaller Companies Are Profiting from Flexible Benefits Plans," *Inc.*, March 1984.
25. Drucker, *Turbulent Times*, p. 123.
26. William Meyers, "Child Care Finds a Champion in the Corporation," *New York Times*, August 4, 1985.
27. "Companies Start to Meet Mothers Halfway," *Business Week*, October 17, 1983, p. 191.
28. *Ibid.*, p. 195.
29. The Today Show, February 26, 1986.
30. "Ninety-Two Percent Say Women's Jobs Should Be Guaranteed After Maternity Leave," *Glamour*, February 1985, p. 33.
31. Jessie Bernard, *The Future of Motherhood* (New York: Dial Press, 1974), pp. 268–69.
32. *Glamour*, February 1985, p. 33.
33. Meyers, "Child Care." For a comprehensive discussion of day care and corporate responsibility, see also Dana Friedman, "Child Care and the Corporation," *Harvard Business Review*, March/April 1986, p. 30.
34. Naisbitt, *Year Ahead*, p. 219.
35. Meyers, "Child Care"; Margaret Engel, "New Day Care Options: How Companies Are Meeting the Needs of Working Parents," *Glamour*, May 1985, p. 136.
36. Jennifer Bingham Hull, "Women Find Parents Need Them Just When Careers Are Resuming," *Wall Street Journal*, September 9, 1985.
37. Anne H. Oman, "Washington Update: The Latest Laws That Affect You and Your Family," *Ladies' Home Journal*, December 1985.
38. Drucker, "Growing Mismatch."
39. "Companies Start to Meet Mother Halfway," *Business Week*, October 17, 1983, p. 191. The article went on to say, however that "attitudes have changed sharply from the days when each arrangement was treated as a rare exception to the role of full-time, on-site work or no work at all"—an insight that our interviews did not support.

40. "Influx of Women Changing the Workplace," *Los Angeles Times*, September 14, 1984.
41. Drucker, *Turbulent Times*, p. 122.
42. "An Alma Mater for Columbia," *Picture Week*, January 1986.
43. "Now Hear This," *Fortune*, June 10, 1985. Home Box Office CEO Michael Fuch's quote from "Swap the Old Lady for a New Woman," *New Woman*, March 1986.
44. "Women Are Moving Into Management—Slowly," *Chemical Week*, December 21, 1983.
45. Fraker, "Getting to the Top."
46. Alan L. Otten, "Young Professionals' Retirement May Be Brighter Than They Think," *Wall Street Journal*, December 10, 1985.
47. *Ibid.*
48. *Ibid.*
49. John A. Byrne, "Some Thoughts From the Best and Brightest M.B.A.'s," *Forbes*, June 3, 1985.
50. *Ibid.*
51. As Betty Friedan points out, "These and other signs of second-stage movement in industry seem to be happening for reasons that have nothing to do with women—but they facilitate, even demand, the new flexible mode and the transcending of sex roles"—*The Second Stage* (New York: Summit, 1981), p. 270.
52. Adam Smith, "Unconventional Wisdom: Yesterday's Yuppies," *Esquire*, May 1985, p. 107.
53. Quoted in Glenn Collins, "Future M.B.A.'s Learn Value of a Home Life," *New York Times*, October 16, 1985, p. C1.
54. Psychologist Carol Gilligan supports Hennessey's point of view, arguing against "a division of ethics into 'human versus female,' " urging instead an approach "where our energy is devoted to finding the inclusive solution"—quoted in Elisheva Urbas, "The Pirate Who Lives Next Door: Carol Gilligan and the Ethics of Caring," *Second Century Radcliffe News*, April 1985.
55. Friedan, *Second Stage*, pp. 28, 133.
56. Lisa Collins, "More Firms Giving New Fathers Time Off to Share Chores and Joys of Infant Care," *Wall Street Journal*, July 5, 1985.

BIBLIOGRAPHY

The following sources have been of aid in the compilation of a comprehensive look at women and the impact of corporate experience. While space considerations prohibited quoting all of them in the body of the book, many provided valuable background insights into the current dilemma.

Baker, Nancy. *The Beauty Trap*. New York: Franklin Watts, 1984.

Baruch, Grace, Roslind Barnett, Caryl Rivers. *Lifeprints: New Patterns of Love and Work for Today's Women*. New York: McGraw Hill, 1983. An excellent discussion based on a three-year study funded by the National Science Foundation of how contemporary woman is coping with a menu of choices.

Beauvoir, Simone de. *The Second Sex*. New York: Vintage Books, 1974.

Bellahm, Robert N., Richard Madsen, William M. Sullivan, Ann Swindler, and Steven M. Tipton. *Habits of the Heart: Individualism and Commitment in American Life*. Berkeley: University of California Press, 1985.

Bernard, Dr. Jessie. *The Future of Motherhood*. New York: Dial Press, 1974.

Bernikow, Louise. *Among Women*. New York: Harmony Books, 1980.

Bernstein, Paula. *Family Ties, Corporate Bonds*. Garden City, N.Y.: Doubleday, 1985.

Blotnick, Dr. Srully. *The Corporate Steeplechase, Predictable Crises in a Business Career*. New York: Facts on File, 1984.

————. *Otherwise Engaged: The Private Lives of Successful Career Women*. New York: Facts on File, 1985.

Bolen, Dr. Jean Shiroda. *Goddesses in Everywoman: A New Psychology of Women*. San Francisco: Harper & Row, 1984.

Brownmiller, Susan. *Femininity*. New York: Fawcett Columbine, Ballantine Books, 1984.

Bryant, Gay. *The Working Woman Report: Succeeding in Business in the 1980s*. New York: Simon and Schuster, 1984.

Bryne, Robert. *The Other 637 Best Things Anybody Ever Said.* New York: Atheneum, 1985.

Charlton, James. *The Executive's Quotation Book: A Corporate Companion.* New York: St. Martin's Press, 1983.

Cosell, Hilary. *Woman on a Seesaw: The Ups and Downs of Making It.* New York: Putnam, 1985.

Cowan, Dr. Connell, and Dr. Melvyn Kinder. *Smart Women, Foolish Choices: Finding the Right Men and Avoiding the Wrong Ones.* New York: Clarkson N. Potter, 1985.

Claremont de Castijello, Irene. *Knowing Woman.* New York: Harper & Row, 1974.

Donahue, Phil. *The Human Animal.* New York: Simon & Schuster, 1985.

Drucker, Peter E. *Managing in Turbulent Times.* New York: Harper & Row, 1980.

Ehrenreich, Barbara. *The Hearts of Men: American Dreams and the Flight from Commitment.* Garden City, N.Y.: Anchor Doubleday, 1983.

Ehrenreich, Barbara and English, Deirdre, *For Her Own Good: 150 Years of Experts Advice to Women.* Garden City, N.Y.: Anchor Doubleday, 1978.

Forster, Margaret. *Significant Sisters: The Grassroots of Active Feminism 1839–1939.* New York: Alfred A. Knopf, 1985.

French, Marilyn. *Beyond Power.* New York: Simon & Schuster, 1985. An exhaustive study of the impact of male-dominated values on society, including several pertinent chapters on the price corporate culture exacts from men.

Freudenberger, Herbert, and Gail North. *Women's Burnout: How to Spot It, How to Reverse It and How to Prevent It.* Garden City, N.Y.: Doubleday, 1985.

Friedan, Betty. *The Feminine Mystique.* New York: Laurel Books, 1983.
——————. *The Second Stage.* New York: Summit Books, 1981.

Gallese, Liz Roman. *Women Like Us: What Is Happening to the Women of The Harvard Business School Class of 1975.* New York: William Morrow, 1985.

Gilligan, Carol. *In a Different Voice, Psychological Theory and Women's Development.* Cambridge, Mass.: Harvard University Press, 1982. Gilligan's theories of women's moral development, applied here for the first time to corporate culture, help immeasurably in explaining how women's perception of their corporate experience diverges substantially from that of male managers.

Ginzberg, Eli, and George Vojta. *Beyond Human Scale: The Large Corporation At Risk.* New York: Basic Books, 1986.

Goldberg, Dr. Herb. *The New Male-Female Relationship.* New York: New American Library, 1983.

Gould, Dr. Roger L. *Transformations: Growth and Change in Adult Life.* New York: A Touchstone Book, 1978.

Halas, Dr. Celia, and Dr. Roberta Matteson. *I've Done So Well—Why Do I Feel So Bad? Conflicts in the Female Experience and What Women Can Do About Them.* New York: Macmillan, 1978.

Harding, M. Esther. *The Way of All Women.* New York: Harper & Row, 1970.

Harragan, Betty Lehan. *Games Mother Never Taught You: Corporate Gamesmanship for Women*. New York: Warner Books, 1977.

Heilbrun, Carolyn G. *Reinventing Womanhood*. New York: Norton, 1979.

Hennig, Margaret, and Anne Jardim. *The Managerial Woman*. New York: Pocket Books, 1977. This is still the seminal how-to book for women managers. We hope we have added dimension to their early research, and raised some red flags as well.

Hisrich, Dr. Robert D., and Candida Brush. *The Woman Entrepreneur: Starting, Financing and Managing a Successful New Business*. New York: Lexington Books, 1986.

Iacocca, Lee with William Novak. *Iacocca, An Autobiography*. New York: Bantam Books, 1984.

Kanter, Rosabeth Moss. *Men and Women of The Corporation*. New York: Basic Books, 1977.

Kanter, Rosabeth Moss, and Barry A. Stein. *Life in Organizations: Workplaces As People Experience Them*. New York: Basic Books, 1979.

Keyes, Ralph. *Chancing It: Why We Take Risks*. Boston: Little, Brown, 1985.

Klein, Carole. *Mothers and Sons*. Boston: Houghton Mifflin, 1984.

Korda, Michael. *Power!* New York: Ballantine Books, 1975.

Kreps, Juanita. *Sex in the Marketplace: American Women at Work*. Baltimore, Md.: Johns Hopkins University Press, 1971.

Lasch, Christopher. *The Culture of Narcissism: American Life in an Age of Diminishing Expectations*. New York: Warner Books, 1979.

Lenz, Eleanor, and Barbara Myerhoff. *The Feminization of America: How Women's Values are Changing Our Public and Private Lives*. Los Angeles: Tarcher, 1985.

Levinson, Daniel with Charlotte N. Darrow, Edward B. Klein, Maria H. Levinson, Barton McKee. *The Seasons of a Man's Life*. New York: Ballantine Books, 1979.

Levinson, Harry. *Executive Stress*. New York: New American Library, 1975.

Litwin, Susan. *The Postponed Generation: Why American Youth Are Growing Up Later*. New York: William Morrow, 1986.

Loden, Marilyn. *Feminine Leadership: Or How to Succeed in Business Without Being One of the Boys*. New York: New York Times Books, 1985.

Maccoby, Michael. *The Gamesmen: The New Corporate Leaders*. New York: Simon and Schuster, 1976.

Macklowitz, Marilyn. *Inside Moves: Corporate Smarts for Women on Their Way Up*. Boulder, Colo.: Career Track Publications, 1984.

Marshall, Megan. *The Cost of Loving: Women and Their Fear of Intimacy*. New York: Putnam, 1984.

Mayer, Nancy. *The Male Mid-Life Crisis: Fresh Starts after 40*. New York: New American Library, 1978.

McCormack, Mark H. *What They Don't Teach You at the Harvard Business School*. New York: Bantam Books, 1984.

Miller, Dr. Jean Baker. *Toward a New Psychology of Women*. Boston: Beacon Press, 1976.

Mitchell, Charlene and Thomas Burdick. *The Right Moves*. New York: Macmillan, 1985.

Naisbitt, John. *Megatrends: Ten New Directions Transforming Our Lives.* New York: Warner Books, 1982.

Newhouse, Nancy, ed. *Hers: Through Women's Eyes; Essays from the "Hers" Column of The New York Times.* New York: Villard Books, 1985.

Nickles, Elizabeth with Laura Ashcraft. *The Coming Matriarchy: How Women will Gain the Balance of Power.* New York: Seaview Books, 1981.

Pascale, Richard Tanner, and Anthony G. Athos. *The Art of Japanese Management: Applications for American Executives.* New York: Warner Books, 1981.

Peters, Thomas J., and Robert H. Waterman, Jr. *In Search of Excellence: Lessons from America's Best-Run Companies.* New York: Harper & Row, 1982.

Roberts, Moss. *Chinese Fairy Tales and Fantasies.* New York: Pantheon Books, 1979.

Rowan, Roy. *The Intuitive Manager.* Boston: Little, Brown & Co., 1986.

Rowes, Barbara. *The Book of Quotes.* New York: Ballantine Books, 1979.

Rubin, Lillian. *Intimate Strangers: Men and Women Together.* New York: Harper & Row, 1983.

Sargent, Alice G. *The Androgynous Manager.* New York: Amacom, 1983.

Scarf, Maggie. *Unfinished Business: Pressure Points in the Lives of Women.* Garden City, N.Y.: Doubleday, 1980.

Schenkle, Susan, Ph.D. *Giving Away Success: Why Women Get Stuck and What To Do About It.* New York: McGraw Hill, 1984.

Sheehy, Gail. *Pathfinders.* New York: Bantam Books, 1982.

————. *Passages: Predictable Crises of Adult Life.* New York: Bantam/ E. P. Dutton, 1977.

Shorris, Earl. *Scenes From Corporate Life: The Politics of Middle Management.* New York: Penguin Books, 1984.

Susman, Warren. *Culture As History: The Transformation of America in The Twentieth Century.* New York: Pantheon, 1984.

Thompson, Anne McKay, and Marcia Donnan Wood. *Management Strategies for Women, or Now that I'm Boss, How do I Run This Place?* New York: Simon and Schuster, 1980.

Tiger, Lionel. *Men in Groups.* New York: Random House, 1969.

Toffler, Alvin. *The Third Wave.* New York: Bantam, 1981.

Ulanov, Ann Belford. *Receiving Woman: Studies in the Psychology and Theology of the Feminine.* Philadelphia, Pa.: Westminster Press, 1981.

Walker, Barbara G. *The Crone: Woman of Age, Wisdom, and Power.* New York: Harper & Row, 1985.

Warren, Robert Penn. *All The King's Men.* New York: Bantam, 1971.

Whyte, William H., Jr. *The Organization Man.* New York: Simon and Schuster, 1956.

Wright, Frank Lloyd. *Writings and Buildings.* New York: A Meridian Book, World Publishing, Times Mirror, 1972.

Wyse, Lois. *The Six Figure Woman: And How to Be One.* New York: Fawcett Crest Book, Garret Press, 1983.

Zolla, Elemire. *The Androgyne: Reconciliation of Male and Female.* New York: Crossroad Publishing, 1981.

Zweig, Paul. *Three Journeys.* New York: Basic Books, 1976.

INDEX

Rowan, Roy, 150, 224
Rubin, Lillian, 142
Rutgers University, 121
"Ruth" (interviewee), 28, 298, 299, 353

St. Joe Minerals, 150, 364
Salary discrimination, 126–127, 370–371
"Sally" (interviewee), 60, 310–312, 313, 365
"Sam" (interviewee), 147
Sargeant, Alice, 45, 222, 398–399
Savvy magazine, 17, 220
Scarf, Maggie, 26, 58, 70, 79
Schenkle, Susan, 194–195
Schlosser, Herb, 167, 215, 236, 398
Schroeder, Patricia, 430
Schulz, Charles, 121
Search for approval, female, 78
Seduction, male fear of, 159–164
Self-betrayal, in corporate career cycle, 241–271
Self-esteem, sense of, 91–104
Self-owned businesses, 278–290
Seltz, Christine, 405–406
Sensitivity and emotion, female, 145–151
Sequential careers, 385–387
Service industry, 216–218, 219
Sevareid, Eric, 290
Sex preference, for offspring, 42–43
Sexual antagonism, 127–129, 135–171
Sexual harassament suits, 212
Sexual tension in corporate relationships, 43–44, 127–129, 135–171
Shalala, Donna, 420
Shearson Lehman Brothers, 76
Sheehy, Gail, 5, 24, 93, 195, 196
"Sheila" (interviewee), 23, 33, 37, 38–39, 54, 95, 97, 109, 117, 177–178, 188, 244, 376, 390
Siegal, R. L., 400
Simpson, Carole, 230, 232
Single-sex environment, 71–72
Sissy syndrome, 143–145

Small Business Administration (SBA), 288
Small Business U.S.A., 279, 395
Smith, Adam, 428
Smith, James P., 11
Smith College, 65, 72, 76, 85
Solomon, Steven, 286, 395
Something Happened, 35
Sorority house stigma, 118–119
Southland Corporation, 410, 411
Staff versus line jobs, 245–247
Stanford University, 73, 335
   Business School, 393
Star Is Born, A, 77
Staying with the corporation, 321–358
Steensma, Connie, 291
Steiger, Paul, 101
Steinbacher, Roberta, 43
Steinberg, Saul, 227–228
Steinem, Gloria, 16, 170–171
"Steve" (interviewee), 285, 290
Strober, Myra, 394
Student loans, 86
Success, male/female definitions of, 209
Suicides among women in corporate jobs, 260–261
"Sunny" (interviewee), 117, 341, 346, 382
Superwoman, 97, 333–339
Susman, Warren, 26
"Suzanne" (interviewee), 278, 284, 285–286, 290

Tattle, Peter, 400
Teachers Insurance and Annuity Association, 316, 410
"Ted" (interviewee), 47, 75, 161, 249, 296
"Terry" (interviewee), 137
Thatcher, Margaret, 229, 333
Thomas, Marlo, 389
Tiger, Lionel, 165
Time, Inc., 169, 250
Time clock, female, 50–52, 103, 182, 253, 339, 346
Time magazine, 11

Timetables, male/female, 234–238, 384–388, 399–401, 416
"Tina" (interviewee), 28, 53, 69–70, 72, 270, 280, 352
Title Seven, Civil Rights Act of 1964, 105
Toffler, Alvin, 400, 415
Tokenism, 105–110, 229–230
Tomlin, Lily, 52, 331
Total Woman (Marabel Morgan's), 20
Touborg, Margaret, 27, 55, 64, 86, 99, 203, 308, 310, 327, 427
Townsend, Robert, 290
Transfer, corporate, 99–101, 198–199, 402
Transformations, 348
Trans World Airlines Incorporated (TWA), 80
Trappings of success, 98–99, 176–177, 197, 406
Travel fantasy, 81–82, 197–198
"Trish" (interviewee), 186, 190, 328–329, 342, 344, 354
Turner, Ted, 215
Twentieth Century Fox, 216
Two-career couples, 327–330, 402

Ulanov, Ann Bedford, 373, 380
Unemployment among corporate executives, 332
Union Carbide Corporation, 401
USA Network, 215
University of California, Los Angeles (UCLA), 64, 69, 86, 85, 270
University of Chicago, 75, 86, 137, 202
University of Pennsylvania, 68
University of Texas, 24
Unlimited potential, myth of, 23, 26–27, 92, 105, 113, 188, 311, 367–370
Up the Organization, 290

"Valerie" (interviewee), 267, 275, 312–313
Value system, female, 48–50, 102, 186–188, 247–248, 322, 401–402

Vietnam war, 16

Wage inequity, 126–127, 370–371
Walker, Barbara, 332
Wall Street Journal, 12, 101, 185, 209, 269, 308, 389, 399, 413, 424–425
Walters, Barbara, 333
Warren, Robert Penn, 96
Waterman, Robert H., Jr., 398
Webster & Sheffield, 150
Wells Rich Green Incorporated, 215
Wexler, Anne, 207, 294, 422
Wexler, Reynolds, Harrison, and Schule, 207
Weyerhauser Company, 400
Wharton Business School, 11
"Who's the Boss," 158
Who's Who in America, 386
Williams, Mary Alice, 215
Wolf, Rosalie, 408
Women's Burnout, 259
Women's colleges, 71–72
"Women's fields," 47
Women's Institute, 28, 181, 250, 253, 365
Women's liberation, 16–18, 136, 120–121, 170, 352
Women's magazines, 16–17, 363
Women's rights, 388–398
Women workers, statistics on:
    executives, 11–12, 222
    managers, 105, 222
    marital status, 269
    professionals, 393
Working Woman, 17, 217–218
Wright, Frank Lloyd, 323
Wriston, Walter, 59, 312
Wyse, Lois, 89, 143, 169, 215, 232, 281, 373, 422
Wyse Advertising Incorporated, 89, 143, 215

Yale Business School, 393

Zehnder International, 380
Zuckerman, Diana, 327
Zurawik, David, 158
Zweig, Paul, 205

...ion male managers! Here is a ...primer on the hidden forces that ...women upward in business, and ...n trigger their disillusionment. You'll be surprised by the lessons this fascinating book contains for both businessmen and businesswomen."

Roy Rowan, *author of*
The Intuitive Manager

In little more than a decade, women have climbed the corporate ladder into middle management, only to bump heads against a glass ceiling. Corporate life has both dazzled women far beyond their most ambitious expectations, and failed to measure up to any of their early dreams. Is the ceiling real or perceptual? Are corporations failing women? Are women failing themselves?

Success and Betrayal is the first book about women in corporations written by two successful corporate managers. Their insider's perspective challenges previous assumptions about how far women will rise and the value of the rewards bestowed by America's biggest and best corporations. Most important, *Success and Betrayal* answers questions posed by the large segment of businesswomen who are ambivalent about their "success"—and are not sure why. Through comprehensive, candid interviews with women managers from all industries and America's top companies, their male peers, psychologists, and many chief executive officers, the authors gained rare access to the complex dynamic between women's expectations and fulfillment within the corporation. The very real barriers women encounter coupled with a second, hidden agenda women bring to

(continued on back flap)